MIRRORS AND REFLECTIONS

MIRRORS AND REFLECTIONS
Processes of Systemic Supervision

Editors
Charlotte Burck and Gwyn Daniel

Taylor & Francis Group
LONDON AND NEW YORK

First published 2010 by Karnac Books Ltd.

Published 2018 by Routledge
2 Park Square, Milton Park, Abingdon, Oxon OX14 4RN
711 Third Avenue, New York, NY 10017, USA

Routledge is an imprint of the Taylor & Francis Group, an informa business

Copyright © 2010 by Charlotte Burck and Gwyn Daniel

The right of Charlotte Burck and Gwyn Daniel to be identified as the authors of this work has been asserted in accordance with §§ 77 and 78 of the Copyright Design and Patents Act 1988.

All rights reserved. No part of this book may be reprinted or reproduced or utilised in any form or by any electronic, mechanical, or other means, now known or hereafter invented, including photocopying and recording, or in any information storage or retrieval system, without permission in writing from the publishers.

Notice:
Product or corporate names may be trademarks or registered trademarks, and are used only for identification and explanation without intent to infringe.

British Library Cataloguing in Publication Data

A C.I.P. for this book is available from the British Library

ISBN-13: 9781855756007 (pbk)

Typeset by Vikatan Publishing Solutions (P) Ltd., Chennai, India

*"This book is dedicated to the memory
of our dear friend and colleague, David Campbell"*

CONTENTS

FOREWORD   xi

THE CONTRIBUTORS   xiii

INTRODUCTION   xix
Charlotte Burck and Gwyn Daniel

SECTION I: EVOLVING THEORIES   1

CHAPTER ONE
Theories of change and the practice of systemic supervision   3
Paolo Bertrando and Gabriella Gilli

CHAPTER TWO
The three faces of supervision: Individual learning,
    group learning, and supervisor accountability   27
Paula Boston

CHAPTER THREE
Creating reflexive relationships between practices of systemic supervision and theories of learning and education 49
John Burnham

CHAPTER FOUR
Three gasps behind the screen: Exploring discourses of emotion in systemic supervision 79
David Spellman and Gerrilyn Smith

CHAPTER FIVE
Exploring emotions: A critical incident for a supervisor 103
Sumita Dutta

SECTION II: GROUP PROCESSES 121

CHAPTER SIX
Minding the group: Group process, group analytic ideas, and systemic supervision—companionable or uneasy bedfellows? 123
Julia Granville

CHAPTER SEVEN
From hazardous to collaborative learning: Thinking systemically about live supervision group processes 141
Charlotte Burck

CHAPTER EIGHT
Times past, present, and future: Revisiting a supervision group experience 163
Gwyn Daniel, Grania Clarke and Reena Nath

CHAPTER NINE
Keeping the family in focus: Doing and reflecting in supervision groups 185
Sara Barratt, Claudia Camhi, Sumita Dutta, Antonina Ingrassia and Guy Larrington

SECTION III: POWER AND DIVERSITY — 201

CHAPTER TEN
"Voice entitlement" narratives in supervision: Cultural and gendered influences on speaking and dilemmas in practice — 203
Elizabeth Boyd

CHAPTER ELEVEN
Addressing issues of race and culture in supervision — 225
Yvonne Ayo

CHAPTER TWELVE
Putting a face to institutionalized racism: The challenge of introducing a live-supervised training programme for black social workers in a predominantly white institution — 249
Sharon Bond

CHAPTER THIRTEEN
The power of delegated authority and how to deal with it — 267
Mojca Brecelj-Kobe and Dubravka Trampuz

SECTION IV: AGENCY AND PROFESSIONAL CONTEXTS — 287

CHAPTER FOURTEEN
Managing multiple relationships in supervision: Dealing with the complexity — 289
Angela Abela and Clarissa Sammut Scerri

CHAPTER FIFTEEN
Systemic supervision in agency contexts: An evolving conversation with clinical psychologists in a mental health trust — 309
Karen Partridge

CHAPTER SIXTEEN
Competition, cosiness, collaboration? Peer relationships in family therapy teams — 337
Jeanne Ziminski

CHAPTER SEVENTEEN
Supervising across a theoretical divide:
    Systemic ideas in action   359
Gwyn Daniel, Maria Eyres, Sarah Majid and Andrew Williams

INDEX   381

FOREWORD

This book is a welcome addition to the series in more ways than one as the editors have gathered together in one volume contemporary topics of relevance for clinicians and service managers alike who cannot not be concerned in these days of ever increasing regulation and diminishing funds for professional development with maintaining high standards in supervision. The editors and contributors are experienced practitioners who know their craft and how to interest readers in new ideas. I am confident readers will find the topics addressed provide both interesting and relevant reading and the book taken as a whole to provide a comprehensive up-to-date survey showing how supervisory practices can be seen to be grounded in theory and how 'theory in action' can be visible and practices transparent.

The book is innovative in three main areas as firstly it provides theoretical chapters which are integrative and address cutting edge issues; secondly the emphasis throughout the book on describing the process of supervision provides readers of any theoretical persuasion with a systemic understanding of group processes which until now has not been clearly articulated in the literature on supervision; thirdly the editors have ensured contributors tackle issues of diversity, power and authority within supervision as well as key practice issues within social services and health contexts. The contributors represent a number of European countries and training contexts and have all in their own way been pioneers in their supervisory practice which brings a wealth of experience to the reader in these pages.

For systemic practitioners and supervisors concerned about their own professional development and supervisees concerned to have a supervisory experience that not only challenges them in ways that enhances their practice but at the same time is experienced as a safe container for working with the increasingly demanding, complex and diverse issues they encounter in their everyday practice, this book will I believe provide a rich resource. The many case examples from a variety of agency contexts provides the reader with an impressive reference book with examples both of the sophistication and creativity now typically associated with the field of systemic thinking and practice.

The editors' choice of the title *Mirrors and Reflections* will I think pique the interest of many professionals both systemically trained and not systemically trained but for whom, regardless of their preferred modality, the complexities of 21st century professional life requires that they think at a meta level and take into account multiple contexts when supervising trainees and colleagues. This book will be a resource for them. For this reason I hope the book will be recognised as an important text in the field of psychotherapy supervision in general and not just systemic thinking and practice and as such be congruent with 21st century aims of this book series.

Ros Draper
Hampshire 2010

THE CONTRIBUTORS

Angela Abela is director of the Centre for Family Studies at the University of Malta, where she is also course director of the Professional Masters Programme in Clinical, Counselling and Educational psychology. She is a clinical psychologist and United Kingdom Council for Psychotherapy (UKCP) registered family therapist and supervisor, supervising professionals working in public social agencies with children and families. She holds a PhD from the Tavistock Clinic and the University of London and a Masters degree in Clinical psychology from the Université de La Sorbonne Paris V. She has published in the area of children and families and supervision practice and is an associate editor on *Clinical Child Psychology and Psychiatry*.

Yvonne Ayo Since qualifying as a family therapist Yvonne Ayo has worked in the voluntary sector with families whose children were excluded from school, and in child and adolescent mental health services in London. She has an interest in community based work and currently works at the Tavistock Centre and in two secondary schools in Camden. In her work as a therapist she has developed interests in issues of race and culture in systemic practice and mixed heritage families. She has undertaken a small research project which explored the extent to which therapists consider the mixed ethnicities of clients and has now embarked on a doctoral programme to research mixed ethnicities in step families.

Sara Barratt is a trainer and team leader of the fostering, adoption and kinship care team at the Tavistock Clinic. She also works in general practice.

Mojca Berelj-Kobe is a child and adolescent psychiatrist and systemic psychotherapist. She is head of the Child Psychiatry Department at the University Medical Hospital Ljubljana. Her interests include work in multi-disciplinary liaison teams. She is founder member of the Institute of Family and Systemic Psychotherapy Ljubljana and works as course co-coordinator for systemic therapy training and supervision.

Paolo Bertrando MD, PhD, psychiatrist and psychotherapist, was trained in systemic family therapy by Luigi Boscolo and Gianfranco Cecchin in the 1980s. Currently he is the director of the Episteme Centre for Systemic Therapy in Turin (Italy). His latest book, published in 2007, is *The Dialogical Therapist* (Karnac). Dr. Bertrando has travelled widely holding workshops and seminars on several topics related to systemic therapy throughout the world.

Sharon Bond is of African-Guyanese heritage. She received her primary and secondary school education in Hackney, where she grew up. Sharon qualified as a social worker in the 1980s. While working in the Psychiatric Social Work Service, she trained as a family/systemic psychotherapist at Kensington Consultation Centre. She is currently director of Chiron Consultation & Therapy Service Ltd and teaches at the Tavistock Clinic and the Institute of Family Therapy.

Paula Boston, MSW, UKCP Family Psychotherapist, AFT registered supervisor is an American, who originally trained as a Family Therapist at the Tavistock Clinic. She has been supervising in qualifying training programmes for more than twenty years. Her interests include narrative therapy and its connection to other approaches, teaching and training issues, organizational consultation and research into self-harm. She is currently director of the University of Leeds Family Therapy Training.

Elizabeth Boyd has worked in the London area for over twenty years, initially as a field social worker and then in Child and Adolescent Mental Health Service where she trained as a family therapist in the late nineties. She qualified as a systemic supervisor in 2004. Elizabeth continues to work with children and families in Child and Adolescent Mental Health in the East End and is also a tutor on the MSc in Systemic Psychotherapy at the Tavistock Centre London. She can be contacted at: elizabethvboyd@yahoo.co.uk

Charlotte Burck is a consultant systemic psychotherapist, trainer and researcher at the Tavistock & Portman NHS Foundation Trust, where she runs the family therapy supervision course and is co-organizing tutor of the Doctoral research programme. Her interests, among others, lie in the areas of multilingualism, supervision and consultation, research, and developing clinical work with families who have experienced violence. She can be contacted at cburck@tavi-port.nhs.uk

John Burnham is a systemic psychotherapist working in the independent and public sectors. His practice includes therapy, supervision, training, consultation and writing. His main clinical work is with children, young people and families at Parkview Clinic, Birmingham Children's Hospital where he is consultant systemic and family psychotherapist and director of the Systemic Training Programme. He was a trainer and director of training at Kensington Consultation Centre (KCC) in London and a Visiting Fellow at Northumbria University. As well as training in the UK he teaches in a variety of contexts including Scandinavia, Netherlands, the USA, and South America.

Claudia Camhi worked until recently within the NHS including settings such as hospitals and Child and Adolescent Mental Health Service. She practiced for several years as a clinical psychologist in Chile working with children, young people and their families before moving to the UK.

Grania Clarke is a consultant clinical psychologist/systemic psychotherapist and supervisor, and at the time of writing was working at the Tavistock Clinic, London. Currently she is the director of psychology, St Michael's House, Dublin.

xvi THE CONTRIBUTORS

Gwyn Daniel has practised as a systemic psychotherapist, trainer and supervisor at the Oxford Family Institute, the Institute of Family Therapy and the Tavistock Clinic. She currently works at the Tavistock Clinic and in private practice in Oxford. She is the author (with Charlotte Burck) of *Gender and Family Therapy* and is co-author of *Growing up in Stepfamilies*. She can be contacted at danielgwyn@googlemail.com

Sumita Dutta is a systemic psychotherapist and supervisor. She works in a London Child and Adolescent Mental Health Service and at the Institute of Family Therapy.

Gabriella Gilli, PhD, psychologist, trained in philosophy in Turin and in Psychology in Milan. She is professor of psychology at the Department of Psychology of the Università Cattolica del Sacro Cuore in Milan.

Julia Granville is a consultant systemic psychotherapist and social worker in the Adoption, Fostering and Kinship Care Service at the Tavistock Clinic. Julia is a clinical supervisor on the Tavistock MSc in systemic psychotherapy and has a special interest in psychotherapy with family members in non-traditional family constellations.

Anto Ingrassia is a consultant child and adolescent psychiatrist. She works with Greenwich Child and Adolescent Mental Health Service, with the specialist looked after children team and with one of the Tier 3 teams.

Guy Larrington works as a systemic psychotherapist on a Child and Adolescent Mental Health Inpatient Unit.

Sarah Majid (MBBChir, MRCPsych) trained in medicine at Cambridge University and the London Hospital Medical School prior to postgraduate training in psychiatry at the Maudsley Hospital, London and further specialist registrar training in psychotherapy at the Tavistock Centre, London. She has an MA in social anthropology and is currently completing the interdisciplinary training in adult psychoanalytic psychotherapy at the Tavistock Centre.

Reena Nath M. Sys. Psych. is in private practise in New Delhi. She has set up a counselling centre at Modi hospital, and was a trainer and supervisor at Sanjivini, a mental health facility, and was secretary of the Indian Association of Family Therapy, prior to training as a systemic psychotherapist at the Tavistock Clinic. She is a consultant psychotherapist with the British High Commission. Currently she is involved in setting up a Masters course in family therapy at the Indira Gandhi National Open University.

Karen Partridge is a systemic psychotherapist and clinical psychologist who has worked in the NHS for over thirty years. She discovered systemic ideas whilst researching into organizational change in hospitals and has been interested in the interface between people and organizations ever since. She is passionate about training and working to create contexts where people can perform and elaborate their preferred versions of self to expand choice and flexibility in their lives. She works as a systemic supervisor and trainer in Central and North West London NHS Foundation Trust and at The Kensington Consultation Centre Foundation, London.

Maria Podlejska-Eyres is a psychiatrist and psychotherapist. She obtained her medical degree in Poland in 1991 and trained as a junior doctor at Royal London Hospital. She completed the foundation year at the Institute of Family Therapy, London. She spent six years in the Adult Department of the Tavistock Centre training in psychoanalytic psychotherapy and is now working as a consultant at the East London Foundation Trust. She has three children.

Clarissa Sammut Scerri is a counselling psychologist and UKCP registered family therapist and systemic supervisor. She has been past head and clinical supervisor of the Family Therapy Services, Appogg, within the Foundation for Social Welfare Services, Malta. She is also a systemic supervisor to professional teams working in schools within the area of domestic violence and family therapy services. She is currently an assistant lecturer within the Department of Psychology at the University of Malta and is reading for a PhD at the University of Surrey, UK.

Gerrlyn Smith is currently Head of a Child and Adolescent Mental Health, Looked After Children Service in Alder Hey Children's NHS Foundation Trust. She is a clinical psychologist and systemic psychotherapist. She has supervised training family therapists over many years with a number of training institutes—currently with the Leeds Programme.

Dave Spellman Dave has worked with children and families as an NHS Clinical Psychologist in the UK (Merseyside and Lancashire) since 1988. He currently works as a consultant clinical psychologist at Lancashire Care NHS Foundation Trust with children who are looked after and their carers. Dave has also trained as a Family Therapist and Family Therapy Supervisor. He can be contacted at: Davescunningplan@aol.com

Dubravka Trampuz is a psychiatrist, systemic psychotherapist and group analyst working in the National Health Service and privately. She is director of the Institute of Family and Systemic Psychotherapy Ljubljana and works as a systemic and group analytic trainer and supervisor.

Andrew Williams is a specialist registrar currently completing a dual training in forensic psychiatry and psychotherapy at the Portman Clinic and the Forensic Directorate of West London Mental Health Trust. His main area of clinical interest is in the application of psychoanalytic principles to working with forensic patients and institutions.

Jeanne Ziminski has a background in generic and Child and Adolescent Mental Health Service social work and family therapy, undertaking her systemic psychotherapy training at Institute of Family Therapy and the Tavistock Centre, where she qualified in 1999. She completed her doctorate in systemic psychotherapy at the Tavistock Centre in 2004 and has subsequently published on her thesis topic—negotiating dilemmas in the kinship care of children. She is a qualified systemic supervisor, and currently works in a Child and Adolescent Mental Health Service team in South London, as a trainer at Institute of Family Therapy and the Tavistock Centre, and as a supervisor in private practice.

INTRODUCTION

Charlotte Burck and Gwyn Daniel

In this volume, as the title indicates, the focus is on understanding and elaborating what might be said to be "going on" in supervision as well as a further exploration of what could be said to be distinctive about systemic supervision. Looking at processes within systemic supervision involves engaging with the different contexts within which this supervision takes place and engaging with a range of theories, some developed and applied within therapeutic contexts and others drawn from theories of learning.

Various theoretical frameworks have emerged and been described as underpinnings for systemic supervision. Social constructionist and narrative ideas have been vital in the creation of supervisory practices that promote open dialogues, multiple perspectives, and the interrogation of traditional assumptions about expertise and hierarchy. This has inevitably led to a discussion of tensions and contradictions: unease about implicit practices of power, the problematics of assessment and evaluation, and issues concerning the allocation of clinical responsibility. Positioning theory, dialogic theories, and ideas from the field of adult education have also contributed helpful theoretical concepts for use by systemic supervisors.

This book takes many of these ideas further as they are grappled with, critiqued, and operationalized in different settings—within agencies and training institutes. What we see as most exciting in these contributions is the way in which contemporary systemic supervisory practice makes use of a creative interplay between different theoretical models and thus demonstrates the versatility necessary to relate to multiple contexts and different levels of system. This is not so much eclecticism, but, as Burnham (Chapter three) elegantly puts it, the ability to create and develop reflexive relationships between practices and theories, and between different theoretical frameworks.

We have been struck by how the literature has often tended to lack accounts of what we might call the "particularities of supervision", that is, the relationships between group members, experiences of diversity and difference, dilemmas of power and authority and, above all, the emotional experience of live supervision, where our visceral responses to the clinical work can erupt and create perturbations in unexpected and unpredictable ways in our struggle for self-definition as either supervisee or supervisor. Live supervision is an intimate process and many of the chapters in this book aim to convey some of the flavour of this intimacy and intensity. What is examined and tangled with here is the interplay between context, the interior processes within supervisory relationships in their interactions with families, and the sense of effectiveness and personal agency of supervisor and supervisees. Yvonne Ayo (Chapter eleven) in her chapter examines the complexities involved in sustaining talk of the meanings of racialized difference and cultural diversity within supervision groups; Sharon Bond (Chapter twelve) provides a powerful account of the impact of developing supervisory relationships in the context of institutional racism; and Angela Abela and Clarissa Sammut Scerri (Chapter fourteen) are concerned with the dilemmas posed when supervisor–supervisee relationships are situated within multiple relationships in a closely connected community.

As well as widening the frame to include new contexts within which processes in systemic supervision can be elaborated, we have aimed to bring to life some of the more fraught and challenging processes within supervision itself, which have often been ignored in more generalized descriptions.

Our overall focus on processes means, we hope, that those chapters which relate specifically to training contexts will be relevant to supervision in agencies where professionals may not be trained systemically. Equally we hope that the "agency-based" chapters will be relevant to training institutes and inform those who are training supervisors. Thus we take the overall view that supervision in whatever context is inevitably a learning process. Additionally, one of the most dynamic developments in recent years has been the growth of training courses in systemic supervision and the research and writing that has emerged from these courses, offering critiques and exploring new contexts, and thus renewing and refreshing established practices within systemic supervision. Several contributions from this context are included in this volume (chapters by Dave Spellman and Gerrilyn Smith [Chapter four], Sumita Dutta [Chapter five], Julia Granville [Chapter six], Elizabeth Boyd [Chapter ten], Yvonne Ayo [Chapter eleven] and Jeanne Ziminiski [Chapter sixteen]).

Theoretical developments

The book begins with Paolo Bertrando and Gabriella Gilli (Chapter one) setting the context by examining the evolution of supervision theory and practice over time and across models, attempting to answer the question, "How does supervision work?" They offer fresh ways of considering the isomorphism between supervision and therapy, which other writers (Paula Boston [Chapter two]; John Burnham [Chapter three]; Sharon Bond [Chapter twelve]; and Gwyn Daniel, Maria Eyres, Sarah Majid, and Andrew Williams [Chapter seventeen]) take up and explore further in their own settings.

Paula Boston (Chapter two) draws distinctions in her use of theoretical frameworks by highlighting responses to different supervisory dimensions and exigencies. Her examples of supervisory practice, allowing the reader to "watch" her theories in action, are particularly engaging as she not only describes creative and helpful practices, but also tackles more problematic sequences in supervision processes within a training institute.

John Burnham (Chapter three) offers new ways to incorporate and transform adult educational ideas into relational and collaborative systemic and narrative supervisory practices, challenging us to examine our own preferred ways of learning and extend these as readers, supervisors, and supervisees.

Dave Spellman and Gerrilyn Smith's chapter (Chapter four) breaks new ground in exploring the place of emotion in systemic supervision and the links they make between theoretical formulations of emotions and the different ways that emotions may be performed and responded to within supervision. This connects powerfully with another aim of the book which is to highlight the fact that supervision, and especially live supervision, is usually a powerfully emotional process, whether or not this emotion is overtly elicited. Sumita Dutta (Chapter five) explores in-depth how a moment of intense emotional resonance in supervision can be theoretically formulated at diverse levels as well as demonstrating how she and her supervisee found a helpful way to reflect on it in practice.

From the perspective of agency supervision, Karen Partridge (Chapter fifteen) adds to the richness of systemic ideas through delineating four different constructions of supervision and analysing the grammars and cultures that the supervisor needs to attend to within diverse contexts, which enable her to connect creatively with professionals for the benefit of clients. Her use of supervision as primary participative research opens up interesting ways for the whole field to develop further in this critical period for the psychotherapies.

Links between psychodynamic and systemic approaches to supervision

We consider it important to engage with approaches to supervision from other theoretical frameworks, including that of psychoanalysis. The relationship between systemic psychotherapy and psychoanalysis has often been polarized through discourses of conflict and competition and sometimes compensated for by an over-eager accommodation. We are pleased that in this volume theoretical and practical differences are unpacked and explored in a spirit of openness and curiosity. Paolo Bertrando and Gabriella Gilli (Chapter one) engage with psychoanalytic methods in the context of the evolution of supervision, highlighting dilemmas regarding power in both systemic and psychoanalytic approaches. Julia Granville (Chapter six) describes psychoanalytic concepts that she has found helpful in understanding group processes within the framework of systemic supervision. Mojca Bercelj-Kobe and Dubravka Trampuz (Chapter thirteen) look at how both psychoanalysis and systemic supervision have responded to challenges of postmodernist ideas. Gwyn Daniel, Maria Eyres, Sarah Majid, and Andrew Williams (Chapter seventeen) provide an account of how tensions between the models were experienced within a systemic supervision group provided for psychoanalytically trained psychiatrists, providing lively multiple narratives of the ways in which differences were managed.

Power, authority, and collaborative practice

Concerns to make power transparent and to work towards developing more collaborative relationships within supervision are evident in many of these chapters. This stands in interesting juxtaposition to the task of claiming one's authority as a supervisor. Mojca Bercelj-Kobe and Dubravka Trampuz (Chapter thirteen) refer to the anxieties and dilemmas involved in developing supervisory relationships in their psychiatric context in Slovenia where the development of the supervisor's own authority was a challenge. Wider contextual power relationships are also played out within supervision processes as Angela Abela and Clarissa Sammut Scerri's (Chapter fourteen) further elaborate in their description of the dilemmas involved in managing overlapping and closely connected relationships in Malta.

These two chapters grapple with the risks that their dilemmas of supervisory practice are being read against a "colonizing eye", positing an imagined space of secure and regulated professional hierarchy and boundaries which can act to problematize multiple relationships rather than embrace and explore their complexity. However, the effects of taken-for-granted power practices can be seen much closer to home as Sharon Bond's chapter (Chapter twelve) demonstrates, drawing our attention to the often "unwitting" forms of institutionalized racism which contextualize and give rise to contested discourses around a training initiative. Bond explores how the generally unacknowledged processes of institutional racism can create "status contradictions" for a black supervisor and contribute to feelings of failure despite having carried out a successful supervisory initiative.

Yvonne Ayo (Chapter eleven) explores the intricacies of the processes of discussion and silencing of the differences of racialized identities and culture in supervision groups, and their effects, and raises questions of how supervisors most helpfully share responsibilities with supervision groups for sustaining this talk. Supervision groups are places where some voices can loom larger and louder than others and Elizabeth Boyd's chapter (Chapter ten) explores the question of voice entitlement and its complex relationship to family history and position as well as to cultural and gendered rules and precepts regarding talking and silence. She uses Bakhtin's (1973) idea of ventriloquation—the process through which one speaks through the voices of others—to evoke past and imagined audiences to trainees' speech acts to enable their increased manoeuvrability as clinicians and team members. All of these processes have immense emotional resonance.

Group process

It has been striking how processes within supervision groups have been under-theorized in the systemic supervision literature. Several chapters in this volume address this gap and move our understanding of systemic supervision from a focus on dyadic interactions (which tend to privilege the supervisor's position) to a foregrounding of the group itself. Positions taken include paying more explicit attention to group processes: Julia Granville (Chapter six) discusses how psychodynamic frameworks enable her to understand group processes and intervene within a systemic and social constructionist model while Charlotte Burck (Chapter seven) draws on systemic, social constructionist and narrative theories and methods to enable supervisors and supervisees to become more attuned to this level. Conversely, Sara Barratt, Claudia Camhi, Sumita Dutta, Antonina Ingrassia, and Guy Larrington (Chapter nine) argue that the work-group ethos of a supervision group, prioritizing the service to families, can in itself enhance group process and further the learning environment. Examples of difficult group processes and their impacts on supervisors as well as on supervisees are also included, as Gwyn Daniel, Grania Clarke, and Reena Nath (Chapter eight) revisit and reflect on their experiences together. The experience of failure in supervision and the struggle to regain a sense of trust, connection, and confidence do not usually make it into the public domain. These different punctuations of this multi-levelled endeavour, alongside the challenges of the work with families, may offer ideas to enable supervisors, supervisees, and supervision groups to reflect on their own positions and situate themselves differently.

Writing about group processes from the perspectives of supervisor and supervisees, as the three multiple-authored chapters (eight, nine, and seventeen) in this volume do, enables both triumphs and tribulations to be named in a more direct, relational, and egalitarian spirit than supervisor-authored papers which perhaps tend to be more cautious in conveying the emotions of pride, shame, competence, and incompetence that the public context of live supervision can evoke.

Agency contexts

While the attention to process highlighted in this volume can hopefully straddle many different supervisory settings, attending to the particular environments created by different agency and different professional contexts remains crucial. Dave Spellman and Gerrilyn Smith (Chapter four) describe a form of supervision structured to develop consultancy skills and to contribute to team building in an agency where practitioners have wide differences of experience. Karen Partridge (Chapter fifteen) demonstrates how in a clinical psychology context, different treatment modalities, different team cultures, and specific client needs create "grammars" that the systemic supervisor needs to "enter" in order to be helpful, and provides a number of useful and creative examples of how she does this. In the Child and Adolescent Mental Health Services (CAMHS) context, Jeanne Ziminski (Chapter sixteen) explores the beliefs, myths, practices, and possibilities of peer supervision and asks questions to enable systemic therapists to review and re-examine these arrangements, many of which risk becoming routine and taken-for-granted. The particular issues for psychoanalytically trained groups in engaging in learning about systemic psychotherapy are tackled by Gwyn Daniel, Maria Eyres, Sarah Majid, and Andrew Williams (Chapter seventeen).

Time

We have been interested in the way that the passage of time can itself create a new context from which to revisit and process difficult and painful experiences in supervision and learn from them. Gwyn Daniel, Grania Clarke, and Reena Nath (Chapter eight) and Sharon Bond (Chapter twelve) explicitly take a retrospective view of supervision processes from a distance of several years to generate ideas which may be helpful for others as well as recuperative for the writers themselves. Paula Boston (Chapter two), John Burnham (Chapter three), and Charlotte Burck (Chapter seven) all allude to how moments of powerful emotional resonance in supervision can be left open for revisiting and reworking over time. These contributions all raise possibilities for supervisors and supervision groups to engender such potential for themselves in the future.

What we anticipate will be evident to the reader, as became apparent to us from our experience of editing this volume, is that systemic supervision is itself very much a work in progress. Taking up interesting and relevant ideas from therapy and other fields to develop creative ways of supervising in different contexts, systemic supervision expands notions of collaborative practice and renews its theoretical base. Hopefully it will keep tangling with difficult and challenging episodes and relationships which in turn will call forth new learning and new approaches. We hope that you, the reader, whether or not you agree with what is presented here, will recognize interesting "edges" in the supervisory process that will lead you to both take some of these ideas and practices further and develop new ones, not yet formulated by us or any of our authors.

SECTION I

EVOLVING THEORIES

CHAPTER ONE

Theories of change and the practice of systemic supervision

Paolo Bertrando[1] and Gabriella Gilli[2]

As psychotherapists, whether experienced practitioners or not, we have all been in supervision, and periodically we go back to it. Supervision is considered essential to good training and good practice, although its precise boundaries, and even its usefulness, have been questioned (see Storm et al. 2001). Now, what is the main characteristic of such a key aspect of therapeutic practice? Probably the fact that the supervisor, more than any other professional in therapy, is "presumed to know". The general idea of supervision involves the prejudice that the supervisor is the one who can (must) correct the supervisee's mistakes. Thus—especially in cases where the supervisory relationship is one-to-one—the supervisor tends to act so as to constantly frustrate her supervisee.[3] As a colleague of ours once happened to say: "I feel my duty

---

[1] Director, Episteme Centre, Turin, Italy. Corresponding address: Paolo Bertrando, MD, PhD, piazza S. Agostino 22, 20123, Milano, Italy. Tel. 00390243511443. E-mail: gilbert56@libero.it.
[2] Associate Professor, teacher of Psychology of Personality, Università Cattolica del Sacro Cuore, Milano, Italy.
[3] For the sake of clarity, we will use throughout the female gender for the supervisor, and the male for the supervisee.

is to help some people to understand when it's the case for them to change their job." This at least justifies the anxiety—sometimes the terror—experienced by supervisees in some circles. It can, however, at times, make the practice of supervision controversial, as this statement from an experienced psychoanalytical psychotherapist testifies:

> In my work in recent years, I have found supervision becoming more and more of a problem, a challenge, and a reason for dissatisfaction to me ... when I asked others what they remembered about their own experience of being supervised, several of my senior colleagues ... said in effect: "I always saw to it that I went to a supervisor who would interfere with me as little as possible."
> (Grotjahn cited in Schuster, Sandt, and Thaler, 1972: 77–8)

All this, however, sharply contrasts with both the theory and practice of systemic therapy, where the emphasis lies on strengths rather than limitations, and on the development of personal competence rather than on teaching some pre-existing wisdom (Bertrando, 2007). Thus, although the field of systemic therapy is by no means free from the exercise of authority (sometimes to the point of being authoritarian), the development of supervisory modalities shows some peculiarities that we would like to deal with in the following pages.

Questions

What is the influence of theoretical models on the practice of supervision? Of course, in order to discuss such an influence, the preliminary question has to deal with the nature of supervision. About which, as it happens, opinions differ. Rather than reviewing the vast existing literature on the subject, we will begin with a short definition which suits our aim. The basic purpose of psychotherapy supervision is to help supervisees develop an experiential expertise, useful in treating their clients.

Supervision (like training) is also a way to embody a theory in practice for trainees, or to refresh the theoretical basis for experienced practitioners. The supervisory experience thus cannot be detached from theoretical models. This does not mean, however, that the supervisor should always make the use of any model(s) explicit to the supervisee, but rather that such models inevitably shape her work. There should be some coherence between general theory, clinical theory and practice, training theory and practice, and supervision. This is what is called an isomorphic perspective: in optimal supervisory practice, supervision is isomorphic to therapy, in the sense that they both obey (more or less) the same set of rules (Liddle, 1988).

The important issue here is that the supervisee will learn (or in Gregory Bateson's [1973] terminology "deutero-learn") not from the content of supervision, but from the form that it takes. His practice will be influenced by the practice experienced in supervision. This is why the particular form given to the supervision is crucial.

> If a supervisor implies that a therapist's personal problems are interfering with the progress of a case, the therapist will suggest, directly or indirectly, to the client that his or her deep emotional problems are interfering with the progress of the therapy.
> (Haley, 1988: 362)

Haley, in the article quoted, criticizes all insight-oriented, non-directive models of supervision. In his view, if the supervisor does not accept being in charge of the supervisory situation, the therapist will learn to not take responsibility for her case. We could say, conversely, that a supervisor too keen to take responsibility for a case will create therapists who do not accept the views of their clients. The fact is, the position that the supervisor brings into the supervision is the position that the supervisee will tend to learn.

> Using the isomorphic perspective, the supervisor can transform this replication into an intervention, redirecting a therapist's behaviour and thereby influencing interactions at various levels of the system. Supervisors are not passive observers of pattern replication, but intervenors and intentional shapers of the misdirected sequences they perceive, participate in, and co-create.
> (Liddle, 1988: 155)

Should supervision models, then, be consistent with the premises of each theoretical model and with the practice of therapy? Or is it better for us to consider some basic issues—namely, focus, goals, and modalities—that any supervisor, sooner or later, has to face?

As to focus, supervision may be focused, roughly speaking, either on the therapist, on the client(s), or on the therapist–client(s) relationship. As to goal, it may (mainly) concern solving some of the supervisee's personal issues which may interfere with existing abilities; helping the supervisee to learn abilities and techniques; enhancing the supervisee's awareness of his own context and positioning; or supporting the supervisee in stressful therapeutic situations. This last goal is often overlooked in the professional literature, although it may be considered one of the most important in some cases, such as the supervision of therapists working with abuse, violence, and trauma: "It cannot be reiterated too often: no one can face trauma alone. If a therapist finds herself isolated in her professional practice, she should discontinue working with traumatised patients until she has secured an adequate support system" (Herman, 1992: 153). Regarding modalities, supervision can be held in an individual or group setting, and it can either use case reports, or various modalities of direct observation. Each supervision model tends to have its specific focus, goal, and modality. In Table 1 we have summarized the most usual combinations, although we have

Table 1. Characteristics of supervision and theoretical models

Focus	Goal	Modality	Models
On therapist/ trainee	Therapist's personal and professional development Therapist's support	Case report	Psychoanalytic Intergenerational
On family/ client	Problem-solving	Direct (live) supervision	Strategic Structural Early systemic
On client–therapist relationship	Awareness of context and positioning	Case report Direct supervision	Postmodern systemic Narrative Conversational

to emphasize that other combinations are possible (and indeed frequent occurrences).

Focus of supervision

On the therapist

If the supervision is focused on the therapist, the supervisor is mainly interested in the supervisee's development as a therapist and, except for serious contingencies, leaves to the supervisee the whole burden of therapy without excessive intrusion. The quality of a specific client's therapy is supposed to improve as a side effect of the supervisee's overall professional growth. Such a focus is usually consistent with the goal of dealing with the supervisee's presumed personal problems, which may interfere with him effectively implementing what he (in some way) already knows.

Probably the most time-honoured supervisory tradition is one where the focus is mainly on the person of the supervisee, namely psychoanalytic supervision. From its very beginning, psychoanalytic supervision has tended to privilege the resolution of personal issues. Supervision thus became a way of working on the person of the analyst, a further step after personal and training analysis. Already in 1926, the Committee of the International Psychoanalytic Association stated that: "Instructional analysis is the most important part of the training but it does not constitute the whole. It is absolutely essential that we should demand and give opportunity for further training, including, above all, the conducting of analyses under supervision" (International Psychoanalytic Association, 1926: 130). Thirty years later, the American Psychoanalytic Association added further determinants to supervision, aiming it very directly to the person of the analyst:

> The aims of the supervision are: 1. To instruct the student in the use of the psychoanalytic method. 2. To aid him [sic] in the acquisition of therapeutic skill based upon an understanding of the analytic material. 3. To observe his work and determine how fully his personal analysis has achieved its aims. 4. To determine his maturity and stability over an extended period of time.
> (American Psychoanalytic Association, 1956: 718)

Such a position has remained more or less the same through the years, as Eckstein and Wallerstein testify:

> [Supervision is] not simply ... the transmission of knowledge and skills, but rather ... a complex process that goes on between the supervisor and the student. This process is a helping process in which the student is being helped to discover his [sic] problems as a psychotherapist, to resolve them with the help of the supervisor, and to develop toward higher integrations as a learner and as a psychotherapist. This process includes affective problems, interpersonal conflicts, problems in being helped, as well as in helping, and is therefore truly itself a helping process.
> (Eckstein and Wallerstein, 1972: 251)

From the point of view of method, psychoanalytic supervision is a typical example of the use of the case report. To each session the supervisee brings news of what happened between himself and his clients since last meeting with their supervisor. The supervisor listens and makes comments about specific points. This very method, however, can be considered one potential source of authoritarianism, and has triggered a growing body of criticism, especially from authors such as Levine (2003) and Kernberg (2004). McCormick comments:

> Verbatim reporting is a fundamentally persecutory set-up in which the only possibility of safety is the beneficence of the supervisor. In this—best—case, the student iatrogenically develops a strong bond of dependency to the supervisor, which is at odds with psychodynamic therapy's aim of fostering personal autonomy.
> (McCormick, 1994: 15)

Of course, it would be unfair to the psychoanalytic method of case report supervision to consider this as its only potential effect. Other, more positive effects, are the absorption by the supervisee of the very method that he has to learn and improve. Already in 1935, Helene Deutsch suggested the use of free association during supervision in order to make it more consistent with the basic rule of analysis:

> The candidate's unconscious actually absorbs the material given
> him [sic] by the patient at a time when he is still completely free
> from understanding its importance. If the candidate is allowed
> to reproduce the material in free association, one can see how
> much more wisdom his unconscious shows in the reproduction
> than does his conscious knowledge.
>
> (Deutsch, 1935: 62)

This means that psychoanalytic supervision is like a subset of analysis, and it varies little according to the clinical experience of the supervisee: the process is the same, whether one is an experienced therapist or a trainee.

Within the field of family therapy, intergenerational supervision shows processes strikingly similar to the ones we have just described. In Bowen theory, for example, the emphasis is on differentiation of the self:

> Role play and live supervision fall into the category of techniques that are employed to help people learn what to do. ... The thrust of Bowen theory has always moved toward helping people to think and to go as far with their cognitive abilities as possible toward differentiation of self in their own families.
>
> (Papero, 1988: 72)

Therefore, no direct techniques are employed in Bowenian supervision. Videotapes too are seldom reviewed, as they typically focus on skills and lead supervisees to imitation. The supervisee, instead, is helped to understand his position in his own family, and, at the same time, his position in relation to the family with which he is working. Techniques and skills are secondary to such an understanding. The main difference to analytic supervision is the emphasis on a comprehensive understanding of intergenerational theory. Bowen therapists should focus on maintaining their differentiation during family work, and not on changing the family: "The effort to change another person is characteristic of anxious families. Training in Bowen theory works always to clarify one's own role in a situation and to step beyond the inclination to change another person" (Papero, 1988: 72).

Problematic families are seen as "trigger" families, that is, families that trigger problematic issues the supervisee has with his own family of origin. This leads, in supervision, to parallel work on the trigger family and the supervisee's family, through comparison of the two genograms to find similarities, and so on.

> It is my impression that even a small amount of time spent in defining and shifting patterns in one's own family is a much more efficient way of learning to deal with [difficult therapies]. Understanding one's functioning in his/her own family seems to facilitate the ability to understand the operation of other natural systems and the ability to generate hypotheses about families on a systems level.
> (McGoldrick, 1981: 19–20)

On the client(s)

Since the early days of strategic and systemic family therapy, supervision tended to be focused principally on families rather than on therapists. In this kind of supervision, the supervisor tends to directly tell the supervisee what to do in order to effectively help the clients. The main goal is to teach him what he does not already know, in order to overcome errors made out of ignorance. The risk here is that the family gets therapy from the supervisor "by proxy", with the supervisee left with the role of message-carrier. Initially performed using verbatim reports, supervision focused on clients was boosted by the introduction of one-way mirrors, which shifted the preferred modality to live supervision:

> Live supervision is a term describing a process by which someone guides the therapist while he [sic] works. ... our experience suggests that it enables the trainee to learn techniques of therapy more rapidly and economically.
> (Cade and Seligman, 1981: 174)

Alongside one-way mirrors came video recordings (see Bodin, 1972), and with them new opportunities:

> Videotape provides three unique opportunities. First, it freezes time so that after the session a crucial sequence can be played and replayed. ... Secondly, the therapist can see himself [sic]

> objectively as one of the contributors to the whole system. ...
> Thirdly, the effect of an intervention can be studied and its success evaluated.
>
> (Whiffen, 1981: 39)

The introduction of video recording and live supervision changed all procedures in family therapy during the late 1960s and early 1970s, allowing a quicker grasp of techniques, and a new notion of self-awareness for therapists. It also led to a therapeutic style geared towards technique: live supervision became the perfect tool to help trainees (rather than experienced therapists) to learn a set of techniques.

All of these features were well attuned to strategic and structural models, where the emphasis was on problem solving (see Haley, 1976). In the case of psychoanalysis, isomorphism is located in the fact that both analysis and supervision are conceived as personal growth processes. In this case, isomorphism stems from a constant attempt by the supervisor to influence her supervisee by all (legitimate) means, exactly as happens during strategic therapy sessions:

> It would seem to be best for the supervisor to influence trainees outside their awareness, particularly if making them aware of an intervention would oversimplify or interfere with their learning to do it. ... The principle is the same when conducting therapy. The difference is that a therapist-in-training must learn to influence many kinds of people in many situations, and so needs an education as people changer.
>
> (Haley, 1988: 366)

The earphone (the "bug in the ear") was invented by Jay Haley and Salvador Minuchin to teach "lay" therapists, and soon became the typical strategic and directive supervision tool (see some lively accounts in Richard Simon's interviews with Haley and Minuchin in Simon [1992]). It is even more directive than the telephone connecting the two rooms. Through this method, the supervisor, to a certain extent, becomes the therapist and vice versa.

> The family responds to the trainee's intervention as if it were entirely his [sic], not someone else's. This provides immediate

> experience of the effects of various interventions; a much quicker way of learning techniques. ... (It) also allows the supervisor to add intensity to the intervention by blocking the trainee's own homeostatic and diffusing techniques and by suggesting more potent interventions. ... The disadvantages come from the fact that it is a powerful tool and deceptively easy to use. The supervisor, who is usually a therapeutic enthusiast, may get caught up in the therapeutic excitement because he can get very close to being the therapist himself.
>
> (Byng-Hall, 1981: 47–48)

The method has, of course, its disadvantages, which lie exactly in its intrinsically directive character. Former supervisees reported

> problems about self-exposure and self-esteem, autonomy and loss of ego boundary, and compliance and authority. [...] The presence of other team members continuously reminds the therapist/trainee that he [sic] is only part of a total thinking and feeling system. He is no longer independent in his work, and there are times when his own judgement will have to be suspended.
>
> (Freud Loewenstein, Reder, and Clark, 1981: 116)

On the therapist–client(s) relationship

The focus on the client–therapist relationship has been adopted mainly by the systemic model (see Boscolo et al. 1987), as it developed after the splitting of the original Milan systemic group. Such an approach, deeply influenced by Gregory Bateson's (1972) emphasis on relationship, shifted its attention from relationship within the client system to relationships within the therapeutic system, that is, the system created by the interaction of therapists and clients. Later on, therapists accepting the various models that are defined, on the whole, as postmodern approaches (Gardner et al. 2003), went one step further. Together with the emphasis on the therapeutic relationship, postmodern supervision tends to deconstruct the authority of the supervisor, which it substitutes with a collaborative relationship with the supervisee:

> In contrast with the hierarchical position adopted by conventional models, strength-based models of supervision attempt to sidestep

hierarchy in favour of co-constructing ideas with the supervisee. A non-hierarchical supervisory relationship is one where there exists a give and take, where the supervisor does not assume to have more "correct" or privileged knowledge of both the supervisee's and clients' goals, intentions or views, and where the supervisor works intentionally to create a strength-based supervision.

(Edwards and Chen, 2004: 353)

Once again, isomorphism is clear. Just as postmodern therapy stresses the clients' expertise (Anderson and Goolishian, 1992) and their potential to become narrators of their own stories (White and Epston, 1992), so postmodern supervisors deliberately use concepts that reflect a non-hierarchical relationship with supervisees. Other relevant features concern the positioning of the supervisor within her context, thus describing where her ideas came from (Bertrando, 2007), rather than focusing on a fixed set of assumptions and techniques, and an orientation towards resources and strengths, rather than dysfunction and pathology.

For supervision these premises imply that the supervisor is an expert in an exploratory conversational process, in which she or he engages collaboratively with the supervisees in the telling, inquiring, interpreting, and shaping of the supervisee's narrative. Such a supervisory position implies that the supervisor is not the expert on the supervisees, but that the supervisee is the expert on his or her own life and on his or her own narratives, experiences, and knowledge.

(Anderson and Swim, 1995: 2)

This position—as many postmodern predicaments—is extremely correct on the one side, and, on the other, slightly paradoxical (see also Trampuz and Berelj-Kobe, this volume). We may define supervision as "co-vision", or "inter-vision", in order to delete the "super" prefix, which unavoidably speaks of superiority. What happens is still supervision anyway, just as strength-based conversation is still therapy. Most of all, supervisees still ask their supervisors something they are presumed to know:

Supervisors might therefore choose to decenter themselves from the process of supervision, bracketing their expertise as

> just one way of knowing the world. However, supervisees are just as likely to want to center the therapist, to hear about his or her experiences, to engage the supervisor in everything from consultation to advocacy.
>
> (Ungar, 2006: 59)

Such paradoxes are difficult to escape if we see postmodernism as a prescription ("I must behave in a postmodern way") rather than a description ("I cannot but be postmodern") (Bertrando, 2000). They, in turn, generate problems for the supervisor that stand exactly on the opposite side from the ones elicited by a strategic approach: rather than feeling a sense of dependency and constriction, the supervisee may risk feelings of indeterminacy and not being supported. Here, concepts like "safe uncertainty" and "authoritative doubt" (Mason, 1993: 189–190) may be more helpful for a supervisor than the often abused (and misunderstood) terminology of "not knowing" (see Anderson and Goolishian, 1992: 25).

Supervision modalities

Group supervision

Group work is quite common in supervision, usually for economic reasons. It also became popular in systemic, structural, and strategic therapy because it allowed for live supervision to be demonstrated and performed in a hands-on way. In structural (Montalvo, 1973) and strategic (Haley, 1988) models, the structure of the supervision group is hierarchical: the supervisor, leader of the group, knows more than the group members; the group as such knows more than the supervisee; the latter has to conform to the group's decision (and the last word is to the supervisor).

The group approaches we want to review now are somewhat different in this regard: here the group itself is the supervisor, whereas the leader (the formal supervisor) should be considered more of a catalyst, with a different role compared to individual supervision. Also, the group is not necessarily presumed to know more (or better) than the supervisee.

> To develop in our students a systemic approach to therapy ... we must create a context where there is a continual flux between

linear and circular thinking, simple linear hypothesizing and circular hypothesizing. Team work is essential to achieve this result and is the basic tool of our training programme. ... Members of a team working together can offer, almost simultaneously, different punctuations of the relationships and behaviours under observation, and can be corrective to one another, so that circular views can more easily occur.

(Boscolo and Cecchin, 1981: 155–164)

This is consistent both with the systemic (Boscolo et al. 1987) and narrative (White, 1995) models and has been fully developed by Tom Andersen with the practice of the reflecting team, which has become one of the most important ways of doing systemic supervision (Andersen, 1991).

We now describe the model of case report supervision devised by Boscolo and Cecchin.[4] The format is that of a small group ranging from six to eighteen persons. Within it, a person or a subgroup is identified, who bring a specific problem. Now the supervisory system involves: the problem-bearer(s), the group, and the supervisor. The latter dictates the working rules and distributes the speech turns (participants only speak when it is their chance). This is the procedure:

1. The problem-bearer describes the problem, its nature and history, the context where—according to him—it developed.
2. When the problem-bearer has the feeling of having told it all, the group members can ask questions. The questions may concern anything that is unclear or where it is felt that extra details would be useful. The problem-bearer, in turn, can add in this period other things that came to their mind during the questions that they believe could be helpful.
3. When the questioning phase is concluded, the group members begin discussing between them what has been said. Their aim is to generate hypotheses about the problem and the possibilities for a solution. There are no limits to the nature of these hypotheses:

---

[4] Although this method has been created and widely used by the two Milan associates, they never published anything on the subject. We describe it here out of our personal experience as both supervisees and supervisors.

they may regard the presenting problem; the relationship between the problem-bearer and their client (or the problematic situation); the context (especially in institutional cases); the relationship between the colleague and the group; or even the analogies between different kinds of relationship. All this time, the problem-bearer cannot speak, but must listen to the group working. The discussion goes on until one or more major hypotheses emerge, or, more frequently, until the supervisor feels that there has been exploration of a sufficient number of different hypotheses.
4. At this point, the problem-bearer can give some response to what has been said, or, in turn, ask questions of the group.
5. After this last moment, the supervision is terminated.

The aim of this kind of supervision is not to offer the supervisee an "authoritative" solution, since the nominal supervisor, the one presumed to hold authority, acts minimally in the first person. What actually happens is that the peer group puts the supervisee in front of a multiplicity of points of view, thus allowing them to observe their work from different positions, constructing at the same time hypotheses, "neither true nor false" (Selvini Palazzoli et al. 1980) about their work, their relationships, and the context of their relationships.

Deliberately, the model does not compel participants to seek one kind of hypothesis (for example, the therapist–client relationship, or the supervision group–supervisee relationship), because the multiplicity of views itself enhances and widens the range of competences for the therapist. Although it has been objected that in such a situation the group may overlook serious shortcomings in evaluation or treatment, this has not been confirmed by experience: usually the supervision team is sufficiently attentive to recognize mistakes due to obvious failures of ethical and professional responsibility, rather than to autonomous theoretical choices. Also, of course, if the team fails, the supervisor always has the chance to recover her authority. Most importantly, the supervisee perceives his colleagues in the team as a strong support, and also as a window on his way of working: not receiving a definitive "verdict" often has the effect of boosting the supervisee's reflection on himself and on the network of relationships that he is embedded in (Bertrando, 2007).

If we consider the shape of a typical reflecting team discussion, we may discern a similar pattern. In reflecting teams, a therapist interviewing an individual client or a family is observed, usually through a one-way mirror, by a team composed (usually, but not necessarily) of three colleagues.

> Each member of the reflecting team listens quietly to the conversation. The members do not talk to each other but each of them talks to him/herself in a questioning manner. [...] The team members then talk to each other about their ideas and questions about the presented issue(s), with the members of the interview system listening to them. [...] This procedure gives the members of the interviewing system [...] a possibility of having an inner dialogue as they listen to the versions the team presents.
> (Andersen, 1991: 40)

Afterwards, therapist and client(s) discuss what they have listened to. The process may be described as a layering of comments and observations, each one about that which has preceded it. The basic idea is that the procedure helps therapists and clients to become more silent and more thoughtful, allowing more room for listening: which was marked a substantial change, a difference that made a difference, for systemic therapy, where listening had never been one of the core abilities of therapists.

Still another variation on the group modality is the narrative group supervision developed by Hugh Fox and his colleagues (Fox et al. 2003) following Michael White's (1995) ideas. In this case supervision is neither direct nor reported, but rather performed over an audiotape of a therapy session. This is the procedure:

Stage One: A group member ("the worker") is interviewed by another group member ("the interviewer") to elicit the background to the piece of work the worker is bringing. The rest of the group listen.

Stage Two: We all listen to a piece of audiotape of an actual session where the worker is talking with the person who is consulting them, usually for around five or ten minutes.

Stage Three: The rest of the group discuss their responses.

> *Stage Four*: The interviewer and the worker talk some more.
> *Stage Five*: Everybody talks together.
> *Stage Six*: The discussions are audiotaped and the worker takes the tape back to the person at the centre of the discussions.
>
> (Fox et al. 2003: 27)

Here, the group process is not centred on hypotheses following one another, nor on the different positions of group members, but rather on what the authors describe as the "telling and retelling" of a story. The person(s) "at the centre" is not the supervisee, it is his client(s). One of the most important stages of this process is the moment when the taped discussion is brought back to the clients. At the same time, in this process, too, it is important for group members to be sensitive to their own personal and emotional responses to what happened during the supervision. Not surprisingly, Fox and his colleagues report that this "stage" of the process is the most difficult to achieve.

These three methods, despite their apparent similarity (in their use of the group, their non-authoritarian stance, their dialogical perspective), also show differences, due to the different models that they embody. In the first, the emphasis is on the construction and proposal of different hypotheses; in the second, it is on the offering of different viewpoints, and on respectful mutual listening; in the third, on the telling and understanding of stories and life experiences. Even with important formal and theoretical analogies, the underlying model still deeply influences the supervisory practice.

Ideas of supervision

We can say, then, that supervision has been (and is) conceived of in different ways, depending on the model of therapy, and also on the specific context and situation of each supervision. Before attempting to take into account the common mechanisms that we see at work in any supervision, we would like to summarize the different ideas of supervision we have so far encountered.

- Supervision as *increase of knowledge*. This is true of analytic as well as strategic supervision: the supervisor knows better, she has the knowledge. The supervisee has only to learn.

- Supervision as *intervention on the person of the therapist*. This is the other side of analytic and intergenerational supervision: the cumulative effects of a series of supervisions produce a lasting change on the supervisee as a person.
- Supervision as *giving directives*. This is typical of strategic and structural supervision: the supervisor is the holder of know-how, rather than abstract knowledge, and instructs the supervisee to act accordingly.
- Supervision as an *increase of points of view*. This is the description of systemic group supervision and reflecting team: it activates a group process that gives the supervisee a multiplicity of points of view.
- Supervision as *open dialogue*. In postmodern systemic supervision, the supervisor engages in a dialogue where the position and point of view of the supervisee have equal (albeit not identical) relevance.

How supervision works (possibly)

How then does supervision work? If we look at therapy and supervision processes with naive eyes, we may think that theory dictates a world vision and a series of techniques that the therapist should simply put into practice. In this way, the unbelievable complexity of the world could be reduced to the simplicity of one theory. In such a perspective, supervision is just a way of constraining the supervisee in the Procrustean bed of theory—a process which would be limiting, and even potentially dangerous.

If we take a closer look at the way any therapist does therapy, we will probably draw the opposite conclusion: in what a therapist does there is always more than is contained in their theory, and also more than they are able to describe. All therapists work from some theoretical standpoint, but in their practice there is much that is neither contained nor containable in their models. We have to look at how models are embodied in practice (see Bertrando, 2008).[5] This is what Donald Schön (1983) calls the reflective practitioner model.

Interestingly enough, Schön himself used as one of his examples in his book a session held by a psychoanalytic supervisor with a

---

[5] Which does not mean that theories are superfluous for therapy. Therapists need theories in order to give sense and consistency to their actions, although we cannot take for granted that theories tell much about the actual clinical situation of clients.

resident in psychiatry. He noticed that the supervisee in his session was focused on content and on the client, whereas the supervisor constantly brought him back to process, to his role in it, and to his own reflections.

> At the very beginning of the session, when the Resident describes his patient as stuck in her relationship with her boyfriend and "getting nowhere in therapy", the Supervisor asks: "In what way did she get stuck with you, I mean, in terms of the same way she got stuck in the relationship?" With this slight change in question, the Supervisor restructures the puzzle. Centering attention on the connection between "stuck in relationship" and "stuck with you", he anchors the inquiry in the patient's transference, where the relationship between patient and therapist can serve as a window on the patient's life outside therapy.
> (Schön, 1982: 118–119)

This means that supervision has to do with Schön's reflection in action rather than with "pure" clinical theory. Supervision becomes essential in making the supervisee aware of his implicit (tacit) knowledge (see Polanyi, 1966), thus achieving a higher order of reflexivity (Burnham, 1993). In order to articulate implicit competences and theories, any therapist needs to be seen from the outside. Here introspection is not sufficient, as implicit theories are embedded in what he does, rather than what he thinks about or reflects on. It is impossible for him to see himself from the outside, which means that he needs somebody else: the supervisee has to accept that the supervisor "knows more" than him, not necessarily because she is more competent or experienced, but simply because she is in a different position.

The importance of the position, of the otherness of the supervisor as such, had been grasped many years ago (albeit within a very different context) by Mikhail Bakhtin:

> [T]he other person's *I* is also experienced by me in a manner which is completely different from the manner in which I experience my own *I*: the other person's *I* is also subsumed under the category of the *other* as a constituent feature of him [*sic*].
> (Bakhtin, 1923–1990: 38; emphasis in original)

In Rom Harré's terminology, the very position of the supervisor as "other" from the supervisee may be sufficient to make the latter more aware of his positioning in the wider sense:

> "Position": a cluster of rights and duties to perform certain actions with a certain significance as acts, but which also include prohibitions or denials of access to some of the local repertoire of meaningful acts. In a certain sense, in each social milieu there is a kind of Platonic realm of positions, realized in current practices, which people can adopt, strive to locate themselves in, be pushed into, be displaced from or be refused access, recess themselves from and so on, in a highly mobile and dynamic way.
> (Harré and Moghaddan, 2003: 5–6)

This implies that the supervisee is (should be) well aware of the fact that he positions himself (and is positioned by others) as a therapist. But he positions himself and is positioned in a variety of other ways too, sometimes outside of his own awareness. For example, a therapist may position himself as a figure of authority, but at the same time be positioned by his clients as a hired help, and by other members of institutions he may be working in as a simple employee. Also, in our examples the model therapist is male and the model supervisor female, thus leaving out all the complexity of gender positioning (see Wilkinson and Kitzinger, 2003). The position of the supervisor as an outsider makes her more aware of the therapist's position, and to be able to articulate it in full.

Possibly, the very process of supervision elicits a reflection that trespasses the contingent themes of the specific case brought into supervision, and that may touch all the different positions the therapist enacts (sometimes outside of his own awareness) within the relationships he is embedded in. We could define this as a sort of halo effect of supervision. Such implications of the various positions the therapist holds (that, in turn, co-operate in the construction of his way and style of working) may or may not be the main overall theme of any supervision, depending on the supervisor's general attitude. If it is not thematized, though, the risk is to lose the very essence of supervision, thus reifying the presented case. We can refer here to George Kelly, who, in the 1940s, when required to meet "problem children" at a school, refused, and insisted instead on meeting the teachers, because he aimed at understanding their positions in regard to the problem children—that is, the premises, attitudes, and representations that constructed the "reality" of the problem:

> Kelly's early clinical experience was in the public schools of Kansas. He found that when teachers referred pupils to his travelling psychological clinic, their complaints appeared to say something about not only the pupils, but the teachers themselves. Kelly tried to understand the teacher's reports as an expression of the teacher's construction or interpretation of events. For example, if a teacher complained that a student was lazy, Kelly did not look at the pupil to see if the teacher was correct in the diagnosis; rather he tried to understand the behaviors of the child and the way the teacher perceived these behaviors, that is, the teacher's construction of them that led to the complaint of laziness. This [...] led Kelly to the view that there is no objective, absolute truth—phenomena are meaningful only in relation to the ways in which they are construed or interpreted by the individual.
> (Cervone and Pervin, 2008: 414–415)

This still allows for the differences among models of supervision. They may be more prescriptive, descriptive, or reflective. Probably, however, all of them put the supervisee face-to-face with the unwanted (or unaware) implications of his way of working. It will then be the supervisor's choice to work in a more or less authoritative and directive manner. And it will be the supervisee's choice to accept or refuse the supervisor's indications, and what use, if any, they make of them.

At the same time, such relevant forms of positioning may help to explain why supervision is generally useful (and perceived as such) in a way that is relatively independent of the type of supervision that is actually performed. It is not (not only), we feel, the type, nor the modality of the supervision that is useful: it is rather the very fact that the supervisor, or the supervision group, is *other* than the supervisee that grants the efficacy of the work.

References

American Psychoanalytic Association (1956). Minimal Standards for the Training of Physicians in Psychoanalysis. *Bulletin of the American Psychoanalytic Association.* 12: 714–721.

Andersen, T. (1991). *The Reflecting Team: Dialogues and Dialogues about Dialogues.* New York: Norton & Company.

Anderson, H. (1997). *Conversation, Language and Possibilities: A Postmodern Approach to Therapy.* New York: Basic Books.

Anderson, H. and Goolishian, H. (1992). The Client is the Expert: A Not-knowing Approach to Therapy. In: McNamee, S. and Gergen, K.J. (eds) *Therapy as Social Construction.* London: Sage. pp. 25–39.

Anderson, H. and Swim, S. (1995). Supervision as collaborative conversation: Connecting the Voices of Supervisors and Supervisee. *Journal of Systemic Therapies.* 14: 1–13.

Bakhtin, M.M. (1923–1990). Author and Hero in the Aesthetic Activity. In: Holquist, M. and Liapunov, V. (eds) *Art and Answerability: Early Philosophical Essays by M.M. Bakhtin.* Austin: Texas University Press. pp. 4–256.

Bateson, G. (1972). *Steps to an Ecology of Mind.* San Francisco: Chandler Publishing Company.

Bertrando, P. (2000). Text and Context: Narrative, Postmodernism and Cybernetics. *Journal of Family Therapy.* 22(1): 83–103.

Bertrando, P. (2007). *The Dialogical Therapist: Dialogue in Systemic Practice.* London: Karnac Books.

Bertrando, P. (2008). The Cognitive and the Narrative. A Theory of Clinical Practice. *Journal of Family Therapy.* in press.

Bodin, A. (1972). The Use of Video-tapes. In: Ferber, A., Mendelsohn, M. and Napier, A. (eds) *The Book of Family Therapy.* New York: Jason Aronson. pp. 318–337.

Boscolo, L. and Cecchin, G. (1981). Training in Systemic Therapy at the Milan Centre. In: Whiffen, R. and Byng-Hall, J. (eds) *Family Therapy Supervision: Recent Developments in Practice.* London: Academic Press. pp. 153–166.

Boscolo, L., Cecchin, G., Hoffman, L. and Penn, P. (1987) *Milan Systemic Family Therapy: Conversations in Theory and Practice.* New York: Basic Books.

Burnham, J. (1993). Systemic Supervision: The Evolution of Reflexivity in the Context of the Supervisory Relationship. *Human Systems.* 4 (Spec. Iss. 3–4): 349–381.

Byng-Hall, J. (1981). The Use of the Earphone in Supervision. In: Whiffen, R. and Byng-Hall, J. (eds) *Family Therapy Supervision: Recent Developments in Practice.* London: Academic Press. pp. 47–56.

Cade, B. and Seligman, P. (1981). Teaching a Strategic Approach. In: Whiffen, R. and Byng-Hall, J. (eds) *Family Therapy Supervision: Recent Developments in Practice*. London: Academic Press. pp. 167–181.

Cervone, D. and Pervin, L.A. (2008). *Personality, Theory and Research* (10th edn). New York: John Wiley & Sons.

Deutsch, H. (1935/1983). On Supervised Analysis. *Contemporary Psychoanalysis*. 19(1): 59–67.

Doherty, W.J. (1995). *Soul Searching*. New York: Basic Books.

Eagle M.N. (1984). *Recent Developments in Psychoanalysis: A Critical Evaluation*. New York: McGraw-Hill.

Eckstein, R. and Wallerstein, R.S. (1972). *The Teaching and Learning of Psychotherapy* (2nd edn). Madison, CT: International Universities.

Edwards, J.K. and Chen, M.-W. (2004). Strength-Based Supervision: Frameworks, Current Practice and Future Directions: A Wu-wei Method. *The Family Journal*. 7: 349–357.

Fox, H., Tench, C. and Marie (2003). Outsider-witness Practices and Group Supervision. *International Journal of Narrative Therapy and Community Work*. 4: 25–32.

Freud Loewenstein, S., Reder, P. and Clark, A. (1981). The Consumers' Response: Trainees' Discussion of the Experience of Live Supervision. In: Whiffen, R. and Byng-Hall, J. (eds) *Family Therapy Supervision: Recent Developments in Practice*. London: Academic Press. pp. 109–114.

Gardner, G.T., Bobele, M. and Biever, J.L. (2003). Postmodern Models of Family Therapy Supervision. In: Todd, T.C. and Storm, C.L. (eds) *The Complete Systemic Supervisor: Context, Philosophy, and Pragmatics*. New York: Authors Choice Press. pp. 217–228.

Haley, J. (1976). *Problem-Solving Therapy*. San Francisco: Jossey-Bass.

Haley, J. (1988). Reflections on Supervision. In: Liddle, H.A., Breunlin, D.C. and Schwartz, R.C. (eds) *Handbook of Family Therapy Training and Supervision*. New York: The Guilford Press. pp. 358–367.

Harré, R. and Moghaddam, F. (2003). Introduction: The Self and Others in Traditional Psychology and in Positioning Theory. In: Harré, R. and Moghaddam, F. (eds) *The Self and Others: Positioning in Individuals and Groups in Personal, Political, and Cultural Contexts*. London: Praeger. pp. 1–11.

Herman, J.L. (1992). *Trauma and Recovery*. New York: Basic Books.

Hoffman, L. (1998). Setting Aside Models in Family Therapy, *Journal of Marital and Family Therapy*. 24(2): 145–156.

International Psychoanalytic Association (1926). Report of the Ninth Psychoanalytical Congress. *Bulletin of the International Psychoanalytic Association*. 7: 119–143.

Kernberg, O.F. (2004). Discussion: "Problems of power in psychoanalytic institutions". *Psychoanalytical Inquiries.* 24: 106–121.

Kutchins, H. and Kirk, S.A. (1997). *Making Us Crazy: DSM—The Psychiatric Bible and the Creation of Mental Disorder.* New York: The Free Press.

Levine, F.J. (2003). The Forbidden Quest and the Slippery Slope: Roots of Authoritarianism in Psychoanalysis. *Journal of the American Psychoanalytic Association.* 51S: 203–245.

Liddle, H.A. (1988). Systemic Supervision: Conceptual Overlays and Practical Guidelines. In: Liddle, H.A., Breunlin, D.C. and Schwartz, R.C. (eds) *Handbook of Family Therapy Training and Supervision.* New York: The Guilford Press. pp. 153–171.

Mason, B. (1993). Toward Positions of Safe Uncertainty. *Human Systems.* 4 (Spec. Iss. 3–4): 189–200.

McCormick, B.R. (1994). *Communication: The Social Matrix of Supervision of Psychotherapy.* UMI Dissertation # 9511956, Columbia University Teachers College, New York.

McGoldrick, M. (1981). Through the Looking-glass: Supervision of a Trainee's "Trigger" Family. In: Whiffen, R. and Byng-Hall, J. (eds) *Family Therapy Supervision: Recent Developments in Practice.* London: Academic Press. pp. 17–38.

Montalvo, B. (1973). Aspects of Live Supervision. *Family Process.* 12: 342–350.

Papero, D.V. (1988). Training in Bowen theory. In: Liddle, H.A., Breunlin, D.C. and Schwratz, R.C. (eds) *Handbook of Family Therapy Training and Supervision.* New York: The Guilford Press. pp. 62–77.

Polanyi, M. (1966/1983). *The Tacit Dimension.* Gloucester (Mass.): Peter Smith.

Schön D.A. (1983). *The Reflective Practitioner: How Professionals Think in Action.* New York: Basic Books.

Schuster, D.B., Sandt, J.J. and Thaler, O.F. (1972). *Clinical Supervision of the Psychiatric Resident.* New York: Brunner/Mazel.

Selvini Palazzoli M., Boscolo L., Cecchin G. and Prata G. (1980). Hypothesizing-circularity-neutrality. *Family Process.* 19: 73–85.

Simon, R. (1992). *One on One: Conversations with the Shapers of Family Therapy.* New York: The Family Therapy Network/The Guilford Press.

Storm, C.L., Todd, T.C., Sprenkle, D.H. and Morgan, M.M. (2001). Gaps between MFT Supervision Assumptions and Common Practices: Suggested Best Practices. *Journal of Marital and Family Therapy.* 27: 227–239.

Ungar, M. (2006). Practicing as a Postmodern Supervisor. *Journal of Marital and Family Therapy.* 32: 59–71.

Whiffen, R. (1981). The Use of Videotape in Supervision. In: Whiffen, R. and Byng-Hall, J. (eds) *Family Therapy Supervision: Recent Developments in Practice*. London: Academic Press. pp. 39–46.

White, M. (1995). Reflecting Teamwork as Definitional Ceremony. In: White, M. (ed.) *Re-Authoring Lives: Interviews and Essays*. Adelaide: Dulwich Centre Publications.

White, M. and Epston, D. (1992). Consulting your Consultants: The Documentation of Alternative Knowledges. In: White, M. and Epston, D. (eds) *Experience, Contradiction, Narrative & Imagination*. Adelaide (Australia): Dulwich Centre Publications.

Wilkinson, S. and Kitzinger, C. (2003). Constructing Identities: A Feminist Conversation Analytic Approach to Positioning in Action. In: Harré, R. and Moghaddam, F. (eds) *The Self and Others: Positioning in Individuals and Groups in Personal, Political, and Cultural Contexts*. London: Praeger. pp. 157–180.

CHAPTER TWO

The three faces of supervision: Individual learning, group learning, and supervisor accountability

Paula Boston

Introduction: Three faces of supervision

Hecate, the Greek Goddess with three faces, associated with (among other things) keeping travellers safe through crossroads and facilitating rites of passage, seems promising as a metaphor for describing

the work of a family therapy training supervisor. The faces could be seen in the following way. One face points towards relational supporting of the individual student's development, another attends to the group process of the training team, and a third faces the evaluative aspect and professional gatekeeper function of supervision. The thesis of this chapter is that the supervisor must draw upon a variety of perspectives to respond to the diverse points of focus inherent within the training context. It will describe how some of the more prominent therapy models can be adapted for appropriate use in relation to the various foci. The family therapy models that have been adapted from clinical practice to supervision were derived primarily from Narrative (Monk et al. 1997; White, 1988; White and Epston, 1990) and post-Milan (Campbell et al. 1991; Jones, 1993). The chapter will also examine the movement between a more collaborative supervisory position and one where hierarchy and "expertise" are called upon. It will draw on the concept of domains (Maturana and Varela, 1987) and positioning theory (Davies and Harré, 1990) to examine the area of supervision where there are irreconcilable perspectives between the supervisor and the student.

The context of this chapter is primarily that of providing live supervision on a family therapy qualifying course. The professional body requires 300 team hours (Association for Family Therapy Blue Book). This is usually with four students and one supervisor and, in our training programme, the arrangement is for a two-year contract with consistent team members and the same supervisor. The usual practice includes a pre-session discussion about the case to be seen in which the student therapist offers reflections on the previous session, thoughts about the coming session, and may request supervisor support and/or attention to particular learning issues. The session occurs, a few ear bug messages are sent through, and there is usually a reflecting team conversation with the family. The post-session time is spent considering the case, the therapist's and team's relationship to the case, revisiting identified learning points, and possibly considering new ones. In the spaces between live therapy sessions, the team does many other things: mapping the family of origin; student learning narratives interview (Aggett, 2004); skills practice; exploration of group themes or preoccupations; and a group review of taped sessions. In addition, individual students meet separately with the supervisor to review progress at least twice per year.

Facing forward together

The first "face" refers to the times when there is full accord between the aims of the student and those of the supervisor: they have a shared vision and purpose. To a large extent, there is isomorphism between the theoretical approach and the praxis of supervision (White and Russell 1997; Schwartz et al. 1988). That is, the way in which a clinician understands and engages with a family is replicated within the supervisor–supervisee relationship. This pattern includes a sense of shared interest in theory and techniques between the supervisor and supervisee and an awareness of the supervisor's response and behaviour as offering an element of modelling for the supervisee's experiential learning. Clarity and coherence of approach is emphasized by many trainers (Boscolo and Bertrando, 1996; Falicov, 1998; Shimabukuro, 2003) and a shared model between supervisor and supervisee is noted as significant (Storm et al. 2001).

As a training supervisor, my own orientation is primarily postmodern, with a particular interest in narrative ideas and practices. I privilege this orientation and encourage students to immerse themselves in it in order to develop a coherent foundation from which to eventually develop other approaches. Having a shared orientation appears to accelerate learning and develop depth. In many ways, this training orientation has proved to be productive and has generally received positive feedback from students. For the most part, the supervisees were either amenable to concentrating on this narrative framework from the start or became so with the agreement to "branch out" later in the supervision. As the supervision progressed, the students often added a more dialogic approach in order to expand their repertoire. Other approaches in the field are outlined and a basic appreciation of these is assumed.

In this "face", the supervisor works alongside the student; the student sets the learning agenda and the team and supervisor go about trying to support these aims. There is an implied agreement that they are autonomous learners, having the authority and self-knowledge to determine their professional learning priorities within the general systemic and family therapy arena. This notion is augmented by theories of adult learning (Knowles, 1968). Within this frame of reference, there is appreciation that individual aspirations are products of the concurrent surrounding discourses; this is not deconstructed. Specifically, these discourses, particularly those of the supervisor, team, course, and profession, serve to create a sense of "sanctioned" theories and skills to be learned. Individual learning preferences are taken at face value and the belief in the "agency" of the student enacted. This supervisory stance would be similar to the "decentred" position of narrative therapists in the attention they give to clients' preferred ways of being, rather than therapists' assumptions or notions of what change should be (White, 2007).

The supervisor clarifies the student's learning preferences and these areas are respected and honoured. When the student has expressed his/her particular hopes for learning in conversation with the supervisor, the supervisor is positioned as mentor and the student as "learning from". While the student sets the agenda as an autonomous learner, this is done in the knowledge that learning can be supported. White's adaptation of Vygotsky's thinking on relational learning and the zone of proximal development and Bruner's metaphor of scaffolding (White, 2007) are employed, with attention to the potential of the mentor relationship to take the student's learning further than it would have progressed in isolation. The "scaffolding" supervisor offers a conversation that assists the student in moving from a concrete learning objective to a clearer definition of the issue: constraints on therapeutic activity; occasions where learning may have already been occurring; and how interest in learning this particular skill or concept fits into the student's personal philosophy and ethics. The process is one of small steps leading to increasing independence in the learning process and additional levels of abstraction. The student's experience of being involved in this process connects theory in a much more personal way. The likelihood is that the issue identified is one that the student sees as problematic, but it could also be an exploration of success. Two examples of this kind of supervision are offered below.

Externalizing interview

My supervisee had reviewed a tape of his practice and saw an aspect that he felt dissatisfied with in the light of new learning from the course. He agreed to be interviewed as a means of moving his perspective and practice but also as a way of demonstrating the use of externalizing.

I asked the supervisee how he would define the difficulty. What would he name it? He said that the problem is a sense of "steering the conversation too actively". I asked him for examples of that occurring in the session. He thought and then answered "when the family seemed to be in a crisis and when I am anxious about the case". I then explored the effect of "the steering" on his relationship with the client and he responded by saying that it obscured important information and took the conversation in another direction. "How had this affected his sense of himself as a therapist?" I asked and he responded that he felt that he was being insensitive and not really using narrative ideas. I asked more about what he would be doing if he were not "steering" and he thought he would be able to ask questions about the dilemmas which would clarify the polarities or be better able to offer multiple perspectives. I then asked an "exception" question: "Was there a time when he noticed himself moving away from 'steering'?" He replied that he had noticed it in the middle of the session when questioning about a particular event (mother and daughter had mentioned avoiding a conflict and going to a function together). He experienced himself as genuinely interested and content to let the conversation take itself in its own direction. When asked more about what he noticed in himself, he was able to connect with a sense of patience. He felt interested but open; he was not in a rush to get somewhere and didn't have the feeling he knew the answers ahead of time. I asked if the moving away from "the steering" was connected to theory and he mentioned taking a stance of curiosity. He then linked therapeutic curiosity with intellectual curiosity related to learning on the course. In the final part of the discussion, the student was asked to think about how this learning might be experienced by his clients and the other members of the team. He hoped it would be seen as risk-taking and a commitment to learning. This interview lasted forty-five minutes. The other team members offered their reflections on the interview itself and also identified aspects of their own practice along the same themes that they hoped to alter.

An interview around the issue of student responsibility

One of the students was involved with a case in a way that stood out from those of the other students. With this case there was a greater frequency of sessions, numerous contacts between appointments, and the student had a high degree of involvement outside of the training clinic. This became the focus of a group discussion related to clinical responsibility and use of the team. The student agreed to explore the issue and it was decided that another student would interview her in order to map the various influences on her high level of responsiveness: the nature of the family difficulties; the professional and organizational discourses around responsibility; and the influence of her personal experiences (family of origin and contemporary family). This particular family exerted significant pressure in terms of their high status and overlapping professional network links. In our discussion, professional identity did not seem so influential. Although the organizational issues did contribute to more diffuse boundaries, the more powerful connections for the student arose from the conversations about the "self of the therapist". As a child, this student had suffered the traumatic effects of an unresponsive NHS in relation to the care of a parent's chronic health problems. This pattern of organizational neglect had become something that this student was determined not to replicate. The strength of this personal value became apparent in the interview. The student was then able to reflect on this, consider how helpful it was to her capacity to engage difficult clients, and also explore the limitations of such a strongly held conviction. She felt that the interview was very useful for a repositioning with clients, as well as being emotionally moving for her and the team. It enabled her to consider how responsibility could be distributed more throughout the team and supervision process and how the in-depth discussion itself epitomized what could be gained from a more integrated connection to the team.

Facing each other

Group process

The second face of supervision is that of attending to group process. Group supervision has been a cornerstone in the training of family therapists; however there is relatively little written about group process in the systemic supervision literature (Proctor and Inskipp, 2001; Burck, this volume; Granville, this volume). It is generally agreed that the individual's ability to learn is affected by context, and that learning within a group constellation contains complexities additional to those where this is not the case. Supervision groups aim to be both safe and supportive while offering challenges and opportunities for substantial growth. Individual needs must be met while, for the sake of team work, there is adaptation and sacrifice for the needs of others. Members must grapple with a high level of exposure and scrutiny as well as enjoying having an audience to witness their progress.

A narrative "flavoured" approach would involve conceptualization of the group in relation to the stories constructed and constituting future ways of relating. The focus is to draw out events that have shaped the individual aspects of "selves" that contribute to a shared and richer description of the nature of the group at that point in time. I have written previously about using a narrative style interview of a supervision group in order to facilitate a story of cohesion and responsiveness between members and the supervisor (Boston, 2006).

Strengthening identities of competence

It would be highly unusual for a beginning training group to form without experiencing some anxiety and fear of failure. Narrative therapy suggests that unique outcomes and alternative stories often reside in the past and may need excavating (Monk et al. 1997). Additionally, value is placed on the dual process of speaking and writing to augment the development of alternative identities (Epston, 1994; Penn, 1994).

A useful exercise in the beginning of the life of the supervision group is for the supervisor to ask group members to meet together to create a map of their "pre-knowledges". That is, to create together a written list of the strengths and resources each brings to the group. They do so by considering a number of categories: their professional and clinical experience, their learning style, their personal attributes, and their ways of working in a group setting. The exercise aims to support the construction of a "rich description" of themselves as contributors to the learning, rather than the "thinly described" version of themselves as anxious and inexperienced new students. The feedback from the students was that this was an extremely interesting and energizing event. They were delighted with their new appreciation of the group members, as well as having their own abilities noted by others. A sense of openness and shared enthusiasm was generated. They had reconnected to a sense of ability and confidence.

A group stuck around assessment issues and boundaries

Over the course of a two-year training, it is not always the case that the group process is experienced as positive. In more fraught moments, a difficult group issue can also be externalized. The issue can be named, mapped in terms of its influence on individuals, their learning, and their relationships with others. Preferences can be explored and exceptions noted. Problematic meanings can be deconstructed and recontextualized. It may be that this is best done by a "consultant", so that the supervisor can participate fully in the discussion.

Students get individual feedback on a formal basis at least twice per year. In one conversation with a student, one particular aspect of practice was seen as problematic and there was a somewhat unsatisfactory conclusion to the conversation. There were differences in the two perspectives about the seriousness of the issue and the relative weight of contributory factors. The student was upset by this feedback and confided in another team member. (While the supervisor is ethically obliged to uphold the privacy of each student's evaluation conversation, the student is free to share their version of events with other students.)

Each supervision group on the training has a mid-year consultation, facilitated by a senior family therapist from another institution. In the course of this meeting, the student who had been confided in felt that they needed to bring up the issue for discussion, as an advocate for the first student. The "confidant" trainee described feeling "unsafe" after hearing of the nature of her team mate's conversation in individual supervision. The third student was unaware of the issue and had no feelings of dissatisfaction. He had been excluded from some of the discussion between the other two and seemed to prefer it that way. The bind for the supervisor was that, if details of the situation were given, that would have transgressed boundaries, but without knowing the content of the original discussion, the anxiety of other students had increased.

Numerous themes were explored in the consultation: the impact of varying degrees of awareness and inclusion/exclusion in the issue; loyalties and boundaries; gender and professional loyalties; transparency of the group; and notions regarding responsibility as a supervisor and as a group member. The theme of safety and lack of safety was explored, while respecting the boundaried conversation with the student. The conversation became more creative when there was movement from "feeling unsafe from material which could not be discussed" to more abstract group process phenomena. Different accounts emerged, with the original student finding herself less anxious and a bit confused about the amount of angst expressed by her confidant and advocating colleague. This situation took time and structure to allow the theme to move from the "not discussed sense of lack of safety" to the discussion in which different boundaries were respected and a "safe enough" conversation could take place. The specific content of the individual's assessment review was never disclosed to the group but there was a sense that the group could recall periods of smoother sailing and could move towards a more open relationship. The tracking of various positions in the group around the issue also illuminated group dynamics in a helpful way. The issue resolved itself over the subsequent months. The examples above are considered from a narrative orientation but could also have been seen through other theoretical lenses.

Narrative therapy calls for a consideration of ideas and practices that become marginalized and, therefore, must examine its own contributions to that process. It also makes a point of distinguishing between the story told and the story lived. There have been times when a narrative framework failed to accurately represent the supervisory activities or concerns. There are times when other explanations have proved preferable; systems and cybernetics often offer us the conceptual tools for attention to context, pattern and feedback, interactional sequences, and analogic communication.

Observed patterns: Toilet breaks and blushes

Transparency about the position you are taking is a very appealing idea. The concept of therapists' transparency has been considered and evaluated from a relational and contextual perspective, rather than as a blunt and rigid ideology (Roberts, 2005). This more subtle reading provides a repertoire of responses in the supervisory domain. There may also be pragmatic reasons: lack of time, competing priorities, and so on, in which one decides to observe the pattern and intervene to alter it. The amount of time for focusing on group process is actually very limited and sometimes one just has to "carry on". There also may be times when it seems best to act on an observation of process without publicly accounting for it. There may be times when a supervisor notices a pattern and decides not to make this observation explicit for the sake of the relationship.

In a supervision group, a new student, who is approximately 35 years old, very bright and able to stand up for her training needs, twice asked me if she could go to the toilet. Internal hypotheses were generated: Was she feeling as if she was in primary school again, seeing me as the headmistress of her youth? Was she trying to work out the rules of the group and didn't want to miss anything? Was she making a statement about the pressure of time? Did she have a different idea about my responsibility as a supervisor, had we not coordinated as a team around individual and group personal requirements? Fascinating as the exploration of such conjectures may have been, I wanted to interrupt this pattern and used humour to do so: I jokingly asked her permission to go to the loo. I felt that the relationship was good enough that that this episode would be construed as a joke based on mutual regard. A group norm was thus established—"when needs must" was allowed.

To give another example, a student had just completed a splendid session and, when the post-session discussion commenced, there was a spontaneous outburst of adulation and compliments. The student blushed. The blush is an anatomical response which arrives without sanction and calling attention to it might have induced a secondary and deeper shade of blush. The supervisory response was to ignore it, and to ask a deliberately bland question designed to guide her back towards composure. For example, "How did she want to use the post-session discussion?" To have focused on the embarrassment at that time would have seemed inappropriately intrusive and the original intention of providing positive feedback would have been negated.

The opportunity to reflect on the experience of being embarrassed by praise would be potentially more relevant and tolerable at some future time. The team members might discuss different responses to praise/compliments from a family of origin and cultural perspective. This was an episode in which the supervisor attended simultaneously to an individual concern and to team members' relational responsibilities.

The reflexive group

There are times when a supervisor wants to invite students to become more observant of the group functioning, meaning-generation, and interaction. The post-Milan model offers a way to conceptualize both beliefs and behaviours as well as offering a range of helpful questions. It provides a theory that helps actively connect people in a group in an equal way and with the emphasis on what occurs between them.

There was a marked difference in abilities in one group; one student excelled in theoretical explanation and delighted in clarifying the understanding of others, while another student drew upon intuition and clinical experience. The difference was heightened in relation to case discussions, with a hint of symmetrical competition in terms of which quality was most useful. The return of a course essay, in which the theorist had done rather well and the intuitively inclined student had done less well, sharpened this conflict and it was suspected that there was some comparing of marks between them. The intuition-orientated student was presenting a case and the student with theoretical leanings offered a theoretical solution. The intuitive student felt frustrated and put down. An interactional reframe with an embedded suggestion was offered by the supervisor: "When a therapist is struggling with a case, it is natural to offer one's own pathway out of confusion, but if it is not the natural path for the therapist, further confusion usually follows. If the team were to decide to try to offer pathways to each other, based not on their own preferences but on that of the one presenting, what would that be like?" Questions could map interactional patterns around each team member's preferences and the fit of responses of others. Clinical experience and intuition as well as theory could thus both be seen as useful and important.

The following example is drawn from supervision training rather than the qualifying level. The group concerned were agency-based generic mental health professionals with varying amounts of exposure to family therapy ideas. The supervisor-in-training had a particularly challenging group, which she presented as part of her supervisor's course. Her team was one where the conversational process was quite askew; there were many episodes of people talking over each other, disrespectful certitude, and increasing volume and withdrawal in post-case discussion. The women tended to be increasingly dominant, while the men in the group became silent. There was a lot of distracting physical activity, restlessness, and leaving and returning to the room. Fortunately, agreement had been gained to tape the post-session process and the supervisor suggested that it might be useful to watch. The group was invited to notice who talked, who listened, and what the pattern was, and to consider the possible external influences on this way of relating. The group agreed and became intensely interested in the process. They were able to speculate about how gendered positions were being played out, how family dynamics might have been replicated by the team's behaviour, and how they might wish to respond to each other in different ways in the future. They agreed to view another tape of themselves in discussion to see if they were moving in the preferred direction. This served as a significant turning point.

Facing the other and keeping an eye to domains of accountability

This third face of Hecate has an eye to responsibility and represents a view of student practice with the external criteria as foreground. Hierarchy is unavoidable, as are changes in form, as the relationship and context require. Despite embracing collaborative practices and postmodern sensibilities, supervisors must also participate, literally, in two of Foucault's practices of power, hierarchical observation, and normalizing gaze (Foucault, 1979). The endemic use of one-way screens in family therapy training concretely epitomizes the process of observation and gaze. This has to do with the supervisor being placed in positions of ultimate authority for both clinical decisions in the training clinic and for evaluation of the individual student by the relevant institutions (the National Health Service, Association for

Family Therapy, the training institution, and so forth). Supervisors are tasked as professional gatekeepers and as purveyors of privilege and, as such, step into positions of accountability and judgement (Bernard and Goodyear, 1992; Brady et al. 1995; Lumadue and Duffey, 1999; Russell et al. 2007).

Evaluation as enhancement

One of the less articulated perspectives in current debates about power is the positive aspect of hierarchy. The role of supervisor and professional gatekeeper offers the opportunity to lend support to the development of confidence and credibility. Feedback from sessions, confirmatory comments in the group, and written evaluation reports, are often opportunities for noting strengths in practice, capacity to learn, and contributions to the group. The team, including the supervisor, function as an audience to the enhanced standing and developing professional identity. One highly capable psychologist said that she had always been told that her practice was excellent by previous supervisors, but had always felt a bit of a fraud, as it had been retrospective supervision based on her own accounts. The positive feedback received from live supervision was experienced as much more specific and direct; consequently she regarded it as more valid and influential in her own personal assessment of her capacity. The comments from her fellow students were also highly significant.

If the damaging effects of power on supervision are to be minimized, it is helpful to students (and supervisors) to develop a more transparent and coherent account of its workings. Several central theoretical perspectives can elucidate this seemingly opaque process. The Coordinated Management of Meaning theory with its notion of layered contexts determining meaning, allows for a discussion of an episode of practice as either being in the context of learning or assessment (Cronen, Johnson, and Lannamann, 1982). For example, an episode of "poor practice" can be seen as an opportunity for learning. If the learning does not develop and the "poor" practice is frequently repeated, then an implicative force develops which recontextualizes the episode as poor practice within the assessment context. Another example of attention to context is how a supervisor might consider different experiences of feedback based on the effect of having an audience. A supervisor may emphasize the appreciative aspect of feedback in group discussion and give fuller formative feedback in a one-to-one communication with the student. This difference would be based on a respect for privacy and an awareness of the potential amplification of discomfort and loss of face when critique is offered publically. Thus, audience is a context marker for the detail and tone of feedback.

Another theoretical tool is the work done by Lang et al. (1990) on the use of Maturana's notion of domains. The domains of aesthetics, explanation, and production are differentiated in terms of ways of relating and focus. Domains of production refer to a social system reproducing itself according to objective standards, which can usefully be employed in relation to the profession of family therapy. The supervisor may comment on a therapeutic activity in terms of the domain of aesthetics, noting the creativity and reflexivity demonstrated in the therapy, and then shift to the domain of production, inviting the student to evaluate the session from a different theoretical approach. In this domain, the supervisor will have an expectation that this case discussion should be conducted with a certain level of knowledge and competency.

A more contemporary orientation, which, in my view, fits well with a narrative approach, is that of positioning theory. It evolved from role theory and suggests that we are positioned within various social discourses with prescribed story lines and associated rights and responsibilities in relation to others (Davies and Harré, 1990). These positions shape the interaction and meaning-making process between people. People converse from within a discourse which encounters the other who may stand within the same discourse and respond accordingly, or may respond from another discourse which is less congruent. Discourses contain "position calls". People either acquiesce, contest, or subvert the position calls that are offered (Harré and Gillett, 1994). Discourses and positions shift rapidly; this is not a static phenomena. For example, a student initiates a conversation about personal difficulties which have interfered with a deadline requirement. The supervisor has been invited to offer sympathy, support, and to authorize an extension. The supervisor may chose to step into another discourse related to accountability and course requirements and equity among all students. It may be that the supervisor responds from an initial position of compassion but then shifts to a conversation about the management of the "mitigating circumstances" procedure; moving from one position to another within a conversational exchange. Examples are provided below.

Clinical responsibility

Supervisors are understandably reluctant to directly override the strongly held preferences of a student therapist; most often differences are negotiated with poise and tact. But, according to ethical standards, the needs of clients must take priority over the training needs of students and, occasionally, these are mutually exclusive. A very talented young therapist was seeing a husband and wife. The therapy had included numerous challenging aspects but was generally being well managed. At one point in the session, the husband mentioned having recently put a gun under the marital bed with thoughts of committing murder/suicide. This information was told in the session with a casual tone, while the wife was obviously distressed at hearing, for the first time, that her life had been in danger. The therapist moved the conversation on to how things had been between them in the following days. The husband's tone (and a subsequently described personal resonance for the therapist) had numbed the therapist into avoiding questions of immediate risk and responding to the wife's emotional reaction. The conversation in front of the screen and among the team members behind it was divergent in the extreme.

At this point, I sent an ear bug message to the therapist in the room to take a break. During the break the team discussed the situation and it was agreed that I and the team would have a reflecting conversation about our serious concern and ask further questions that would help us to more fully appreciate any risk and discuss potential safety strategies. At the time, the therapist was mildly disconcerted but later, after watching the videotaped session, was alarmed by her original response and relieved that the supervisor had intervened. The relational task for the supervisor then became that of assisting the student therapist in reclaiming her sense of competence and recovering her standing with the team. The way in which the situation evolved proved to be a highly positive and productive episode of learning. From a Coordinated Management of Meaning (CMM) perspective, the episode of therapy was initially contextualized by "usual practice" and "low risk"; at the relationship level, the therapist was defined as having responsibility for the management of the session and a direct relationship with the family. The event of the therapist failing to identify an episode of high risk placed the supervisor and observing team in a direct relationship with the family. Safety thus became a higher context marker than the therapist's confidence or relationship with the family. The therapist's impressive capacity to reflect on the case and the demanding "use of self" issues were part of a process that re-established her work firmly within the context of competence.

Supervisor expectations

One of the expectations of students on the course is to create a pro-forma for each session based on the material from the preceding session, the post-session discussion, and the tape review. The format alters with the various preoccupations that develop within the supervision group over the two years, but there is a clear requirement for students to invest time in preparation. In addition, they are expected to identify learning issues, potential ethical dilemmas, theory and practice links, and so forth. This is reviewed in the thirty-minute pre-session discussion before the family arrives. One particular student failed to provide the pro-forma for the pre-session discussion on two occasions, without explanation. I saw him as ignoring a practice that I thought was significant to individual and team learning. With some attention to timing, I asked him to elaborate on his thinking about this and asked whether he would be agreeable to being interviewed. What transpired was that he was very unhappy about his work base's antiquated practice of pre-session criticism of family members and of the pathologizing talk. I asked him what was behind this reaction and he described his personal frustration with the nature of the team talk and his ethical concerns. I wondered whether our pre-session talk would have the same feel to him and how we could address the ethical issues. We also spoke of the difference in practices for training and how this might connect the team. This conversation was very helpful and moved us all along. This supervisory event might be explained as having shifted from a consideration within the domain of production to one of aesthetics.

Discordant discussions

The most difficult exchange is when, in the context of evaluation, the supervisor believes that a student's practice needs to develop in significant ways and the student does not share this view. One supervisee, when watching a family session from behind the screen, had an intensive emotional reaction. This memory was one of an abusive situation in his childhood and was connected to the activities related to the case. The impact of the episode made it impossible for the student to contribute to the team work for the remainder of the session. The reaction itself was very dramatic for the whole team and the initial response was of surprise and then support for the student. But the impasse arose when the student refused to engage in any further discussion or reflection on the episode. Whilst I could appreciate how this situation was very difficult for the student, and was aware of the potential risks of engaging in further discussion of this episode, I considered that, when a supervisor has an awareness of the problematic connection of the personal to the clinical, this conversation is within the remit of supervision. Personal history and issues that do not show themselves in relation to the therapy or team work are, in my opinion, beyond the boundary. I took a position both as someone who could mentor the progression of this difficult event and as an evaluator of his capacity to do so. As supervisor, I was drawing on discourses of ethical practice (Association for Family Therapy [AFT] guidelines no. 14), themes of the "self" of the therapist, and ideas about the importance of making the "unsaid" available for discussion within the group, as they had experienced the initial shock reaction of their colleague. I aimed to have a conversation, not specifically in relation to the traumatic personal history itself, but to encourage reflection on the reaction. I believed that this understanding might be helpful in clinical practice, especially in facilitating the student's capacity to regain a sense of equilibrium, should such an event reoccur. I felt I was being positioned by the student as another perpetrator of an abusive episode and, despite proclaiming a respect for individual privacy in relation to the event itself, I could not engage the student in a reflexive discussion.

While several different supervisory approaches were adopted, the difference of opinion about whether the issue was "on or off limits" for discussion/reflection was never sufficiently resolved. I believe that both the student and I, as supervisor, experienced a sense of disappointment, together with an ironic appreciation of the serendipitous nature of the event (another family/a different day; the episode may never had emerged) and a conviction that our own positions were justified. No doubt, we were both in identifiable discourses: professional accountability, commitment to meaning-making together versus post-structural critique of interiority and oppressive practices in educational institutions. I would describe this event in terms of Harré and Gillett's (1994) contested position calls. There seemed to be no bridging of the two positions.

Individual feedback conversations

The power differential between supervisor and student is most keenly evident in formal feedback situations. The formal assessment document on the qualifying course has two functions: providing a narrative of the progress in designated categories (general practice, theory and technique, and team contributions) and as documented supporting evidence of the assessment procedure. This process is associated with the marking of each student. The students provide their own written perspectives, the supervisor responds to their accounts and offers their own feedback, and then there is a meeting together to seek clarification, amplify themes, and discuss points of agreement and difference.

Conversational tone and agenda is often set by the first speaker, so students are asked to offer the first perspective on their progress in the review meeting. Students are encouraged to specify their aims for the coming months, with the document as a reference point. Supervisory questions are aimed at bringing forth episodes of progress. When the supervisor offers comments that suggest the need for different practice or development, it is important to provide a fuller account of the supervisor's thinking. For example, in relation to professional standards, I point out to students that it is necessary to comment on their capacity to work cross-culturally.

Questions are asked such as, "What in the student's past or future practice would provide evidence of these abilities?" It may be that the student contributes to the discussion in a way that leads to a marked change of view. If not, the supervisor invites the student to elaborate on their different point of view. This may provide useful feedback about the way in which the supervisor can better support the student's development. It is important to try to hold on to the notion of "separating the evaluation from the person". Difficulties are seen as punctuation in relation to this point in time, based only on what has been observed, and a product of current expectations. Given the appreciation of multiple perspectives and the isolated nature of much of the live supervision, it is helpful to invite additional supervisory views from colleagues. Tapes of practice can be viewed by other supervisors as a form of "double marking" to aid a sense of equity.

Conclusion

The three faces description was an attempt to represent the different supervisory gazes. Management of these different aspects represents the art and craft of live group supervision in a training context. Clearly, the theoretical elements in the mind of the supervisor are only one small aspect of the supervision. Trainees bring to training their own theories, life experiences, and past and concurrent relationships. No doubt, there are many highly significant contributors to the experience that are beyond theory.

Family therapy has a history of offering many different theories of change and, at points, competition between them. Over time, some of these theories drop out of the frame and others become so established that they become tacit and, as such, difficult to notice. Eclecticism was critiqued in favour of theoretical coherence, which in turn led to the increased differentiation and competition between the various approaches (narrative, solution-focused, collaborative, post-Milan, and so on). As a result, present discussions are more concerned with the similarities among approaches and achieving an integrative stance. The field of systemic supervision is less developed but no doubt contains the same tensions.

The intention of this article was never to develop a "meta" theory of supervision which would provide clear indications of what theory was best employed in the many possible circumstances. Rather it has provided the opportunity to bring forth some of those tacit theories alongside the more current models. Over the course of writing this article, I have moved from someone who would have described my supervision with more of an emphasis on theoretical coherence to someone who has developed a greater appreciation of the active part played by a diversity of models. There is no neat correlation between the different supervisor foci and the most useful approach. Nor could it be said that some of the same encounters could only be described in a singular theoretical frame. Situated somewhere between a purist and eclectic orientation is the pragmatic case that suggests some theories just seem, at the time, better suited for the task. Given the complexity of the supervisory position and the need to attend to multiple and sometimes contradictory domains, it does seem important to keep an eye on the many useful approaches which are contained in the field.

References

Aggett, P. (2004). Learning Narratives in Group Supervision: Enhancing Collaborative Learning. *Journal of Systemic Therapies*, 23(3): 36–50.

Andersen, T. (1995). Reflecting Processes: Acts of Forming and Informing. In: Friedman, S. (ed.) *The Reflecting Team in Action*. New York: Guilford Press. pp. 11–37.

Bernard, J.M. and Goodyear, R.K. (1992). *Fundamentals of Clinical Supervision*. Boston, MA: Allyn & Bacon.

Bess, M. (1988). Interview with Michael Foucault. History of the Present. Issue 4. http://www.vanderbilt.edu/historydept/michaelbess/Foucault%20Interview (accessed Sept 2008).

Boscolo, L. and Bertrando, P. (1996). *Systemic Therapy with Individuals*. London: Karnac Books.

Boston, P. (2006). Once Upon a Time in a Supervision Group: The Narrative Approach in Training. *Context*. June. 16–18.

Brady, J.L., Guy, J.D. and Norcross, J.C. (1995). Managing Your Own Distress: Lessons From Psychotherapists Healing Themselves. In: Vandecreek, L., Knapp, S. and Jackson, T.L. (eds), *Innovations in Clinical Practice: A Sourcebook*. Sarasota, FL: Professional Resource Press. pp. 293–306.

Campbell, D. Draper, R. and Huffington, C. (1991). *Second Thoughts on The Theory and Practice of the Milan Approach to Family Therapy*. London: Karnac Books.

Cronen, V., Johnson, K. and Lannamann, J. (1982). Paradoxes, Double Binds, and Reflexive Loops: An Alternative Theoretical Perspective. *Family Process*. 21: 91–112.
Davies, B. and Harré, R. (1990). Positioning: The Discursive Production of Selves. *Journal for the Theory of Social Behavior*. 20(1): 43–63.
Epston, D. (1994). Extending the Conversation. *Family Therapy Networker*. 18: 31–63.
Falicov, C. (1998). From Rigid Borderlines to Fertile Borderlands: Reconfiguring Family Therapy; Commentary On Lynn Hoffman's "Setting Aside The Model In Family Therapy". *Journal of Marital and Family Therapy*. 24(2): 157–163.
Flaskas, C. and Humphreys, C. (1993). Theorizing About Power: Intersecting the Ideas of Foucault with the "Problem" of Power in Family Therapy. *Family Process*. 32(1): 35–47.
Foucault, M. (1979). *Discipline and Punish*. New York: Vintage Books.
Harré, R. and Gillett, G. (1994). *The Discursive Mind*. London: Sage Publications.
Harré, R. and van Langenhove, L. (1999). The Dynamics of Social Episodes. In: Harré, R. and van Langenhove, L. (eds) *Positioning Theory: Moral Contexts of Intentional Action*. Oxford: Blackwell. pp. 1–13.
Jones, E. (1993). *Family Systems Therapy: Developments in the Milan Systemic Therapies*. Chichester/New York: Wiley.
Knowles, M.S. (1968). Andragogy, Not Pedagogy. *Adult Leadership*. 16(10): 350–352.
Lang, P., Little, M. and Cronen, V. (1990). The Systemic Professional: Domains of Action and the Question of Neutrality. *Human Systems: The Journal of Systemic Consultation and Management*. 1: 39–55.
Lumadue, C.A. and Duffey, T.H. (1999). The Role of Graduate Programs as Gatekeepers: A Model for Evaluating Student Counselor Competence. *Counselor Education and Supervision*. 39: 101–109.
Maturana, H. and Varela, F. (1987). *The Tree of Knowledge*. Boston/London: New Science Library.
McNamee, S. (2004) Promiscuity in the Practice of Family Therapy. *Journal of Family Therapy*. 26(3): 224–244.
Monk, G., Winsldae, J., Crocket, K. and Epston, D. (1997). *Narrative Therapy in Practice: The Archaeology of Hope*. San Francisco: Josey-Bass.
Oliver, M.N.I., Bernstein, J.H., Anderson, K.G., Blashfield, R.K. and Roberts, M.C. (2004). An Exploratory Examination of Student Attitudes Toward "Impaired" Peers in Clinical Psychology Training Programs. *Professional Psychology: Research and Practice*. 35: 141–147.
Penn, P.F.M. (1994). Creating a Participant Text: Writing, Multiple Voices, Narrative Multiplicity. *Family Process*. 33: 217–231.

Proctor, B. and Inskipp, F. (2001). Group Supervision. In: Scaife, J. (ed.). *Supervision in the Mental Health Profession*. Hove: Brunner Routledge.

Rober, P. (2005). The Therapist's Self in Dialogical Family Therapy: Some Ideas About Not-Knowing and the Therapist's Inner Conversation. *Family Process*. 44(4): 477–495.

Roberts, J. (2005). Transparency and Self-Disclosure in Family Therapy: Dangers and Possibilities. *Family Process*. 44(1): 45–63.

Russell, C., Jared DuPree, W., Beggs, M., Peterson, C. and Anderson, M. (2007). Responding to Remediation and Gatekeeping Challenges in Supervision. *Journal of Marital and Family Therapy*. 33(2): 227–244.

Rycroft, P. (2004). When Theory Abandons Us—Wading Through the "Swampy Lowlands" of Practice. *Journal of Family Therapy*. 26: 245–259.

Schwartz, R., Liddle, H. and Bruelin, D. (1988). Muddles in Live Supervision. In: Liddle, H.A., Becker, D. and Diamond, G.M. (eds). *Family Therapy Supervision: Handbook of Psychotherapy Supervision*. New York: Guilford Press.

Shimabukuro, S. (2003). Models, Truth and Utility. *Journal of Systemic Therapies*. 22: 60–64.

Shotter, J. (1996). "Now I can go on" Wittgenstein and Our Embodied Embeddedness in the "Hurly-Burly" of Life. *Human Studies*. 19: 385–407.

Simon, G. (2006). The Heart of the Matter: A Proposal for Placing the Self of the Therapist as the Centre of Family Therapy Research and Training. *Family Process*. 45(3): 331–344.

Storm, C.L., Todd, T.C., Sprenkle, D.H. and Morgan, M.M. (2001). Gaps Between MFT Supervision Assumptions and Common Practice: Suggested Best Practices. *Journal of Marital and Family Therapy*. 27: 227–239.

White, M. (1988). The Externalizing of the Problem and Re-Authoring of Lives and Relationships. *Dulwich Centre Newsletter*. pp. 8–14.

White, M. (1997). Supervision as Re authoring Conversation. *Dulwich Centre Publications*. pp. 148–171.

White, M. (2007). *Maps of Narrative Practice*. London: Norton and Co.

White, M. and Epston, D. (1990). *Narrative Means to Therapeutic Ends*. New York: Norton.

White, M.B. and Russell, C.S. (1997). Examining the Multifaceted Notion of Isomorphism in Marriage and Family Therapy Supervision: A Quest for Conceptual Clarity. *Journal of Marital and Family Therapy*. 23(3): 315–333.

CHAPTER THREE

Creating reflexive relationships between practices of systemic supervision and theories of learning and education

John Burnham

Introduction

Supervision has many functions in relation to: establishing and maintaining clinical governance; promoting the ethical responsiveness of both supervisor and supervisee (Bennett et al. 2002); and evolving the personal and professional development of trainees, junior colleagues, and peers. A practitioner's journey to "becoming a supervisor" or "doing supervision" may be via a range of pathways. Some may imperceptibly "drift" into doing it, others may be "drafted", and some may even have an irresistible desire to become a supervisor. A convenient shortcut to developing one's practice as a supervisor is to use ideas and skills learnt as a practitioner in the doing of supervision. In a comprehensive review of systemic supervision, Liddle (1991) found that most supervisors quoted references from therapy, rather than supervision literature, and so he kindly pointed supervisors in the direction of the literature available at that time.

In an act of transparency, I confess that, up until 1995, I was one of those people. Never mind! Around 1995, as programme leader of Kensington Consultation Centre's (KCC's) Diploma in Systemic

Teaching, Training and Supervision (DSTTS), I began to explore the educational literature. Up until that time I, and colleagues, had relied on isomorphism, sometimes imaginatively, to train supervisors. I engaged in this exploration with some trepidation, since I feared that I may find that the practices of supervision developed within our field might be found wanting within a "proper" educational framework. To my delight, however, I found that the systemic practices of supervision and training developed over many years could readily be understood within, and supported by, educational theories. Some of the early discoveries readily provided connections with a systemic approach: for example, Knowles (1990) stressed how adult education is influenced by the students' storied experience of education; Brookfield (1995) proposed that culture may be as important as age in creating contexts for education; and Belenky et al. (1986) reviewed how the delivery of adult education had been based on research with male students. Belenky et al. (1986) repeated this research with women and suggested a move from the "banking" model of education, to "connected" teaching in which the trainer/supervisor is the "mid-wife" to the trainee's/supervisee's emerging abilities, as a metaphor within which to organize learning relationships. bell hooks (1994) writes passionately about creating learning communities through compassionately deconstructing the social context of learning, in terms of, for example, race, gender, sexuality, and power. Donald Schön (1987: 47), addressing the education of professionals, shows how "knowledge-in-action", without reflection, leads to taken-for-granted practices; distinguishes between reflection-on-action and reflection-in-action; introduces the concept of "professional artistry"; and promotes coaching as a way of consolidating difference. David Kolb (1984), turning the focus onto the learner as expert in their own training, emphasizes how, in his view, experiential learning is more important as a process than as an outcome. Jerome Bruner (1986), using the narrative metaphor, proposes that education is *both* a cultural forum, *and* a forum in which culture is examined. Lev Vygotsky (1986) focuses on learning as a relational achievement, between teacher and learner, within a social context. A learner/supervisee engages with a "more knowledgeable other" (supervisor, peer, book, software programme), in moving from "what they know", through the "Zone of Proximal Development" (ZPD) to reach towards, and grasp "what is not yet known/what it is possible to know". Vygotsky's ideas have been usefully translated into our field by White (2007) and Hayward (2007). Boston et al. (2008 personal communication) has used this explicitly in the area of supervisory/training practices.

With some excitement, these ideas were gradually introduced into the DSTTS curriculum, at the KCC Foundation, with a variety of effects. In preparation for this chapter I canvassed the views of past graduates and current students. Many trainees have spoken of how useful educational theories have been to them during DSTTS training and beyond.

Influence on trainees' experience ... doubtful curiosity ...

"I have to say that at first I struggled a bit with the educational theories and trying to integrate them into a systemic model." (Emily Strang)

... through ... interested curiosity ...

"[As the course progressed] it became clear to me that this [educational theories] offered an extra dimension to the course in terms of richness ... ... educational theories have become of great interest. More so than I would have expected and it was one of the pleasant surprises of the course!" (Pete Brown)

to a ... reflexive relationship ... beyond the end of the course. More of their views will be interspersed through the text with the intent of enhancing a reflexive process.

This chapter looks at how the efficient process of isomorphism can be extended by developing a reflexive relationship between a) a model of supervisory practice, and ideas from education and learning; b) supervisors and supervisees.[1]

Making the move from therapist to supervisor

During a career, practitioners "make the move" from positioning themselves as therapist to supervisor in a variety of ways, and for dif-

---

[1] In this chapter I am particularly grateful to Kerri Newnes, Anne McDonald, Emily Strang, Pete Brown, Gillian Hughes, and Semra Akan for contributing their time, thoughts, and energy to sending me written feedback which I include in this chapter; to Jo Everill for contributing the case example on writing; and to Alison Roper-Hall for her patient and helpful suggestions.

ferent reasons: by default of time or seniority, by design, by ambition, or by preference. To "make the move", back and forth, successfully, I would propose that practitioners can benefit from both utilizing their skills as a therapist (supervisor as experienced therapist), and developing new skills (supervisor as trainer/educator).

Isomorphism: Making the most of what you already know

"I hear you're doing some systemic training. I've got a really difficult family; can I talk to you about it?" Such an invitation can lead to the beginning of experiences in "speaking from a supervisory position". All the philosophies, passions, values, working practices, and competencies developed at levels of Approach, Method and Technique (AMT) (Burnham, 1992; 1993), through a process of isomorphism (White and Russell, 1997) can be useful in the practice of supervision. Most models of therapy transfer their intrinsic ideas, values, practices, and skills into supervisory practices, for example, Psychoanalysis (Martindale et al. 1997), Cognitive Behavioural Therapy (CBT) (Milne, 2008), Systemic (Burnham, 1993), Solution Focused (Lowe and Guy, 1996), and Narrative (Behan, 2003). Isomorphic transfer may happen in a variety of ways, including: non-intentional (happening outside of immediate awareness); imposed (without choice); or rigorous (exact replication).

Effectively transferring practices from therapy to supervision has many advantages. Transferring the effects of training across contexts is generally rated as one of the hallmarks of success in adult education. It is convenient, efficient, and can enhance the coherence and trust between a practitioner and their model, as they experience its usefulness in more than one context. It also gives the supervisee a richer/deeper experience of the skills that they are learning to use as a therapist, when those same concepts and practices are used by the supervisor to assist them in the process of learning.

Potential disadvantages, including inhibition of the process of supervision, may arise if supervision is conducted in a language and practice too richly associated with therapy. Supervisees may wonder if they are in therapy or supervision. Supervisors may find themselves acting more as experienced therapists than as emergent supervisors. Supervisors may act effectively from the position as experienced therapists when the supervisee works in the same agency/discipline and is willing to act as an apprentice to the supervisor. This position is limited especially when a supervisee works in a different agency, or with quite a different client group. Resources as therapist can sometimes be restraints as supervisor. Interaction between supervisor and supervisee may become a pursuit of self-replicating images (Hare-Mustin, 1994) and the discourse of therapy can become inappropriately dominant in the domain of supervision. It can be useful for a supervisor to ask themselves: What are the qualities I have as a practitioner? How might these be a resource to the practice of people who come to me for supervision? How might they be a restraint to the practice of people who come to me for supervision?

Imaginative isomorphism: Extending current practices into different contexts

I use the term "imaginative isomorphism" to express what happens when a practice is transferred into a different context in ways which can avoid the potential disadvantages of direct transfer by maintaining the benefits of the practice *and yet* aesthetically and pragmatically fitting the "new" context. As a general principle this process uses the pattern of the practice while situating the practice in language and activities relevant to the new context. Examples of familiar/reliable concepts and practices from therapy which can be used effectively in supervision include:

- Analysing the multiple levels of context involved in episodes of supervision (Burck and Campbell, 2002; Fruggeri, 2002).
- Social GRRAAACCEEESS (Gender, Race, Religion, Age, Ability, Appearance, Class, Culture, Ethnicity, Education, Employment, Sexuality, and Spirituality) as an influence in training and supervision (Burnham, Alvis Palma, and Whitehouse, 2008).
- Exploring narratives of learning (Aggett, 2004).
- Hypothesizing about the significance of this supervisory relationship in the context of other supervisory relationships in the supervisee's career so far.
- Externalizing experiences that can promote or inhibit learning (Lee and Littlejohns, 2007).
- Rituals for trainees to facilitate the rites of passage involved in supervision and training (Roberts, 2003).

These theories and practices have developed within the context of systemic and narrative therapy and are made more versatile by paying close attention to the grammar, vocabulary, and activities relevant within the new context. It is always an exciting development when something familiar is used in unfamiliar ways or in a context that extends its usefulness. Making connections between a practitioner's current systemic abilities and the grammar, vocabulary, and activities of education can create a context for extending supervisory practice.

Extending supervisory practice through engaging with theories of education and learning

What inspires learning? How do we learn? ... Learning theories, particularly Kolb and Schön ... now form part of my "as if rough guide", mapping emerging abilities as a facilitator of learning. The theories loosened up my previously tight holding of the developmental model of supervision and they continue to free up my thinking in the co-creation of more spacious, fluid learning sites. (Ann McDonald, experienced supervisor, in further training)

Theories that were developed within the context of education and learning can add different dimensions to supervision, especially when supervisors create a reflexive relationship with systemic practices, in which there is mutual influence between the two "traditions". The rest of the chapter explores these possibilities.

Kolb's experiential learning: Relating to experience and transforming experience into learning (Kolb, 1984: 68–69)

I chose to illustrate this model as it is one of the most versatile, and can be used to coordinate many of the other educational influences. In a critical review Rogers (2008), proposes:

> Kolb's contributions cannot be underestimated. Whatever their limitations, by presenting a model of experience in a scientific form, he has helped move educational thought from the locus of the instructor back to the learner. ... experience has once again become a viable topic of discussion.

An important contribution the systemic tradition can make to extending Kolb's model is for systemic supervisors to make a distinction between a) Kolb (1984) as a "first order" tool in the "classification" of supervisee learning styles (personal coherence) and b) as a "second order" process in which supervisor and supervisee compare their narratives of supervision and learning, and their preferred practices of supervision. Thus begins a process of achieving an interpersonal co-ordination through practices of relational reflexivity (Burnham, 2005). During this process the supervisor's preferences must also be explored, although in this chapter I am privileging the supervisee's experience. In addition, since that time there have been many developments in our field, and it is necessary for readers of the original text to update the model within the contexts of important developments such as Social GRRAAACCEEESS within the supervisory relationship (Burnham, Alvis-Palma, and Whitehouse, 2008).

Kolb proposes that people have two complementary ways of *relating to experience* as well as two complementary ways of *transforming their experience* into learning.

Relating to experience through concrete experience and abstract conceptualization

Kolb proposes an inclusive continuum from *concrete experience* to *abstract conceptualization*. This refers not to the activity one is engaged in but how one senses, and makes sense of, the particular activity.

Concrete experience: (sensing) "immersing oneself in experiences, through affect, feelings, intuition, and relating to people in specific situations, unstructured, artistic, open-minded" (Kolb, 1984: 68). I have come to think of it as the "unspoken", visceral response to experience: a response experienced as, for example, an increase in heart rate; sweaty palms; a particular facial expression; dry mouth; a physical movement; crying; laughing; an ability/inability to think. As soon as one puts these into words then one has begun to use abstract conceptualization to some extent. According to Brookfield (1994) this affective/emotional aspect of a learner's experience is often the least appreciated/examined during training, and yet according to the research conducted by Skovholt and Rønnestad (1992), is a very significant resource during pre- and post-course periods of practitioners' careers. In the systemic/narrative field the work of Griffiths and Griffiths (1994), Scaife (2001), Fredman (2004), and Bertrando and Gilli (2008) refresh our views/practices about the emotional and spiritual aspects of therapeutic practice. Dutton and Turner (2007) apply this directly to the supervisory process. Schön's (1987) distinction "knowing-in-action" (intuitive action, without reflection, difficult to describe in words), seems to relate to this punctuation in a learning process.

Abstract conceptualization: (making sense of) "responding to experience through analysing it through, logic, theory, symbols, rigor and discipline, aesthetic quality of a neat conceptual system" (Kolb, 1984: 68). I most commonly associate this with responses that are more "intellectual", "cognitive", "linguistic", expressed in both word and tone. The less sense I have about an emotional response to an experience the more it seems situated in abstract conceptualization (and vice versa). Responses may tend towards either end of the continuum but are likely to contain both aspects. Someone may express their response in theoretical words whilst simultaneously demonstrating a visceral/emotional response. Similarly, someone may be discussing emotions in a very theoretical way. Some metaphors wonderfully combine both: "My heart leapt—through multiple levels of context!"

Videotape review is an excellent opportunity to "reflect-on-action" (Schön, 1987: 47). Pausing a tape, during supervision, I asked the supervisees (who were doing a systemic placement of 100 hours, whilst training in psychoanalytic psychotherapy), "What is your response?" (If I had asked, "What do you *feel*?" or "What do you *think*?" I would have been privileging one kind of response over another.) One supervisee audibly *gulped*. Another supervisee responded: "That is a clear case of 'projective identification'." Using Kolb's model I hypothesized about the ways in which they were experiencing the material on the tape, and the task of reviewing it. It is important to validate and explore each kind of response before, at some point, inviting each person to reflect on and experiment with other ways of experiencing the material. For example: "If that 'gulp' were to speak, what would it say?" "What kind of gulp is that?" "What feelings do you associate with the concept of 'projective identification'?" "How does that concept move you?"

How a person speaks can indicate the relative influence of concrete experience and abstract conceptualization in how they are experiencing an activity, and the connections between these two positions/punctuations. For example, if a supervisee uses a phrase such as, "I have butterflies in my tummy," "I had a lump in my throat," or "I was treading on eggshells," then I would understand this as using a metaphor (abstract conceptualization) to express their visceral experience. The chosen metaphor provides some clue as to which position the person is speaking from. The person who says, "I have butterflies in my tummy," doesn't actually have butterflies in their tummy, but the chosen metaphor is more closely situated within their visceral experience. Similarly, a person who says, "That is a clear case of 'projective identification'," indicates that they are speaking from a position of abstract conceptualization, as the words give me no clue about their bodily/emotional experience, but their tone of voice and other analogic communication may offer some expression of their visceral experiences.

In the process of supervision we can explore this inclusive continuum.

"As you begin this clinical session are you more aware of your feelings or your theoretical orientation?"

"As a supervisor would you prefer me to talk with you from the position of emotion or metaphor/theory?"

"I notice that when you are talking about optimism in your work with this family, you are using many theoretical concepts. Which concept makes you feel most optimistic about the work you are doing with them?"

Similar questions may be used to explore the process of the supervisory experience, as well as the clinical content of the supervisory conversation.

If this is how people grasp their experience both viscerally and abstractly, then how might they transform experience into learning?

Transforming experience into learning through reflective observation and active experimentation (Kolb, 1984)

Experience by itself does not necessarily lead practitioners to learning. It requires the ability to reflect on that experience in ways which lead to active experimentation with difference in the performance of their practice.

Reflective observation: This focuses on *learning through examining a practitioner's intention* and may be closely related to self-reflexivity, an ability much sought after by systemic practitioners. It is often demonstrated by practitioners who show, or express, an explicit preference towards spending time trying to understand ideas, events, how things happen, the implications, and different perspectives; appreciating other points of view; being patient; and making considered judgements. "I am wondering what that might mean for the client?" "I find it hard to listen when the client tells me about the relationship with her father, and I would like to spend this supervision session thinking about that issue."

Donald Schön's (1987) distinctions on the ability to reflect are particularly helpful. Reflection-*on*-action, refers to looking back on an event, for example, in a post-session, a video review, or case discussion. This kind of reflection cannot change the action being reflected upon, but is likely to involve thinking about the action in the context of concrete experience and/or abstract conceptualization, and planning/scaffolding for active experimentation in a future episode of practice, through, for example, imagination, future-oriented questions, or coaching through role/real play. In comparison, reflection-*in*-action refers to the ability to create, through immediate reflection, the potential to change an action, as it is happening. This may occur through an initiative of the practitioner, an invitation from a supervisor during live supervision, the ear bug, a telephone call, a call out, or a reflective supervision in the presence of the family. Each form of reflection may be done personally, or relationally.

Active experimentation: (Kolb, 1984) This focuses on learning through extending practices beyond a practitioner's current "comfort zone" (Wilson, 2008: 15), or perhaps through the "zone of proximal development" (Vygotsky, 1986). It is often demonstrated by practitioners who show, or express, an explicit preference towards spending time trying to influence people and who try to change situations through practical application of theory or metaphor; using their emotional response to inspire themselves and clients to do something different; looking for what works; and concentrating on getting things accomplished. Practitioners are often willing to take risks to achieve objectives, and are often willing volunteers to be the first to role play, or try a new technique that they have read about or seen in a workshop!

"I would like some practical suggestions about what to do in today's session." "I find it hard to listen when the client tells me about the relationship with her father, and so I need to know what to do differently. What do you suggest?"

In the process of supervision we can explore and work with this inclusive continuum:

> "Following the session do you feel more in a 'let's take time to reflect about what happened' mood, or a 'let's do something different' mood?"
>
> "We've given quite a bit of thought to your intentions towards doing something different in this piece of work, how might you/ready are you, to express those intentions in practice?"
>
> "I notice that when you are talking about this family you seem focused on what you might do differently. If we pause to think about what you have done so far, which practices have the clients responded to most enthusiastically?"

Whilst each practitioner will have their regular preferences, particular habits, comfort zones, and areas of exceptional ability, so the process of supervision should invite practitioners to explore other areas of practice and learning that they visit less often, especially in the phase of professional training.

Influence on trainee's practice ... emerging appreciation ...

> *However I did come to appreciate quite a lot of the ideas. One of the important ideas for me was thinking about the trainees' learning styles*

and my own, and how you accommodate different learning styles within a group. I suppose I became aware that I based my teaching on my preferred ways of learning so it was good to think about the impact of that and try to be more flexible and accommodating. It also helped me feel a bit less frustrated when they didn't seem to get some of the ideas and concepts I was trying to communicate. I found Knowles's ideas helpful in thinking about the stories adult learners bring with them from their own educational experiences. I found that it has been useful to explore these issues with trainees. (Emily Strang)

Developing a relationship with Kolb's model

In tune with the idea that people learn in different ways, I am offering two different ways of feeling your way through Kolb by reflecting on it as an abstract concept (Figure 3.1) and/or through active experimentation (Exercise 1).

Kolb's model is perhaps, in its own terms, situated in abstract conceptualization and trainers have to work hard in order to make it practically useful. When I have presented the model through "talk and chalk" (or even PowerPoint!) it has appealed to those who

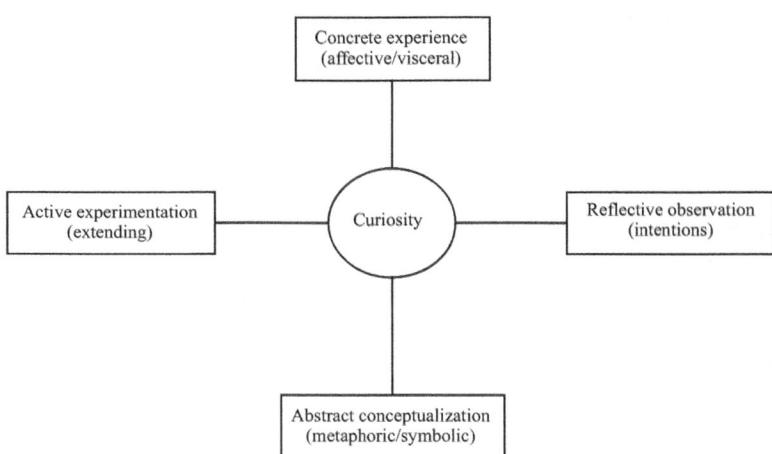

Figure 3.1. Kolb's model presented as an abstract concept (based on Kolb, 1984: 42).

love diagrams, but "turned off" those for whom diagrams act like an anaesthetic for learning. Up until that feedback from supervisees, I had naively thought that "everybody" would like diagrams in the same way that I did! This was a nodal point for me in my relationship with Kolb's model, and the persons I was using it with. Placing curiosity in the centre of these quadrants, helps the map to become a "curiosity compass", and can inspire a relationship with our systemic/narrative questioning skills. More practical methods/techniques are necessary to appeal to/engage with the range of preferred approaches to learning. Here is an exercise that supervisees and supervisors have said is useful.

Developing positional abilities, and abilities to position within the Kolb's model (Musical chairs without the music)

In a group for an exercise that lasts between thirty minutes to an hour, this is a practical way to engage/experiment with the model in a group, which was devised by the late Penny Lewis. Place four chairs back-to-back as follows:

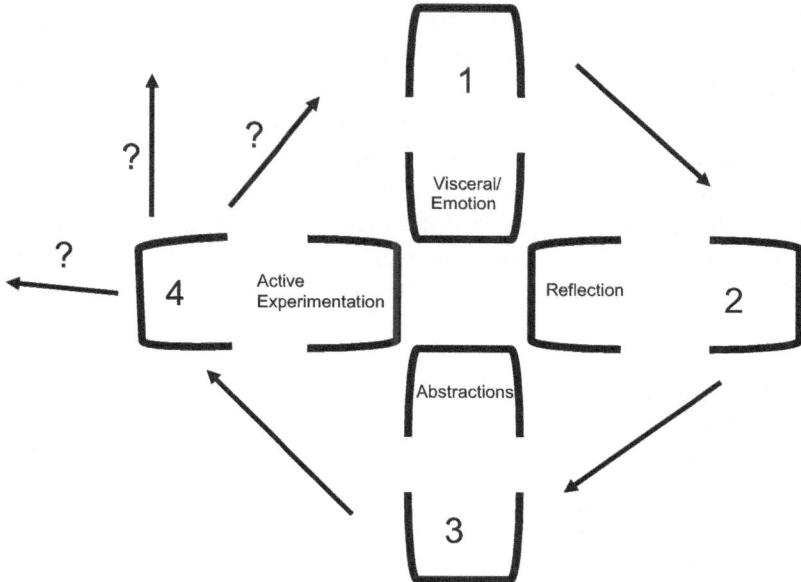

Figure 3.2. Kolb's model as a practical exercise.

A person sits in each chair, representing the voice of each aspect/position/punctuation of Kolb's model. A person presenting an issue for supervision (presenter) takes their numbered chair and sits in front of one of the positions. The supervisor usually suggests "concrete experience" (visceral/emotional) first, although this can be experimented with. The presenter engages in conversation about their "issue" with the person sitting in that position, whose job it is to stay with and rigorously explore the issue for that punctuation of the supervision/learning process. After a period of time (perhaps decided in advance, for example, five minutes in each position and ten minutes for discussion about the whole process), the presenter rotates to each position/punctuation in turn. The conversation can follow the "thread/theme" throughout each position, or can start as if the previous conversation had not been heard. The supervisor can help each person to stay focused, keep time, and so on.

Learning, development, taking up different perspectives and practical ways forward often occur for all involved in the exercise, the presenter, the persons in the interviewing "positions" (Harré and Van Langenhove, 1998), and any observer/witnesses to the exercise. For this to be effective the "position person" has to, initially, stay focused on speaking from the position in which they are seated/situated, and speak about the other positions from the context of their own. This can be hard work if a) they are not in their own "favourite"/preferred position and so do not have a repertoire of exploratory questions/comments to use and/or b) they are tempted to "drift" into other aspects of the experience prematurely, because they see connections. When the exercise is used regularly (albeit in different forms) each member of the group tends to find that they develop:

- an acceptance of difference between group members' ways of "doing" supervision;
- an appreciation of each aspect of their own, and each other's, learning process/narrative;
- abilities in exploring each position through noticing, listening, and explorations; and
- ambitions to experiment and extend their repertoires.

As the group works, its members often become more fluent in speaking from each punctuation, (Head, Heart, Reflect, and Experiment), more adept at moving along the arc between positions and more skilled at constructing relationships between different positions. There will be many other ways to develop the ability of those involved in a supervisory relationship to position and re-position in the context of Kolb. Each time I take a supervisee through this, or a similar exercise, I learn more about: my relationship with the model; my current preferences and what I need to learn more about; and those supervisees' I am similar/different to. These experiences help it to become a second order, relational tool within the supervisory relationship.

Developing through time

The above exercise takes place in the space of a single session of supervision or training. This is, as many will know from their own practice, not always possible and the process may take a few weeks to work through in relation to particular issues. Boscolo and Bertrando (1993) make a helpful distinction between chronological time and personal time. As an example, a young female therapist beginning a new job following completion of training went in to conduct her first session with live supervision from her more senior/experienced colleagues. She was working in a context that was familiar to her, and she was reasonably confident in her own competence. She felt that the session did not go well at all. The family shouted/argued loudly with one another; the father walked out of the session; the children said that the questions were stupid. Everything that "could go wrong did". Near the end of the session the therapist chose to come out to be with the team behind the screen, and promptly burst into tears. At this point, I as a supervisor felt concerned that the visceral experience of the therapist was so strong that any attempt to invite reflection, theorizing, or active experimentation would be cruel (my own emotional experience?). I asked, "If you were on your own, without us here, what would you do?" She replied, "I would end the session with a few comments about how difficult things had been for them, and then invite the parents on their own to the next session." To which I responded, "OK, that sounds OK. Do just that." Without further discussion she returned to the room and ended the session in the way that she was familiar and confident with. Immediately following this experience there was ample opportunity for reflection (video review, reflecting team, discussion, being interviewed, and so forth). The effects of the visceral experience seemed so strong, expressed verbally as, "I feel such a fraud when that kind of thing happens; it's as if they made a mistake when I passed the training," that it was agreed to postpone an extended reflection until the therapist felt more able. She requested some immediate reassurance that it wasn't "too awful". Colleagues responded with stories of similar experiences, with similar effects of feeling incompetent.[2] As supervisor, I opted to "withold" (Burnham and Harris, 2002: 40) the many questions I could have asked, and suggested instead a range of ways the process of reflection could begin (view video alone/with another, telephone conversation, and so on). She looked at the video alone, with limited success as the same feelings emerged (she saw/experienced the session in much the same way). A video review with colleagues introduced a polyphonic, multi-versal reflection, and some humour and theorizing, which led to a plan for how to extend her repertoire in similar situations (being more active, taking initiative, looking for patterns within the "chaos", and so forth).

Developing reciprocity between Kolb and systemic/narrative practices

The following table illustrates some of the systemic questions that can be used for/from each position.

---

[2] See Brookfield 1994 for an in-depth exploration of this phenomenon, which he calls the fear of "impostership", as in "If only there was a real therapist/supervisor, they would know what to do." This can be thought of as the self-critical stage in the development of self-reflexivity.

Developing reciprocity between Kolb and systemic/narrative practices

Position	Explore within the position	Relate to other positions (only after exploring "within" the position)
CE: Immersing oneself in experiences, through affect, feelings, intuition, and relating to people in specific situations, unstructured, artistic, open-minded.	What was the feeling that you were most aware of with this issue? How did/do you experience that physically? How do you remember sitting/looking at that time? How are you feeling now that you are talking about it (same or different to being there?)? Was that a new emotion for you with this family, or in your work in this agency?	Does that feeling lead more towards reflecting or more towards doing something practical? What does it do to your ability to theorize? What name would you give to that feeling?
RO: An orientation towards understanding ideas and events, how things happen, the implications, different perspectives; appreciating other points of view; patient, considered judgements.	How does the issue seem with the passage of time? Do you think you have sufficient distance from it to reflect about it? As you look at it from a distance, what did you like about what you did, and what would you have done differently? How did you use that feeling in the session to alter the way that the session went? How do you think your colleagues might have viewed how you handled things? How would the "you" of a year ago have handled the situation?	At that moment in the session/work, in what ways were you being guided by your feelings/intuition, and in what ways by a theory or metaphor? Would you usually reflect in the context of CE or AC? What about doing it differently today?

(*Continued*)

Developing reciprocity between Kolb and systemic/narrative practices

Position	Explore within the position	Relate to other positions (only after exploring "within" the position)
AC: Analysing experience through logic, theory, symbols, rigour, and discipline; aesthetic quality of a neat conceptual system.	What is your preferred/favourite theory or metaphor that you use to understand your work in general or this kind of situation in particular? What metaphor comes to your mind to describe this family, you and the relationship between you and this family? Of all the theories/readings that we have been learning about this term, which one seems most likely to help you? You said earlier that you enjoyed recalling the clinical work, but were not sure how to theorize it. As I was listening the idea of 'curiosity' came to mind. Would you be interested in using that as a concept to understand the work?	You said, to begin with, that you "could not see the wood for the trees", and while you were reflecting you said that "now there was light at the end of the tunnel". Which metaphor would you prefer to use to understand the situation?

AE: Orientation towards actively influencing people and changing situations. Emphasizes practical application, what works; getting things accomplished. Willing to take risks in order to achieve objectives.

After this process do you think you will be trying to influence how the family are, or yourself? If we were watching the next session what do you hope we would see you doing differently? If the family had been listening to this conversation what changes do you think they might be expecting/hoping for? Which of the new methods and techniques you have been learning about on the course will you be introducing to the client?

Now that you have reflected about your feelings and your thinking about the work, what is emerging as the direction you would like to take? How might you introduce that to the family, in a new way? As you were going through this process did you notice your self experimenting, or taking any risks compared to your usual supervisions? If so, which position was that? You said that this process has helped you to externalize your anxiety about using externalization. Do you feel more confident to experiment with doing that with a client, or in a role play situation?

Developing supervisory writing practices as a space for reflection in the context of Kolb and Schon

Writing is recognized as a useful tool for reflection in supervision (Walker, 1985; Burnham, 1993; Scaife, 2001). Jo Everill, a trainee on our Birmingham MSc in Systemic Psychotherapy, sent me a written self-reflexive commentary on her clinical development during her first term of qualifying level systemic training (required as part of the course). Using Kolb transparently, within this written form of "reflection-on-action", helped me to attend to each aspect of her experience and create a context for the written exchange between us as, respectively, supervisor and supervisee. I responded as follows:

"This is a very encouraging beginning to the training process. I like it that you have a clear idea about your abilities, as well as creating a vision for the continuous development of current skills and some discontinuous learning of new skills. There is strong and clear evidence of both the desire and ability to take a self-reflexive posture in relationship to your practice, and that relational reflexivity is an area for active experimentation."

"I was thinking about this task within Kolb's learning cycle, and my thoughts and curiosities are as follows: The whole piece is very reflective about your experience. I looked at the words you use to describe your reflections about experiences and hopes for the future. I noticed that you use more words that are related to theory or abstract concepts, than words or metaphors that relate to feelings or emotions. This is also related to the ways in which you express your learning aims. I wonder if this is a feature of the way the feedback form is structured and what we invite you to reflect upon? Did you find yourself wanting to describe your feelings or emotional experience but didn't find a 'section' (on the feedback form) for it? I would be interested in hearing from you about the place of emotions and emotional language, in therapy and supervision. How often do I invite you to talk about this aspect of the supervision or training? You said it is not easy for you to introduce 'spirituality', does this apply to emotions also?"

You expressed one of your goals as:
"I find it relatively easy to connect theory to practice (depending on the theory) when I am in a context that privileges the theory. When I am in sessions I tend to work at the level of method and

technique and this is something I would really like to be different. I am interested in identifying and exploring links to theory more spontaneously when in clinical situations to inform my practice and encourage me to consider different ideas and hypotheses. I now mostly do this work in supervision, but would like it to be part of what I naturally do in sessions or in pre/post discussions." (Direct quote from the supervisee's written account)

I interwove my supervisory curiosities with some of her ambitions, again using Kolb to remind me to include different aspects of the learning process:

"If we take what you say, and try to create a relationship between theory and emotions: What feelings or emotions do you associate with doing something *'more spontaneously'*? What feelings/emotions might you have/do you think you need to have, if you begin to actively experiment with *'identifying and exploring links to theory more spontaneously when in clinical situations to inform my practice'* and when this becomes *'part of what I naturally do in sessions...'*? Perhaps this can be part of our on-going conversations...?"

Supervisee response (one week later):

"I found it quite fascinating to receive your feedback and until then I had not realised that my report was quite so devoid of emotions. After giving this some thought I realise that I tend to approach these things in a very 'clinical' way focusing on skills and knowledge and not really thinking very much about my relationship to this learning. I am certainly not averse to introducing emotion (mine or other) into conversation in a therapeutic environment but in a learning situation, such as on the course and in supervision perhaps I privilege this information less. In relation to the form, perhaps if it was mentioned explicitly as something to be included it would have cued me in to this.

"I really liked the idea of thinking about what emotions would be associated with doing something 'more spontaneous' or when it becomes 'naturally [what I] do in session' although I am finding this tricky and will need to give it some thought (I'm not sure how telling that is?!). It seems easier for me to think about the emotions associated with starting to do something different—such as when actively experimenting. Using this model has certainly made me think about my use of emotion and of recognizing my embodied experience in a learning context."

This example shows how writing as a form of reflection-on-action between supervisor and supervisee becomes a context in which all parties experience change, and in which, during our "face-to-face" episodes of supervision, we may be more able to "reflect-in-action" as we have "warmed the context" (Burnham, 2005: 9) for this to happen. I, as supervisor, was changed in that, by using Kolb, as a "curiosity compass", I paid attention to multiple aspects of the supervisee's experience, and opened space for the trainee to notice the apparent "absence" of emotion in her theoretical description of her experience (though not in her actual/concrete experience). Our relationship became a resource for exploring this area, with other supervisees in the group, as well as with her. Creating this kind of relationship is what Belenky and colleagues refer to as "connected teaching" (Belenky et al. 1986: 32). The influence of this event went beyond this group. The form used for recording clinical experience is being changed to invite trainees to more explicitly document their emotional experience in the process of learning and supervision.

This method of placing a concept or activity at the centre of Kolb's quadrants (or any other quadrant grid) to explore the "landscape" (Bruner, 1986: 14) of that concept or activity, using each pointer on the compass, can work with other methods of supervision. For example, videotape supervision may seem to "obviously" fit into the "reflective observation" position. Placing video supervision in the centre of the diagram enables the exploration of this supervisory activity within the context of each point of the compass, and the creation of exercises for development, emerging from the video supervision.

Continuing influence of educational theories on the individual development of graduates' supervisors

Graduates of the KCC, DSTTS course had continued to use the educational theories and developed their own unique blends with other abilities. For example:

Kerri Newnes

"Schön's (1987) concept of 'coaching' I still find useful for the reason that it constructs a collaborative and creative approach to learning. I've extended the use of educational grammars to include dramatic theatrical terms referring to the different postures available to the application of teaching, training and supervision. For example, I now use and demonstrate the action methods and techniques of adopting a coaching/freeze framing/pause/play positions to create contexts which facilitate opportunities to develop the skills of reflection in action/on action and critical reflection (Schön, 1987) allowing the trainee to think in the moment about what he/she was doing whilst practising a specific skill/ability. It also creates a context for safe uncertainty (Mason, 1993), allowing for relational risk-taking (Mason, 2005) on both our behalfs. Recent feedback from a trainee when I coached her in the technique of internalized other interviewing (IOI; where a person is interviewed as someone else with the intention of developing a better understanding of someone else's point of view) explained how she experienced this as:

"surprisingly comfortable ... where I was stuck, if I was on my own ... I wouldn't have got to the relationship between ... even when you prompted me, I needed that question ... but now I've done it I'm quite surprised ... I can see myself using this whereas before I didn't think I'd ever use this ..."

Gillian Hughes offers these thoughts:
"I have to say, one of the theories I come back to time and again is Kolb in both training and supervision. It is simple and easy to apply and while I was training, I think it helped me maintain rigor in my work. Similarly, I find as a supervisor, it is incredibly useful in helping people create theoretical frameworks around what they do 'instinctively' (their words) so that they can apply what they know more effectively in new contexts. The discipline that Kolb's model invites of constantly weaving between theory and practice I think helps maintain ethical and reflective practice. I have come to realize that I don't find it useful identifying individual learning styles—at least following Kolb's categories, as of course people have many different styles which depend on the learning context."

Samra Khan contrasts the usefulness of the theories during training and afterwards
"During training, theories were more related to addressing anxiety of 'getting it right', each-and-every-time kind of feeling and so on. But after training the theories turned into real tools that

could be referred to both in teaching and supervision, and they continue to be helpful in my professional development as a tutor and supervisor."

Summary and discussion

Most practitioners give and receive supervision at some point, be that at significant times or throughout their professional career. Practitioners may experience giving supervision as a duty, a developmental activity, or a career ambition. Developing one's practice/identity as a supervisor often begins through using ideas and skills learnt as a practitioner, and the experience of being supervised. Supervisory practice can be extended through adopting/adapting ideas from education and learning. Both supervisors and supervisees can use Kolb's model (1984), personally and interpersonally, to bring forth both the visceral/emotional and symbolic/narrative punctuations of the experiences each of them has during supervision. These complementary aspects of experience can be transformed into learning/development through reflection and active experimentation in the contexts of the narratives of learning of both the supervisor and supervisees. This dated but still influential model can be used in its own right, as well as being a "coat hanger" for other ideas within the educational and systemic fields. Using systemic and narrative practices (for example, questions, externalization, internalized other interviewing, exercises, rituals, and curiosity) to navigate within and contextualize around the model may enhance the confidence/abilities of systemic practitioners to use the model and, I think, extends the model itself in directions perhaps not considered by its originator.

Isomorphic transfer from therapy to supervision is an efficient form of self-reflexivity, while connecting practices of supervision to educational theories can prevent a model from becoming too self-referential. Relational reflexivity (Burnham, 2005) can be useful in developing relationships between a model of therapy and theories of education/learning in ways which can enhance both. Being able to explore with rigour a particular position, whilst being able to imagine the consequences for, and potential within, the other positions, can achieve what Kolb calls "wisdom", and what Schön terms "professional artistry": "the kinds of competence practitioners sometimes display in unique, uncertain, and conflicted situations of practice" (Schön, 1987: 22).

References

Aggett, P. (2004). Learning Narratives in Group Supervision: Enhancing Collaborative Learning. *Journal of Systemic Therapies*. 23(3): 36–50.

Austin, K.M., Moline, M.E. and Williams, G.T. (1990). *Confronting Malpractice: Legal and Ethical Dilemmas in Psychotherapy*. London: Sage.

Behan, C.P. (2003). Some Ground to Stand On: Narrative Supervision. *Journal of Systemic Therapies*. 22(4): 29-42.

Belenky, M. et al. (1986). *Women's Ways of Knowing*. New York: Basic Books.

Bennett, M., Gower, M., Maynerd, C. and Wyse, G. (2002). Supervision and Clinical Governance. In: Campbell, D. and Mason, B. (eds). *Perspectives in Supervision*. London/New York: Karnac Books.

Bertrando, P. and Gilli, G. (2008). Emotional Dances: Dialogues as Embodied Systems. *Journal of Family Therapy*. 30(4): 362–373.

Boscolo, L. and Bertrando, P. (1993). *The Times of Time: A New Perspective in Systemic Therapy and Consultation*. New York: Norton Press.

Boston, P. et al. (2008; personal communication).

Boud, D., Keogh, R. and Walker, D. (eds) (1985). *Reflection: Turning Experience into Learning*. London: Kogan Page Ltd.

Breunlin, D.C., Karrer, B.M., McGuire, D.E. and Cimmarusti, R.A. (1988). Cybernetics of Videotape Supervision. In: Liddle, H., Breunlin, D. and Schwartz, R. (eds) *Handbook of Family Therapy, Training and Supervision*. New York: Guilford Press.

Brookfield, S. (1994). Tales from the Dark Side: A Phenomenography of Adult Critical Reflection. *International Journal of Life-long Education*. May–June: 203–216.

Brookfield, S. (1995). Adult Learning: An Overview. In: Tuinjman, A. (ed.) *International Encyclopaedia of Education*. Oxford: Pergamon Press.

Bruner, J. (1986). *Actual Minds, Possible Worlds*. London/Cambridge Mass: Harvard Press.

Burck, C. and Campbell, D. (2002). Training Systemic Supervisors: Multi-layered Learning. In: Campbell, D. and Mason, B. (eds) *Perspectives in Supervision*. London/New York: Karnac Books.

Burnham, J. (1992). Approach—Method—Technique: Creating Distinctions and Creating Connections. *Human Systems*. 3: 3–27.

Burnham, J. (1993). Systemic Supervision. Special Edition: Voices from the Training Context. *Human Systems*. 4: 3–4.

Burnham, J. (2005). Relational Reflexivity: A Tool for Socially Constructing Therapeutic Relationships. In: Flaskas, C., Mason, B. and Perlesz, A. (eds) *The Space Between: Experience, Context, and Process in the Therapeutic Relationships.* London/New York: Karnac Publications.

Burnham, J. and Harris, Q. (2002). Cultural Issues in Supervision. In: Campbell, D. and Mason, B. (eds) *Perspectives in Supervision.* London/New York: Karnac Books.

Burnham, J., Alvis Palma, D. and Whitehouse, L. (2008). Learning as a Context for Differences, and Differences as a Context for Learning. *Journal of Family Therapy.* 30(4): 529–542.

Campbell, D. and Mason, B. (2002) (eds) *Perspectives in Supervision.* London/New York: Karnac Books.

Cave, M., Hanney, S., Henkel, M. and Kogan, M. (1997). *The Use of Performance Indicators in Higher Education: The Challenge of the Quality Movement.* London: Jessica Kingsley Publishers Ltd.

Down, G. (2000). Supervision in a Multicultural Context. In: Gorell-Barnes, G., Down, G. and McCann, D. (eds) with contributions by Nuala Sheehan and Paul Blackburn. *Systemic Supervision: A Portable Guide for Supervision Training.* London: Jessica Kingsley Publishers.

Dulwich Centre Newsletter (1989/90). *Family Therapy Consultation and Teaching.*

Dutton, J., El Hadi, A., Gray, P., Erskine, R. and Cox, B. (1999). Personal Development in Relation to Race, Ethnicity and Culture in Family Therapy Training. *Context*:(AFT), 44: 35–42.

Dutton, J. and Turner, A. (2007). *The Emotional Aspect of Supervision.* Proceeding of IFT/TAVI Conference on Supervision.

Fredman, G. (2004). *Transforming Emotions: Conversations in Counselling and Psychotherapy.* London/Philadelphia: Whurr Publishers.

Fruggeri, L. (2002). Different Levels of Analysis in the Supervisory Process. In: Campbell, D. and Mason, B. (eds) *Perspectives in Supervision.* London/New York: Karnac Books.

Gorell-Barnes, G., Down, G. and McCann, D. (eds) (2000). With contributions by Nuala Sheehan and Paul Blackburn. *Systemic Supervision: A Portable Guide for Supervision Training.* London: Jessica Kingsley Publishers.

Griffiths, M. and Griffiths, J. (1994). *The Body Speaks: Therapeutic Dialogues for Mind-Body Problems.* New York: Basic Books.

Grosch, W.N. and Olsen, D.C. (1994). *When Helping Starts to Hurt: A New Look at Burnout among Psychotherapists.* New York: Norton.

Hardy, K.V. and Laszloffy, T.A. (1995). The Cultural Genogram: Key to Training Culturally Competent Family Therapists. *Journal of Marital and Family Therapy.* 21(3): 227–237.

Hare-Mustin, R. (1994). Discourses in the Mirrored Room: A Postmodern Analysis of Therapy. *Family Process.* 33:19–35.

Harré, R. and van Langenhove, L. (eds) (1998). *Positioning Theory: Moral Contexts of International Action.* London: Wiley-Blackwell.

Hawes, S. (1993). *Reflexivity and Collaboration in the Supervisory Process: A Role for Feminist Poststructural Theories in the Training of Professional Psychologists.* National Counsel of Schools of Professional Psychology Midwinter Conference on Clinical Training in Professional Psychology, La Jolla, California. Unpublished Manuscript.

Hawes, S.E. (1998). Positioning a Dialogic Reflexivity in the Practice of Feminist Supervision. In: Bayer, B.M. and Shotter, J. (eds) *Reconstructing the Psychological Subject: Bodies, Practices and Technologies.* London: Sage.

Hayward, M. (2007). Proceedings of Workshop "What is Narrative Therapy?" Birmingham.

Hedges, F. and Lang, S. (1993). Mapping Personal and Professional Stories: The Personal Development of Psychotherapy Trainees: Contributions from within a Social Constructionist Discourse. *Human Systems: The Journal of Systemic Consultation & Management.* 4(3–4): 277–298.

hooks, B. (1994). *Teaching to Trangress: Education as the Practice of Freedom.* London: Routledge.

Knowles M. (1990). (4th edn) *The Adult Learner: A Neglected Species.* Houston: Gulf Publishing.

Kolb, D.A. (1984). *Experiential Learning.* New Jersey: Prentice Hall.

Lee, L. and Littlejohns, S. (2007). Deconstructing Agnes: Externalization in Systemic Supervision. *Journal of Family Therapy.* 29: 238–248.

Liddle, H.A. (1991). Training and Supervision in Family Therapy: A Comprehensive and Critical Analysis. In: Gurman, A. S. and Kniskern, D. (eds) *Handbook of Family Therapy.* (2nd edn) New York: Bruner/Mazel.

Lowe, R. and Guy, G. (1996). A Reflecting Team Format for Solution-Oriented Supervision: Practical Guidelines and Theoretical Distinctions. *Journal of Systemic Therapies.* 15(4): 26–45.

Martindale, B., Morner, M., Cid Rodriguez, M.E. and Videt, J-P. (eds) (1997). *Supervision and its Vicissitudes.* London: Karnac Books.

Mason, B. (1993). Towards Positions of Safe Uncertainty in "Voices from the Training Context": A special edition of *Human Systems: The Journal of Systemic Consultation and Management.* 4(3&4): 189–200.

Mason, B. (personal communication). Calls Creating a "Culture of Contribution".

Mason, B. (2002). A Reflective Recording Format for Supervisors and Trainees. In: Campbell, D. and Mason, B. (eds) *Perspectives in Supervision*. London/New York: Karnac Books.

Mason, B. (2005). Relational Risk-taking and the Training of Supervisors. *Journal of Family Therapy*. 27: 298–301.

McLeod (2007). Vygotsky's Theory of Social Development http://www.simplypsychology.pwp.blueyonder.co.uk/vygotsky.html

Milne, D. (2008). CBT Supervision: From Reflexivity to Specialization. *Behavioural and Cognitive Psychotherapy*, 36: 779–786.

Montalvo, B. (1973). Aspects of Live Supervision. *Family Process*, 12(4): 343.

Pearson, M. and Smith, D. (1985). De-briefing in Experienced-based Learning. In: Boud, D., Keogh, R. and Walker, D. (eds) *Reflection: Turning Experience into Learning*. London. Kogan Page Ltd.

Polkinghorne, D.E. (1992). Postmodern Epistemology of Practice. In: Kvale, S. (ed.) *Psychology and Postmodernism*. London/New Delhi: Sage Publications.

Roberts, J. (2003). Rituals and Trainees. In: Imber-Black E., Roberts J. and Whiting R. (eds) (revised edn) *Rituals in Families and Family Therapy*. New York: Norton Press.

Rogers (2008) Experiential Learning Articles and Critiques of David Kolb's Theory http://reviewing.co.uk/research/experiential.learning.htm

Rudes, J., Shilts, L. and Berg, I.K. (1997). Focused Supervision Seen Through a Recursive Frame Analysis. *JMFT*. 23(2): 203–215. Special Edition of *Journal of Systemic Therapies*. 14(2): 1–13.

Scaife, J. (1995). *The Use of Audio and Videotapes in Supervision*. Training Link: Newsletter of the Universities of Leicester and Sheffield Clinical Psychology Training Course. No. 7.

Scaife, J. (2001). Learning Logs in Supervision. In: Scaife, J. (ed.) *Supervision in the Mental Health Professions: A Practitioner's Guide*. With contributions from Francesca Inskipp, Brigid Proctor, Jon Scaife, and Sue Walsh. London/Philadelphia: Brunner-Routledge.

Scaife, J. and Scaife, J. (2001). Supervision and Learning. In: Scaife, J. (ed.) *Supervision in the Mental Health Professions: A Practitioner's Guide*. With contributions from Francesca Inskipp, Brigid Proctor, Jon Scaife, and Sue Walsh. London/Philadelphia: Brunner-Routledge.

Scaife, J. and Walsh, S. (2001). The Emotional Climate of Work and the Development of Self. In: Scaife, J. (ed.) *Supervision in the Mental Health Professions: A Practitioner's Guide*. With contributions from

Francesca Inskipp, Brigid Proctor, Jon Scaife, and Sue Walsh. London/ Philadelphia: Brunner-Routledge.
Schön, D.A. (1987). *Educating the Reflective Practitioner*. San Francisco: Jossey Bass Publishers.
Schön, D.A. (1992). The Crisis of Professional Knowledge and the Pursuit of an Epistemology of Practice. *Journal of Interprofessional Care*. 6(1): 49–63.
Skovholt, T.M. and Rønnestad, M.H. (1992). *The Evolving Professional Self: Stages and Themes in Therapist and Counsellor Development*. New York: J. Wiley and Sons.
Vygotsky, L. Supervision. *Journal of Family Therapy*. (2007). 29: 238–248. http://sciencehack.com/videos/view/634376752589779456
Vygotsky, L. (1986). *Thought and Language*. MA: MIT Press.
Walker, D. (1985). Writing and Reflection. In: Boud, D., Keogh, R. and Walker, D. (eds) *Reflection: Turning Experience into Learning*. London: Kogan.
Weeks, P. (1996). *The Teaching Portfolio: A Professional Development Tool*. The International Journal for Academic Development. 1: 170–74.
White, M. (1992). Family Therapy Training and Supervision in a World of Experience and Narrative. In: *Selected Papers of David Epston and Michael White (1989–1991)*. Dulwich Centre Publications. South Australia.
White, M. (1997). *Narratives of Therapists' Lives*. Dulwich Centre Publications. South Australia.
White, M. (2007). *Maps of Narrative Practice*. New York: Norton Publications.
White, M.B and Russell, C.S. (1997). Examining the Multifaceted Notion of Isomorphism in Marriage and Family Therapy Supervision: A Quest for Conceptual Clarity. *JMFT*. 23(3) 315–333.
Wilson, J. (2008). *The Performance of Practice*. London: Karnac.

CHAPTER FOUR

Three gasps behind the screen: Exploring discourses of emotion in systemic supervision

David Spellman and Gerrilyn Smith

This chapter examines a variety of ways to understand "emotion discourses" that position supervisors, therapists, and clients in systemic practice.

Therapists are expected to be receptive (Andersen, 1987) and alive to all the experiences of the people who consult with them, as well as being reflective (Rober, 2005). We aim to listen to and talk with clients, engaging with them in their experience, as well as being outside of it. Supervision could be seen as helping the supervisee improve his or her effectiveness by managing the tension of getting close to clients' experiences and simultaneously maintaining some distance. Emotions seem central as an experience that clients communicate with and about. What are the dominant discourses of emotion both in therapy and in supervision? How might we make each discourse of emotion more visible so that we can better evaluate the effects on our work as supervisors and as therapists? Can we move to a "feelingful understanding" (Swedenborg cited in Keeney 2005: 169) of the systems we work with?

In *Transforming Emotion*, Glenda Fredman (2004) highlights how therapists routinely see it as their responsibility to name, describe, and locate emotions, but that as systemic practitioners we need to reconsider these taken-for-granted approaches to emotion. Thinking and practice around emotion are often rooted in other theoretical perspectives as if they fall outside a "truly" systemic perspective. In developing systemic perspectives on emotion we can, as supervisors, be more helpful to supervisees and embed emotional discourses into systemic theories and frameworks. In preparing this chapter we are reminded of the gap between systemic practice as it is written about in books and journals and the practice that people employ every day in their work: something narrative therapists might call the difference between "storied" and "lived" experience.

We are interested in the idea of deconstructing "emotion discourses" as part of the work in a supervisory relationship and in this chapter we provide examples from our work.

Defining emotion

Emotion is often distinguished from reason in the phrase "the heart rules the head" yet it remains difficult to define. It is primarily a felt experience. Ekman (2003) has shown that at least some facial expressions and their corresponding emotions are universal across human cultures and are not culturally determined. These universal emotions include anger, disgust, fear, joy, sadness, and surprise.

Neuropsychological research indicates that emotional literacy is located predominantly in the right hemisphere of the brain and that this early maturing right hemisphere is dominant for the first three years of life. Our basic primitive affective responses predate our capacity to verbalize them (Schore, 2003). This is important in considering that our affective understandings are likely to be more immediate than our cognitive/intellectual constructions.

Is putting our feelings into words important? Selvini-Palozzoli et al. (1980: 4) took a pragmatic position regarding hypotheses that "they are neither true nor false but rather more or less useful". We could apply this to our discussion of wording emotions. More recently, Paolo Bertrando (2007: 166) in *The Dialectical Therapist* adds: "In dialogue emotions are created, not just discussed." Words alone may not always convey emotion; hence the emergence of emoticons for text messages and emails. Messages based on words alone need to be embedded in a feeling in order to be appropriately understood. The early research on double bind theory clearly understood that messages can be received on two levels simultaneously and, when these levels were contradictory, it induced severe confusion and distress. There is also a common assumption that we all use the same emotional lexicon. With both of us working with looked-after children, who often have issues regarding emotional literacy, we have come to realize that this is not always so. Charlotte Burck's (2005) work on multilingual living also gives a clear indication of the languaged nuances of emotions.

> Because Di-Yin could only express anger in English, she only experienced it in English. Her different languages (and cultures) named, differentiated, and allowed different emotional states.
> (Burck, 2005: 115)

Emotions tend to be talked about as if they exist "inside" a person and that it is a therapist's job to "get them out". This of course minimizes the role that context plays in generating emotions—especially important in understanding the issue of emotion and the supervision process. Fredman (2004) plots some of the dominant discourses of emotion in the therapy world and Bertrando (2006) details "commonplace" ideas about emotion including the idea that emotions are an expression of "inner states" and the "true" self. Such discourses of individualism have been dominant in the general field of psychotherapy, although some family therapists neglect the evidence of the more relational dimensions in other approaches (see, for example, Mitchell, 1988).

Defining supervision

In reflecting upon how we might approach the issue of emotions in systemic supervision we need first to reflect on what we understand by "supervision" and what we think it is for. This provides an opportunity to remember all of the supervisors/supervisees who have influenced us. As reader you might find it helpful to take a few moments to do this yourself as an exercise.

Encouraging new supervisees to similarly reflect on their histories of supervision as part of the context setting at the beginning of a supervision relationship can be very helpful. Burnham and Harris (2002) more recently ask if there is such a "thing" as supervision at all, whereas in his earlier introductory text, Burnham (1986) saw a supervisor as primarily there to develop and maintain a "meta-view".

Supervision is often seen as the "sanctuary" of two people in a room away from a hectic work schedule, talking about the dilemmas experienced seeing families, and generating constructive ideas and practices. It is an activity that all psychotherapies value whichever theoretical framework is used. A common assumption is that you supervise to the model, an example of isomorphism (Liddle and Saba, 1983; see Bertrando, this volume).

If one component of therapy is, as Flaskas (2005) says, the emotional task of tolerating powerful emotions, then the challenge for supervision may be how to help supervisees position themselves to remain connected to emotion (even be moved by it) without being so overwhelmed by it that they cannot think or move between levels of therapeutic discourse—from feelings to ideas recursively.

In reading the "emotional tone" of a session, we must be aware of our own emotional tone. Wilson reminds us "to be extraordinarily mindful of the appropriateness of our emotional intimacy with our clients. The emotionally attuned therapist … [is] able to be in touch with the client's feelings and on the basis of feedback, decide safe enough emotional distance to make the client feel at ease" (1993: 153). How can supervision help with this, especially when it may be retrospective, the emotional "in the room" experience having faded? It is important to remember how radical it was to open out the therapeutic space to video and live supervision groups. Not surprisingly, there was a huge amount of material that came under scrutiny that previously would have gone unnoticed and perhaps unreported if systemic psychotherapy had opted solely for a retrospective model of supervision.

Whilst reflexivity is an important feature of contemporary family therapy and supervision, perhaps it is important to recognize that it is not inevitably helpful. Burnham (1993) warns us against confusing self-reflexivity with self-preoccupation and this subtle distinction may be one way of introducing some observation of the effects of our self-reflexivity. We may be too interested in ourselves when in a therapist position just as we may not be interested enough. Self-reflexivity needs to be in service of our clients. Supervision may be the training ground for developing self-reflexivity so that it becomes more habitual in the clinical setting. Supervision may also offer a space to reflect on emotional discourses noticed during therapy but not developed on at the time.

Should the way we deal with emotion in therapy inform the way we deal with it in supervision?

Jones (1996: 223) says: "The training experience offers a template in which trainee therapists can learn, via the relationship with the supervisor, much that is also of relevance to their own relationships with clients. Can we make space, in the construction of supervisory models, to attend to the many interlinked and overlapping complexities that affect the supervisory relationship as much as they do the therapy relationship?"

Supervision groups offer a multiplicity of views for families to consider. This richness can introduce difference or can perturb the system. Additionally the supervision system acts as one mind for the client/s with the therapist in the room functioning as a conduit between two systems united (hopefully) in a healing experience:

> It may then be helpful for therapists, especially when stuck, to look to what is happening in their own relational and emotional lives (internal, personal and professional) but also to look at their emotional responses as a source of information about what it is like to be a member of this family–therapist system.
> (Jones, 1996: 222)

Flaskas (2002) similarly points out that therapeutic impasse (the material often taken to supervision) requires attention to the therapist's emotional self. Pocock (2005: 128) prefers the phrase "feeling self" to "emphasize the ordinary human capacity for feelings and the way that the self is regulated, both internally and in relationships, on the basis of which feelings come to be experienced as acceptable in both domains". He remarks that he is not confident that the feeling dimension is adequately represented alongside the "more cognitively framed relational or narrative self of contemporary family therapy".

What kinds of prejudices exist around emotion, therapy, and supervision?

The naming of emotions and their discourses is seen by Fredman (2004) as a powerful and sometimes helpful act. There is the potential that as part of a wish to help people to move to new positions, therapists may unwittingly coerce others into accepting "our" labels and concepts. It is not unusual for people, including supervisors, to name emotions on behalf of others ("You are feeling angry aren't you?"). Risks of coercion may need most attention where there are issues of hierarchy such as in the case of an evaluative supervisor or when working cross-culturally.

According to Fredman (2004), who draws heavily from social constructionism, a relational emotions discourse (as opposed to a non-relational, autonomous one) assumes that there is no direct correspondence between sensation and meaning. In other words, the meaning has to be made as part of a social process. Emotions are not perceived as universal and they cannot be classified according to bodily and facial expressions—they need to be seen in context. But as Parker (1992: 4–5) writes: "Once an object has been elaborated in a discourse, it is difficult not to refer to it as if it were real." That is, the relationship in which the emotion emerged or was constructed can be forgotten but the emotion remains. The change of context or emerging new relationships do not generate a change of emotion. There is no news of difference (Bateson, 1973). This is often the case for traumatized children who continue to feel fearful even in "safe" situations.

Campbell and Groenbaek (2006) say: "Rather than attributing the source of our behaviour to individual, internal factors such as attitudes, emotional states or personality, we take the view that our sense of who we are and how we want to behave results from the positions we choose and are given, within the range of discourses society offers us." This analysis can be extended to how we feel.

Jim Wilson (2007) in his book *The Performance of Practice* outlines a framework that includes a number of emotional scales to consider in one's practice that could easily be adapted to the supervision context. These include, for example, Scale 1 Systemic Humility/Passionate Conviction and Scale 5 Emotional Closeness and Distance, covering the range of preferred emotional proximity to our clients. Like positioning theory it offers a series of polarities to consider in your practice.

Semantic polarities (Campbell and Groenbaek, 2006) are used to promote the interplay of meaning by the contrasting of positions along a continuum rather than less helpful either/or dichotomies.

For example, as a supervisor I (DS) have explored the significance of "anxiety" on performance of the therapist when working with a supervisee behind the screen. We drew up the polarity as follows:

Anxiety of the therapist
Hinders   Doesn't help or hinder   Helps
|_____|_____|

A person is encouraged to take a position on the polarity and explore the consequences for the work. Others can be invited to take their positions on the polarity which can then form the basis for discussion on the merits of each position. Feelings are regarded here as a result of positions we take and are put in by others.

Another example from a cross-cultural supervision session is when the supervisee brought to supervision the issue of how to be an effective therapist and black. She felt doubtful that she could be effective when all her "feelings" (seen as connected to her ethnicity) "keep getting in the way". Helping the supervisee move to a both/and position (having feelings and being effective) was important in her professional development and in claiming her expertise. It also required a discussion about the process of self-censorship that can emerge in certain contexts and cultural stereotypes of feelings.

These examples also demonstrate how our emotions are connected to the particular construction of self most prominent in any one interaction. Given that we have multiple constructions of self to choose from, it may be important to preface comments with, for example, "If I hear this as a mother I feel this way … "

Semantic polarities help someone consider a both/and position. They encourage looking at the possibilities *between* polarities and not just the meanings at either extreme. In the cross-cultural example above the trainee was able to talk within the reflecting team about how *as a black woman* she heard the descriptions of the client, who was also a black woman. It enabled her to change the view of the white professional system and allow a different view of this black family to emerge. This view and the conversations that followed with the family were so different that court proceedings were not initiated, whereas at the point of original contact the local authority was about *to remove an unborn child*. This can also be seen as demonstrating passionate conviction—the supervisee was so moved by her first experience and her feelings that she sought supervision. Having started by feeling unprofessional about her feelings, she moved towards claiming her expertise.

It can be helpful to draw a continuum of how "central" therapist emotional experiences might be seen:

Importance of emotional experiences of the therapist
Central   Significant   Marginal
   1   2   3
   |_____|_____|

Here position 1 could be linked to the view that personal therapy may be the best way to pay attention to emotions in a way that promotes more effective therapy. Position 2 is the dominant emerging view in the systemic field where development of awareness and reflexive "use of self" represent the preferred way to attend to emotion, but where personal therapy is not usually seen as the only way to achieve this. The third position may be where great emphasis is put upon technical skill development of the therapist and emotional experiences seen as largely irrelevant to the task. Although three key positions are identified there are clearly any number of positions one might take. It may be that a position statement from a supervisor (an example of transparency) may help a supervisee position themselves and make best use of the supervision within the framework available. It may be that positions are context specific (for example, at times of being stuck, an exploration of the emotions of the therapist becomes more important).

In reflecting on our own experiences of supervision as supervisees, feelings were not explored in detail. It is not possible to predict how feelings will come up or be dealt with over the course of a supervisory relationship, but some families we see generate a powerful emotional response because of a shared personal experience. Talking in supervision about how, when, or whether to share this information with families is important. Is it helpful for families to know that you as a therapist have experienced particular kinds of trauma and distress in your personal life? We can be overcome by emotion or just distracted from the therapeutic task. Sometimes this can come up in live supervision where the supervisee, perhaps prompted by the supervisor, can move into self-disclosure. Often this occurs around issues such as bereavements.

How much supervisees might share about personal experiences in supervision will vary, but the respectful and sensitive responses of a reflecting team (as a supervisory activity) guided by a supervisor can in our experience be very helpful. This is rarely a neat and tidy experience; it can feel very uncomfortable. However, it can encourage supervisees to reflect on how they are positioned by emotional experiences, how this affects their work, what they might need to do about it, and how they might choose to position themselves in the future.

The supervision group can seem to have an emotional life of its own that can influence the therapeutic process. Laughing behind the screen may be at odds with what is going on in the room. Excessive supervisory comments may become irritating and may disrupt the flow of the session to the point of disrupting it all together. Some supervision groups can be very cohesive where people have intimate conversations but for others the supervision group is not the right context for them.

Some ideas for practice development

There are a number of ways that systemic practice may be developed. This can include appreciating emotional contexts, deconstructing discourses, challenging emotional prejudices, or a more reflexive use of "feeling" self. The different points of entry for practitioners may depend on theoretical preferences but clearly supervisors can open up these discourses.

Personal and professional development

Scaife (1993) emphasizes the importance of negotiating as much as possible as early as possible in the supervisory relationship. One possibility for making emotion discourses more visible is to develop the cultural genogram (Hardy and Laszloffy, 1995) to track a person's experience of "emotional" cultures both within their families, and within the various communities that they identify with. It may also be helpful to specifically address stories of "family shame", as this emotion so dominates clinical work and is an especially difficult one to share. In linking feelings to actions it is feelings of shame that seem to make us hide.

A supervisee, Lilian,[1] came to supervision with some reflections on the joyous and energetic way in which she often interacted with people, what she came to call her "enthusiasm". In many senses this was a positive influence for Lilian, but she began to wonder whether there were times when it was a hindrance (for example, to her being taken seriously). After generating some options for further reflection with her in one-to-one retrospective supervision, Lilian decided that she might like to experience an externalizing interview (White, 1988) with the rest of the family therapy team. We did this, and with each person taking a turn at asking questions. Lilian said that she found this helpful in reviewing the effects of "enthusiasm" on her life and the various influences upon the "life of enthusiasm". She went on to identify which effects she preferred and which got in the way. She described being able to begin to revise her relationship with enthusiasm, tracking it over time. Although in this case the supervisee benefited from the externalizing discourse approach, O'Hanlon (1993) prefers a both/and position. He argues that it is not inevitable that internalizing discourses will be oppressive, blaming, pathologizing, or discouraging.

A trainee in supervision discussed her feeling of wanting to give up. She described feeling defeated by the training course she was on. As a black and minority ethnic trainee she said that she felt isolated and disconnected from the wider course membership and the whole ethos of the training. She felt she was "faking it" to get through. In supervision she was asked, "Do you think Rosa Parks[2] had a moment of doubt as she sat there on that bus?" This question, framed as it was, accessed a new dimension of thinking for the trainee. It focused not on Rosa Parks' actions but on her feelings. It seemed to allow the trainee to see herself as a ground-breaking pioneer and to accept that doubt almost certainly was part of the training process. It connects to a wider cultural story of courage and struggle and opened the door to a wider repertoire of coping strategies.

---

[1] All names are pseudonyms.
[2] Rosa Parks was a black woman in Alabama, USA, who in 1955 refused to give up her seat on the bus for a white person when the whites-only section of the bus had filled up. Her civil disobedience sparked the Montgomery Bus Boycott and was seen as pivotal in the American Civil Rights Campaign.

Supervisory practice

Some training and on-going supervisory practices may help us prepare for our work by building up a bank of ideas and resources to be deployed. However, preparation is not always possible. Sometimes ideas and practices need to be picked up as we go along in response to specific contexts. Wilson (2007: 154) draws on the metaphor of a well—"the emotional well within us"—and how we draw upon it to "provide the refreshment required to think anew about what is occurring in the room".

Fredman (2004) describes a pre-session preparation ritual called "emotional pre-supposing" where all parties anticipate likely emotional flow in a session by thinking about which postures they are likely to bring and which postures they can expect to find. The team with a supervisor can help the therapist transform unwanted physical and emotional postures to be more helpful to the people attending the session. I (GS) remember discussing this with a male supervisee who was very tall and who occupied a large space in what was a small room—had he thought how this might feel for children and women attending therapy with him? This example also highlights how gender issues in relation to both emotion and supervision are interwoven.

Fredman suggests inviting postures of tranquillity. It may be helpful to become more mindful of how we sit when we work with clients, including ideas of feet flat on the floor to "ground", chest open and relaxed to receive, arms and hands pre-embrace as opposed to folded across the body. The same could be said for supervision.

Timing is also an important issue. How long should one linger in this area of emotion? How quickly or forcefully should the therapist invite a step out of the "old" and into the "new" language being offered (for example, externalizing the relational and development of counterplot)? The dangers of what Fredman (2004: 3) and others have called "colonizing" are clear; we can be in too much of a rush and too pushy in trying to promote change. It is also possible for an emotion discourse to be hijacked and to become a way of closing down discussion rather than opening it up—crying can do this sometimes.

Gasps behind the screen

The following two examples (the first from DS and the second from GS) describe moments in therapy where in response to something in a session the members of the observing team gasp (a sudden, short intake of breath, to express emotion such as shock or surprise). Perhaps there is something about the screen that allows the expression of emotion that in the room might be more difficult to deal with. The shared chorus of gasps also adds to the weight of emotion, perhaps positioning it as the dominant emotion of the process. Just because everybody gasped does not necessarily mean that it is the emotion that should be the focus of further discussion.

1. During a family therapy session, Jessica, the therapist, was interviewing a couple (Mr and Mrs Clarke) as parents, in a session arranged without the children. To set the context, all four supervisees were white women, three clinical psychologists (two trainees, one two years post-qualified) and the other a social worker with many years experience, and the supervisor a white male (DS). This is an example of supervised practice in the context of a UK child and family clinical psychology service. Jessica had been asking how they worked together as parents. The issue of "communication as parents" was discussed and Jessica asked Mrs Clarke if she would like to work with her and the team on that issue, to which she responded she would. Jessica then asked Mr Clarke if he thought it was something he thought they needed to look at. He said it might well be, but that Jessica did not have the skills to help them with it. This is when the three team members (Lavinia, Lilian, and Grace) gasped behind the screen. There was little time to explore this immediately, so the next week we agreed to look at it in a slot when we didn't have a family to see, although two members of the team were absent (Jessica and Grace).

Lavinia and Lilian said that they had "felt for the therapist", that Mr Clarke's remark was blunt and critical of Jessica as the therapist, and that they felt a degree of shock by the remark. Lavinia felt that in the position of observer behind the screen her emotional experience was generally more heightened and she felt freer to react, whereas as a therapist she was much more focused on the task of interviewing and less "emotional". Lilian, on the other hand, reported generally feeling more emotionally aware in the session itself compared to behind the screen.

Lavinia said that if she was to choose a word to describe her emotions it would be "sympathy". Lilian chose "disheartened". Since two team members were absent (including Jessica, the therapist) they took a guess as to what the others would say and agreed that Grace would say she felt "angry" and Jessica "exhausted". For the exercise it was helpful to have such a range of descriptions even though some were hypothetical. We explored the meaning of these words for each person ("What is in the word 'sympathy' for you?") and the finer, more subtle detail within their descriptions. A "pure" emotion may be rare since it is possible to discover many feelings within feelings if they are unpicked in this way.

Lavinia could recall stories of "sympathy" from her own life relating to a recent bereavement, but decided that she didn't want to say any more about it at that point. Lilian was able to recall feeling "disheartened" when, as a child, her parents split up, and that this related also to feelings of "injustice". These stories were elaborated on.

Explorations were then extended to emotion in relation to the parents and the family and what stories of sympathy and feeling disheartened (and a sense of injustice) we might see. Both Lavinia and Lilian were able to generate discourses based on their own identified emotion, but also a cross-fertilization developed in that each began to get interested in the emotion named by the other and then make use of each other's named emotion as a lens through which to see the family processes. How was the perceived emotion connected to the hypothesis? Lavinia felt sympathy for the parents who were invited to look at their own communication when perhaps they had only expected to talk about their child's behaviour. She sympathized for how "stuck" they felt as a family and their apparent dissatisfaction with each other as a couple. Lilian wondered if Mrs Clarke might have felt disheartened by Mr Clarke's response to Jessica's invitation to explore parental communication. After all Mrs Clarke had wanted to do it there and then whilst her husband's challenge and apparent lack of faith in the therapist's skills seemed to curtail such an exploration. Their struggles to agree on a number of issues also seemed to make it difficult for them to progress as parents together in relation to the challenges of managing their child's behaviour.

The effects of the various emotion discourses were then explored, paying particular attention to the positioning of the therapist. The disheartened discourse helped Lilian see an opportunity for the therapist and team to join with the parents as she imagined what they might feel disheartened about. This could take the form of opening up space to name something not yet spoken of. Such actions can build rapport in the way that empathic comments can. This could position the therapist much more alongside a family and in a greater spirit of collaboration. However, Lilian also identified the danger that such a discourse could generate or intensify feelings of hopelessness, which might make it difficult to generate a context for positive change. The injustice discourse might have been an opportunity to join together in the way that a common cause sometimes can.

Lavinia thought that if overly organized by her sympathetic feelings she might as a therapist or team member begin to feel overly sad (because of the personal resonance with her bereavement) and that would interfere with her position as a therapist.

I shared my own reflections as supervisor. I too had felt some shock at the bluntness of Mr Clarke's remarks. However, I didn't gasp and very quickly became curious about the meaning of what Mr Clarke had said and how the team had responded. As the supervisor you are, in part, required to attend to two systems simultaneously: the family therapist on one side and the team behind the screen on the other.

After the gasps, Lilian had asked me what I made of it and I felt reluctant to discuss that immediately. My own response was to hold back in a rather dispassionate way to "sort out my feelings" about the remark, the therapy, and the team process. I explained that although I will register feelings, I do not always express a feeling straight away just because I experience one. The issue for me would be what purpose would it serve and how might it position me and others. I may feel freer to do this with my own supervisor, but as a supervisor myself I would probably exercise more caution here. I have found Rober's (2005) development of the voices metaphor helpful, the notion of "inner conversation", and a multi-faceted notion of self. For me there is a helpful distinction between my intellectual self and my feeling self. I imagine them having conversations. Rober summarizes a therapist's essential dilemma as one of how to use his or her inner voices responsibly. Lavinia could have used her curiosity and asked the family, "What is it about me that makes you feel I lack experience? What kind of skills do you think would be needed here? Who might have such skills?"

The above exercise took the best part of an hour, but feedback was that it helped supervisees first tune in to, and then process, some complex feelings using a framework that helped them position themselves. My own experience was similar and it encouraged me to reflect more on my positioning as a supervisor.

2. The second example is an extract from team supervision. One team member (M) is being supervised by GS with three team members (B, L, and N) observing. We are discussing a very difficult case of a 12-year-old boy who was looked after in residential provision. The supervisee had made a recent visit to Michael. The gender balance of the team is three females to two males; three white and two black practitioners. The supervisor (GS) is white and female. It is a multi-disciplinary team but on this occasion includes a preponderance of clinical psychologists from assistant to consultant grade. The supervision dialogue is taken from a recording in numbered sequence for the reader to follow. The comments from the observers were written retrospectively while observing the extract. It is laid out in table form to convey the multiplicity of emotion and ideas arising simultaneously. M's emotional pre-supposing was a posture of self-protection from Michael's violence.

The excerpt has been selected to demonstrate the richness and complexity of the emotions generated. As the supervision session progressed, the reflecting team joined M and I to discuss what they had heard. We then viewed the recording of our supervision. This allowed us to privilege certain interactions and emotions depending on the context—behind the screen, in front of the screen, discussing the supervision with M and I listening, and then discussing all together.

The team discussed how much easier it was for them to voice their feelings in the "privacy" of the supervision room. None of them would have felt able to gasp had they been sitting in the room with us.

In leading the supervision discussion I wanted to explore with M his many roles. Which of the feelings discussed were more or less

In-front-of-screen dialogue		Behind-screen dialogue and reflections		
G Supervisor	M Supervisee	B	N	L
1. "Michael has very effectively created this violent aura around him that is always active … he doesn't have to do anything … he doesn't even have to get out of bed … to activate it.				1. Felt responsible for B and N. 2. Felt uncomfortably hot in room. 3. Annoyed at care Michael was receiving.
2. People are so *relieved* when he doesn't get up or attend sessions … It is hard to engage; to knowingly walk into this kind of engagement … it is so exhausting.				
	3. Even getting ready for work I thought … training shoes to run away … Pop buttons so he won't destroy the shirt.		Reminded me of needing to be permanently alert, contemplating my exits, and positioning myself in non-threatening ways.	
4. When we think about ourselves as clinicians and the impact of this work on us … I'm interested in your reflections. Are there bits of Michael that resonate for you?				

THREE GASPS BEHIND THE SCREEN 95

	5. He is not completely alien because of my previous work in secure …	*This was an invitation for M to access different aspects of self. He chooses to remain in professional mode.*
	6. "Michael doesn't touch the Father part of you?"	*This is a prompt to move into a personal role—accessing parental feelings. It evokes a strong emotional tone which is followed up by further questioning.*
	7. No.	I felt a maternal instinct to want to try to help Michael—change in a positive way. Seeing Michael as a lost little boy not knowing any other way to cope. Unexpressed feeling. Accessing roles—promoted by supervisor's question to see it differently.
	8. There's something about him that doesn't touch that part of you?	*Again a strong emotional tone in the response.*
	9. There is definitely something about him … I've worked with a lot of distraught and dangerous kids. To me Michael is the Hannibal Lecter of kids.	We were discussing how M's description of Michael brought up horror film characters that were calculated and had a presence, and none of us could remember Hannibal's name so we did the noise.

(Continued)

96   MIRRORS AND REFLECTIONS

In-front-of-screen dialogue		Behind-screen dialogue and reflections		
G Supervisor	M Supervisee	B	N	L
		At this point there were three gasps from behind the screen.		
		Maternal instinct came up for me after the feeling 'he's a monster'. I felt he needs a female touch— a mother figure brought into his life. A woman who isn't *scared* of him, a real 'black mama' to sit down and be fed.	The gasp moment for me was one of cementing the idea of Michael as Hannibal followed by guilt at having fit Michael into the Hannibal role and in effect having written him off to a certain extent as untreatable. On a superficial level there was a momentary wow ... Did M hear what we said or pick up the vibe of the three of us talking about Hannibal?	The gasps came when almost instantly Mark named him. This was a magical moment. We *felt a real connection* with the process going on in the other room. It *validated us* that we were on the ball and for a moment the screen was irrelevant.

THREE GASPS BEHIND THE SCREEN   97

It seemed like we were there with M following his thought processes and arriving at the same ideas at practically the same time. I think there is more to what happened than coincidence. What was happening in the supervision activated similar associative pathways in all of us. I think what was important is the exploration of this. Which is why it is so important to have a skilled senior therapist to manage and participate in the discussions.

At the same time as being a 'kapow' moment, that we all came to that idea about a 12-year-old boy is really quite *sad.*

useful for the therapist working with Michael? At point 6, when I ask him about being a father, I am inviting M to explore his feelings towards the young person from a different, personal perspective. This invitation to parental reflexion evoked parental responses in both B and N. When talking later with the whole group, M described how he reflected for a moment about discussing his paternal feelings at work, but then felt that he wanted to take a risk and move into this territory in supervision.

The supervision structured as it is, is aimed at team building and developing consultancy skills as we consult in pairs. It is a clear example of supervision being isomorphic to the service's overarching systemic model of intervention. Because of the large difference in experience levels within the team, it is important to find a way to be involved and use curiosity or not knowing creatively. This discussion of feelings in supervision is intended to increase confidence in discussing feelings in therapy sessions with clients.

The reflections about the gasp also show the multiple layers of feeling, first about the team consensus and simultaneous arrival at a point of view about this boy and then, rapidly, the feelings of hopelessness and despair the boy has evoked in the treatment team.

The three gasps in this example were gasps of surprise, reflecting a degree of emotional tuning within the team (Bertrando, 2007). The previous gasps were of shock. This supports the idea that feelings arise in contexts or through relation rather then existing inside (inhaled gasp) waiting to get out (exhaled gasp).

Concluding comments

To broaden systemic approaches to include emotion we need to encourage turning towards and "tuning-in" to feelings within supervision and clinical practice. From here we can find words for experiences of emotions and consider their influences on our work. These emotion words and experiences can then be explored using a systemic framework. Malik and Krause (2005: 108) suggest:

> While this aspect may be outside an individual's awareness, it is none the less a requirement of training that the therapist is someone who is skilled in becoming aware of his/her own

sensations, feelings and emotions and how these interact with the sensations, feelings and emotions of the client/s.

This is an interesting privileging of "outside awareness" where perhaps the affective response is "inside" and the intellect "outside". Our emotional responses are activated before we *know* they have been and before we can label them. Perhaps we need to privilege the emotional (often visceral experience) over the intellectual articulation of it without reifying emotions.

Engagement of families must include an emotional attunement of therapist plus family system. A large part of the therapeutic relationship involves a capacity to empathically mirror the emotional states of others. Something we are "hard wired" to do (Schore, 2003).

Systemic theory needs to move beyond the dominant discourse of dyadic attachment thinking if it is to develop a theory of "emotion discourse" that is sufficiently robust for systems of more than two. This is especially important within the supervision context. Much of systemic supervision occurs through a "one-way screen". While dialogue and visual input may transfer across glass, "the feeling in the room" is often less available to the supervision group. This can lead to dystonic supervision discussions where the supervisee and the rest of the supervision group are not attuned to each other.

The privacy of the observation room can allow certain feelings to emerge or be expressed before being raised for discussion more transparently. This should work towards developing personal reflexivity. It could be argued that a supervisor's role is to provide a context that makes it safe enough for supervisees to express and use feelings within the supervision group but working towards the utilization of them in a therapeutic context.

The supervisory relationship within a systemic framework is a place and relationship in which these issues can be explored further. A systemic framework can and does allow for feelings to emerge without losing the frame of multiple contexts. These multiple contexts operate simultaneously and require some degree of privileging/ordering to allow discourses to develop into a dialectic as the clinical examples of group supervision show.

Fredman (2004) and Campbell and Groenbaek (2006) show how systemic frameworks can be developed to include explorations of emotion discourses and we have experimented with how the supervision context can be central to such an exploration. Whilst some other therapeutic traditions may have a longer history of exploring emotion as a more central theme we feel systemic psychotherapy and its supervision process are precisely what is needed to appreciate the multiple levels of meaning and context in emotion discourses.

Our theoretical reach should move beyond the gasp.

References

Andersen, T. (1987). The Reflecting Team: Dialogue and Meta-dialogue in Clinical Work. *Family Process*. 26: 415–428.
Bateson, G. (1973). *Steps to an Ecology of Mind*. London: Paladin.
Bertrando, P. (2006). *Emotional Systems: Managing Emotions in Systemic Practice*. 5.6.06. One Day Conference at Leeds Family Therapy and Research Centre, UK.
Bertrando, P. (2007). *The Dialectical Therapist*. London: Karnac Books.
Burck, C. (2005). *Multilingual Living: Explorations of Language and Subjectivity*. London: Palgrave Macmillan.
Burck, C. and Daniel, G. (1995). *Gender and Family Therapy*. London: Karnac Books.
Burnham, J. (1986). *Family Therapy: First Steps Towards A Systemic Approach*. London: Routledge.
Burnham, J. (1993). Systemic Supervision: The Evolutionary of Reflexivity in the Context of the Supervisory Relationship. *Human Systems*. 4: 349–381.
Burnham, J. and Harris, Q. (2002). Cultural Issues in Supervision. In: Campbell, D. and Mason, B. (eds) *Perspectives on Supervision*. London: Karnac Books.
Campbell, D. and Groenbaek, M. (2006). *Taking Positions in the Organization*. London: Karnac Books.
Casement, P. (1985). *On Learning from the Patient*. London: Routledge (imprint of Taylor and Francis Books Ltd).
Ekman, P. (2003). *Emotions Revealed: Understanding Faces and Feelings*. New York: Times Books.
Flaskas, C. (2002). *Family Therapy beyond Postmodernism: Practice, Challenges, Theory*. Hove: Brunner-Routledge.
Flaskas, C. (2005) Sticky Situations, Therapy Mess: On Impasse and the Therapist's Position. In: Flaskas, C., Mason, B. and Perlesz, A. (eds) *The Space Between: Experience, Context and Process in the Therapeutic Relationship*. London: Karnac Books.

Fredman, G. (2004). *Transforming Emotion: Conversations in Counselling and Psychotherapy*. London: Whurr Publishers.

Hardy, K. and Laszloffy, T. (1995). The Cultural Genogram: Key to Training Culturally Competent Therapists. *Journal of Marital and Family Therapy*. 21: 227–237.

Jones, E. (1996). Changing Systemic Constructions of Therapeutic Relationships. In: Flaskas, C. and Perlesz, A. (eds) *The Therapeutic Relationship*. London: Karnac Books.

Keeney, B. (2005). *Bushman Shaman: Awakening the Spirit Through Ecstatic Dance*. Rochester Vermont: Destiny Books.

Liddle, H. and Saba, G. (1983). On Context Replication: The Isomorphic Relationship of Training and Therapy. *Journal of Strategic and Systemic Family Therapies*. 2: 3–11.

Malik, R. and Krause, I-B. (2005). Intercultural: Where the Systemic Meets the Psychoanalytic in the Therapeutic Relationship. In: Flaskas, C., Mason, B. and Perlesz, A. (eds) *The Space Between: Experience, Context and Process in the Therapeutic Relationship*. London: Karnac Books.

Mitchell, S.A. (1988). *Relational Concepts in Psychoanalysis: An Integration*. New York: Harvard University Press.

O'Hanlon, W.H. (1993). Commentary on Epston. In: Gilligan, S. and Price, R. (eds) *Therapeutic Conversations*. London: Norton.

Parker, I. (1992). *Discourse Dynamics: Critical Analysis for Social and Individual Psychology*. London: Routledge.

Pocock, D. (2005). Systems of the Heart: Evoking the Feeling Self in Family Therapy. In: Flaskas, C., Mason, B. and Perlesz, A. (eds) *The Space Between: Experience, Context and Process in the Therapeutic Relationship*. London: Karnac Books.

Rober, P. (2005). The Therapist's Self in Dialogical Family Therapy: Some Ideas about Not-knowing and the Therapist's Inner Conversation. *Family Process*. 44: 477–495.

Roberts, J. (2005). Transparency and Self-disclosure in Family Therapy: Dangers and Possibilities. *Family Process*. 44: 45–63.

Scaife, J. (1993). Setting the Scene for Supervision. *Human Systems*. 4: 161–172.

Schore, A.N. (2003). *Affect Regulation of the Self*. (Norton series in Interpersonal Neurobiology.) New York: W.W Norton and Co.

Selvini Palazzoli, M., Boscolo, L., Cecchin, G. and Prate, G. (1980). Hypothesizing: Circularity and Neutrality. *Family Process*. 19: 73–85.

White, M. (1988). The Externalization of the Problem and the Reauthoring of Lives and Relationships. *Dulwich Centre Newsletter*. 5–7.

Wikipedia, http://en.wikipedia.org/wiki/Emoticons (accessed April 2010).

Wilson, J. (1993). The Supervisory Relationship in F.T. Training: Constructing a Fit between Trainee and Trainer. *Human Systems*. 4: 140–159.

Wilson, J. (2007). *The Performance of Practice: Enhancing the Repertoire of Therapy with Children and Families*. London: Karnac Books.

CHAPTER FIVE

Exploring emotions: A critical incident for a supervisor

Sumita Dutta

Introduction

"The thing is Sumita I don't know what it is but I ummm really dislike Carla ... "

This chapter explores a supervisory moment occurring at the end of a live-supervision session in which the interviewing therapist (Lisa) expressed a strong dislike for the child (Carla) being seen. As a supervisor I believe that this challenges us to consider the ways in which we conceptualize and utilize emotions within the supervisory encounter.

The process of supervision, like the process of therapy, can evoke a myriad of emotions. As supervisors this calls for us to develop our ideas about emotionally sensitive practice and consider the constructs that we draw upon to understand emotional experience and communication within the supervisory domain.

The chapter divides into two parts. In the first I give an overview of some of the pertinent issues currently being debated within systemic thinking regarding emotions. In the second, I look at an extract of my own supervisory practice, drawing upon the literature to evaluate my supervisory response. In doing so, I hope to draw attention to the interconnecting considerations that emerge and highlight some of the wider implications for supervisory practice and research.

Part 1: Exploring emotions in systemic supervision

In the seventeenth century, a division was posited between reason and emotion with emotion being viewed as a primeval aspect of human life to be overcome in favour of rationalization and progress. Universalists, from a Darwinian perspective, argued that emotions are fixed and internal states of being which are identifiable in behavioural sequences (Fiumara, 2001). From this perspective it is possible to make linear links between observed behaviours and their inner correlating emotions as long as rational and objective observation is pursued (Stearns, 1995).

The obvious parallels to be drawn with systemic thinking are between universalist positions and first order systemic theorizing and positioning. Both hold as a central tenant the modernist belief in universal truths and linear causality. Importantly a blue print for human behaviour is available to the objective observer with the correct knowledge and expertise. From this privileged position, supervisors become experts on any emotions arising within the therapeutic encounter while the personal life of the therapist is viewed as something that needs to be overcome in favour of professionalism and the attainment of technical expertise (Fletcher, 2002). Importantly, emotions were only viewed as a necessary consideration for supervision in so much as they pertained to issues of therapeutic engagement and it is therefore not surprising to find that most of the early thinking in systemic supervision placed the supervisor in a hierarchical position above the supervisee, teaching or transmitting technique whilst occupying a meta-position to the work.

From these perspectives Lisa's dislike of Carla would be viewed as a barrier to the therapeutic engagement with the family and my role as a supervisor would be to decipher the true meaning of Lisa's emotions, from a finite number of possible explanations, in order to be rid of it.

Emotions as relational and contextual

The counterbalance to universalist definitions of emotions are constructionist and relational explanations which seek to broaden descriptions of emotion to acknowledge the social construction and regulation of emotions. Within this framework, emotions are seen as something we learn to do in relationships, rather than a fixed reality (Harré, 1986). This links to early systemic thinking about multiple levels of meaning (Bateson, 1972) and draws upon Watzlawick et al.'s (1967) suggestions that each (emotional) communication is simultaneously a communication on two levels—content and relationship—with the latter being the context for the former. Cronen and Pearce (1980) frame this slightly differently by proposing that there are an indeterminate number of levels of contexts that influence our meaning-making, all of which exert different degrees of contextual force.

These new ideas brought with them a correlating shift in systemic supervision in which emotions were no longer seen as problems that need to be managed but as an important source of contextual and relational information to be used as a resource. Drawing on postmodern sensibilities, the myth was dispelled that the supervisor has privileged access to a priori knowledge about emotions and attempts to place the supervisee at the heart of the meaning-making process began to emerge. Certainly White (1997) proposed that supervision, with the implication that one party has a "super vision" status over another, is more helpfully described as "co-vision" as this acknowledges combined authority and expertise. Fruggeri (2002) sees this distinction reflected in two competing models of supervision: supervision as teaching or supervision as a practice of reflection. Within this later framework, and as Bobele et al. (1995) point out, the supervisor's expertise therefore shifts from the ability to convey a venerated body of information towards concentrating on the way in which the conversation (about emotion) is conducted.

From this point of view, emotions are seen as a potential resource within the supervisory encounter. The emotion of dislike expressed by Lisa is viewed as a social and relational communication and it is Lisa, not myself, who is viewed as the expert in deconstructing the multiple possible meanings available.

Limitations of language

One of the limitations of the social constructionist view is that not all meaning and understandings can be negotiated between participants in language alone (Boscolo and Bertrando, 1996). Indeed Wittgenstein

(1953) proposes a game analogy to highlight the centrality of shared game rules in enabling successful communication of meaning. He asserts that confusion can arise when one person's language is interpreted according to the rules of another. Fredman (2004: 14) believes that emotional utterances and mannerisms will be deeply influenced by the belief structures that people hold about emotions, be it that they fall somewhere in the continuum between universalist and relational views. It is the co-ordination of these belief structures into a good enough fit that, she argues, allows for one's "local emotional grammar" to become co-ordinated and for successful understanding to take place.

The idea that "there is nothing outside of text", as quoted by Derrida (1965: 158) has been misinterpreted to imply the notion that all texts are open to multiple possible interpretations, all of which are equally valid. Of course, whilst this may be possible, Pocock (1997) points out that it ignores the power differentials which render some readings more valid than others. Malik and Krause (2005) illustrate this point when discussing the way in which embodied communication of emotion is often obscured or minimized by Western practitioners, despite the experiences of many Eastern societies who consider emotional experiences to be part of the biological entity of their bodies. The Western conceptual framework of emotions assumes a body—mind split and as such renders invisible emotions outside of the mind. This dishonours the idea that in many cultures and societies language and texts are not privileged over experience. Here we intersect with Lyotard's concept of the Differend (1988: 9), a term used to highlight the suffering of phrases that remain unphrased. Put in another way, we also fall straight into the heart of identity politics where the naming of one experience over another is viewed to be a political act (Gergen, 1991).

This thinking highlights the importance of attending to emotional expression through language, analogical, and embodied communication. It also proposes an awareness of the belief systems being drawn upon to co-ordinate communication and the impact of privileging one belief system over another.

Second order considerations

The advent of second-order cybernetics brought with it the recognition that the therapist is both visible and influential within the therapeutic systems of which they are a part (Von Foerster, 1981). The self of the therapist came to be viewed as a community of internalized others (Tomm, 1998) and a new premium was subsequently placed on making room for these "inner conversations" to emerge as a vital therapeutic resource (Rober, 1999). The dilemma that this thinking posed for supervisors was to consider to what extent the self of the therapist could be explored within supervision without mimicking therapy for the supervisee and whilst maintaining a focus on client work at hand (Woodcock and Rivett, 2007). Indeed, and as Aponte (1992) points out, the role of personal and professional development (PPD) within family therapy training has a long and debated history and the field is still divided on whether PPD slots should be integral or separate from live supervision spaces. Similarly Jones (2003) illustrates this tension when arguing for a distinction to be made between supervision and consultation. She marks out the former as primarily responsible to the development of the client therapy, whilst the latter, free of clinical and statutory responsibility, allows a focus on the self of the therapist to be fully maintained.

A correlating development to these ideas was the growing acknowledgement that the therapeutic system is likely to mirror structural, relational, or emotional aspects of itself within the supervisory relationship (Liddle and Saab, 1983). These parallel processes or isomorphic tendencies highlight the view that supervisors are not simply passive observers of pattern replication but, as Hardham (1996) writes, are both "embodied" in their subjective experiences and "embedded" in their relational contexts. Within this framework, curiosity is no longer unlimited but needs to be continually maintained, a position akin to that of Cecchin et al.'s (1991: 125) position of "irreverence". Indeed, Anderson and Swim (2001: 10) propose a framework of "self-supervision" through which the supervisor maintains an "inner dialogue" or critical perspective to their preferred ways of working, in order to maintain spaces for new ideas to emerge. Similarly, Browne and Bourne (1996) have written an interesting chapter on 'The Making of a Supervisor' in the context of social work, which categorizes aspects of the supervisor's own experiences that may intersect with their practice. These include considerations of the influence of the supervisor's own formative experiences of authority, their professional experiences as a practitioner, and their own experiences of being supervised.

These ideas highlight the ways in which the self of the therapist and supervisor can be used as a resource to consider aspects of the therapeutic and supervisory systems of which they are a part. This includes remaining alert to replication between the therapeutic and supervisory system and asking the question: what personal and relational resonances do Lisa's feelings of dislike create?

Ethical considerations

One of the difficulties with postmodern supervision is that it risks simply replacing expertise from one system (supervisor) to another (supervisee). This split reflects the many other dichotomies that emerge when reviewing systemic supervisory ideas, many of which I have already touched upon: modernism versus postmodernism; realist versus social constructionist; knowledge versus language; teaching versus reflection; and fixed truth versus emergent truth. In my view nowhere do these splits become more visible than when thinking about the supervisor's ethical responsibility.

Stewart and Amundson (1995) propose that all ethical dilemmas include competing value systems, of which a blue print of preferred value systems is available and preferable; for example, child protection legislation. Indeed, Philip et al. (2007) argue that one must practice from the solid ground of modernist certainty when managing the "real" definitions and dilemmas of abuse. In these situations, the supervisor activates their hierarchical positioning in the supervisory relationship and owns their own knowledge and experience as being helpful to the dilemma at hand. Far from the supervisee being central to the meaning-making process, Rest (1983) argues that it is supervisees' ability to de-centre themselves enough from the given behaviours, and to consider the actual or potential consequences, which characterizes an appropriate response.

This touches on the tension between a view of supervision as a learning and development space for the supervisee as opposed to a view of supervision being a professional gate-keeping activity with a primary responsibility to client welfare and the interest of the profession/public at large. Whilst supervision can of course be both of these things, Storm and Haug (1997) believe that the ethical dilemma for the supervisor arises when the latter necessarily overrules the former. Turner and Fine (1997b: 233) describe this hierarchy in terms of situated realities, ethics being part of the "centrally situated realities" which sit on the top of the professional hierarchy and are often the least flexible and the most far removed from the supervisor/supervisee. Swim et al. (2001), however, emphasize the local and relational processes in which ethics are negotiated within therapeutic relationships and propose that even these distantly located realities or ethical guidelines can be usefully deconstructed at a local level to keep ethical thinking alive.

This thinking emphasizes my ethical and professional obligations as a supervisor to intervene to protect client welfare should Lisa's dislike of Carla have the potential to cause harm. Part of this response is also to consider the ways in which I relate these ethical considerations to Lisa at a local level.

Here I will pause the thinking so far and summarize the ideas already discussed by drawing out some of the key questions to bear in mind when thinking about emotions from a supervisor's perspective (see Figure 5.1). I will then move on, in Part 2, to look at a small

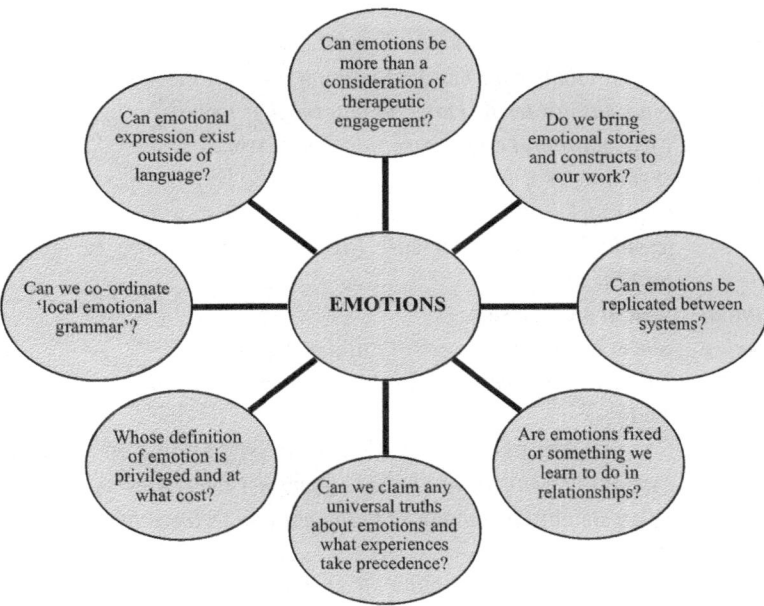

Figure 5.1. Questions to bear in mind when thinking about emotions from a supervisor's perspective.

extract of my supervisory response to Lisa's comments, drawing upon these ideas in order to reflect upon and critically evaluate my practice.

Part 2: Practice reflections

The following extract has been taken after the third session of live supervision with the Brown family. Carla Brown, aged eight, has been referred to our child and adolescent mental health service with concerns about her angry outbursts at home. She is an only child who lives at home with both of her parents. In each session so far Carla has been very tearful, and in the last the parents began to indicate strong signs of ambivalence towards continuing to attend.

Lisa: *The thing is, Sumita, I don't know what it is, but I, ummm, really dislike Carla ...*

Sumita: *(laughs) Ohh! You have ummm caught me off guard. I wonder am I laughing in response to what might feel like quite a taboo subject?*

Lisa: *Ohh God yes. I know this is a bit shocking but I am really filled up with dislike for her. Did you not see it in the session?*

Sumita: *No I did not see it. How did you think it looked?*

Lisa: *I felt, ummm, I could hardly look at Carla.*

Sumita: *It sounds as if you were working hard to keep it covered.*

Lisa: *Oh yes! I wonder if she knows. I know it sounds really unprofessional and I'm not sure this is the right thing to say but ummm ...*

Sumita: *Lisa, it's Ok to say.*

Lisa: *She is ummm really getting under my skin.*

Sumita: *I thought we were staying away from the right thing to say? (laughs)*

Lisa: *(laughs) Yes we are, but it's not the right thing to say is it? I wouldn't want to be seen by a therapist who hates me.*

Sumita: *What usually helps you to manage these feelings when they get inside you?*

Lisa: *Ummm, I suppose I blow off steam somewhere. Can I use the PPD space today to think about this? I would quite like some space.*

Drawing upon my understanding of the different belief structures that people draw upon to inform their emotional expressions, Lisa appears to be referring here to a more universalist framework that situates emotions as internal to the body and in need of a fixed explanation ("I'm really filled up, she is really getting under my skin, I don't know what it is ... "). When Lisa asks me whether I saw the dislike in the session she is inviting me to respond to an idea that it is possible to make linear links between her behaviours and some correlating inner emotions. Lisa's question may also assume that as a supervisor I have access to privileged knowledge that enables me to make an expert reading of her emotions. Rather than take up these invitations, I ask Lisa what she thinks her dislike would have looked like in the session and in doing so try to open up a conversational space in which Lisa is viewed as the expert of her own life and experiences. Here I am privileging a postmodern commitment to de-centring practices (Gardner et al. 1997) and favouring a view of supervision as a reflective space in which multiple ways of knowing can emerge (Fruggeri, 2002).

What is interesting is that, as a South Asian woman supervisor supervising a white UK woman supervisee, I do not pursue my own constructs of emotion, which are more constructionist and relational. Instead I mirror some of Lisa's universalist thinking by asking her to comment on what usually helps her to manage these feelings when they "get inside" of her. This can be seen as my attempt to co-ordinate, what Fredman (2004: 14) describes as, our "local emotional grammar" and to find a way of joining alongside Lisa in the search for shared meaning (Harré 1986). However this understanding does not obscure the possibility that I may also be "self-silencing" my experiences from a disadvantaged position as a woman (Goode, 1982: 143) and indeed, despite my privileged position as a supervisor, aspects of my racial and cultural identity may be less privileged within the supervisory relationship. Akamatsu (1998: 25) refers to this as the "multiplexity" of power relationships that exist in cross-cultural working and it could be seen that it highlights also the issue of visibility when managing differences in a (supervisory) relationship (Thomas, 2002).

When Lisa comments that she knows that her dislike "sounds unprofessional" and that it is "not the right thing to say", this conveys a view of emotions as something that must be overcome in favour of progress and professionalism. Indeed my supervisory response can be interpreted as upholding this universalist view as I display both discomfort and surprise in the way that I use my laughter and I name the subject as "taboo", implying that this is out of bounds. This is a good example of how Lisa and I are communicating together about emotions, both in the words that we use but also beyond them in our dialogical communication and in the emotional constructs we convey.

What is interesting is that I do not challenge Lisa's request to use the PPD slot to discuss these feelings and to "blow off steam", thus maintaining the idea that emotions need to be separated from the clinical work from which they have arisen. Indeed the initial negotiations around Lisa's supervision placement with me included separating out the PPD slot from the live clinical supervision space under the assumption that some links to the work may feel more personal than others. I think this segregation connects to the wider dilemmas of how to meaningfully incorporate aspects of the self within systemic supervision and training, especially given the time constraints of the clinical slots themselves.

Drawing upon Browne and Bourne's (1996) ideas in which one's own supervisory, training, and professional experiences are seen as a valuable resource to the task of supervision, I am not convinced that my own experiences of having separate PPD slots in training have been as useful as talking about the feelings in the actual moments that they arise in the clinical work (see Barratt et al., this volume). This relates to the concept of "emotional heat" (Real, 1990: 267) and implies a belief that learning from emotional intensity is both possible and helpful. Indeed feminists such as Turner and Fine (1997) have proposed that voicing personal and collective pain about gender oppression is the first step to meaningful reflection and resolution of differences. Further to this, and thinking from a practitioner point of view, although I am now very confident in resisting fixed "either–or" positions, this approach has taken me many years to develop. Perhaps my own embeddedness as a fledgling supervisor in a supervision course makes it more difficult to access my clinical confidence and relational risk-taking abilities from a learning position (Mason, 2005). Or indeed, perhaps the desire to learn to get things "right" is not just a preoccupation for Lisa but is also an isomorphic tendency shared between the therapeutic and supervisory systems, given that we can all be said to be influenced by the desire to be the "right" sort of parent, therapist, supervisor.

Drawing upon Cronen and Pearce's (1980) Co-ordinated Management of Meaning (CMM) framework, an important consideration for Lisa and I was to think about the contextual influences of the "family stories" of emotion that we bring to the work. For the Brown family, "sorting out" Carla's distress is one of the reasons that they are attending therapy and indeed Carla has been very tearful throughout the sessions so far. For Lisa, she has spoken informally and within PPD sessions about the effort that she and her husband are making to try to shelter their two young boys from the terminal illness of their grandfather. She has also spoken about how important it is to them as parents to be able to be in control of at least one aspect of this painful experience. For me, managing the distress of family members has been a defining aspect of my role in my family and one that has gained me praise and positive reward from a very early age. If we go with the constructionist idea that emotions are something that we learn to do in relationships, then the family's ambivalence about continuing with therapy can be seen as a reflection of their disappointment with therapy "not working" and not making Carla any happier. Similarly, Lisa's dislike of Carla and her inability to look at her in the session can also be seen as a desire not to see Carla's distress, given Lisa's own struggles to protect her children from emotional pain. Further my affirming and protective response to Lisa, which is to acknowledge how hard she has been working to keep her feelings "covered" can be interpreted as a communication about Lisa's clinical work, her family life, and my own efforts to manage emotional pain within my family. Here thinking about the family stories of emotion that we bring to the work, and drawing upon the self as a "community of internalized others" (Tomm, 1998) allows for inner and outer conversations to merge as an important therapeutic resource (Rober, 1999). Indeed Lisa was able to use her uncomfortable experience of disliking Carla as a way to connect to Mr Brown's ambivalence about continuing to attend therapy, empathizing with the sense of failure that Carla's continual unhappiness provokes.

Drawing upon Watzlawick's (1967) belief that communication is primarily influenced on the level of relationship, it is interesting to note that I do not immediately respond to the content of the conversation, despite the intensity of words such as "dislike" and even "hate" being used. Instead I choose to focus on nurturing Lisa's ability to take risks within the relationship by assuring her that "it's okay to say these things" or reminding her that "we were staying away from the right things to say". This nurturing and relational positioning may well be a highly gendered response, given the socialization of women into caring roles (Reid et al. 1987). Similarly, and as Hare-Mustin and Marecek (1988) have argued, a more relational focus can also be a reflection of wider experiences of oppressions, gender being just one aspect in intersection with others. Of course this is not to imply that a relational focus should be viewed as lacking, for indeed it is the interpersonal qualities of the supervisor which have been identified in research with supervisees as being of primary importance in creating helpful supervision experiences (Anderson et al. 2000). It is also not to obscure the particular aspects of the supervisory relationship that may be evoking such nurturing and protective responses. Indeed, I am aware that Lisa is in the process of managing terminal illness in her family, an experience made infinitely more personal between us given my own experiences of loss during systemic training. It is exactly these elements of human connection that Turner and Fine (1997b: 232) draw upon when describing supervision as a "venture in goodwill", an expression that favours the emotional content of all human and professional collaborations.

This idea of supervision as a venture of goodwill should not however obscure the power hierarchy that exists between Lisa and I, nor be seen to imply that good will exists without limit. For example, although I am focusing on certain aspects of our relationship at this stage, this does not mean that I do not also go on to explore with Lisa the extent of her dislike for Carla. Should Lisa talk about Carla in negative ways that I thought would bring harm to her or the family I would activate my hierarchical positioning as a supervisor and intervene to protect client welfare. I would also attempt, as Jones (2003) points out, to give Lisa permission to stop her work with the family, should the level of her own distress become concerning. Here my ethical responsibilities and professional gatekeeping role takes precedence over all other considerations and as such I would draw upon the "centrally situated realities" of professional guidelines and protocols to guide my practice (Turner and Fine, 1997b: 233).

Interestingly, the issue of "dislike" is not mentioned in the Association of Family Therapy (AFT) code of ethics and practice (December 2000), although much is said about the positive aspects of therapeutic engagement and reference is made to over-intimacy in the form of sexual relationships. Nonetheless I was still able to draw upon the guidelines in my conversation with Lisa the following week to keep my ethical thinking transparent and to keep ethical considerations on the supervision agenda. Drawing upon Swim et al.'s (2001) very useful distinction between "content" and "process" ethics, I asked Lisa what she thought about the lack of ethical guidelines on dislike in the therapeutic relationship. By focusing on both the content and the process in which ethical thinking is formulated at a professional level, I was able to be transparent about my professional responsibilities and open up a conversational space at a local level to process these ethical ideas. This type of ethical deconstruction fits well with me, as it connects to my experiences as a child protection social worker where one has to take up definite positions of power and authority whilst simultaneously making one's thinking as open to scrutiny as possible It also provides a possible bridge across the old dualities of social constructionist and realist thinking, enabling supervision to be both a space in which ethical action and reflection is simultaneously possible.

Ending thoughts

Thinking about emotions and writing this chapter has been an emotional process. It has invited me to consider the constructs I draw upon to understand emotional experience and communication, given that these are deeply ingrained in my cultural, familial, and relational histories. Thinking about emotion in supervision is intimately connected to ideas about the use of self, the influence of the "multiplexity" (Akamatsu, 1998) of our supervisory relationships and the management of our ethical responsibilities. It is in these subtle and complex intersections that we can begin to develop our ideas about emotionally sensitive practice.

More needs to be written from a systemic perspective on the supervision of emotions (see also Spelman and Smith, this volume). Although I have drawn from a wide range of literature in this chapter it is worth noting that less than a third of this thinking has been written exclusively about systemic supervision. Given the priority that systemic practitioners place on considering mutual influences within relationships, it is important that we enhance our existing ideas about the emotions by seeking out and researching supervisee descriptions and experiences.

One of my continuing challenges as a supervisor is to consider the impact of privileging some emotional views over others, especially given the challenges that this poses for cross-cultural working. This requires that the supervisor's "inner dialogue" (Anderson and Swim, 2001: 10) remains open to new ideas at all times, including those that feel less comfortable. I would argue that this is not a task that can be taken lightly, or indeed on one's own. On one level it requires supervisors to privilege their self-reflexivity skills as well as drawing upon their own peer and individual supervision as resources for self-reflection. On another level, and as a field, we also need to consider the way in which we embed considerations of emotionally sensitive practice within our training and on-going professional development.

References

Akamatsu, N., Basham, K. and Olson, M. (1996). Teaching a Feminist Family Therapy. *Journal of Feminist Family Therapy*, 8(2): 21–36.

Anderson, H. and Swim, S. (1993). Learning as Collaborative Conversation: Combining the Students' and Teachers' Expertise. *Human Systems*, 4: 145–160.

Anderson, S.A. et al. (2000). Family Therapy Trainees' Evaluations of their Best and Worst. Supervision Experiences. *Journal of Marital and Family Therapy*, 26: 79–91.

Aponte, H. (1992) Training the Person of the Therapist in Structural Family Therapy. *Journal of Family Therapy*, 18(3): 269–281.

Bateson, G. (1972). *Steps to an Ecology of Mind*. New York: Ballantine Books.

Bobele, M., Gardner, G. and Biever, J. (1995). Supervision as Social Construction. *Journal of Systemic Therapies*, 14: 14–25.

Boscolo, L. and Bertrando, P. (1996). *Systemic Therapy with Individuals*. London: Karnac Books.
Browne, B. and Bourne, I. (1996). *The Social Work Supervisor*. Buckingham: Open University Press.
Cecchin, G., Lane, G. and Ray, W. (1991). From Strategising to Non-Intervention: Towards Irreverence in Systemic Practice. *Journal of Marital and Family Therapy*, 17(1): 125–136.
Cronen, V. and Pearce, W.B. (1980). *Communication, Action, and Meaning: The Creation of Social Realities*. New York: Praeger.
Derrida, J. (1974). *Of Grammatology*. Baltimore: John Hopkins University Press.
Fiumara, G.C. (2001). *The Mind's Affective Life: A Psychoanalytic and Philosophical Inquiry*. Hove: Brunner-Routledge.
Flecther, P. (2002). *Re-engaging with Emotion in Systemic Therapy and Supervision*. Unpublished dissertation. Tavistock Clinic.
Fredman, G. (2004). *Transforming Emotion: Conversations in Counselling and Psychotherapy*. London: Whurr Publishers.
Fruggeri, L. (2002) Different Levels of Analysis in the Supervisory Process. In: Campbell, D. and Mason, B. (eds) *Perspectives in Supervision*. London: Karnac Books. pp. 3–20.
Gardner, G.T. et al. (1997). Postmodern Models of Family Therapy Supervision. In: Todd, T.C. and Storm, C.L. (eds) *The Complete Systemic Supervisor. Context, Philosophy and Pragmatics*. London: Allyn and Bacon. pp. 229–240.
Gergen, K.J. (1991). *The Saturated Self: Dilemmas of Identity in Contemporary Life*. New York: Basic Books.
Goode, W. (1982). Why Men Resist. In: Thorne, B. and Yalom, M. (eds) *Rethinking the Family: Some Feminist Questions*. New York: Longman. pp. 131–150.
Hardham, V. (1996). Embedded and Embodied in the Therapeutic Relationship: Understanding the Therapist's use of Self Systemically. In: Flaskas, C. and Perlesz, A. (eds) *The Therapeutic Relationship in Systemic Therapy*. London: Karnac Books. pp. 71–89.
Hare-Mustin, R.T. and Marecek, J. (1988). The Meaning of Difference: Gender Theory, Postmodernism and Psychology. *American Psychologist*, 43(6): 455–464.
Harre, R. (1986). An Outline of the Social Constructionist Viewpoint. In: Harre, R. (ed.) *The Social Construction of Emotions*. Oxford: Blackwell. pp. 2–14.
Jones, E. (2003). Working with the "Self" of the Therapist in Consultation. *Human Systems*, 14(1): 7–16.

Liddle, H.A. and Saba, G.W. (1983). On Context Replication: The Isomorphic Relationship of Training and Therapy. *Journal of Strategic and Systemic Family Therapies*, 2(2): 3–11.

Lyotard, J.F. (1988). *The Differend: Phrases in Dispute*. Translated G van Den Abbeele. Minneapolis: University of Minnesota Press.

Malik, R. and Krause, I. (2005). Before and Beyond Words: Embodiment and Intercultural Therapeutic Relationships in Family Therapy. In: Flaskas, C., Mason, B. and Perlesz, A. (eds) *The Space Between: Experience, Context, and Process in the Therapeutic Relationship*. London: Karnac Books. pp. 95–109.

Mason, B. (2005). Relational Risk-taking and the Training of Supervisors. *Journal of Family Therapy*, 27: 298–301.

Philip, K. et al. (2007). Social Constructionist Supervision or Supervision as Social Construction? Some Dilemmas. *Journal of Systemic Therapies*, 26(1): 51–62.

Pocock, D. (1997). Feeling Understood in Family Therapy. *Journal of Family Therapy*, 3: 283–302.

Real, T. (1990). The Therapeutic Use of Self in Constructionist/Systemic Therapy. *Family Process*, 29 (3): 255–272.

Reid, E. et al. (1987). Taking it Personally: Issues of Personal Authority and Competence for the Female in Family Therapy Training. *Journal of Marital and Family Therapy*, 13(2): 157–165.

Rest, J.R. (1983). Research on Moral Development: Implications for Training Counseling Psychologists. *Counseling Psychologist*, 12: 19–29.

Rober, P. (1999). The Therapist Inner Conversations in Family Therapy Practice: Some Ideas about the Self of the Therapist, Therapeutic Impasse and the Process of Reflection. *Family Process*, 38(2): 209–228.

Stearns, P. (1995). Emotion. In: Harré, R. and Stearns, P. (eds) *Discursive Psychology in Practice*. London: Sage.

Stewart, M. and Amundson, J. (1995). The Ethical Postmodernist: Or Not Everything is Relative all at Once. *Journal of Systemic Therapies*, 14(2): 7–78.

Storm, C.L. and Haug, I.E. (1997). Ethical issues. Where do you draw the line? In: Todd, T.C. and Storm, C.L. (eds) *The Complete Systemic Supervisor. Context, Philosophy and Pragmatics*. London: Allyn and Bacon. pp. 26–40.

Swim, S., St. George, S. and Wulff, D. (2001). Process Ethics: A Collaborative Partnership. *Journal of Systemic Therapies*, 20(4): 14–24.

Thomas, L.K. (2002). Ethnic Sameness and Difference in Family and Systemic Therapy. In: Mason, B. and Sawyerr, A. (eds) *Exploring the Unsaid: Creativity, Risks and Dilemmas in Working Cross-Culturally*. New York: Karnac Books. pp. 49–69.

Tomm, K. (1998). A Question of Perspective. *Journal of Marital and Family Therapy*, 24(4): 409–413.

Turner, J. and Fine, M. (1997a). Gender and Supervision: Evolving Debates. In: Todd, T.C. and Storm, C.L. (eds) *The Complete Systemic Supervisor: Context, Philosophy and Pragmatics*. London: Allyn and Bacon. pp. 229–240.

Turner, J. and Fine, M. (1997b) Collaborative Supervision: Minding the Power. In: Todd, T.C. and Storm, C.L. (eds) *The Complete Systemic Supervisor: Context, Philosophy and Pragmatics*. London: Allyn and Bacon. pp. 229–240.

Von Foerster, H. (1981). *Observing Systems*. Seaside, CA: Intersystem's Publications.

Watzlawick, P., Beavin, J. and Jackson, D. (1967). *The Pragmatics of Human Communication*. New York: Norton.

White, M. (1997). *Supervision as Re-authoring Conversation: In Narratives of Therapists' Lives*. Dulwich Centre Publications. pp. 148–171.

Wittgenstein, L. (1953). *Philosophical Investigations*. Oxford: Blackwell.

Woodcock, J. and Rivett, M. (2007). Bringing the Self into Family Therapy Training: Personal and Professional Consultations with Trainee Families. *Journal of Family Therapy*. 29(4): 258–265.

SECTION II

GROUP PROCESSES

CHAPTER SIX

Minding the group: Group process, group analytic ideas, and systemic supervision—companionable or uneasy bedfellows?

Julia Granville

To what extent should supervisors take responsibility for being group facilitators and can they ever avoid this role? Can the dynamics that inevitably arise in group contexts be ignored or left to supervisees to work out, or is it essential to address these explicitly? Group supervision is not, after all, group therapy and there is also the constraint of available time. If group process, that is, the pattern of interactions and exchanges between group members, between the group and the supervisor, and the group and the outside world, is not attended to, does this matter? My experience thus far suggests that attention to these questions is important, not just when difficulties arise in a group, but in order to promote a context where development is maximized and a link between the personal and clinical practice is made in a live context. Attending to and making group process more explicit can offer particular opportunities for learning and development. It is an additional tool for addressing anxieties about performance and evaluation and an aid to developing reflexivity and collaboration. It can aid "group relational reflexivity" (Burck, this volume). I also suggest that an essential component of the demanding and complex activity involved in being a supervisor/group facilitator, is to explore the interactional nature of this role and the powerful expectations that come with this position.

Writings that connect to group experience in family therapy have tended to be those that touch on self and emotion, and address therapists' stories and areas of self-doubt (White, 1997; White, 2002; Clifton et al. 1990). Parry and Doan (1994) refer briefly to experimenting with these ideas in training groups. They and Proctor (1999) develop the use of reflecting teams specifically in relation to the trainee therapist. Proctor (1999) considers the group process in supervision and highlights the inner conversations of self-doubt that can take place during a supervisory group. Ratliff et al. (2000) look interestingly in their research study at examples of lack of consensus in supervision. Despite these, there seems to have been a dearth of systemic writing that addresses group experience specifically in relation to training and supervision groups.

Given this paucity, the questions I explore in this chapter are, first, the extent to which ideas from within the extensive psychoanalytic/ group analytic literature could help facilitate thinking and practice in running live supervision groups and, second, how such ideas might fit with systemic thinking and approaches and the particular challenges within clinical supervision groups.

The individual and the group: influences from Foulkes, Dalal, Foucault, and Bion

There is generally a tension for each individual in a group between the sense of self as individual and as a group member. This will shift in emphasis over time and within particular group sessions. Questions might include: Will my individual needs, skills, resources, value, and uniqueness be recognized and acknowledged? How do I fit in with this group? Am I a part of it, or am I marginal, or even outside? At times an individual may feel a connection, a sense of comradeship, and belonging. Being in a group can be a comfortable, comforting, and cosy experience and/or a fractious, challenging, argumentative, embattled one.

Foulkes

S.H. Foulkes sees individuals as essentially social with their personality and psychic structures fundamentally influenced by their social relationships (family and community). "Each individual—itself an artificial though plausible abstraction—is basically and centrally determined, inevitably, by the world in which he [sic] lives, by the community, by the group of which he forms a part" (Foulkes, 1948 cited in Pines, 1983: 268). This sits rather comfortably with a systemic understanding of the social construction of identity and realities. Foulkes' understanding of the importance of communication and especially language in groups relates to his idea of how a communication within a group will make the individual's mental distress more ordinary and allow them to feel more adequate (Dalal, 1998: 57). Foulkes sees a "sick" person as like an isolated, injured part of the social organism and a "symptom as a disturbed expression of the patient's conflicts. ... This leads, inevitably and logically, to the fashioning of a situation in which people can communicate better—more freely—to the small group as a therapeutic framework" (Pines, 1983: 269). Foulkes saw each individual as part of the group to which they belonged, defining the group norms collectively, their uniqueness being their variation from the norms thus created, "within a group, individuality manifests itself as variations upon a common ground" (Pines, 1983: 271). Foulkes explains the way that a group can help with individual struggles and difficulties. "The process of communication moves individuals and the group as a whole from the exchange of autistic un-understandable experiences, communicated by symptoms and by neurotic behaviour patterns, to shared, articulate, understandable communication, so there is a freeing of individual energies and potentialities which can now be used in the creative development of the group process itself and of the individual's own personal growth and change" (Foulkes cited in Pines, 1983: 271). There is a labelling here of individuals, and their communication and behaviour as "sick", "neurotic", or "autistic", language that powerfully pathologizes. It contrasts with systemic perspectives that would see "problematic" communication and behaviour more as serving a function within relationships or the system and as constructed between people. However, the key idea of exploration and process between people as a means to render individual experience more understandable, ordinary, and manageable fits comfortably with a systemic/social constructionist perspective.

In applying this to a supervision context, the experience of sharing struggles and self-doubt within a group can be seen as performing a service on behalf of the group. The resonances for others in the group, of fellow feeling or difference, can be drawn on to enable members to experience their individual issues as both unique and shared. There is a flow between the experience in a group of feeling commonalities and belonging, identification with the group, and an acceptance that all are separate and different.

Dalal

Farhad Dalal (1998), in his book on groups, develops ideas about belonging and identity that, I think, help with an understanding of some experiences in supervision groups. For Dalal, the group is, par excellence, somewhere that notions of the self and identity are socially constructed. Dalal discusses questions of group identity and the ideas of self and other, "us" and "them". He writes, "First, identity is a name, the name of a category. Second, identity is an internal sense of belonging to a name" (Dalal, 1998: 173). Dalal then points to the problem of whether a person identifies him or herself or is identified by another. In particular, how individuals position themselves or are positioned, in relation to the socially constructed dimensions of, for example, race, culture, gender, class, sexuality, and so forth, categorizing that is both more and less visible and open for attention, would be especially pertinent to consider. Dalal discusses the choosing of categorizations from a mass of available similarities and differences, which become identities that position "self" in relation to "other". He discusses how ideology, discourses, and, most importantly, power, influence which categorizations and identities become essentialized and viewed as natural (Dalal, 1998: 201–7). This positioning of self and of others on a multiplicity of dimensions happens in a group from the very outset, although it may get renegotiated and may shift as people get to know each other, show different aspects of themselves, form alliances and oppositions with each other at different times and on different issues.

Dalal goes on to say, "Given that there are a multitude of potential identities, there must be a constant danger of slippage from one to another. In other words, there is a constant danger of 'loss of identity'. Any such threat is indeed an existential crisis. Suddenly, one sort of an 'us' might transmute into another sort of an 'us'. Suddenly and perhaps terribly, one might find oneself belonging together with one of 'them'" (Dalal, 1998: 173). In the context of group supervision, the issues of judgement and evaluation, exemplified in the very term "supervision" itself, I think strengthens this sense of potential slippage that Dalal describes. For example a trainee who has received feedback about an aspect of their clinical skills that may not be at the required standard, may find themselves suddenly feeling apart from the group in which they were only just before very much at home. The spectre of a fall from grace into the category of "failure" looms large, whether realistic or not, and there is the threat of a loss of identification with and belonging to the "us" of the group. I am interested in the way in which inner and outer conversations may influence this and whether this could be explored more explicitly in a supervision group.

To apply these ideas within a systemic training group context, one avenue could be to draw on Peter Rober's (2005) approach to identifying and exploring therapists' internal dialogues during therapy through video review. This could equally helpfully be applied to a review of supervision group discussions to tease out group members' responses, thoughts, choices, identifications, and personal resonances, not only to the work with clients but also to the process in the supervision group itself. Bringing these concerns and themes into the group arena from the private sphere of internal conversation can help to render them more "ordinary" and more "shared". As Foulkes discussed, the group context[1] "simply brings back the problems to where they belong. ... Valuations and norms are restated and modified by comparison, contrast and analysis. Communication leading to a shared experience and understanding is in terms of the group" (Foulkes, 2004: 155).

Foucault

In systemic trainings and therapy the visibility of the work and the person of the therapist as they work, the "goldfish bowl" of live supervision where the therapist is viewed from all angles, heightens the possibility for Dalal's "slippage in identity". The use

---

[1] Foulkes refers mainly to psychotherapy, but also applies the same approach to other groups, such as the family, work, and teaching groups.

of screen and observing team carries with it the potential for this to be experienced as a powerful gaze, exercising what Foucault (1991) describes as normative or modern power, exemplified in the system of the panopticon. Observation and supervision can be a technique of shaping and moulding the developing therapist to fit a variety of norms. Panopticism, argues Foucault, is a system that gets the individuals to "police" themselves to conform to these norms. "The judges of normality are present everywhere. We are in the society of the teacher-judge, the doctor-judge, the educator-judge, the 'social worker'-judge; it is on them that the universal reign of the normative is based; and each individual, wherever he [sic] may find himself, subjects to it his body, his gestures, his behaviour, his aptitudes, his achievements" (Foucault, 1991: 304). In Foucault's formulation, the separation of the individual is an important component of the disciplinary system. I find that engaging in an externalizing of this through the group process is a way to "detoxify" and undermine the judgemental potential of so much observation. Thus conversations about doubt, evaluation, and the positions taken and given in a group will create opportunities for a diversity of alternative narratives to emerge and the possibility to challenge more oppressive stories.

Bion

The ideas of Bion, in my view, offer further valuable ways to understand and facilitate the process of supervision in groups. Bion (1961) in his seminal writing on groups theorizes the relationship between the individual and the group. He sees the group in a sense as an idea or fantasy rather than as an objective entity in itself. His ideas, in contrast to those of Foulkes, tend to see the group as less a psychological entity and perhaps in a less benign light. However, I am struck again by the ease of fit here with social constructionist ideas. Bion sees the group as representing an "aggregation of individuals all in the same state of regression" (Coleman and Bexton, 1975: 11). While the rather pathologizing language of regression may not fit comfortably with a systemic framework, the idea of the group tending to co-construct ways to be a group together does. Bion talks of the tension between individuals and the group when the "group" becomes aware of individual distinctiveness. This, he suggests, gives rise to anxiety and panic. Bion posits that the individual believes that the group has an "attitude" towards them, and that the group has an "attitude" towards both individuals and the group leader. These "attitudes" are seen as unconscious, as influencing group process and behaviour, and as open to interpretation. Bion describes these as basic assumptions that he thinks groups often labour under.

In contrast to the basic assumptions, Bion developed the idea of a particular mode of functioning in a group, which he called the "work group" (1961: 12). This represents the group behaving in its most functional manner. Bion's concept of the "work group" refers to mental activity by the group members that relates to the task that is the agreed purpose of the group. "Since this activity is geared to a task, it is related to reality, its methods are rational and, therefore, in however embryonic a form, scientific. ... This facet of mental activity in a group I have called the Work Group. The term embraces only mental activity of a particular kind, not the people who indulge in it" (Bion, 1961:12). In other words, a group is in work group mode when the activity taking place, the thinking and talking, are based on the "realities" of the situation and context, and face the dilemmas and anxieties of the task of the group. The concept of the work group describes the *quality of the group functioning*, rather than the nature of the group per se, its members or particular tasks.

In a supervision group the agreed task may vary depending on the context but in general will be a combination of providing a good quality, ethical, clinical service to clients/families in combination with developing the practice of the group members. This may include an evaluative component relating to the group members developing to a set standard of qualifying practice and a judgement as to whether this has been achieved.[2] A question therefore is, "What would work group mode look like in supervision groups and how could one maximize this way of functioning?"

A supervision group in work group mode might, for example, be developing a range of thoughts and ideas about a particular intervention with a family. The group could be thinking about how the family would have experienced the therapist, what alternative

---

[2] A supervision group may also encompass elements of line management depending on the context. However, I am not going to be considering this aspect here.

interventions there might have been, what might be the rationale for these and their advantages and disadvantages. In work group mode, the therapist and the group might reflect on the therapist's development in relation to the piece of work under discussion, what was going well, and what developments the therapist, group members, and supervisor might like to see. There would be perhaps some differences and struggles and an acknowledgement of the difficulty in changing ways of working and resonances between group members in relation to this. I think this would encompass exploration of complexity, the struggle to manage anxiety in the absence of simple solutions, awareness of both similarities and differences, being able to bear difficult responses as well as comforting and comfortable ones and the hard work of really putting one's mind to the issues at hand.

A supervision group that was in comfortable agreement, where the main flow of conversation was to reassure and validate the group members, swapping praise for each other's work and minimizing the struggle, difficulties, or moments when the therapeutic work and engagement was less helpful, is not in work group mode. This is not to say that, for the group to be functioning productively, it must be a difficult place to be. Indeed there are certainly times when the group and individuals will need to focus on positives, connections, and similarities. However, for the task of the group to be moved forward, it must be possible to tackle differences, areas of discomfort, and the struggle of learning and change, which will be different for different group members over time.

Bion identified a number of ways in which groups respond to anxieties and escape the task of the group. These "basic assumptions" (BAs) of the group can be defined as those assumptions which underlie behaviour, so that a group might at particular times be operating "as if" such and such were true (Rioch, 1975). Perhaps in systemic terms this might be seen in more conscious terms as the beliefs underlying behaviours. So, for example, there may be a basic assumption that the leader will solve difficulties and nurture the group without the group needing to do anything. The group members will take a position of inadequacy, knowing little, being powerless. This would be what Bion called Basic Assumption dependency. In BA dependency the leader is seen as omnipotent and ultimately bound to disappoint, leading to hostility and perhaps the seeking of an alternative leader. For example, a group might see their supervisor as wonderful or dreadful.

At this point I want to consider how, as a systemic supervisor, these ideas might be put into operation. The examples from practice that follow are an attempt to draw on the ideas from a group analytic frame and to apply them within a systemic approach. For instance, rather than relying on analysis and interpretation, the ideas inform hypothesizing about process and the development of questions and exercises.

Example
An example of BA dependency might be of group members emphasizing how little they know, how they worry about the work, and how they want the supervisor to tell them exactly what to do. Another example might be of group members feeling that there is a right way to do the work and that the supervisor should be more forthcoming in passing on this knowledge. There may be feelings of anger or resentment when this is not taken up. As a systemic supervisor these polarizations in the relationship to the supervisor could be explored by posing them as semantic polarities (Campbell and Groenbaek, 2006). For example,

Supervisor's ideas and knowledge essential for learning.	*Trainee's ideas prioritized and privileged in learning.*

This would give trainees the opportunity to identify their responses and understand those of others as positions with meaning, emotion, and history attached to them. The potential for movement and flexibility is thus increased.

Bion talks of people having a "valency" towards particular basic assumptions, a tendency to be pulled towards a particular form of functioning. For myself, I recognize as a group member the wish for a supervisor/teacher/mentor to tell me the way and to tell me I'm doing ok and so on. As a supervisor, I have recognized a tendency to accept invitations to take up a position as a wished-for (perhaps both by supervisees and by me) all-knowing, all-giving supervisor, too readily wanting to, or feeling I should, provide answers and solutions. Flattering or gratifying though it can be to be seen as holding expert knowledge in an idealized way, in reality there is always the sense that one cannot meet such high expectations and that such a position undermines supervisees' development of, and trust in, their own thinking and development. Being able to recognize one's valency in one's self as supervisor is helpful in avoiding the pitfalls associated with taking up these unhelpful positions.

Bion described two other basic assumptions: Basic Assumption pairing and Basic Assumption fight/flight. BA pairing is in operation when two people take centre stage and the group looks on. Bion suggests that there is a feeling of hope that something wonderful will emerge from this pairing, that something new will be brought forth that will "save" the group. Bion emphasizes that this is a messianic position where the saviour, whether a person, idea, or utopia, is "unborn" and must remain a hope: "only by remaining a hope does hope persist" (Rioch, 1975: 17). This defends against feelings of hatred, destructiveness, and despair. A leader in a pairing group is required to be potentially marvellous, on the verge of coming to fruition. The hope for something to come is the key point here.

Examples in systemic practice
In the supervision group context the structure of consulting partners, a common practice where trainees pair up to support and feed back to each other over a period during clinical training, can become caught up in this. A particular pair of trainees may become very allied with each other which can both be validating for that pair but can also exclude others or leave them feeling somehow envious or spoiling, perhaps not as good, skilled, or creative. A supervisor may also find him or herself engaged more intensely with a particular group member because of a sense of affinity, appreciation, similarity, and so forth. The rest of the group may feel like spectators to that exciting and sparky relationship but ultimately disappointed or excluded. Talk and ideas generated between a pair may seem as if they will lead to some transformation of learning and practice, a new way for the supervision group to be that will somehow make it fantastic or successful. However, these overblown expectations do not in reality materialize and disillusion can ensue.

In BA fight/flight, the group is operating as if it has met in order to fight something or run away from it in order to survive. The leader is called on to provide opportunities for fight or flight. If they do not provide these sorts of opportunities they will be ignored. A leader of a group in fight or flight mode is required to be, respectively, unbeatable or uncatchable (Rioch, 1975).

Examples
In a supervision group an example of fight/flight basic assumption might be when a group becomes focused on the perceived shortfalls of an individual member seen as not pulling their weight or persistently arriving late. Despite significant concerns that this will impact on a group, a focus on this to the exclusion of other issues can become scapegoating. Group members could be avoiding anxieties inevitably experienced by all about their abilities to manage the work and the learning. The person who is attacked has in a way been elected to represent this on behalf of the group. An exercise on polarities around expectations of participation, challenge, and support in the group, interviewing each other on the meaning of lateness, success, and failure in family of origin, work, and personal contexts would explore this within the systemic frame. A further example is when a group resorts to an idealized assertion that they are a "great group" or "the best group". This can be pleasurable but avoids the anxiety that might be provoked by acknowledging differences, competition, or areas of difficulty in their developing practice. Mapping ideas about what they appreciate in this or other group contexts and what they find more challenging would be a way to encourage a more realistic "work group" mode of thinking.

As a supervisor I have felt tempted to fall in with group members in engaging in a battle with the institution about organizational issues such as fees, communication, and consultation. There is comfort in feeling the strength of the group identity in the face of an external threat or enemy. While comfortable it does not, however, facilitate dealing with issues that need to be negotiated and resolved realistically.

In one supervision group, the members talked often about the specialness of the group and put a lot of effort into being positive and reassuring with each other. As the supervisor, and a relatively inexperienced one, at the beginning of the group I was also keen to make sure that all felt supported and that I was seeing and acknowledging their strengths and capacities. However, there was a risk that this way of being as a group could be difficult to challenge and could restrict the stretching, challenge, and acknowledgement of the struggles involved in development. This cosy warmth and appreciation could be understood in Bionic terms, at least partly, as a flight from the discomforts of both giving and receiving more challenging feedback necessary in order for development to take place.

In Bionic theory, the BA group mode is seen to be present in groups both fleetingly and persistently at different times. Work group mode similarly is seen as coming and going within groups and operating alongside the basic assumptions. In BA mode there may be a cosy feeling of oneness, but it does not put great demands on the individual. Rioch describes work group function being related to the real task of the group. "The group takes cognizance of its purpose and can define its task. The structure of the group is there to further the attainment of the task." The work group members co-operate as separate and discreet individuals. The work group "seeks for knowledge, learns from experience and constantly questions how it may best achieve its goal" (Rioch, 1975: 23).

The position of the supervisor

In the systemic and group analytic literature, a number of terms are used to name the role: group leader, conductor, facilitator, and supervisor. These terms construct the identity and activities of the supervisor in terms of directiveness, influence, and observation versus exploration, facilitation, and participation. Group analytic writing suggests that the facilitator's role is to create an "analytic" stance where what is communicated, through language and non-verbally, is available to be explored and understood—"work in communication" (Foulkes, 2004: 156). This seems to be akin to what in a systemic frame could be called a "reflective space", one where, to use Mason's (1993: 189) term, a context of "safe uncertainty" is created that enables openness and trust to develop recursively with a willingness to take risks and try new things (Mason, 2005).

A group analytic facilitator might take a communication expressed by an individual and understand this in terms of a function or communication on behalf of the whole group. To use this in a systemic frame is not a great distance to travel. Rather than an interpretative response, introducing a possible hypothesis, bringing individual dilemmas into the arena of the group to be considered collectively, to map members' relationships to an issue is a systemic activity that makes the group an ideal location to recognize and accept a whole range of responses to a particular issue.

I think, from an ethical position, the supervisor has a responsibility to do what they can to make the group experience a learning one for all, where it is possible and "safe enough" to explore, experiment, and extend development. However, exploration of group dynamics has the potential to be an unhelpful distraction from the primary tasks at hand. In Bion's terms, could it be a flight from the anxiety of being a work group? There is the potential to lose sight of the main aims of supervision if the group gets over-involved in exploration of their internal relationships. A supervisor would need to be mindful of that possibility, and be prepared to move the group on in order to resume a work group mode, the supervisor moving between explanation and challenge of basic assumptions and promoting work group functioning.

Example
I have suggested that a group sculpts their relationships using a basket of beach pebbles, with members sculpting the group relationships over time. This activity was suggested at a point of transition in the group and was in my mind an opportunity to identify some of the risks and constraints that might be influencing the trainees and the alliances and affinities that flowed between the group members as well as stirring up some creative energy. Sculpts using objects or themselves can be a useful active tool for exploration of areas such as risk-taking, self-disclosure, certainty, emotional expression, theoretical positions and any number of themes around which groups may split or coalesce.

Some deconstruction of group members' experience of being in a group, how they see this group, how they individually and collectively interact with issues such as competition, success, criticism, or feedback, how they see their own, the supervisor's and the group style, would provide the opportunity to understand some of the influences at play and promote the work group functioning through the deconstruction of potential splits.

Contexts that influence positioning in groups

As a final thought, I briefly want to raise the way in which people bring their previous experiences to the groups that they are in. For both supervisors and supervisees, it is helpful to use the opportunity to explore group members' preferred or habitual positions in groups in general and in this particular group. A supervisor can provide the context in which to consider how this reflects patterns and scripts from other systems such as family of origin, social, educational, and professional contexts. Burck (this volume) explores this further. Aggett's (2004) work on supervisees' relationship to experiences and preferences about learning offers a wealth of ideas for this. The supervision group can be a venue to explore the relationship to authority, leadership, and followership and the relationship to challenge, exploring similarities and differences in the group around these. As an example of a relevant context, one could helpfully suggest discussion of sibling relationships, position in family of origin, or experience of being an only child, and how these might influence ideas about the self in groups.

The following are some questions it might be helpful to pose about sibling experiences. They could form the basis of individual thinking, mapping, and group discussion.

> *What are group members' experiences with brothers and sisters?*
>
> *What was it like as an only child?*
>
> *What are the narratives in your family about sibling relationships? In your family how much value was attached to individual or family needs and desires?*
>
> *How does this influence your expectations of being in a group? For instance, did/do you fight for attention/approval/things? On a continuum about the relative prioritization of others' views and your own, where do you tend to find yourself? How do you make decisions with others?*
>
> *How have these experiences constructed or invited feelings and ideas about being in the limelight, or one of the gang?*
>
> *How do you relate to competition and rivalry, being special or not standing out?*
>
> *What is your relationship to authority figures, to hierarchy, to being told what to do?*

Conclusions

Systemic psychotherapy training is a uniquely transparent and visible form of clinical training in the psychotherapies. In live supervision or video review the minutiae of our practice is open to scrutiny. The level of feedback we receive about our work and ourselves is potentially huge and can be reassuring as well as discomforting and at times disturbing to our beliefs and sense of ourselves. In groups, informal, non-therapeutic, and family groups as well as in formal group psychotherapy, we give and receive feedback on how we come across to others, and how this may coincide or differ from our overt intentions. In a group context, our interactions and the conscious and unconscious thoughts and feelings that influence our ideas about others and ourselves and construct our identities, can be explored. The ideas from group analytic theory provide a rich source of understandings and insight into these processes. Drawing on them from within a systemic frame and practice provides a coherent way to explore process in a systemic group within systemic training.

Yet, how important is it to enter into this arena of group process and how does this fit with the debates about personal and professional development in family therapy? There needs to be a reasonable balance between the focus on the actual therapeutic work, personal development as a practitioner, and the process within the supervision group. I would argue that, as a therapist, to have personal experience of a therapeutic process, in the broadest sense, within a group context, enables greater empathy with the position of a client coming for therapy. The experience of risk-taking, sharing intimate aspects of the self, and exploring interactions with others in a group, offers an important preparation for the experience of offering these opportunities to others. Experiencing change in oneself as a result of such experiences is likely to support a developing therapist in the project of helping others to change during the therapeutic endeavour. Having a systemic group process focus would perhaps offer trainees an opportunity to address the impact of the work on themselves and to experience the vulnerability and openness to new insights and experiences of the self in relation to others that is akin to a therapeutic encounter.

The disadvantages are that, unlike personal or training therapy, a supervision group is not a confidential space. In a training context the exploration is taking place in a context where how an individual "performs" could form part of their evaluation for fitness to practice. This is bound to constrain. In addition there is the factor of time constraints. The multiple tasks of a supervision group are considerable and perhaps this extra dimension could be an overload that would mean that group process could only be addressed in a superficial way and would therefore add little.

Overall, however, I believe that the use of a group process lens, can, and has, enhanced learning and development within my own supervisory practice. Do we need to import another theoretical framework? I have certainly found that some of the ideas have helped and changed my thinking and practice. I have been surprised at how well the ideas of Foulkes and even Bion sit with a social constructionist approach. The ideas can enrich our thinking, without us becoming too reverent, and can be incorporated into systemic exercises and conversations that open up learning. When a group is going well, the group aspect enhances the opportunities to move between positions, to develop capacities to work with similarities and difference. Using the group process facilitates working with, and understanding the power of, the inner narratives of doubt, matching up, and competitiveness. Attending to group process can enable anxieties to become exterior, interpersonal, and held collectively by the group, rather than being held internally by an individual. Groups, at the moments when working at their best, provide tremendous opportunities for creative exploration, cooperation, and dynamic thinking. Attending to the group process can, I think, only enhance this.

References

Aggett, P. (2004). Learning Narratives in Group Supervision: Enhancing Collaborative Learning. *Journal of Systemic Therapies*. 23(3): 36–50.

Bion, W.R. (1961). *Experiences in Groups*. London: Tavistock Publications.

Bion, W.R. (1975). Selections from Experiences in Groups. In: Coleman, A. and Bexton, W.H. (eds) *Group Relations Reader*. Florida: AK Rice Institute. Chapter 2.

Campbell, D. and Groenbaek, M. (2006). *Taking Positions in the Organization*. London: Karnac Books.

Clifton, D., Doan, R., and Mitchell, D. (1990). The Reauthoring of Therapist's Stories: Taking Doses of our Own Medicine. *Journal of Strategic and Systemic Therapies*. 9(4): 61–66.

Coleman, A. and Bexton, W.H. (1975). *Group Relations Reader*. Florida: AK Rice Institute.

Dalal, F. (1998). *Taking the Group Seriously*. London: Jessica Kingsley.

Foucault, M. (1991). *Discipline and Punish*. London: Penguin Books.

Foulkes, S.H. (ed.) (2004). Some Basic Concepts in Group Psychotherapy. In: Foulkes, S.H. and Foulkes, E. (eds) *Selected Papers of S.H. Foulkes*. London: Karnac Books. Chapter 15.

Fredman, G. (2004). *Transforming Emotion Conversations in Counselling and Psychotherapy*. London: Whurr.

Mason, B. (1993). Towards Positions of Safe Uncertainty. *Human Systems*. 4: 189–200.

Mason, B. (2005). Relational Risk-taking and the Therapeutic Relationship. In: Flaskas, C., Mason, B. and Perlesz, A. (eds) *The Space Between: Experience, Context and Process in the Therapeutic Relationship*. London: Karnac Books. Chapter 11.

Parry, A. and Doan, R. (1994). Re-visions of Therapists Stories in Training and Supervision. In: Parry, A. and Doan, R. (eds) *Story Re-visions: Narrative Therapy in the Postmodern World*. London: Guilford Press. Chapter 6.

Pines, M. (1983). The Contribution of S.H. Foulkes to Group Therapy. In: Pines, M (ed.) *The Evolution of Group Analysis*. pp. 265–285.

Proctor, K. (1999). The Bells that Ring: A Process for Group Supervision. *Australian and New Zealand Journal of Family Therapy*. 18: 217–220.

Ratliff, D.A. et al. (2000). Lack of Consensus in Supervision. *Journal of Marital and Family Therapy*. 26(3): 373–384.

Rioch, M. (1975). The Work of Wilfred Bion on Groups. In: Colman, A. and Harold Bexton, W. *Group Relations Reader*. Florida: AK Rice Institute. Chapter 3.

Rober, P. (2005). The Therapist's Self in Dialogical Family Therapy: Some Ideas About Not-Knowing and the Therapist's Inner Conversation. *Family Process*. 44(4).

White, M. (1997). Supervision as Re-Authoring Conversation. In: White, M. (ed.) *Narratives of Therapists' Lives*. Adelaide: Dulwich Centre Publications. Chapter 7.

White, M. (2002). Addressing Personal Failure. *International Journal of Narrative therapy and Community Work*. 3: 33–76.

CHAPTER SEVEN

From hazardous to collaborative learning: Thinking systemically about live supervision group processes

Charlotte Burck

Systemic psychotherapy relies heavily on the use of live supervision groups, often without question, for training purposes and clinicians' continued professional development (CPD). When live supervision groups work well they involve fruitful and satisfying processes at every level, with the supervisor, team, therapist, and family learning from and enhancing each other. However, when they run into difficulties, they can constitute, at the very least, a headache, and, at worst, a nightmare, for all concerned. Finding ways to think about live supervision group processes within systemic and narrative frameworks in order to help group participants manage themselves well seems crucial, as these form such a significant part of the therapeutic process.

Of central importance here is how to pay attention to the ways in which group processes are affected by, and affect, the therapy and the family. The importance of the development and maintenance of supervisors' and therapists' self-reflexivity is strongly emphasized in the processes of systemic therapy and supervision (Burck and Campbell, 2002; Burnham, 1993; Rober, 2005). Yet the development of self-reflexivity in relation to one's membership in a group and group processes (that is, "group relational reflexivity", to extend Burnham's "relational reflexivity") has almost completely been ignored. Many qualifying courses in systemic psychotherapy/family therapy in the UK include the criteria of being a "good" supervision group member as part of the clinical assessment. Being a "good" team member will be intimately bound up with participating in the creation of helpful group processes. However little explicit attention has been paid to group processes in the systemic field, as Granville in this volume also notes. In this chapter I elaborate some applications of systemic and narrative ideas to live supervision group processes and generate some questions which may be important to consider and dilemmas which may arise.

The literature on the reflecting team (Andersen, 1991; Anderson and Jensen, 2007; Friedman, 1995) has mainly focused on the generative quality of having a multiplicity of views, to the exclusion of a discussion of the actual group processes involved and how to manage when reflecting teams are not working well together. It is as if the idea that individuals will usually be able to link their ideas with each other helpfully can in itself be sufficient to produce useful conversations. It is interesting that Robert Reich, economic adviser to Barack Obama, said recently about him: "My sense is he genuinely believes that people can come to a rough consensus about big problems and work together effectively" (Baker, 2009). Such beliefs enable persistence and engender an atmosphere that enables links to be forged at different levels. This is somewhat similar to the process when supervisors-in-training move from feeling at a loss of what to offer a supervisee who comes out of the room with a family, to having faith that something helpful will be generated from the discussion with the therapist and the group, which has its own effects. But is this always sufficient?

Live supervision groups

The live supervision group often provides the most intensive and intimate grouping in the learning environment of a training programme. This is the group who learn most about each other's clinical work and the personal resonances which each member brings to their clinical practice. Group members will be involved in each other's learning processes, giving and receiving feedback to each other, as well as observing the supervisor's input to each. It is here that individuals' vulnerabilities are most likely to be revealed and their strengths and leaps in development noted and shared. This is also the group in which trainees spend the most time during their training course, and often at close quarters in a darkened room.

Family therapy clinics within child and adolescent mental health services or other settings are often run as live supervision groups with members taking it in turn to be the therapist and the rest of the group providing supervision with or without a designated lead supervisor (see Ziminski, this volume). The therapist's development and personal resonances may not appear explicitly on the agenda as it is in a training context but still may be observed. Often considered a way to maintain and develop systemic and narrative practice in public sector and voluntary organizations they can veer between sustaining overworked clinicians and replicating tensions and conflicts from the wider setting.

Some of the thinking about systemic and narrative therapy groups and retrospective group supervision can easily be applied to live supervision groups, but there are also significant differences which need to be taken into account. One of the most crucial is that a live supervision group needs to "act in the moment" with the family and with the therapist, and not simply reflect on the work—it is required to operate in the domain of action as well as exploration. This sense of urgency, of needing to make decisions with a deadline, intensifies group interactions as well as making differences more challenging to manage. However this need to act in the immediate interests of the family session which is central to a live systemic supervision group also helpfully keeps this as the highest order context of the multiple tasks to be managed (see also Barratt et al., this volume).

Alongside the need to act "in the moment" with the family, live supervision groups have times when they process their work. It is here that ideas about the narratives of self and group, discourses of equality, similarity and difference, notions of polarization and positioning, and the development of group relational reflexivity can best be attended to.

The most important distinguishing feature of systemic and narrative groups (see Asen, 2002; Burck et al. 1996; Monk et al. 1997; Vassallo, 1998) is that group leaders take charge of their formats, actively structuring and harnessing the group to enable processes to develop which facilitate the emergence of multiple perspectives and disrupt redundant ways of thinking. The posing of reflexive questions, use of interviews, reflecting processes and outsider-witness practices are commonly incorporated in such group work. This is in stark contrast to a group analytic tradition of commenting on group processes. Such interventive use of group processes transfers well to managing processes in live supervision groups.

Recursive connections between families and groups

Much of the complexity in live group supervision involves the number of levels of interactions to be kept in mind (Burck and Campbell, 2002). Keeping the family's clinical interests at the heart of the matter involves finding ways to keep an eye on the impact of the family on the therapist and the group, and vice versa, the impact of the supervision group on the family.

One of the most helpful concepts in this task is that of isomorphism (Liddle and Saba, 1983; White and Russell, 1997), which has most often been elaborated in relation to the isomorphism between therapy and training (see Bertrando and Gilli, and Burnham, this volume). Being able to identify similar processes in the group and in the therapist and family system is a task which will be primarily the supervisor's responsibility but is usefully shared by all the group members. The linking between family and team concerns processes and patterns that connect (Bateson, 1970) as well as mutuality of responsiveness. Responsiveness between families and teams is closely bound up with the nature of dialogue which is possible between them. As families often come to therapy with narratives which are unhelpfully fixed or experience themselves as if locked into repetitive interactional patterns, the supervision group's ability to find ways to sustain and demonstrate flexibility of positioning becomes a vital part of the therapeutic process, in order to enable the family to generate more helpful ideas.

It is when families and teams have very difficult processes going on that it is most challenging to know how to proceed. Given the recursive nature of the mutual influences between the family and the therapeutic team, it can be difficult to untangle how each is affecting the other, but finding a way to take into account the supervision group process can be a key. A therapist came out of a very difficult session with a family to find that the team were very perfunctory in their responses to her and then rushed off leaving her on her own. She felt terrible—both that they must think the session had gone badly (that is, that she had managed it badly, as she herself feared), and that they had not shown interest or concern in finding out how things had been for her. Helping her to become curious about how these group processes might interlink with family processes became a frame which enabled her to name this group process in the group and explore its meanings, and allowed the group to help her explore how she might also take a different position in the therapy.

When we are most emotionally invested in our perspectives and positions in the group and least appreciative of different views, it is most difficult to maintain a stance of group relational reflexivity and of course most crucial. How do supervisors and groups facilitate this stance throughout their working together? What I will argue is that explicitly putting on the agenda ways to ensure that group narratives do not become frozen and group interactions too predictable is central.

Paying attention to the wider context

Supervision groups, therapists, and families meet each other in different settings, and these contexts as well as wider societal meanings impact on their interactions and the therapeutic experience. When we are involved in intense processes it is often easy to forget to consider this wider context. When two supervision group members are applying for the same job, when the clinic is under threat, when the clinical examination on the training course is imminent, all have an impact on group interactions and thus on the therapy. Remembering to consider the question of what might be pertinent contextual issues and making a space to flag these up for the group as a whole gives them a chance to be taken on board explicitly rather than implicitly.

Live supervision groups in training

Entering family therapy training can be experienced as somewhat overwhelming by trainees, as Nel (2006) reported in a qualitative study of the impact of a training course on trainees' identities. The visibility of the learning and evaluation process in systemic trainings is likely to be a contributing factor to the anxiety. One of the enduring ideas about live supervision is how helpful it is for therapists to experience a mirroring of the experience of a family in family therapy, that of demonstrating/doing your relationships as well as speaking about them. The usual concerns in joining a group in relation to how we want to be perceived by others and how much we want to be in or out of the group are heightened by the fact that both our therapy and learning are being observed.

One of the most important aspects of groups referred to in the literature of whatever theoretical orientation is the effect of taking part in a "community": the advantages of sharing common experiences, learning that this is not just an individual challenge, struggle, or issue but one shared by others, alongside which it is possible to establish a mutuality in giving and receiving help. This emphasis on connectedness and collaboration with implications for relational identity and identification facilitates the recognition of resourcefulness and the lessening of shame. It is also said to have the effect of lessening power differences between group leader and group members. This aspect is much less focused on by trainees who often view the evaluative context as all encompassing, conferring power on the supervisor to make or break careers. This stance both under-emphasizes and under-estimates the power of a group, of being able to challenge the supervisor in their role as observers of the supervision. As many supervisors currently seek ways to work collaboratively alongside their evaluative role, this aspect of group power and process can be made more use of.

In joining a live supervision group individuals can be preoccupied with questions about both individual and group identity. Which identities are important to us and do we want to have validated: clinical identities or academic identities or relational identities? Being respected for our work at whatever level may be the most over-riding concern. The group identity at this point is often reported as a "we're all in this together" narrative—a sense of mutuality and vulnerability as individuals frequently begin to experience themselves as de-skilled in the challenge of taking on new ways of thinking and practice (Nel, 2006). This group narrative is often accompanied by individual positions of being very polite and supportive to each other. This connection through shared vulnerability will inevitably also involve differences. The question of how individuals "do" anxiety, for example, may be usefully explored early on in a live supervision group—whether toughing it out, going blank, rejecting supervision, taking a position of certainty, or performing with confidence—and may help avoid these positions and their accompanying group interactions becoming fixed and therefore hazardous. This exercise also enhances the building of respect as supervisor and supervisees begin to understand the contexts which inform individuals' ways of working with families and of managing their own development.

The individual and group narratives, which supervisees and the supervisor construct together, will be informed by ideas about what an ideal family therapist, an ideal supervisor, and an ideal supervision group are like. It was not until I was involved in training family therapy supervisors that I really learned how constrained some course participants felt at points in their qualifying training, because their own questions about whether they were "fit to become therapists" were often all-consuming. Trainee supervisors spoke of monitoring what they revealed and how they presented, fearing that aspects of themselves or their family of origin experiences would be considered a criteria to disqualify them. Ratliff et al.'s (2000) research exploring supervision where there was a lack of consensus between supervisor and supervisee found that supervisees needed to manage a fine balance between "performing competence" as a therapist and "performing cooperation" with their supervisor by being a "good" learner. We can extend this to include supervisees' need to "perform cooperation" with their peers which might include the following rather daunting list: contributing "good" ideas and validating others' ideas; balancing talking and listening; being able to give and receive feedback; being sufficiently supportive and challenging; and disclosing enough but not too much. When does the "performance" become something you own? And what happens when we feel irritated, angry, disqualified, fed up, or bored? What happens when we start to feel that we have to leave out aspects of ourselves and our experience? There is anecdotal evidence that there are a number of family therapists who experienced chronic and unresolved difficult relationships in their supervision groups during their training, which impacted on the therapy offered as well as their learning. How can supervisors and supervisees best sense and attend to the unsaid in group relationships and its effect on the work?

Taking the risk of telling someone in the supervision group that they annoy you will usually only happen if there is an idea that something can be done with this (hopefully that they will stop!). One of the most frequently discussed ideas in the supervision literature is the importance of setting up a context in which it is safe to take risks. However, the processes involved in building a sense of safety are among the least well elaborated. Communicating a sense of respect for all points of view appears to be one of the most crucial components and as the supervisor's view is often given most weight, their ability to do so is probably key. However, being able to acknowledge the validity of different perspectives is different to finding a way to link these perspectives together helpfully. And if polarization occurs between two positions this can sometimes take time to unpack. A helpful guideline for systemic supervisors, to "keep talking about the complexities" (Burck and Campbell, 2002: 71), applies particularly to the development of group relational reflexivity. When there is tension, it is useful to create time and a structure within which it is possible to "keep talking", thus enabling the talk across differences to take place, in the belief that this will lead to some helpful understandings. Two trainees consulting found themselves becoming constrained and uncomfortable with each other, when one finally said that she often found the other's way of presenting ideas problematic. Deciding to see what we could all learn from how to manage this, we agreed as a group that they should continue with the conversation, with some questioning of how each had taken up the position in the group that they had. It emerged that both trainees had developed their different ways of presenting themselves in relation to experiences of oppression. This understanding came as a surprise and indeed connected them, which in turn shifted their emotional experience of the other. What the group as a whole learned was the importance of being able to identify the contexts which inform how individuals position themselves and that being able to talk "through the tension" led to an ability to find significant links at a different level. This has resonances with the work of the public conversation project which aims to create dialogue between people whose views are very polarized (Becker et al. 1995). However, it can also be important at times to stop talking and to trust that people will move things forward without the supervisor.

Evaluation and group processes

In a training context where the supervisor and group are working to give every individual's contribution equal value, the evaluative context can at the same time give different weight to different individuals' contributions. When a supervision group contains supervisees with very different levels of clinical experience, this difference may be named initially and then "forgotten" and become experienced as "personal failing". In the process of "forgetting", an identity of incompetence rather than inexperience can be constructed and this positioning/identity may contribute to the individual withdrawing from offering ideas and relying more heavily on the supervisor and the rest of the group for their therapeutic work.

As a supervisor I learned much later that when one of the trainees failed the first year clinical exam, the whole supervision group had felt a failure, although this was not expressed explicitly at the time. The mutuality of the learning project with everyone reflecting on and contributing to each other's therapy may have led to a sense of shared responsibility. The importance of respect and mutual liking which had contributed to positive team processes may have over-ridden the appreciation of different learning paces. This highlighted for me how crucial it is to include discussion of differences of experience and different paces of learning which can often accompany this as an on-going factor to be taken into account within individual and group struggles, and especially when a group relishes focusing on similarities.

Connections within groups

Individuals often join live supervision groups in their agency settings, as well as in training institutes, which include people with whom they have relationships in other contexts including the supervisor. Naming these connections at the beginning of a group by mapping individuals' links with others allows questions to be considered in the whole group about what impact these may have on everyone's development and interactions, as well as how the group can manage the impact of these multiple relationships (see Abela and Sammut Scerri, this volume). Such a mapping exercise can also identity the similarities and differences in the group and consider how these may impact on experimentation, on relationships and interactions, on disclosure, and on therapy and supervision. It can also immediately raise issues of belonging and otherness, if one or more individuals have no connections to others, and provoke questions about how the group and individual can make use of this position, or find other ways to make connections. Questions of belonging involve both one's sense of connectedness—the experience of one's self-narrative corresponding well enough with the group narratives ("this is the kind of group I want to belong to") as well as how we are seen by, and connected to, others. Those who are considered central in a group may not even notice this, while those who experience themselves as marginal may not communicate this explicitly. We can view group membership as an on-going fluid process, never to be taken for granted. Exercises to consider this aspect of a group, such as asking supervision group members to sculpt the group in relation to a particular family, can free up this positioning to allow more fruitful and flexible talk.

But which of our similarities and differences do we want to have noted or not in a live supervision group? As discursive psychologists have highlighted we are continually taking up or refusing subject positions and offering positions to others in constructing our narratives with each other (see Wetherell, 1998). These subject positions can be untroubled or troubled—are we happy to be the one who challenges, the one who does not speak, the one who always addresses issues of race, the person who does theory, the one who looks after relationships, to be central or at the margins? There are many other contexts that influence our positioning in groups which include our family and sibling relationships (Granville, this volume), our gender, our racialized identity (Bond, Ayo, this volume), our cultural identity, our learning narratives (Aggett, 2004), our voice entitlement (Boyd, this volume), and our professional scripts. At what point does a position tend to become an identity and a pattern of relating in a group become fixed rather than fluid? How can we disrupt the development of unhelpful rigidities?

Agazarian (2000) proposed that it is most useful to help individuals to claim subgroup alliances around similarities and that the ability to claim multiple subgroup memberships is a fruitful way through which similarities and differences can be explored and used by the group as a whole. This idea is readily applied to a live systemic supervision group and although challenges remain when there is a sole black member in an otherwise white group, or a single man in an all female group, for example, the invitation to claim multiple subgroup memberships incorporates a claiming of multiple and therefore fluid identities, and may therefore facilitate differences to be named and made use of. One constraint in pursuing a discussion about differences is located within the discourse of equality which sometimes becomes conflated with similarity. This may be an attempt to counter the way difference has so often been constructed as inequality and experienced as discriminatory in the wider context. Paradoxically the minimization of difference in a supervision group ends up replicating unhelpful disqualifying processes, such as when different meanings of racialization are not taken into account to the detriment of the black and minority ethnic professionals (see Ayo, this volume).

Visible differences such as those of gender and "race" are unavoidably disclosed (Hurst, 2008) but there are always differences which we can choose to let others know or not—such as our sexual orientation, religious beliefs, and physical health—which may have profound importance in the way that we construct our identities, and how we might be constructed by others. Differences have highly variable emotional loadings, particularly when they involve experiences of disqualification and discrimination as in racist and homophobic processes. Although the question, "Which differences in the group are easiest to manage and which hardest?" may not always be easy to answer, asking it can provoke discussions of the assumptions which group members are making.

Group narratives and group reflexivity

Individuals' previous experiences of groups also influence their positioning and narratives. Finding ways to identify these early on may help develop relational reflexivity regarding the ways in which this group will work together. Questions for everyone, including the supervisor, can be posed such as: What has been your worst group experience? What has been your best group experience? How do you explain this? What will need to happen for this group to work well for you and for others? What will you need to do to contribute? Such questions may help individuals and the group as a whole to locate themselves in a self-reflective space in relation to the workings of this new group.

It is useful to make time to review the narratives of the group from time to time. Chen and Noosbond (1999) propose that it is helpful to use an outside team to observe and reflect on a group's working together to "unstick" group processes which are handicapping (although of course, we need to be able to identify the stuckness first—work with particular families can often illuminate this). The language the group uses and its ways of thinking can be reflected on, as can group patterns and narratives. This can help group members think about their own positions and how they might position themselves differently in the group. As supervisors we don't often have the resources of such a team available, although supervision groups on a training course are able to do this for each other, and supervision groups in work settings can link to one in a different setting. Incorporating such an observing/reflecting process within a supervision group can also be useful, by allocating a couple of group members to observe a supervision session and then reflect on group talk, interactions, and positioning, alongside talk of the family and the therapy. However insiders may face more constraints in identifying and questioning shared assumptions and in opening up more challenging issues.

At the same time as we are constructing our own and others' positions we are participating in constructing an identity of our group and our relationship to it. What assumptions do we make about others which allow us to feel a group? When has a group become a group? Who is our "imagined community"? Which other imagined communities impact on this grouping? We may feel much more connected to another reference group. Some groups feel more of a group than others who might characterize themselves as a loose collection of individuals. This touches on our beliefs about groups and their characteristics, as well as what kind of a group we want to belong to, or want to help construct. Which dominant discourses about group-ness and group processes inform our thinking and practice as group members? Commonly it is thought that a group should be safe, should enable risk-taking, do "great" therapy, be good for learning, be creative, be fun, be interesting, and contain diversity. What do these discourses disallow? Are there any advantages of being in a group in which we can hide, or be bored, or in which there is a "tricky combination" of people? Can we find a way to make any of these group processes helpful to the therapy and to us at some level? How do we get into a position where we can do so?

A consultation with Jo about having to participate in a working group with whose agenda she did not agree and during which she was often bored and frustrated, posed the question of how she could best survive. Identifying the ways in which her preferred identity and positioning, that of challenging and questioning practices which she found problematic, were not experienced as helpful to herself or taken up by the rest of the group, she was then able to identify how she might use this experience to learn how to experiment with different positions, for example keeping silent, which she would be able to make use of in therapy and in her supervision group membership, among other contexts.

Playfulness can also help illuminate positioning and patterns of group interactions. Mason's (1994) idea of asking team members to put names in a hat, draw them out, and "perform" as one of their peers can lead to identification with a different position as well as experimentation with new ones.

Competition, conflict, and consensus

Proctor and Inskipp (2001) have argued that it is the supervisor's responsibility to manage group responses, addressing conflict, competitiveness, and other interactions which may hinder the group's work, as well as being responsible for creating a culture conducive to good group alliances and work, modelling respect, empathy, and straightforwardness. This argument raises two important questions for me: Who is responsible for what in a live supervision group? What assumptions about conflict and competitiveness are embedded in this proposition?

It does seem important that a supervisor takes charge of setting up the context for the supervision group, of holding conversations about the ground rules, the expectations, and the contract. Alongside clarifying issues of accountability and responsibility for the therapeutic work and for therapist development, it seems useful to flag up the task of how to keep an eye on group processes and functioning. Supervisors are responsible for trying to maintain their self-reflexivity in relation to the many different levels involved in live supervising a group, but they also strive to make transparent the components of supervision and work towards more collaborative positions.

In training supervisors, I became interested in the meanings which "competition" and "conflict" hold for individuals, as these notions often act as constraints for therapists and supervisors. Proctor and Inskipp, as many other writers, connote these negatively. Spending time unpacking these concepts with trainee supervisors (as well as thinking how they might do this with their supervisees), often leads to surprising conversations. Asking what "competition" means, when it is helpful, and when not, can track back to past contexts within the family and at school, as well as drawing out consideration of how competition might prove helpful or might hinder the supervision group. Finding a range of ways to think about competition as well as finding alternative descriptions for somebody we have defined as competitive can enable different processes to occur. Competition can enable supervisees to push their thinking and their therapeutic skills further. It is often possible to name competition and use it playfully within a group to good effect. Trainee supervisors can be nervous about having a qualified family therapist in their supervision group alongside those with less systemic training, often fearing that they will have nothing to offer, and can easily see the qualified family therapist through a lens of competing with them as supervisor. Being able to consider some of the dilemmas a qualified family therapist might face in terms of their relationship with their colleagues, feeling, among other issues, that they need to represent "good family therapy" or being anxious about the possibilities for their own development, can help a trainee supervisor interact quite differently with such a supervisee, finding ways to use their expertise for the benefit of the group.

Taking on board that we learn different things from different supervisors, different supervisees, and different therapists can often be a profound leap in experiential learning which can contribute to deconstructing competition further. Finding ways to construct such experiences might include swapping supervisors for a time, which can dissolve notions of the "right way" to do things as a lived experience rather than as a theoretical notion.

Supervisees often observe the supervisor closely with regard to exactly whose ideas they take up, and who they engage with most. So what happens when supervisors favour one supervisee and find another hard work? These alliances will have their effect on group processes and the therapeutic work and being able to identify this for oneself as supervisor can help process it in a way which is isomorphic to how one would work to engage all members of a family while feeling drawn to some more than others, although as we spend more time in supervision groups together this can also be more challenging. Finding other contexts which make sense of the ways that supervisees position themselves can be helpful.

Conflict similarly carries negative connotation but it can be very useful in conveying the emotional positioning that can accompany differences in view. The importance of maintaining group relational reflexivity when polarizations occur may be especially challenging if one feels drawn as a supervisor to one of the positions. The question about whether this is a continuation of an on-going polarization within the supervision group or isomorphic with the family is usually crucial to consider. If the latter realization, this can help the supervision group to think about how best to reflect on their own and the families' differences. If the former it can often take time to find ways to make sense of this and experiment with finding different positions or links at a different level. A polarization between two members which we identified in one supervision group was between focusing on resilience and focusing on pain. Using a visual method, such as drawing the semantic polarity—as Campbell and Groenbaek (2006) do in their organizational consultation work—and asking supervisees to take up different positions along its continuum can also work as an externalization of the conflict so that everyone can develop a different view. Sometimes identifying what the central polarity is can be a challenge but can itself be a task on which the group can collaborate.

A different kind of challenge is how to flag up the "pull to consensus" which can happen to groups, as it can to families, where it becomes hard for anyone to take up a different position, and some views go underground. This can result in the group taking up positions of certainty in relation to how the therapy should go and how to view the family. Perhaps live supervision groups need to ask themselves on a regular basis, "What do we agree about, what can we disagree about, what would happen if we were to disagree about this?" The meanings of disagreement can be complex if they pertain to ideas and values which feel central to individuals' preferred identities, but the inability to sustain multiplicity can be stifling for the therapeutic work and everyone involved. Strategic questions such as, "What would be the opposite of this idea? What would three alternative explanations be?" (Burck and Campbell, 2002) can sometimes provoke the group to entertain further difference.

I have also discovered that "challenge" is a word which carries layers of meanings for trainee supervisors, many of them problematic. It is as if trainee supervisors and supervision groups lose sight of the many ways they have found to be challenging within their therapeutic work, the many different things that can create a challenge (for example, asking a naïve question), which they can also use in supervision. It is as if, at times, "collaborative practice" and "challenge" are considered to be mutually exclusive. Being collaborative, of course, can in itself be experienced as challenging of certain beliefs.

Using personal resonances in group processes

The narrative and group supervision literature highlights the power of having conversations about personal and professional responses to each other's work, to disrupt unhelpful group patterns, and to generate new thinking for the therapist as well as the family (Proctor, 1997). "Outsider-witnessing practices" involve group members reflecting together on the work of one of their peers with a particular focus on the values and commitments they identify in it. This includes discussion of how these may influence members' own lives and work and can create generative and energizing processes for therapists and families (Fox et al. 2003).

How is the creativity of such processes best sustained? Asking supervision group members to address particular questions (for example, concerning values) in relation to the family and therapist can be very useful. However it may be helpful to consider whether feeding back in such a specific way creates any constraints, such as group members feeling that other ideas need to be excluded. On the other hand, not everything needs to be spoken; there will always be "inner conversations" (Rober, 1999: 209), inner dilemmas and questions which will ripple into the future. Acknowledging this may be the very thing which can help groups manage themselves well (Daniel, personal communication). Being aware of the limitations of falling into group rituals and ensuring variation in the ways in which personal resonances and other feedback are elicited will also be important.

Having permission to identify other contexts, such as family of origin or professional experiences, which inform one's contributions to group processes (Boland, 2006; Granville, this volume) can also enable the supervision group to understand group members' different positions in relation to the families they see.

Supervisor dilemmas

Supervisors often need to take charge of and make decisions when differences in groups cannot be easily reconciled. This may be an easier task in a training institute where it is clearer that the supervisor is accountable for the clinical work, than in an agency setting where these negotiations around responsibility and accountability may have been left vague. However, a supervisor's intervention of this kind can leave supervisees feeling disqualified or even disturbed if the decision made was counter to their own view. Being able to deconstruct one's own positioning as a supervisor is therefore important as this can help disrupt notions of "right" and "wrong" in processing these episodes after the session.

Supervisors, as many others in powerful positions, often carry unearned privilege (McIntosh, 1998). At the same time, supervisors (certainly trainee supervisors) often find it difficult to own this power (see also Trampuz and Berelj-Kobe, this volume). And indeed this is not always straightforward, as when the wider context constructs power relationships in contradictory ways (see Bond, this volume). Supervisees give the most weight to the perspectives and behaviour of the supervisor and can find it difficult to challenge them, especially in an evaluative training context. Supervisors therefore need both to name and declare their power, while at the same time finding ways to "really" give permission for supervisees to challenge them. Being able to empower the group, where, as noted previously, there are fewer power differentials than in an individual relationship, is key to de-centring the supervisor, to making it possible to elicit and use the richness of group thinking more productively. Interestingly trainee supervisors are sometimes just as worried about asking for feedback about their supervision and position in the group as they are about claiming their authority, and this affects the feedback they receive. Being able to own one's own mistakes, clumsy interventions, awkwardness, and blind spots as a supervisor can free supervisees to speak about the more uncomfortable processes in the supervision and in the therapy, and supports helpful group processes and resourceful therapeutic work.

How can we really enable "everything" to be examined and explored? The ability not to let misunderstandings close down conversation is as crucial in supervision groups as it is in therapy. And yet there are times when the supervisor needs to stop the talk and "act in the moment". Can our intentionality and belief that we are all doing our best to keep connected through our differences, for the families and our mutual learning, be enough to allow some of the tensions to be resolved in the future? Just as questions posed in a family session can evoke silence in the present and echo months later for family members, questions about the supervision group processes and the therapeutic work can lead to the development of different meanings in the future.

Questions for supervisors

During the work of a supervision group with families, the supervisor's identity too is in a process of construction. What kind of supervisor are we trying to be or trying to avoid being and with what effects? It may be difficult to keep remembering that this is a relational project. It is helpful to identify the kind of group style we prefer (for example, quick, funny, warm), to think why this might be and how this affects the groups we are working with if they correspond to our ideal or if they do not. When we work with a group that makes us feel like a terrible supervisor, are we still able to find a position from which to engage the group in group relational reflexivity?

Maintaining self-reflexivity as a supervisor is a never-ending task. When we are unable to generate this within the group itself, we often need to rely on resources such as having a consultant to our supervision. However, finding the time to pose our own questions can sometimes help create a self-reflective space.

Here are some possibilities:

> How have I engaged the group in paying attention to group patterns, positions, and narratives in relation to the families?

Which families are making us feel that we are a good supervision group? Which ones make us feel like we are a terrible supervision group? What does this mean?

Which supervisees make me feel like a good or terrible supervisor? How does this impact on group processes and work with the families?

How would I recognize when processes are too bland and the group is "over-polite", or conversely too critical, and how do I manage these processes?

How do group members' preferred learning styles fit with my own or create misunderstandings and how does this impact on group process?

What are my ideas about what should be public and what should remain private? How does that inform how I supervise?

What can be left unsaid? Do I always leave this unsaid?
Which alliances do I allow? Which do I disrupt?

Methods to enrich group processes

Systemic therapists have the advantage of being at ease with using structures and exercises to provoke helpful group processes and learning. These can all be brought to bear to address difficulties directly in group processes when these are hindering the work, or to disrupt these processes. A whole array of formats can be implemented at different times: assigning different roles behind the screen; allocating or swapping consulting pairs; using observing positions; holding sequential discussions; having one pair consulting to another pair; interviewing with a particular focus; use of reflecting processes; asking group members to attend to the positions they take up and its effects; setting a task to experiment with different positions; and the use of outsider consultation. Making use of these kinds of resources in combination with the belief that differences and multiplicity are beneficial for the therapeutic work as well as for mutual learning should give supervisors and supervision groups plenty of room for manoeuvre.

Conclusions

I have argued in this chapter for the importance of putting group-relational reflexivity on the agenda and keeping it there, in our therapeutic work with families. Teams who are polarized or cannot speak about critical differences will not find it easy to be helpful to the families who are consulting them, and indeed may be hazardous for them.

If we really believe in the helpfulness of multiple perspectives then we need to be able to "live" this well enough in our supervision groups in order for it to be persuasive for families. This may be isomorphic with the findings of a research study (Frosh et al. 1996) I was involved in some years ago where we found that during "successful" therapy (considered so by the family and the therapist) the family had moved to using a greater number of discourses. If supervision groups are able to offer flexibility and coherence in complexity then they are much more likely to engage and work with families successfully. We therefore need to work to keep them able to do so.

References

Agazarian, Y.M. (2000). *Systems-centered Group Psychotherapy: How to Develop a Working Group*. Good Enough Press.

Aggett, P. (2004). Learning Narratives in Group Supervision: Enhancing Collaborative Learning. *Journal of Systemic Therapies*. 23(3): 36–50.

Andersen, T. (ed.) (1991). *The Reflecting Team*. New York: Norton.

Anderson, H. and Jensen, P. (2007). *Innovations in the Reflecting Process: The inspirations of Tom Andersen*. London: Karnac Books.

Asen, E. (2002). Multiple Family Therapy: An Overview. *Journal of Family Therapy*. 24: 3–16.

Baker, P. (2009). Transition Holds Clues to How Obama Will Govern. *The New York Times*. January 19, 2009.

Bateson, G. (1970). *Mind and Nature: A Necessary Unity (Advances in Systems Theory, Complexity, and the Human Sciences)*. Hampton Press.

Becker, C., Chasin, L., Chasin, R., Herzig, M., and Roth, S. (1995). From Stuck Debate to New Conversation on Controversial Issues: A Report from the Public Conversations Project. *Journal of Feminist Family Therapy*. 7(1&2): 143–163.

Boland, C. (2006). Functional Families: Functional Teams. *Australia & New Zealand Journal of Family Therapy*. 27(1): 22–28.

Burck, C. and Campbell, D. (2002). Training Systemic Supervisor: Multi-layered Learning. In: Campbell, D. and Mason, B. (eds) *Perspectives on Supervision*. London: Karnac Books. Chapter 4.

Burck, C., Hildebrand, J., and Mann, J. (1996). Women's Tales: Systemic Groupwork with Mothers Post-Separation. *Journal of Family Therapy*. 18(2): 163–182.

Burnham, J. (1993). Systemic Supervision: The Evolution of Reflexivity in the Context of the Supervisory Relationship. *Human Systems*. 3/4: 349–381.

Campbell, D. and Groenbaek, M. (2006). *Taking Positions in the Organization*. London: Karnac Books.

Chen, M-W. and Noosbond, J.P. (1999). "Un-sticking" the Stuck Group System: Process Illumination and the Reflecting Team. *Journal of Systemic Therapies*. 18(3): 23–36.

Daniel, G. (personal communication).

Fox, H., Tench, C., and Marie (2003). Outsider-witness Practices and Group Supervision. *International Journal of Narrative Therapy and Community Work*, 4.

Friedman, S. (ed.) (1995). *The Reflecting Team in Action*. New York: Guilford Press.

Frosh, S., Burck, C., Strickland-Clark, L., and Morgan, K. (1996). Engaging with Change: A Process Study of Family Therapy. *Journal of Family Therapy*. 18(2): 141–162.

Hurst, A. (2008). *Systemic Therapists' Use of Self-Disclosure in Therapy*. Unpublished Doctorate in Systemic Psychotherapy Thesis. Tavistock Clinic.

Liddle, H.A. and Saba, G.S. (1983). On Context Replication: The Isomorphic Relationship of Training and Therapy. *Journal of Strategic and Systemic Therapies*. 2: 3–11.

Mason, B. (1994). Experimenting with Change: An Exercise in Team Consultation. *ANZ Journal of Family Therapy*. 15(2): 111–113.

McIntosh, P. (1998). White Privilege: Unpacking the Invisible Knapsack. In: McGoldrick, M. (ed.) *Re-Visioning Family Therapy*. New York: Guilford Press. Chapter 11.

Monk, G., Drewery, W., and Winslade, J. (1997). Using Narrative Ideas in Group Work: A New Perspective. In: Forester-Miller, H. and Kottler, J.A. (eds) *Issues and Challenges for Group Practitioners*. Denver: Love Publishing Company.

Nel, P. (2006). Trainee Perspectives on their Family Therapy Training. *Journal of Family Therapy*. 28(3): 307–328.

Proctor, K. (1997). The Bells that Ring: A Process for Group Supervision. *ANZJ Family Therapy*. 18(4): 217–220.

Proctor, B. and Inskipp, F. (2001). Group Supervision. In: Scaife, J. (ed) *Supervision in the Mental Health Professions*. London: Routledge. Chapter 6.

Ratliff, D., Wampler, K., and Morris. G. (2000). Lack of Consensus in Supervision. *Journal of Marital and Family Therapy*. 26(3): 373–384.

Rober, P. (1999). The Therapist's Inner Conversation: Some Ideas about the Self of the Therapist, Therapeutic Impasse and the Process of Reflection. *Family Process*. 38: 209–228.

Vassallo, T. (1998). Narrative Group Therapy with the Seriously Mentally Ill. *ANZJFT*, 19(1): 15–26.

Wetherell, M. (1998). Positioning and Interpretive Repertoires. *Discourse and Society*. 9: 387–412.

White, M.B. and Russell, C.S. (1997). Examining the Multifaceted Notion of Isomorphism in Marriage and Family Therapy Supervision: A Quest for Conceptual Clarity. *Journal of Marital and Family Therapy*. 23(3): 315–333.

CHAPTER EIGHT

Times past, present, and future: Revisiting a supervision group experience

Gwyn Daniel, Grania Clarke and Reena Nath

This chapter addresses some processes involved when supervisors experience themselves as "unsuccessful" in working with a clinical training group. While this term, is, of course, subjective, partial, and at variance with the orthodoxies of postmodern thought, it is probably a common experience for supervisors. We explore, from the perspectives of supervisor and supervisees, the various contexts and positions that played a part in constructing this experience, one that can be difficult to share within the professional community. Some learning points will be offered as well as reflections on the gap between theoretical ideals and lived practice and on the significance of revisiting these processes after a period of time.

During clinical training in systemic psychotherapy, two years are spent within an intense context of learning and gaining new experiences of self and others. The self of the trainee can feel raw, vulnerable, and open to many challenging understandings. Given the power of the supervisor through her responsibility for the clinical work and her role in the assessment process, supervisees frequently find that relationships to authority are evoked. Within this context, certain aspects of self are performed and expanded while others are constrained or hidden. This, it can be argued, applies equally to supervisors. The evaluative context which gives rise to anxieties and dilemmas over power and authority for trainees can have parallel effects on supervisors, to whom the authority of this aspect of the course is delegated (Trampuz and Berelj-Kobe, this volume).

When experience of clinical supervision is satisfying and rewarding, it can mark a turning point in a professional trajectory and indeed many systemic psychotherapists talk about the profound effect their relationship with the supervisor had on their entire self-narrative as clinician. Certainly a clinician will rarely again receive such intense and focused feedback on their clinical work and this is a unique opportunity for growth. When therapists go on to train as supervisors they will often refer to their "internal supervisor", referring to this crucial period. What can we take this to mean? Does our development continue to be to some extent dominated by the internalized "shadow presence" of the supervisor, evoking a particular narrative of learning and of therapy? Or does the intense learning experience itself create durable tools for self-reflection, self-evaluation, and creative manoeuvring that continue to evolve and adapt and thus serve the new contexts within which the ex-trainee finds him or herself?

What, however, of those experiences in clinical supervision where there was not such a good fit, which seemed to be marked by tension, frustration, or mistrust? How do such experiences live on and can they too become incorporated into useful learning? What of the supervisor who finishes a group feeling that she has been responsible for/immersed in a process that has not gone well? What of trainees who finish training feeling that they could/should have been able to develop their clinical skills more, learnt more, been more successful? Is the supervisor's learning from this only to benefit her next group or is there any value in re-exploring it with the group itself? How does the passage of time serve to rigidify or transform the effects of these learning experiences? It is often only after a period of time that the hidden narratives of trainees' experiences within supervision are spoken out loud. They can, at the least, provide useful hypotheses for supervisors in their subsequent practice and for group members who themselves train as supervisors.

In writing this chapter, after a time lapse of over seven years, we hope to provide some descriptions and understandings of these processes, especially their emotional content, and to highlight gaps in the supervisory literature that could benefit from further elaboration.

First, "failures" in clinical supervision have received scant attention. In the supervisory literature, and, to a slightly lesser extent, the clinical literature, we unsurprisingly find that successful stories are selected out for survival. Difficulties and impasses are generally described as a backdrop to successful strategies in overcoming them. Clinical literature contains rich and detailed descriptions of clients' interactions with therapists within the intimate space of therapy. Sometimes these are anonymized or sometimes co-authored, claiming a public narrative space. This is less evident in the supervisory literature. Most writing tends to outline practices and procedures for effective systemic supervision. Case examples are of a rather brief or generalized nature, or geared towards specific learning experiences rather than emotional impasses or conflicts. In a small field, there may be a greater fear of exposure and breaches of confidentiality with supervision than in clinical work. Additionally, is there an anxiety that exposing difficulties to public scrutiny may lead clinicians to suspect that their training (and therefore, by extension, they) have not been good enough? In a chapter written in the early 1980s from a trainee perspective, Lowenstein and Reder (1982) point to the intense emotions aroused in trainees in live supervision. They describe, as common experiences, high levels of anxiety related to shame of self-exposure, loss of autonomy, and challenges to competence as well as difficulties in relationships with authority, represented by the supervisor's position. A more recent article "Deconstructing Agnes" (Lee and Littlejohns, 2006) points to the impact of self-doubt and anxiety on all levels of the supervision group process.

While there are a few co-authored papers between supervisor and supervisees (Anderson and Swim, 1995; Barratt et al. this volume; Charlés et al. 2005; Daniel et al., this volume) these are more likely to constitute "prideful" stories. Kavner and McNab (2005) have, however, written insightfully about experiences of shame in clinical work and about the relationship between shame, secrecy, and isolation, ideas which can also be applied to supervision. In the more private world of psychotherapy, the therapist's shame may remain hidden, since, unless a complaint is made, he/she can choose whether or not to bring this experience to supervision. In a clinical supervision group, the supervisor's failings are very much in the public domain and may lead to acute anxieties about being judged by colleagues or by the training institution. This easily leads to supervisors generating such defensive descriptions as "a difficult group", trainees who have "problems with authority", or who are "not reflective". These lineal and blaming descriptions may be buttressed by colleagues in an attempt to be supportive to the supervisor. Trainees are also likely to fear that the institute will not address the issues, that it will defend the supervisor or blame them for the apparent failure and may in turn generate descriptions such as "difficult supervisor" or "impossible to please". "Failure" in supervision can be one of the most excruciating and shaming experiences in professional life and yet, like similar experiences in therapy, can be usefully explored in terms of the supervisor's personal, professional, and institutional contexts and the relational processes within the group.

The second gap in the literature relates to the personal position of the supervisor. How do supervisors' own development and past histories of supervision influence them in their task? How is it that they do well with some groups and less well with others? What processes "faze" them and how does their own role within the training organization affect them? Although courses in supervision pay attention to issues of personal development (Burck and Campbell, 2002) the personhood of the qualified supervisor is rarely addressed, possibly because issues of status and prestige weigh more heavily, especially on training courses. One of the most important aspects of the process is the relationship between epistemologies, aspirations, and practices. Supervisors are likely to adhere to a set of guiding theoretical principles which create "ideal practices" against which they judge and evaluate their transactions. Nowhere is this more striking than in the domain of the postmodern supervisor, committed to the bringing forth and enhancement of "localized knowledges", to respectful and collaborative practices, and to diminishing, where possible, the hierarchical distance between supervisor and supervisees. The tensions between the ideal and the actual are also discussed elsewhere in this volume (Bertrando, Boston, Berelj-Kobe and Trampuz).

Third, systemic literature rarely addresses group process itself (Clarke and Rowan, 2009; Granville, Burck, this volume).

Surprisingly in our field, most writing has tended to focus on the supervisor/supervisee dyad rather than on the group itself, implying that the process consists of separate dyadic interactions rather than being contextualized and influenced by the group as a whole. This leads to a tendency to foreground the person of the supervisor and background the relational patterns of the group. How do groups influence supervisors? If we define group process as "the forces in existence that exert influence over all aspects of the events that occur in a group, we need to consider the processes operating in the group as a significant context for the behaviour of that individual" (Thompson and Khan, 1988: 23). Group process theory considers groups to contain ambivalent relationships related to the interplay between group coherence (the forces in the group to continue) and group disruptiveness (the forces in the group to break up). How do groups manage processes in which some members fare better than others, where there is a good fit with the style of the supervisor for some members but not for others? What significant events and histories affect the way that creative learning takes place? What consultation is helpful to groups when they have difficulties, and how should consultants position themselves between the needs of the group and the wish to support a colleague? Experienced systemic supervisors have many helpful strategies for developing positive group interactions, but sometimes, with the best of intentions, these do not have the desired effect because the emotional climate seems wrong or hidden loyalties and strong allegiances to alternative ideas emerge. Selvini and Selvini-Palazzoli (1991) highlight problems occurring in teams which can arguably be applied to supervision groups. They point to competition between members, marginalization of members through coalitions and scapegoating, rigid hierarchies leading to impotence and passivity or alternatively "adolescent disobedience". In addition, they suggest that the supervisor may become an object of criticism for the team, or the team may become passive in their role, leaving all responsibility to the supervisor.

Context

The clinical supervision group took place in the second year of clinical training on a Masters in Systemic Psychotherapy. It was, at the time, the practice for groups to change supervisors at the end of the first year. The group consisted of four trainees: two men and two women. The cultural identities were English, Irish, and Indian. There were two psychologists, one social worker, and one psychiatric nurse. The supervisor, whose cultural identity was Welsh, also had social work as her core training and joined the course and the institution at the same time as taking over the clinical supervision group.

Given that we are here, most unusually for a systemic paper, drawing out the more negative threads of the group's narrative, it is essential to point out that this does not, of course, represent the whole story. The group was certainly not a catastrophe, no complaints were made by trainees to course management, nobody left prematurely and all members have qualified and are achieving success in their various systemic activities. While we could argue that, because of this, it feels safe enough to reflect back on this process, nevertheless raising the spectre of "failure" carries emotional force over the years and demonstrates the risks of using this description. One member said of an earlier draft: *"My response to the opening paragraph of the chapter was a shocking disbelief. For which individuals was the supervision a failure? Reading the negative account of your role of as supervisor I feel as if I was not there at all ... your input has been immeasurable. I don't feel I can say more as it doesn't fit with the theme of failure!"*

Handover

The narrative begins at the moment of handover between supervisors and the events, personal and institutional, that contextualized it will be described from the positions of both supervisors and from various group members.

The first supervisor (interviewed for the conference presentation by GC and GD) describes the experience by positioning both supervisors within a discourse of "directive/non-directive" and evoking the figures of her own past supervisors.

"Thinking about myself as a supervisor I think about the context of my own training where I was definitely situated between X who was very didactic and directive and, Y who was indirectly directive ... at the non-directive end of directive and I'd put myself right in the middle of that and I'd put you (GD) between me and X.

So, unpacking challenging, there are so many different ways of challenging so I think you probably intervene more directly. I'd be more likely to ask questions, do that kind of intervention, whereas you'd be more likely to say 'I want you to do this; not that I don't do the other as well. I thought the group were in for a great treat but no, they weren't going to have it!'"

Group narratives

While obviously our (GC and RN) perspectives on the handover from first to second supervisor are not identical, what we present here are some perspectives we hold in common. It has been an immensely interesting experience trying to "reconstruct" our narratives of the feelings and processes of events that took place all that time ago. It may be that this has resulted in a rather frozen narrative as we have not had the opportunity to reflect on these experiences together from our current positions.

It had long been the tradition on our course to change supervisors at the end of year one. There had been a great deal of resistance to this within the student group as a whole based on the argument that we had developed a "secure base" (Byng Hall, 1995) for learning in the groups and our further learning would be compromised by the instigation of too much change. To some extent our whole course group had taken a rather oppositional stance to the authority of the course as represented by this issue.

We were aware that, although we did not know her, our new supervisor was a close friend and colleague of our "old" supervisor. This led us to be unsure about what sorts of conversations they might have had about us as a group; were these professional conversations or those more akin to those one might have with a close friend?

In some ways our fight to stay together made it difficult for us to openly talk about our differences in style and our beliefs about therapy in particular. It could be argued that focusing on the difference between us as a group and our second supervisor helped us to avoid the perhaps more difficult conversations about our own differences and the levels of competition between us as a group.

As another group member commented: *"I felt a fraud and a small person in that group, because you all had a lot more experience with kids.*

I felt (first supervisor) had a much more engaging warm style. She seemed to spend more time on 'our learning edges' and seemed more interested in coaching. Even though there are so called multiple realities in this business she was clearer in my view what was expected and where the 'Tavi bar' was set. I wasn't very clear of what I had to do at the end of the second year to get a satisfactory report, the objectives were not clear. So I just felt criticized sometimes without the constructive feedback. Sometimes, though, Gwyn was supportive."

As time went on we experienced our supervisor as working hard to forge individual relationships with us and in many ways this lead us to stick together more, almost becoming a sibling-like gang, resisting the authority she represented to us in her role as supervisor. We became more and more resistant to her ideas which at time came across as "orders" and refused comments aimed at opening up a space for difference.

Another group member commented: *"For me the difficulties in year two were coping with the change. It was so unsettling and I missed (first supervisor) but I liked you right off. But a need to be part of the group encouraged me to share the doubts of other group members."*

The supervisor's narrative (GD)

Owing to a family bereavement, I started work with the group two weeks late. This meant that the carefully planned, more leisurely, and reflective ways of carrying out handover and introductions were rushed. I had various dilemmas which gradually crystallized. The first was that, although I was a highly experienced supervisor and had run Masters trainings for many years, I was new to the culture of this particular course. The group were, in many respects, more conversant with the course culture and regulations as well as with the clinical procedures in this particular institution. Normally this would not be an issue; I would have used my "not-knowing" creatively. However we can underestimate what happens when we are not able to access our usual robustness and when we are caught unawares by our anxiety and sense of incompetence. I had a dilemma in talking about my bereavement. I did not want to join this group as a vulnerable person, nor share these feelings in the absence of a prior relationship. Having already lost time, I opted to try to convey to the group that they did not need to worry about me.

This may have had a disempowering effect on the group by not giving them an opportunity to be helpful. In deciding not to discuss these personal issues, I was being loyal to a family story about myself as strong and good at coping and a life-long pattern of not readily asking for help.

Additionally I had a sense of having to live up to the expectations placed on me. Before the handover, the first supervisor told the group how lucky they were to be getting someone who would be very good and was likely to be challenging, something she thought the group needed and would respond well to. "Challenging" is one of the more loaded and ambiguous terms in this context with supervisors often unsure about whether they do too much or too little of it and trainees sensitive to the distinction between "positive" and "negative" challenge. Responding to a subtle injunction to be challenging may involve a supervisor reading her interactions within this parameter and being less tolerant of times when she might deem herself "not challenging enough". This connects with our personal narratives and histories about these processes. Anxiety about making up for lost time added to what may have become an impatient "edge" which did not meet with a positive response from the group. I had not appreciated quite how sorry they were to be changing supervisors at all, nor had I correctly divined that their expectations of the second year were somewhat different from my own.

Assessment

The group developed a "myth" about the nature of our supervisor's evaluation. At the end of the first year we presented our work to a panel of four staff members, including our first supervisor. We had all passed this and had been given detailed feedback about our areas for development.

Assessment of work in the second year consisted of our supervisors presenting an excerpt of our work to the other supervisors. The myth developed that, as we had "made it" through the first year, we were therefore on track for passing at the end of the second year. This myth enabled us, I think, to minimize the level of difference in the group in terms of experience, clinical skill, and confidence as well as appease our anxiety about the process of evaluation.

As the supervisor, I was surprised to discover that there was no "end of course panel" at which trainees showed their own work but that I would present their videos to the other supervisors and the external examiner. In being critical of this, I was being loyal to other more familiar methods of assessment. I was astonished at the group's assertion that they had had their main assessment and that the second year was more about consolidation and developing their clinical style rather than being assessed on whether they had reached a satisfactory level. My response to this assumption, which was to challenge it, must have increased the group's mistrust about how I would represent them at the end of the course. It could thus be said that at this stage there was an almost perfect lack of fit!

Theories, practices, and personal styles

How do we enact theoretical frameworks and how do we account for interactions that seem to depart from our theory? One effect of negative feedback is to find ourselves depicted as, and indeed enacting, the kind of supervisor we do not wish to be. My philosophy draws upon postmodernism and social constructionism in my attention to the power of societal and cultural discourses to define identities, in questioning essentialist assumptions about the way "things are" and my confidence that creative thinking lies in dialogue and in an expansion of discursive repertoires as "team mind" emerges from diverse perspectives and positions. While mindful of the way power and hierarchy contextualize the persuasiveness of some discursive positions over others, I nevertheless believe that supervisors are most effective when they take a position and simultaneously convey that this position is contingent on time, place, and relational context and is open to being challenged. The following feedback was therefore disconcerting to say the least!

"Our experience was of moving from supervisory interventions such as 'which of those ideas do you think it would be most useful to bring back to the family and in what way?' To something more like 'having listened to the ideas I think it would be most useful for you to say ... in this way' and 'I think that this really shook the culture in the group from a very postmodern culture where different ideas (including those of the supervisor) were seen as simply that and the trainee therapist was invited to 'choose' between them a bit like using a reflecting team model with a family. While *this model obviously has its difficulties (in that some ideas are more useful than others and this is at least in part related to experience and the role and position of the supervisor) it had promoted a non critical and free space for 'thinking out loud'."*

In this narrative, both supervisors' positions and "styles" could have been polarized and exaggerated over time with the one being read against the idealized "other" in ways that both would struggle to recognize. However I also reflect that my style, close perhaps to that of Bertrando's (2007) depiction of the therapist as "opinionated partner", needed a context of mutual trust and warm personal engagement in order to flourish and enhance learning. Articulating a theoretical position is one thing; for example, that positions taken are invitations to be interrogated, but the receiving context is another. Given the struggle to gain acceptance by the group, assertiveness was frequently experienced as authoritarian and dialogue closed down rather than opened up. Additionally I reflected back on how much I might have been trying to prove my competence and did not allow enough time and space to get to know the group.

"I think our relationships with each other were stronger than with Gwyn and that was a problem for her initially. She was facing the same challenges as we were about proving your competence yet being free/confident enough to take a risk and be yourself. But it wasn't a helpful parallel process."

This need to prove competence was picked up by the group in relation to the therapeutic work. What is important to highlight is that as well as staying together as a group we also kept working with several families from the previous year. In some ways the experience of seeing the same families with different supervisors highlighted further their contrasting styles. It took us some time to adjust to the style of our new supervisor. As developing therapists we had the expectation of moving towards more autonomy in the therapy session. However the different, more directive stance of our new supervisor created a tension in relation to this expectation. The experience of an increase in the number of interventions and clear directives were incongruent both with the style of our previous supervisor and with our expectations. Our sense is that this led us as a group to be even more resistant to our new supervisor's ideas and suggestions and we at times complained about her "style".

As a group we had different learning styles which presented each of us with different challenges. Kolb (1984) highlights how teachers need to assess student learning styles to find a fit between these and teaching methods. Kolb's model of learning proposes that immediate or concrete experiences provide a basis for observations and reflections which are subsequently assimilated and distilled into abstract concepts. These can then be actively tested and in turn can create new experiences (Burnham, this volume).

Kolb argues that different people naturally prefer different learning styles related to their prior experiences and, we would argue, are heavily gendered (see Gilligan, 1993). An individual's preferred learning style is made up from two separate choices about how one "grasps experience" and how one "transforms" it into something meaningful. Thus, for example, we might prefer to "watch" or "do" in terms of how we grasp an experience and either "think" or "feel" in terms of how we transform the experience. Thus Kolb presents a 2 × 2 matrix of four learning styles as follows: Diverging (watching and feeling); Assimilating (watching and thinking); Converging (doing and thinking); and Accommodating (doing and feeling).

One member of the group was clear from the start that he liked to first try things out and then see how they go. In Kolb's terms this trainee had an "accommodating" learning style and learnt best through hands-on practical experience with space for reflection afterwards. To what extent should supervisors adapt their style to those of trainees or do trainees need to adapt their learning to the style of the supervisor? I think that our view was the former and we felt our supervisor's was the latter! Another tension in the group was the extent to which we wanted to learn "skills" and the amount of reflection and thinking we wanted to do. In the words of one group member: *"With hindsight I think that the focus was (wrongly) on our beliefs about therapy, on our thinking, not on our actual behaviour ... it should be on the basis of what you did or didn't do and what you need to do to put it right. That's how I learn best ... I'm not sure exploring my beliefs about therapy is the best use of my time."* This difference was split mainly along gender lines with the men in the group favouring "skills" and the women "feelings". While this area has been well researched in the area of higher education (Hayes and Flannery, 2000) there has been little written about its effect on supervision groups dynamics. One group member wrote: *"The team did things to the supervision climate too. Some members were more active than others. For example there was a gender split with the women doing more of the tasks of being team members while the men played a less active role, almost to the point of passivity."*

Personal development

As a supervisor, I (GD) was committed to working at the interface between the personal and professional, identifying "learning edges" for trainees, engaging with habitual ways of thinking and acting which may be either resources or constraints in the development of therapeutic range. The personal development side of clinical supervision is designed to enhance therapists' awareness of our responses to different emotional material and to encourage mindfulness about what we do routinely and what is divergent. This involves reflecting on how different aspects of self are brought forth in different contexts and tracking the accompanying physical and emotional markers.

Engaging with and working at these edges involves groups in some intense processes. Woking at this level of intensity may not work for all trainees, especially if the relationship has got off to a mutually mistrustful start. One trainee commented: *"I think she likes intensity and believes that is a powerful learning experience and useful for families. She may be right but at what cost?"*

For this cohort, personal development was run by other tutors in a separate group for all course members; some trainees, especially the two men in the group, had been critical of this group and complained that it had not been useful. While extra time was allocated in the supervision group for processing clinical matters and developing theory–practice links, it was not formally designated as personal and professional development (PPD). The space and indeed the value of the crucial process of personal development were contested, with some trainees valuing it and others declaring it pointless and a waste of time. The supervisor's response was to keep raising these matters; not knowing the trainees' personal histories made this trickier to navigate. The borderline between intensity and intrusiveness may have become troubling for some trainees; for others the lack of a positive group ethos meant a loss of the intimacy that nurtures creative conversations.

Feedback and challenge (GD)

How were the feelings of rebelliousness within the group expressed? Nothing I did quite seemed to work. Interventions in the clinical context seemed to fall flat. As I became more anxious, so I became more directive and so the group seemed to become more stubborn. This increased my anxiety about whether families were getting a good enough service and whether all the trainees would reach the required standard by the end of the course. I would have done well to remember Gianfranco Cecchin's observation (personal communication) about directive supervision—that trainees who don't like being directed but cannot overtly rebel are likely to do so by performing the intervention incompetently! The atmosphere in the group became de-energized, it seemed difficult to access anyone's creativity, and I came to dread the clinical afternoon, feeling myself to be the object of criticism and feeling ashamed that I was not able to "turn things around". While I had various possible responses available, one of which being to ask for help from the staff group, I hesitated, feeling that I "ought" to be able to manage. I did not want to blame the group for the difficulties. I responded by trying harder; yet the way I tried seemed to lead both to taking more control and feeling that I had less. I could be said to have enacted a position analogous to the alcoholic's "pride", as described by Bateson (1973) in *The Cybernetics of "Self"*, where the epistemological error is that of acting as if mind is transcendent rather than immanent, that is, located in the ecology of all the group's interactions within their wider context.

Control and responsibility are recursively linked and it can be argued that over-responsibility on the part of a supervisor risks draining the life force out of a group. *"Gwyn came along, clearly very talented, and I wondered if sometimes she didn't allow the trainees time to find their own solutions and own feet without rescuing too much."* The relationship between responsibility and criticism is a crucial one. When responsibility becomes individualized rather than relational (Gergen and McNamee, 1999) the risk is of implying that others are not good enough and the result is de-motivating. The process of taking more responsibility rather than less also runs counter to the usual developmental trajectory of supervision groups where members gradually assume increased responsibility for their work with the supervisor taking a more facilitative and reflective role.

Acknowledging disappointment

At the group's annual consultation (conducted with another staff member who was not a supervisor) some difficulties were aired and the group able to acknowledge their mutual disappointments. Stating openly that, while she liked group members as individuals, she did not, at this moment, like them as a group, was experienced by the supervisor as crossing a threshold she had hitherto avoided. The group were able to comment on how they did not feel that the supervisor was accessing their competence. While this consultation did not seem to be immediately transformative, it laid the ground for a more open and fluid dialogue.

Two other moments stood out for me as supervisor. One was when I gave a theory lecture to the whole course. Following this, one member of the group told me that another course member said that they had really enjoyed the lecture and could not understand why they (the group) had been complaining so much about their supervisor! The honesty and directness of this comment both exposed and confirmed the fear (that I was being talked about negatively in a public domain) and transformed it into something much more benign and humorous. Feedback such as this from a trainee is a gift because it can act as a context marker for trust and intimacy. Indeed the trainee's later reflection for this chapter that *"had I been aware of the distress you were going through, instead of thinking that you were robustly able to handle our opposition, I could not have made that remark. If I had been really critical I could not said what I did as openly as I did"* has helped me reflect in turn that it was the very assumption of this robustness and the warmth and humour with which the message was delivered that was so helpful to me.

Another significant event was in a skills development session. Following consultation with the group about how they wanted to use this session, and because I would be arriving a little late, I devised an exercise aimed at addressing the issues the group said they were interested in exploring, left a copy for each member, and asked them to prepare so they could start when I joined. When I did so, I discovered that the group did not like this exercise and had decided that it wasn't what they wanted to do after all! Having hoped that this would be another turning point when things might get better, I felt so upset that I told the group to decide for themselves what they wanted to do and walked out, saying I would return in five minutes. Feeling tearful, I walked down the corridor and, as I did so, a memory flashed into my mind of my own supervisor, fifteen years earlier, walking out on my group when we were in a recalcitrant mood and I remembered that it was from this very room. I returned with a broad smile, having made this multi- positional connection over time, and both I and the group were able to engage more creatively.

The two moments discussed above were examples of opportunities to recover a precious aspect of self. In this case humour and playfulness were valued parts of my supervisory persona and being unable to access them was disconcerting and demoralizing. Humour in supervision, as indeed in therapy, is a multi-faceted resource, enabling dilemmas to be named and explored from playful as well as serious perspectives. It involves shifts of context and level (Bateson, 1973) and the subversion of rigid categories of thought. It is especially helpful when giving challenging feedback, allowing giver and receiver to make connections which do not have to seem too toxic. Moments when we recover aspects of self do not occur, however, as a result of searching for them; they are generally random and arise in unexpected ways, in contrast to the dogged search for "turning points" as outlined above.

Learning points

"Decentring" the supervisor

Being in a hurry to "get down to work" had various negative effects. It did not allow time for "not-knowing", to explore the culture and history of the group and, in particular, to address the wider contextual issues. To this end, getting too quickly down to business, which can have positive effects with beginning groups (Barratt et al., this volume) can have the reverse effect when the group as a unit has already worked together. It may lead the group to feel that what they are already doing is devalued. Observing each trainee do a session without intervening at all but simply watching the group interact would have been a wiser course.

What supervisors do can be based on sound systemic/constructionist thinking but is only useful and will only enhance learning if there is a receptive emotional climate. For example, I (GD) find that to invite the group to interview me at the beginning of our relationship normally sets up mutual and more egalitarian processes, but, in this case, it was constrained by, among other things, the group's uncertainty about how they could or should ask about my bereavement. In retrospect, an outside consultant could have allowed more collaborative sharing of mutual expectations and anxieties.

The relationship of both therapists and supervisors to the theme of responsibility deserves further exploration. Enabling group members to take responsibility for what they want to learn is a truism of adult learning but easily eroded by anxieties about standards for qualifying or by a difficulty in addressing widely different levels of experience and capability within the group. Succeeding or failing can be the single most difficult difference to discuss and group loyalties may mean that supervisors are isolated in addressing this. If a person seems unlikely to finish within the time, it is helpful to situate this as part of a learning trajectory where everyone has a developmental time frame which is as much organized by contexts outside the group as within it. I have learnt to locate my own responsibility more within the domain of creating contexts for collaborative dialogue and expanding clinical potential rather than being too fixed on my responsibility for the final outcome.

One important learning point for supervisors is to have the confidence to name processes that do not seem to be working and to invite the group's expertise in finding ways forward. I find it helpful to use this experience to talk with new groups about those processes which are likely to bring out the best in me and those likely to bring out the worst. I am open to being questioned about aspects of my personal history that might give rise to these patterns. One of the joys of clinical supervision is the way that a group which holds each other's narratives and knows each other's "learning edges" can be finely attuned to moments in therapy and in group interaction when a habitual stuck pattern is transcended or conversely when a therapist cannot seem to access their usual range. These processes are equally valid for supervisors so that when we find ourselves acting in ways that seem not to reflect aspects of self we usually rely on, this can evoke curiosity about the context rather than a reaction of defensively "making do".

Conclusion

It will be evident that there were not only multiple narratives within the group about its processes but also multiple levels at which these processes could be understood; the impact of the wider course context, the lack of fit between supervisor and group's expectations, and gender patterns are to name but a few. That the main input has been from the two women in the group, while on the one hand, regrettable, can also be seen as being faithful to the gendered divisions in the group from all those years ago!

Reflecting back on the experience of writing this, Grania comments that there is something to be said about the continued potency of group process even when the group no longer exists! She adds: *"When Gwyn asked me to be involved in the presentation for the conference I was terrified but also felt it was important as a way of thinking about and perhaps resolving some of the issues that had been left. While I had initially thought that we would do the presentation as a group this did not happen for a variety of reasons. Most of the group correspondence has been via e-mail and this had a significant effect on the power of different voices and the resulting positive or negative emphasis of the group descriptions. The attempt to include all voices had the effect of giving the men's voices, through their e-mail comments and reflections more power than perhaps they should as they were simply presented in written form rather than in conversation with all the questioning and challenging that conversations involve—it is such a shame that we could not have had a 'proper' conversation about all of these things—but maybe that has been the enduring pattern of the group? Perhaps another dynamic was the extent to which the negative narrative was capable of being challenged retrospectively and the risk of allowing different views within the group. Reading your (Reena's) e-mail conversations did make me think if I had been too negatively influenced by this—what stopped me from focusing on the more positive memories in the way that Reena had been able to? Were our experiences so different or was it how we held onto them afterwards; is there something to do with style—I know that I learn most by examining what has not gone so well. ... enough said!"*

Reena comments: *"It was immensely gratifying to be a part of the narrative again. This time when I read it I felt like I was back in our Tuesday afternoon clinical room. I recognize the acrid smell of our combined failures to connect. I remember some sessions with families where even as an observer it felt excruciatingly futile, and how the futility was a part of us, the group. I can now understand why it was important to write this paper, and to painfully put together the pieces of what happened then between us. While I have been aware that leaving after the course ended and living so far away has made me more likely to connect to the positive memories that I have of our supervision group, I too have had unanswered questions about what was happening with us that we were not engaging with the families we were seeing. I see now how as our supervisor you would have been very anxious about this and also feeling responsible for our learning (and passing). I really appreciate your persistence, courage and honesty in attempting to put together this account for all our sake's. Your transparency about your feelings, and experiences in the position you were in makes this special. I regret that our group, or the context, did not bring this aspect of you forward then, but you have persisted and given us this gift! Your naming of the processes and contexts that influenced us and the learning points in the chapter helped me to think constructively about what went wrong and what could have made a difference. I agree that spending more time at the beginning of year two in knowing each other would have been good. Reflecting on my contribution to the group processes it could be that my presence as a member added to the 'difference quotient' in our group. After just a year I was still 'new' , you were 'new', some information about passing was 'new', and your style was 'new'. There was just too much difference that needed attention before we rolled up our sleeves and got down to the work of therapy. I am very happy that you have used your learning with us for working with later supervision groups."*

Gwyn comments: *"For me, as the supervisor, the process has been hugely important in opening up a space for me, and hopefully for others, to address some of the more hidden and shaming aspects of our professional experience. In the original presentation and in writing this, I have been reminded of the compelling nature of the successful narrative, the pressure I felt, and decided to resist, to present a 'positive' story to mitigate each 'negative' example. While one member of the group in particular has helpfully challenged my sometimes self-critical tone in this chapter, the effect on me has, paradoxically, been liberating. I have been intensely grateful to my two co-authors for their generosity in travelling this road with me. It has helped me to be aware of how hard we work to maintain our professionally 'prideful stories', how easily the imperative to find a 'better story' can obscure feelings of shame and humiliation but also that there is no such experience that cannot be transcended. Ethical practice in supervision, as in therapy, should involve us in being honest about our mistakes and about our feeling that we cannot find a new position from which to act. Doing this is usually, in and of itself, a new position!"*

Note

This chapter is based on a plenary presentation by Grania Clarke and Gwyn Daniel at the Institute of Family Therapy/Tavistock Clinic Conference on Supervision in December 2005.

References

Anderson, H. and Swim, S. (1995). Supervision as Collaborative Conversation: Connecting the Voices of Supervisor and Supervisee. *Journal of Systemic Therapies*. 14(2): 1–13.

Bateson, G. (1973). The Cybernetics of "Self": A Theory of Alcoholism. *Steps to an Ecology of Mind*. St Albans: Paladin. pp. 309–337.

Bateson, G. (1973). A Theory of Play and Fantasy. *Steps to an Ecology of Mind*. St Albans: Paladin. pp. 177–193.

Bertrando, P. (2007). *The Dialogical Therapist: Dialogue in Systemic Practice*. London: Karnac Books.

Burck, C. and Campbell, D. (2002). Training Systemic Supervisors: Multi-layered Learning. In: Campbell, D. and Mason, B. (eds) *Perspectives on Supervision*. London: Karnac Books. Chapter 4.

Byng-Hall, J. (1995). *Rewriting Family Scripts: Improvisation and Systems Change*. New York: Guilford Press.

Cecchin, G. (1990; personal communication).

Charlés, L.L., Ticheli-Kallikas, M., Tyner, K. and Barber-Stephens, B. (2005). Crisis Management During "Live" Supervision: Clinical and Instructional Matters. *Journal of Marital and Family Therapy*. 31(3): 207–219.

Clarke, G. and Rowan, A. (2009). Looking Again at the Team Dimension in Systemic Psychotherapy: Is Attending to Group Process a Critical Context for Practice? *Journal of Family Therapy*. 31(1): 85–107.

Gergen, K. and McNamee, S. (1999). *Relational Responsibility*. London: Sage.

Gilligan, C. (1993). *In a Different Voice: Psychological Theory and Women's Development*. Cambridge, MA: Harvard University Press.

Hayes, E. and Flannery, D.D. (2000). *Women as Learners: The Significance of Gender in Adult Learning*. San Francisco: Jossey-Bass.

Kavner, E. and McNab, S. (2005). Shame and the Therapeutic Relationship. In: Flaskas, C., Mason, B. and Perlesz, A. (eds) *The Space Between: Experience, Context and Process in the Therapeutic Relationship*. London: Karnac Books. Chapter 10.

Kolb, D.A. (1984). *Experiential Learning: Experience as the Source of Learning and Development*. New Jersey: Prentice Hall.

Lee, L. and Littlejohns, S. (2007). Deconstructing Agnes: Externalization in Systemic Supervision. *Journal of Family Therapy*. 29(3): 238–248.

Lowenstein, S.F. and Reder, P. (1982). The Consumers' Response: Trainees' Discussion of the Experience of Live Supervision. In: Byng-Hall, J. and Whiffen, R. (eds) *Family Therapy Supervision*. London: Academic Press. pp. 115–129.

Selvini, M. and Selvini-Palazzoli, M. (1991). Team Consultation: An Indispensable Tool for the Progress of Knowledge. *Journal of Family Therapy*. 13: 31–53.

Thompson, S. and Khan, J. (1988). *The Group Process and Family Therapy: Extensions and Applications of Basic Principles*. Oxford: Pergaman Press.

CHAPTER NINE

Keeping the family in focus: Doing and reflecting in supervision groups

Sara Barratt, Claudia Camhi, Sumita Dutta, Antonina Ingrassia and Guy Larrington

In this chapter, written from the perspectives of supervisor and supervisees, we describe some aspects of the learning process in a qualifying-level systemic psychotherapy training group. In this context, where the dual purposes of providing a high quality clinical service and enhancing the systemic skills and understanding of the trainees can sometimes sit in tension, we argue that the dilemmas presented by the clinical work itself can and should provide the main context for learning. Looking back on our learning experiences, we reflect on the ways that we developed confidence in our clinical abilities by prompt engagement in the clinical work and by a continued focus on the centrality of those families seen in the supervision group. Drawing upon the rich material provided by families to enhance our learning involved moving through a continuum of "doing therapy", reflecting on our practice in order to connect with therapeutic skills and theoretical knowledge and identifying the emotional impact of the work in order to connect with personal issues. The active pace of the clinical work also generated tensions, resulting in creative ways of giving and receiving feedback as well as attending to personal/professional reflection. In our opinion, there is an ever-present risk of a group becoming too focused on its own processes or on its learning in the abstract so that it becomes detached from the clinical context in which it is based.

Thus in the film *The Mirror Has Two Faces* (1996) Barbra Streisand plays the character of a brilliant lecturer in English Literature, who is trying to help a Maths lecturer (played by Jeff Bridges) to improve his teaching skills. After observing him teaching, with his face entranced by his own ideas and his back constantly facing the meagre audience of very bored students, she immediately spots the problem. "It's like you are having a math party", she says, "but you only invited yourself!"

The team

Our supervision group comprised four trainees from different professional and cultural backgrounds all of whom were established practitioners in their work setting. Three of us, including the supervisor, have a background in Social Work, one of us is a Psychiatrist, and the other a Clinical Psychologist. There were four women, including the supervisor, and one man. Two of us are of White-British origin, one Indian, one Italian, and one Chilean. Out of the five of us three are bilingual and two have English as a second language.

Getting on with it!

In qualifying course supervision groups, there can be high anxiety for trainees prior to seeing the first family and further anxieties about engaging families for more than one session. Inevitably some members work with families with whom they engage quickly, while others have families who do not attend the first appointment or drop out of therapy after only one or two sessions. These experiences can affect the confidence of trainees in the early stages, leading them to question their own abilities and wonder whether, had they been better, the family would have engaged in the work. Given this unavoidable state of uncertainty, it seemed important to invest in getting on with the work as quickly as possible in order to create some security and a sense of shared group purpose. For a group of experienced professionals, privileging their identity as clinicians/ practitioners can create a more secure base than overly focusing on their identity as trainee. Indeed, in our supervision group the supervisor had a strong belief in just "getting on with it" so that she used her authority to commit each group member to seeing families from the second group meeting. By doing this she intended to convey the message to the trainees: "I have confidence in you."

The supervisor was departing from her previous practice which was to use the early sessions for the group to discuss learning goals and link these to personal and professional experience and knowledge. Given the anxiety that can build up about starting the work, she considered that it was more productive to undertake these explorations in the context of family work that was already underway.

The rationale for this position for a supervisor is that students' experience in front of the screen is essential to developing the confidence to open themselves up to the (sometimes difficult) experience of learning. In certain respects she trades on her students' secure identity as professional helpers to help them become more effective learners. Thus the trainee who works with a family engaged in therapy is more likely to feel central to the supervision group, providing material for discussion and thinking within the group and thereby gaining attention and feedback at the different levels of family, group, and supervisor. This hopefully enhances confidence in the learning process and in the creation of self-reflexive spaces as trainees take account of the way that they are positioned by different family members.

Supervision groups quickly establish rules, and trainees may settle into fixed roles which can make it difficult for members to change their position, creating the need for supervisors to challenge them to take on different roles and develop different aspects of themselves within the clinical team. Early immersion in the clinical work, with all its richness, unexpectedness, and intensity can help create more flexible positioning in the group. For example, one author, who experienced a major family illness at the beginning of the group entered the team feeling very unsure about her abilities and whether she could engage both in the work and with the group. In her experience, it was only when she was able to join the "fast pace" of seeing families and the resultant commitment she made to the families, that she felt able to gain a foothold into the group and develop her own clinical confidence and sense of group belonging. She might otherwise have been ascribed an unhelpful identity as a fragile or marginal member of the group. It is therefore essential that all members of the group feel that they are working and contributing, particularly at times when, for a variety of reasons, there may be a hiatus in seeing families.

Inevitably, some trainees are able to engage in the clinical work earlier than others and this can lead to a loss of confidence which affects the dynamics of the team. The supervisor faces the ethical dilemma of whether to keep trying to engage a family that frequently misses appointments in the hope that they will eventually attend, or deciding, possibly precipitously, to prioritize the needs of the trainee to find another family. This may suit the trainee's needs better but giving up too soon on the family may be detrimental to them. As well as holding these different perspectives the supervisor needs to ensure that a trainee without an engaged family is involved in some aspect of the clinical work in each session, either as a member of a reflecting team or as the person conveying the team's ideas to the family and therapist. This means ensuring that a trainee without a family can hold on to their self-confidence and have an active, participatory role in each supervisory session.

The impact of the families on the group

In the early stages of a supervision group, trainees may be more worried about their relationship with the team behind the screen, and the team's views of the trainee as therapist, than with the family per se. Indeed one task of the supervisor at this stage may be in taking a firm lead in holding the family in mind. Hopefully, as the work continues, the relationship with the family is paramount and the supervisor and team come to be seen as supporting the work rather than as criticizing and assessing the therapist. However, this position can only come about through the experience of engaging families and feeling that one can have conversations with families that do make a difference. Given the idea from the Milan approach that "no one can change, at least not easily, under a negative connotation" (Boscolo et al. 1987: 15), the trainee working with a family where positive feedback is in short supply, either in words or action, may struggle to gain confidence. This is a particular issue in a training context based in a Child and Adolescent Mental Health clinic where it is common for the trainee to have to attend to child protection concerns as well as maintain a therapeutic relationship, and where families may be ambivalent about attending for regular appointments. Such events can lead a trainee to lose confidence and to feel that s/he is not doing "real" family therapy. Here the team and supervisor's position is crucial in enabling the trainee, who may experience negative connotation from the family, to identify some aspects of their practice that create more positive openings for change.

We were therefore mindful and interested in the effect of the families on the supervision group. For example, how did some families become "owned" by the group as a whole? How do families affect the dynamics of a supervision group so that they may appear to determine the position different trainees adopt within the group? Some families we worked with had a primary relationship with the trainee/therapist whilst others developed a relationship with the team, saying hello and goodbye at the beginning and end of sessions. For example, a separated mother, concerned about the impact of her partner leaving the family, was working with the only male member of the group. Whilst forming a strong relationship with the therapist, she also had a lively relationship with the female members of the team behind the screen. Important themes such as gender, trust, and betrayal began to emerge in the therapeutic work but also in our discussion with one another. Thus, the mother effectively led us to talk about and take positions on our beliefs about these powerful issues whilst recognizing the possible blind spots that may be created through such a connection. Keeping questions in mind such as whether the women in the team might be in danger of accepting rather than questioning the mother's view that her partner was being too hard on the children was an important way to keep these possible "blind spots" on the table and open to challenge.

We were interested in how the positions taken by the women members of the team supported or constrained the therapist. In fact, the experience of the male therapist here was that this "position taking talk" with his colleagues freed him up to be a better therapist rather than simply perform as a "good man". The team's ability to "open dialogue" about these issues bolstered his confidence to do the same in the room. Indeed the therapeutic talk in the room sometimes opened out to a three-way debate with "the women next door" in a manner that allowed humour to cut through entrenched anger and distress in a helpful manner.

In effect the team began both to create and mirror the same risk-taking behaviours behind the screen as were being tried out in front of the screen with the family. This recursive process helped trainees to experience and appreciate further the sensitivity of the work with the family. It also moved the group into taking more risky or exposed positions with each other, in relation to the work that was being carried out together. In this way, keeping the family central to the supervision became a key element of group cohesion and in establishing our group identity and ethos as a working/learning group, organized by the dual task of working with the particular family and learning more about how to work with families in general.

Anxiety about the families also had an important impact on group development and relationships. For example, one group member worked with a family with complex problems in which we were, at different times, concerned about the physical safety and the mental health needs of individual family members. This family work focused our attention on the diverse cultural backgrounds of the group members and provided a focus for what Campbell et al. (2003: 424) describe as a "significant moment". The family, which contained two teenage children, were talking about an occasion when the father had criticized the younger son who had erupted in anger and hit his father. The father, who felt that he had had a very tough childhood, resented the support that his son received from his wife. His consistently critical digs meant that the son frequently became violent and the mother, who was committed to a very close relationship with her children, moved in to protect her son (a very "familiar" scenario). As a team, we each felt that we wanted to rescue different family members at different times and we also noticed that the more hopeless the family seemed the more active we became. The significant moment emerged when the therapist was struggling to describe the ways in which the family members were relating to one another and struck on a well known metaphor from her country of origin by asking, "Who will put the bell on the cat?"

The saying summarizes a story from Chile that goes:

> *The mice get together to decide what is the best way to protect themselves from the cat. A clever mouse realizes that, rather than one of them always having to stand guard to warn the others about the cat approaching, all they have to do is somehow get a bell on the cat and*

the cat will do it for them. However another wise mouse realizes that, no matter how good the plan is, all of them fear the cat so much that hanging a bell to the cat's neck was out of the question!

This metaphor was used with the family as they appeared to feel intimidated by the father but were unable to comment on it. The team had been struggling to find the best way to help the members of the family explore a different way of relating to one another and had, in particular, been thinking about the patterns of closeness and distance, which led to intense hostility and violence at different times between family members.

In the event, the Chilean saying was met with incomprehension by the family and the team behind the screen alike. The team asked the therapist to explain to the family (and to them) what the saying meant. Burnham and Harris (2002) describe the importance of attending to the different cultural contexts within a training group. In our case this was achieved by naming the confusion, rather than avoiding it with the family and between ourselves, to open up a therapeutic space in which to consider difference.

This story subsequently became part of the team's narrative of itself, carrying in emblematic form both our struggles over translating our differences to each other and our willingness to address them openly. Naming our uncertainty about the meaning of the therapist's Chilean story was a form of risk-taking in which we simultaneously acknowledged the therapist's difference whilst taking up a position of cultural curiosity in relation to what was being said. As a group with so many professional and cultural differences, this making space for differences to be explored was an essential ingredient to our feeling that our differences were acknowledged, listened to, and valued as part of the group.

Within groups it is important to value both the different cultural experiences and the professional knowledge that trainees bring. In our group some members came from a hierarchical professional context in which people looked to them to provide information and others were more used to working in partnership with families and communities. This consideration led us to wonder about the different degrees to which trainees feel (more or less) confident within family therapy training where ideas of co-constructing knowledge sometimes seemed to be at odds with the idea that there is a "right" way to do therapy and indeed to succeed academically. Philip et al. (2007) describe the ways in which supervisees and supervisors can be confronted with ethical issues which seem to challenge the consistent application of postmodern ideas in therapy and suggest that social constructionist supervision has difficulty in freeing itself from realist thinking:

> Students trying to work in a way which embodies social constructionist ideas are confused when they are simultaneously drawn into realist ideas about uncovering "the truth" about clients, finding expert prescriptions for client change and uncritically accepting and aligning with theoretical perspectives.
> (Philip et al. 2007: 53)

Within our group, one trainee was engaged in work with a family where there were pertinent issues around parental drug use and the cultural fit of the family within their community. The risk the therapist took, in this instance a social worker who was used to doing practical social work with families, was to let go of ideas about the "right way" (or truth about how) to do therapy within a training and assessment context and to embrace the practical skills and approaches from her social work background, which moved the work into a more practical domain. In this instance the supervision group were affirming voices for the therapist to utilize her social work skills in order to respond most effectively to the needs of the family rather than stick with the orthodoxy about what a "proper systemic psychotherapist" would do.

Personal connections

A wide range of literature on supervision concentrates on the self of the therapist, the effect of family of origin on the positions taken, and—occasionally, in a safe enough group—on current relationships and patterns (Haber and Hawley, 2004; Hildebrand, 1998; Young et al. 2003). Supervisors are often reticent about negotiating permission to talk about current events in the lives of students. A student may sometimes flag up concerns about working with a family with a referral problem which resonates with a difficulty in their personal life. However, there is a danger that a supervisor, with some background knowledge, may determine that there are connections and resonances for a student which do not actually fit with the student's own perception. This can be experienced as an abuse of power within a relationship where the supervisor has the power of assessment and may have the effect of silencing the student or coercing them into accepting the supervisor's definition.

By prioritizing the interaction with families as the main context for learning, a shared focus is created to build a sense of confidence, expertise, and self-reflexivity through which the trainee can challenge the supervisor's power. If we start by "doing" then we have a focus for reflection. Where a sense of group cohesion develops in the early stages of clinical training, trainees and supervisor have another basis for working on the use of self in the context of a relationship with a clinical family. Put in a different way, when groups start to work on their personal experiences before engaging in the clinical work, one runs the risk of operating in a vacuum, or a space where reflection is cramped by power imbalances, anxiety about criticism and assessment, rather than working with the issues that arise spontaneously in the course of the work.

It is interesting to reflect on the way that our supervisor used the power of her position in a collaborative way; on the one hand she used her authority to set the pace of the work from the start, but, on the other, by doing so, she provided the very context in which her authority could be challenged and a more collaborative approach could be taken. In other words, although seeing families from the start was non-negotiable, this then provided the opportunity to have a debate about all the negotiable ways of doing therapy, that is, what the therapist wanted to do in the room, how often they wanted to see families, who was to be invited, and so forth. The supervisor also quickly exposed herself as a "do-er" of therapy, as her trainees observed her making hypotheses, naming her own prejudices, and suggesting interventions. This provided a basis for a debate in which all group members participated and generated different ideas as well as learning from the way the supervisor noticed which of her interventions and ideas did not sit comfortably with the therapist or family and rectified them. Such an approach embodies the creative co-existence of hierarchy and collaboration suggested by Selicoff (2006), who suggests that both standpoints can co-exist and inform a supervision style.

Although a separate space was provided on the course for personal–professional development, our group thought that it was important to centralize the clinical context in order to understand our responses and to understand one another; this meant that it was important for us to do this work also with our clinical supervisor. The process, both guided and joined by the supervisor, included use of genograms, mapping of current relationships, and thinking about different work contexts and professional expertises.

We talked about our different reactions to families and the connection to our personal experiences. For example, one of the families we were seeing was considering sending a child to boarding school. This lead to a fairly heated discussion amongst the team about the different ideas and prejudices people held about boarding schools. Two group members had been to boarding school themselves; one felt that this had been a positive experience in the context of a separating family, while one felt it was entirely negative. Other group members who had not attended boarding school personally were puzzled by a culture which would consider boarding school as a method of bringing up children; their surprise and curiosity were very helpful to us all in thinking about our values in relation to child care. As a team we remained committed to bringing these beliefs out into the open as a way of helping the therapist recognize the range of beliefs and feelings that can be activated within us by our work, an action which enabled the families' dilemmas to remain central to our own self-reflexive processes.

There is, of course, a danger that trainees may feel that "doing it" is more important than "talking about it". It is important, however, that they can develop confidence in their different ways of knowing and learning (Burnham and Harris, 2002), a confidence that can most creatively be explored through reflections on the clinical experience itself. Thus trainees who need to process information intellectually may understand what is said from a theoretical perspective but may struggle with emotional communication in the therapeutic context. Similarly trainees who rely on intuition may need to engage with a different knowledge base and, through the team's feedback, start to recognize and challenge their own intellectual processes. For example, one author carried out a piece of work that at the beginning relied on her feeling that she wanted to rescue a family member. Indeed she was supported in providing some individual space to this person. As time went on, she and the group revisited the theoretical and therapeutic implications of the way that this decision positioned her within the family system and her responses to this.

Our group became interested in exploring intuitions and how they relate to our personal stories and to our professional experiences. In one family, the supervisor had a speculative idea that there had been coercive sexual practices in a post-separation family which were not spoken about, but which had a strong impact on the children's relationships with both of their parents. The group discussion was significant as it focused not only on the relevance or otherwise of this hunch for the clinical work, but also on the place in our group for "another way of knowing" which was harder to locate theoretically.

While intuition may be thought of as, by definition, "unteachable", it can be used as a new lens through which to look at "problematic" relationships between family members; alternatively it can address the tensions group members experience between "knowing" and "saying" and identify and debate the different "knowings" of each group member. Debate and discussion around our prejudices and emotional responses to the difficulties families presented could thus be activated by the explicit use of intuition and become an essential part of learning. Privileging the impact of families' ways of being on us and on our different certainties meant we were able to connect the personal with the professional in an immediate way—by being in it and then talking about it. This seemed to free group members to develop confidence in their hunches and to try to understand their origins, confident that these hunches would be questioned and debated.

Double feedback

The group ethos of "getting on with the work", which also became weekly "reality" as the demands of the work increased, set a problem for our learning which was that of making room for feedback. Feedback time was constantly squeezed, and group discussion would tend to slide away from the development of the therapist to discussion of the family (or indeed the next family we were seeing, when time was tight between sessions). This was in part due to the competing demands of doing therapy and doing learning on our time and attention, but also probably involved anxiety about giving and receiving feedback in a group context, especially one where students' competence was being assessed. As well as developing our individual confidence as therapists, we had to develop confidence as a learning group.

It may well be that our Chilean saying became a "significant moment" due to the resonance it had for the group as well as the family it was shared with. Deployed as a response to the power struggles of a family, at its heart the metaphor spoke to the different positions taken by the members of a supervision group. It connects with power as part of the supervision process, and the constraints in eliciting and giving team feedback as part of trainees' development as therapists. In this scenario, the supervisor is the most obvious candidate for the cat, equipped as she is with the claws of assessment. Nonetheless, this role may be a mobile one within the play of relationships in the supervision circle, with each member of the group anticipating cat's claws as they get feedback from each other, in a context where the development of a new professional identity (and pass or failure) is at stake.

Finding room for feedback, and managing the anxieties involved, is of course a problem for all supervision groups. Training courses based on live supervision have developed various methods to enable feedback and learning in this context. These methods include pre- and post-session discussion, consulting partners, learning logs, video review, and case presentation (AFT Blue Book, 1999; Gorell Barnes and McCann, 2000).

We utilized all of these methods to varying degrees, but found ourselves repeatedly wishing for "more time" to talk about our work as well as doing it. However, more time conflicted with our ethic of getting on with the work, so that, as much as we grumbled, we kept on booking those families in! Burnham (1993: 350) describes the ritual of traditional family therapy training groups: "During this process reflecting teams, direct comments and supervision notes all facilitate a second order observing system which brings forth multi-versa in the context of a team approach to training. This ritual allows the supervisor direct access to the work of the therapist in training and the therapist in training has direct access to the supervisor as a resource in relation to first and second order positions."

However, our supervision group did not feel that they were allowing themselves sufficient space to develop second order thinking about their positions and they wanted something more. The "clinical doing" aspect of the group's identity meant that we still struggled to keep discussions focused on the therapist rather than the family.

The group's grumbling reflected a tension, and as we moved into the second year of the course, this tension became a creative one. Together we developed a more formalized method for post-session discussion in order to give ourselves space for feedback. In essence we utilized Andersen's (1990) reflecting team to provide group feedback for the therapist but with our own "twist".

Fellow trainee members of the therapy team sat in the therapy room immediately after a session and discussed the therapist's contributions to the session just held. Simultaneously the therapist and supervisor watched through the screen. This meant that the team members were able to develop their different ideas about the trainee in the session before the supervisor gave her feedback. The importance of this structure was that the supervisor was in the position of listening and used this as a basis for her reflections to the therapist. It is tempting for supervisors to "hold the floor" in giving feedback and thus constrain the trainee group from developing their own ideas. It was also easier to focus on the therapist. Furthermore, this method of feedback encourages a collective ownership of each trainee's development rather than this being the exclusive preoccupation of the supervisor. The ability to think simultaneously about the needs of the family and the development of the therapist's skills is an important team function and it communicates to trainees that their learning and development as therapists will not become obscured by considerations of the families' needs. In all of our feedback, we tried to focus on the development of the therapist's skills rather than use the space to reflect upon further clinical considerations for the family. It also enabled each trainee to practice giving reflections to their colleagues in a way which enables them to practice the skills required to give feedback to families as part of the reflecting team.

The team feedback discussion was taped as part of the family session, enabling a further level of reflection for the therapist in between sessions. In shaping their discussion, the team would often take a lead from the therapist's comments in the pre-session discussion about what aspects of their practice they hoped to develop, for example, "I need to make more room for the children in this session—can you track this," or "I want to be able to punctuate the session more this time." By and large team members kept their remarks speculative and positive, but also allowed different perspectives to accrue in the discussion.

In retrospect though, we see that the value of what we had created for ourselves lay not in the feedback per se, but in the practice of a double discussion, where the therapist and supervisor listened and talked about the team's discussions as they occurred. The supervisor might invite the therapist to take a position on the team's reflections or might take one herself, thereby encouraging active, participatory listening. The supervisor might ask the supervisee what she was getting from the discussion they listened to, and help the supervisee articulate what they want from the team.

Dividing up talking and listening in this manner provided a means of involving the group more fully in each therapist's development and of overcoming any constraints in doing so. Importantly it was an arrangement we enjoyed and were enthusiastic about, creating intense curiosity about what the team would say. A listening space was provided for the therapist to hear the team's perspectives on their development, together with the invitation to engage in personal, reflective discussion on the team's reflections.

An interesting aspect of this process was the temporary sub-grouping of the therapist and the supervisor in an intimate space separate from the team, cutting across in a powerful way the usual division between supervisor and supervisees. Intimacy can provide a secure place to ask difficult questions and open difficult conversations. This could of course have been a problematic aspect of the arrangement if the conversations opened had been left in this darkened space, and if the supervisor was not trusted in her use of power. The security of the space that the supervisor and supervisee occupied depended on group confidence, as well as working to develop that confidence. We may not have felt the same way about its use at an earlier point of our group development when that confidence was not in place. Importantly in this respect, this feedback arrangement was one that worked for us when we were ready for it to do so, and because we had created it and felt able to use it as a way of serving our own developmental needs.

Conclusion

In supervision groups, as we learn about new ideas and theories and simultaneously worry about assessments, do we not run the risk of having our very own "family therapy party" without inviting the family?

Supervision groups are unique forums on a systemic psychotherapy qualifying course, in as much as they are also work groups. It is therefore very important to capitalize on this aspect of them as a resource for learning. In our experience, the relationships with the different families and the engagement in the clinical work are central to developing confidence and relationships within a supervision group. We have therefore argued that this crucial process must start as early as possible, to allow the development of true clinical-based learning. By centralizing working relationships with families, self-reflexivity becomes embodied in the work, rather than a prequel or sequel to it, and is, we believe, enriched through this embodiment.

Providing a double feedback space of listening and reflection with the supervisor, whilst the rest of the team provides feedback, also allows the trainee multiple opportunities to make connections and reflect. As the "fast pace" of our supervision group's approach probably reflects the working reality of most family therapy clinics in the National Health Service, this approach to feedback might provide one creative solution to the struggle most clinicians face between doing and reflecting.

References

Andersen, T. (1990). *The Reflecting Team: Dialogues and Dialogues about the Dialogues*. Kent: Borgmann Publishing Ltd.

Association for Family Therapy. (1999). *The Blue Book* (3rd edn) CRED subcommittee. Canterbury: AFT Publishing.

Boscolo, L., Cecchin, G., Hoffman, L. and Penn, P. (1987). *Milan Systemic Family Therapy*. USA: Basic Books. p. 15.

Burnham, J. (1993). Systemic Supervision: The Evolution of Reflexivity in the Context of the Supervisory Relationship. *Human Systems: The Journal of Systemic Consultation and Management*. 4: 349–381.

Burnham, J. and Harris, Q. (2002). Cultural Issues in Supervision. In: Campbell, D. and Mason, B. (eds) *Perspectives on Supervision*. pp. 21–41.

Campbell, D., Bianco, V., Dowling, E., Goldberg, H., McNab, S. and Pentecost, D. (2003). Family Therapy for Childhood Depression: Researching Significant Moments. *Journal of Family Therapy.* 25(4): 417–436.

Gorell-Barnes, G. and McCann, D. (2000). Into the Millennium. In: Gorell-Barnes, G., Down, G. and McCann, D. (eds) *Systemic Supervision: A Portable Guide to Supervision Training.* London: Jessica Kingsley Publishers.

Haber, R. and Hawley, L. (2004). Family of Origin as a Supervisory Consultative Resource. *Family Process.* 43(3): 373–390.

Hildebrand, J. (1998). *Bridging the Gap.* London: Karnac Books.

Philp, K., Guy, G. and Lowe, R. (2007). Social Constructionist Supervision or Supervision as Social Construction? Some Dilemmas. *Journal of Systemic Therapies.* 26(1): 51–62.

Selicoff, H. (2006). Looking for Good Supervision: A Fit between Hierarchical and Collaborative Methods. *Journal of Systemic Therapies.* 25(1): 37–51.

Simon, G. (2005). The Heart of the Matter: A Proposal for Placing the Self of the Therapist at the Centre of Family Therapy Research and Training. *Family Process.* 45(3): 331–344.

Young, J. et al. (2003). Revisiting Family of Origin in the Training of Family Therapists. *Australian and New Zealand Journal of Family Therapy.* 24(9): 123–140.

SECTION III

POWER AND DIVERSITY

CHAPTER TEN

"Voice entitlement" narratives in supervision: Cultural and gendered influences on speaking and dilemmas in practice

Elizabeth Boyd

This chapter describes the experience of supervising an all female and ethnically diverse group of Family Therapy trainees in London. Included is a study exploring trainees' speaking narratives looking at family of origin, school, and adult learning experiences. "Voice entitlement" was a major theme, contextualized by cultural, gendered, and second language effects. Construction of these narratives brought forth dilemmas in trainees' practice. These helped to explore difference, promote trainee's self-reflexivity, and offered opportunities for change, thus providing a valuable "tool" in supervision.

The emergence of "voice entitlement" as a concept

During the early life of a supervision group, one of the trainees, Safria,[1] appeared preoccupied with how to structure a first session: "If a family can't contain things then I get lost ... I can't structure it. If there's a lot

---

[1]All names have been changed in this chapter to protect the identity of the participants.

of information ... you feel "Oh gosh what did we get out of this?" We had already had lengthy discussions about structuring sessions but it seemed I was no nearer answering her question. As we talked Safria raised the notion of respect: *"The way to be respectful is to let the other person lead the conversation ... If there's an Asian man in the room I feel ... it's very difficult to challenge that person ... it's part of my culture ... It feeds into what I've been taught really, where's your respect? For me, even if you don't agree with their opinion you play along with it, in a way. If it satisfies that person, that's fine. You keep your opinion to yourself ..."*

Daunted, I was suddenly aware of a much larger picture for me as supervisor. The issue was not which questions to ask or even how to ask a question, it was about my trainee's sense of whether she had *permission* to ask. This was the beginning of an understanding that trainees came with a history, a narrative about speaking that was deeply embedded in their cultural, gendered, and educational experience. This narrative has a profound impact on them both in the supervision group and the therapy room. I have come to understand this as a "voice entitlement" narrative, which transcends technique and knowledge in systemic thinking. I concluded that to be a more effective supervisor I needed to address the significant meanings that having a voice implied for my trainees.

The Supervision Group consisted of five women. Maria described her ethnicity as white Caucasian and her culture as German working-class Catholic. Safria described her ethnicity as Indian and her culture as Indian/African (childhood spent in Zambia). Sarah described her ethnicity as white British and her culture of origin as complicated, since she is of Romany descent (maternal side) and her father was illegitimate. She spent several of her teenage years in Africa. Simran grew up in the Punjab and described her ethnicity as Sikh Indian and her culture as Punjabi. Manjit described her ethnicity as Sikh Indian and her culture as Indian, although, like Safria and Sarah, she spent a period of her childhood in Africa. Four of the women spoke more than one language. The author/supervisor is of mixed English and Irish heritage and grew up in Wiltshire (semi-rural) and London.

Realizing that supervisees had voice speaking histories that informed their contributions within the supervision group, I became interested in what informed their verbal interventions? When did they offer opinions, make statements, interrupt, and ask questions?

What constraints were they working with and where did these come from?

Gilligan's (1993: xvi) work exploring women's psychological development links voice to the core of the self, describing it as natural, cultural, and intensely relational. To have a voice is to be human, connecting the inner and outer world. "Speaking and listening are a form of psychic breathing. This relational exchange ... is mediated through language and culture, diversity and plurality. ... Voice is a new key for understanding the psychological, social and cultural order—a litmus test of relationships and a measure of psychological health."

These ideas seem crucial when supervising female trainees. "From the age of three ... socio-linguists tell us, girls tend to shift speech style depending on whether they are talking to boys or to other girls" (Brown, 1998: 91). In adolescence girls "struggle to stay with their own experiences and to create space for their own voices in the presence of alternative voices or truths held by those with the power to name, to reconfigure, their reality" (Brown, 1998a: 92). With this history, where are female trainees in their life cycle of development as regards their voice entitlement? Safria was struggling with expressing an opinion, to structure a session.

Also important was the cultural context. Challenging an Asian man went against Safria's interpretation of her culture. Integral to this was the notion of respect, which I learned went to the heart of her sense of being a good person. Parekh (2000: 143) defines culture as "a historically created system of meaning and significance ... a system of beliefs and practices in terms of which a group of human beings understand, regulate and structure their individual and collective lives ... [it] has a practical thrust and is not purely theoretical." Safria articulated powerfully this "practical thrust" in her statement about not challenging Asian men. As her supervisor, I wondered how to help her manage the dilemmas posed by her new role as therapist, coupled with her cultural loyalties.

Exploring difference became a focus in the supervision group. Among others, Down (2000: 73) notes that many papers describing cross-cultural work suggest that "trainees need to become aware and have some understanding of their own culture before being able to understand others". I found this concept helpful. During the process of exploring trainee's culture of origin, the concept of "voice" emerged as useful in empowering trainees. The idea of "learning narratives" (Aggett, 2004: 36) provided a springboard for my thinking and I became interested in trainees' "voice entitlement" narratives. These provided a tool to aid self-reflexivity and address the dilemmas around cultural and gendered experiences. The systemic literature emphasizes the need for informed cross-cultural practice (Krause, 2002; Boyd-Franklin, 1989). However "finding a way in" to trainees' experience remains complex. I will address how "voice entitlement" narratives became a "tool" in supervision: locating dilemmas when making interventions in therapy, "finding a way in" to these complex issues and increasing self-reflexivity for supervisees.

The development of "voice"

"Voice entitlement" begins with the development of language and speech. Babies are tuned into speech from birth or even in utero (Greenfield, 1996). In early mother–child interactions, both take turns in a pseudo-conversation (Stern, 1977). The baby's ability in this turn-taking sequence represents the beginnings of voice development and underlines the relational significance. At one, the baby gives real responses in these interactions (Newson, 1977) and "proper" speech starts in their second year (Carter, 1998). Infants have the potential to speak any language but this diminishes with age. Languages learned later involve different neural mechanisms than primary language (Pinker, 1994). Bilingualism and voice is a fascinating area, one which will be discussed later.

Studies reveal gender differences in language ability and communication. Girls talk earlier, have larger vocabularies, and score generally higher than boys in language tests (Hines et al. 1992). These studies and others (Brown, 1998; Gilligan, 1982), however, found girls inhibited in the company of boys despite their enhanced language ability. This raises questions about the implications for the development of voice. Kimura (1987) emphasizes gender brain differences, with females having superiority in language and males in spatial ability. However this is not supported in all studies (Feingold, 1988). Baron-Cohen (2003) highlights the evidence suggesting female language superiority (Shaywitz et al. 1995) but goes further proposing that, usually, female brains have superiority in empathizing skills and males in systemizing ability. He links this to speaking style: "male style is to assume that there is an objective picture of reality, which happens to be *their* version of the facts ... The female approach seems to assume ... there might be subjectivity in the world. Therefore they make room for multiple interpretations" (2003: 50; emphasis in original). Gilligan (1993: xxi), however, depicts girls as silencing themselves in response to their preoccupation with maintaining relationships. She views females as grappling with dissociation: "the coming not to know what one knows, the difficulty in hearing or listening to one's own voice ... the use of one's own voice to cover rather than convey one's inner world, so that relationships no longer provide channels for exploring the connections between one's inner life and the world of others."

The advent of advanced technologies such as Functional Magnetic Resonance Imaging (FMRI) is providing new evidence regarding language and gender differences in the brain (Frackowiak et al. 2004). This challenges the gender debate given that much feminist thinking locates sex differences in behaviour within a socio-political context (Chodorow, 1974). Whilst attempts to understand genuine gender differences in brain function offer opportunities for further insights, there is a risk of unhelpful generalizations. Gilligan (1993: xix) sees danger in "the reduction of psychology to either sociology or biology or some combination of the two" arguing that it "prepares the way for ... the suffocation of voice". Her appraisal of how developmental theorists (for example, Piaget, 1932) have tended to see males as the norm, viewing female differences as lacking, is important. If females are thought to be "natural" empathizers how can they develop an authentic voice if constructed as biologically determined to see multiple interpretations?

Brown (1998a: 92), in her study of adolescent girls, explored the ability of girls to voice their experiences. She locates herself within a feminist research programme which "is grounded in a notion of voice as a relational, discursive phenomenon—linguistically constituted, socially constructed". She views subjectivity as constructed within on-going power relations (Foucault, 1980) and acknowledges a culture interwoven with inequality and oppression. She concludes that "social, cultural and material location, have profound effects on what voices, fictions and fantasies of femininity are ventriloquized" (p. 109).

The term "ventriloquation" was developed by Bakhtin who argued that, in individual's utterances, the voices of groups and institutions can be heard. He placed dialogue at the heart of every thought and viewed words, as they enter a dialogical relationship, as "double voiced". Even when another isn't present there is hidden dialogicality since "the second interlocutor is invisibly present" (1973: 163–164). Harvey (cited in Brown, 1998: 109) sees this as "a powerful strategy of silencing" since the individual is inevitably affected by group attitudes and beliefs. Brown saw the girls in her study evidencing ventriloquation, but also struggling against appropriation, thus creating the potential for new discourse through disruption, contestation, and infiltration. This optimism for the emergence of new discourse suggests a dynamic process where change is possible and individuals can and do find new voices.

Ideas about "self" feature when an individual's development of voice is being considered. Hermans and Kempen's (1993: 62) "dialogical self" combines the concepts of dialogue and self, viewing self *as* relationship. They like the narrative approach: "the notion of story or narrative assumes the existence of a person who tells and an actual or imagined who listens. The fact that the listener, another person, is always present or implied, makes the self a dialogical phenomenon *par excellence*" (1993: xx). White and Epston (1990) see individuals telling themselves stories about themselves through social exchange. Central is the idea that stories aren't fixed but are selective and can change. An important implication here is that the self is essentially relational as opposed to intrapsychic, transcending the boundaries between the "inside" and the "outside".

If self and voice are relational and inextricably linked to the groups to which individuals belong, membership of a cultural group is important. The systemic literature acknowledges culture as powerful but difficult to define (Brah, 1996). Indeed Kroeber and Kluckholn (1952) identified 164 different definitions. Krause (2002: 17) sees the difficulty (of definition) as "being that culture is both inside and outside persons". "Inside" is not a reference to something intrinsic, rather that culture is internalized. I like this argument since it acknowledges how individuals make their own meaning of culture. Bruner (1990) believes that culture is constitutive of mind and that making meaning is achieved in a public and communal form rather than privately (echoing Bakhtin's ideas). Laird (1998: 20) quotes terms such as "cultural diversity", "multiculturalism", and "cultural competence" as buzz-words of the 1990s but complains about an absence of shared meanings. Gorell Barnes (2002: 1) suggests that it is important to think about ourselves rather than the "other" (Kitzinger and Wilkinson, 1996). There is a richness of ideas in this debate about the meaning of culture but it can leave one still grappling with how to make it "real" within a supervisory relationship. I have found "voice" narratives helpful in situating culture "within" persons as well as acknowledging the relational component.

Examples of "voice entitlement" narratives

I decided to carry out semi-structured interviews with the women in the supervision group to explore their speaking histories using Interpretative Phenomenological Analysis (IPA) (Smith et al. 1999) to analyse the results. In this chapter I have concentrated on three of the women's accounts, however all the women had powerful stories to tell. The narratives reveal the enduring influence of messages that trainees received from their family of origin about speaking, although experiences in education were also important.

Maria's story

Maria's experience of growing up in a German, working-class Catholic family brought strong messages about speaking: "The way we still converse in my family when we disagree we shout, the louder you shout the more likely it is that you are being heard ... my parents run a pub ... and the pub is next to our living room so we could always hear people shouting ... to listen properly what the other person says I think there wasn't much of that really ..." Maria regrets that there weren't rules about speaking: "I would rather learned to ... that there were rules ... that I was told not to shout and to listen ... when you shout there was no conclusion to anything ... no positive outcome." She links this to respect, concluding that if what she had to say had been respected she would have learned how to respect others.

At primary school this style of speaking was positive for Maria. She described herself as "a very lively child ... I didn't have many inhibitions to voice my, raise my [voice], or to express my opinions." At this stage Maria wished others would listen to her: "When I was a child I wanted to be a TV presenter ... I had this fantasy that all these people would have to listen and not contradict [me]." However at High school the experience became painful for Maria: "They shut me up a bit but that was not done in a nice way ... I experienced it as humiliation ... they said: 'You're stupid, you better shut up.'"

When exploring the impact of this experience, Maria talks about compensating for her speaking style by becoming quieter and studying hard. She found school difficult at this level but becomes "extremely industrious ... then had good marks." She takes to heart this powerful message about being quiet and concludes: "The experience I had was shut up, sit down, learn your stuff and have good marks that's why I think a librarianship was a perfect thing to do that, just study." Maria then designs her career choice based on her learning about being quiet and studying.

In adulthood, Maria appears to move between two positions learnt during childhood, one of being quiet and listening and the other of speaking out and being lively. This positioning often poses dilemmas for her as she attempts to hold the two in mind. She expresses this dilemma when talking about her experience of self-disclosure in the supervision group. "I think I just give out too much too easily." She talks of wishing she could hold back and imagines that others don't experience this tension. "My impression is that everyone else knows how to hold back and that this puts me in a vulnerable position ... I'm a bit of an open book."

This dilemma seemed related to how she positioned herself with regard to the cultural mix in the group. "Because we are a multicultural group I think it is important to listen." She sees the others as "bound to have different opinions ..." However she also states: "I say things that others wouldn't dare say." She relates this to her cultural influences and sees it as helpful. "I don't have to overcome hurdles to speak up in a group, as opposed to many people." She later acknowledges the tension and potential advantages between speaking out and holding back: "But I take this risk [speaking out], from my roots, come from a family who speaks before they think, not necessarily a good thing, sometimes a good thing."

Safria's story

Safria described a powerful hierarchical tenet in her family of origin with regard to speaking, which demanded that she listen to those older than herself, particularly the men in the family. "Questions were never encouraged, you just did it [what you're told] ... you just go along with it." Any opinions you held in relation to family issues "would never be taken on board". Safria even doubted how often she had an opinion to express: "Even if you had an opinion ... in my family if you disagree with somebody you don't go and disagree with them openly". However there was room for expressing disagreement, although it had a nebulous quality for Safria: "somehow it gets aired ... but you don't stand up to anyone". This rule was more relaxed in relation to her sisters who were close in age, although only in certain contexts. "As far as offering opinions, I could to my older sister, above me ... whilst shopping with my mum. I could choose for her, materials. She would agree to it." Safria later said (after reading this chapter) that she feels no criticism of family members regarding the "rules" in her family about speaking.

At primary school Safria found voicing opinions impossible: "I couldn't participate in any discussions ever." When answering questions Safria was less constrained. If she "knew the answer to something, I could put up my hand". However the move from Africa to England at age eleven meant her secondary education produced new demands and her confidence diminished. Even when she felt that she knew the correct answer to a question, she wouldn't raise her hand. She decided that: "everyone else was so much more vocal than me; I would go over it in my head ... you might say it like someone else but you didn't have the confidence to say it". She related this to the idea that one "listens because you might make a nuisance" of yourself and the practice in Africa of "having things done for me ... not taking much responsibility". She thought it was "different for youngsters living in England ... here you take responsibilities for yourself. There [Africa] we had ironing done for us, services and so forth."

Later Safria began working as a Health Advocate. She said of this decision: "Imagine, an advocate, someone who has to speak up for others ... something I'm not used to." She thought this increased her confidence, but talking to other agencies was difficult.

Early in her training Safria found it difficult "to share and open up or even think about things". However her experience on a counselling course had a significant effect on her finding a voice: "The group was very different, it really gave me permission to give my input ... It was how they encouraged me. I was the only Asian person ... there was another lady of African origin, the rest were white, British, English. It just felt that from time to time people would note what you said, valued it in a way ... it just had more weight and it made me think, gosh they really value that, it made me realize that I have got some of the things valuable to have an input."

In the supervision group Safria thought she experienced little of her previous inhibition: "When I have got something to share I come in." She talked about feeling able to explore "lots of different things" and associates this with feeling valued: "the more able you are to take part, feel involved in a discussion, the more valued you feel" and this encouraged her to "speak up". She identified this process as the reason "you don't feel you're making a nuisance of yourself".

Safria's experience of not having a voice at home seems linked to her perception of the value placed on her opinions. She worries about whether her contributions are "really going to be connected to what others are talking about". This represents a preoccupying theme that is constraining. She acknowledges though how things are changing and how "my daughter, she's nineteen, said, 'You were a doormat mum.' It rings a bell; it must be. I did feel trodden on in a sense, you let things take place but it's very different now."

Sarah's story

Sarah learned an overriding rule about speaking from her family: "If you can't say anything nice, don't say anything at all." She felt the message included being quiet and "keep that bow in your hair" which seemed connected to ideas about femininity. The importance attached to "being nice" also extended to avoidance of arguments. Sarah was careful to follow the warning: "there's a quarrel down there, don't go down that route". Although Sarah felt that she could converse within her family she also received the message: "Children should be seen and not heard." Interestingly, in a religious context, Sarah was required to speak and this provoked "horrible memories of not speaking as a child". She was taken by her auntie to an evangelical, Pentecostal church: "The preacher would say, 'Put up your hand if you've been saved.' Everyone would look at you." Sarah found this attention very uncomfortable.

Sarah was described at school as conscientious and quiet. She felt small and shy, and talking was difficult: "I wouldn't say boo to a goose." Sarah experienced secondary school as: "worse … I would go bright red if I had to even answer a question; I wouldn't put my hand up even when I knew the answer." Sarah became more vocal when she attended school in Kampala at age 13. This was because "everyone wanted to know about the Beatles and mini skirts". The experience of being the only English pupil in the class meant: "I had no one to compare myself with, critically, unfavourably, whatever … I'm English, I'm different." She described this as having a "very freeing" effect.

Sarah gradually became conscious of having different views from others but "you would be a nice person and agree. I didn't think about it at the time." When disagreeing but not voicing this, she remembers thinking: "what a plonker—or something worse …" She connected this to the strong message from her mother: "It's nice to be important but more important to be nice." In further education Sarah became aware of disagreeing with others but experienced this as a tension: "I would want to argue but struggle with that."

Sarah experienced boys and men as more vocal so she tended "to listen more". Now Sarah advises: "If you want to be assertive you need to be more like a man, say something and not tag it." Tagging is the process Sarah identifies as women's tendency to check with the listener, to gain confirmation of what they're saying: "I believe … *don't you think?*"

In an adult learning context, Sarah concluded that being compared unfavourably to others led to her hesitation in offering an opinion. "When I was asked a question I would assume it was because I was doing something wrong. I realize now that other people were asked similar questions." Sarah acknowledges that when things were going wrong in her learning "people threw me life lines and I ignored them". She talked of worrying that she would antagonize her tutor, that by speaking she ran the risk of arguing and making it "worse". Here there seem clear links to Sarah's maternal teaching: "If you can't say anything nice, don't say anything at all," a lesson which Sarah learnt well. Sarah sees her therapy training as helping her gain an insight into the messages which came from her family of origin and that continue to influence her with regard to disagreeing with others.

Identification of trainee's dilemmas regarding speaking in therapy

Constructing the "voice entitlement" narratives brought forth dilemmas for trainees in how they talked with families in therapy. As a supervisor I became aware of these links in my work with the different women and in our group discussions. I found it helpful to think in terms of experiences for the trainees that "punctuated" their dilemma and through self-reflexivity facilitate a re-storying of the speaking narrative (see Figure 10.1). These "punctuations" presented opportunities in supervision to facilitate change. The following examples demonstrate how this informed my supervision during the life of the group.

During one session Safria expressed anxiety about feeling critical of, and lacking empathy for, the mother in the family who was worried about her son's behaviour. I had noticed that as the session became tense, Safria had begun to ask more and more questions, firing them off to the mother in quick succession. A collaborative dialogue was slowly lost in this process. Safria's technique of asking more questions seemed unhelpful in her attempts to engage the mother. Safria's "voice entitlement" narrative included an early

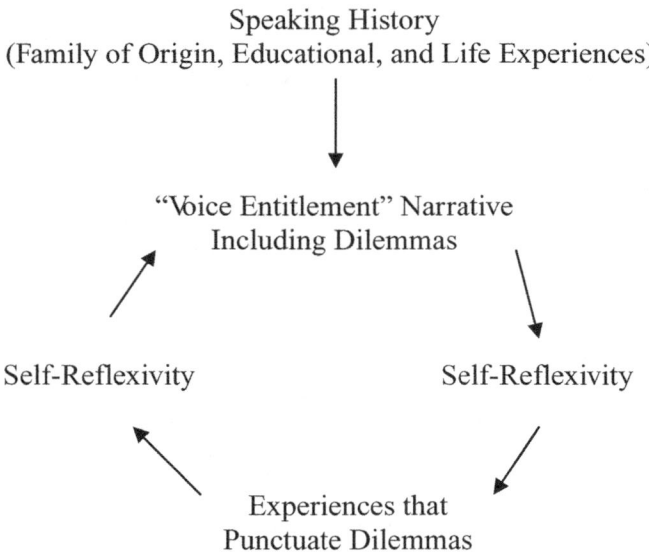

Figure 10.1. Re-Storying Dilemmas.

history where voicing opinions was discouraged. She feels safer asking questions than offering opinions. In the face of her increasing anxiety due to a rising tension in the session, Safria had reverted to asking questions where she feels "safer" rather than offering her views about the son's behaviour. During the break we agreed it was important to "offer" ideas to the mother, so we constructed an intervention and the work became more productive. I also suggested that Safria review the tape of the session, counting how many questions and how many opinions she gave, in order to help her take an "observer" position in relation to her tendency when anxious to ask questions rather than offer opinions.

As a supervisor it was helpful to understand Safria's history. Offering opinions represented a dilemma for her since it held connotations of disrespect (culturally taboo), but equally, offering opinions was equated with feeling valued (experienced on a counselling course), an event which punctuated the dilemma. Exploring the effect (on her client) of asking lots of questions helped Safria self-reflect and reposition.

Maria's preoccupation about whether to "say things others wouldn't dare say" and needing "to learn to listen more" emerged as a significant dilemma in her narrative and represented two positions she often moved between. During a painful therapy session when the mother in a family became tearful and the children looked uncomfortable, Maria became quiet and the opportunity to explore the issue was lost. We discussed possible interventions that could have explored the children's experience. On reflection, I realized that I failed to explore Maria's dilemma, so clearly articulated in her narrative. "Needing to learn to listen more" represented a powerful response to painful educational experiences (and fears of being contradicted as a child). Contextualizing her learning in the supervision group then, was this tenet, which informed her therapeutic response to the mother in this example. Maria's propensity to "say what others wouldn't dare say" could have been usefully deployed (by me as her supervisor) to empower her therapeutic stance. In addition it could also have addressed her desire "to find the words" in therapy which was one of her improvement goals. Holding the trainee's narrative in mind maximizes supervision opportunities for the excavation and re-storying of unhelpful narratives (and exploration of dilemmas) for the trainee.

Sticking with emotionally difficult issues with families was an important learning aim for Sarah. The strong maternal message of being "nice" posed a dilemma for her when painful issues arose for families. She would find herself moving to "nicer" topics, thus losing therapeutic opportunities. Sarah's openness about her wish to challenge this (nice) story meant that it was a feature of our work together. Others in the group equally understood the significance and would offer her helpful insights. Sarah's self-reflexivity promoted the active re-working of new experiences in therapy where she learnt to stay with pain and uncomfortable issues. These successes "re-storied" her speaking narrative and enhanced her voice "entitlement" (see Figure 10.1).

The potential fluidity of a narrative means that developing "voice entitlement" histories offers opportunities for locating meaningful cultural (and other) stories in a way that also allows for positive re-working. I have included below questions for supervisors to aid constructing "voice entitlement" narratives with trainees.

Questions for supervisors to explore supervisees' voice entitlement narratives

How would you define your ethnic origin?

How would you describe yourself in terms of your culture of origin?

What messages do you feel you heard from your family of origin about talking in the family—close/extended, with friends, neighbourhood, to authority? Were there rules about interrupting, offering opinions, asking questions, agreeing or disagreeing? Do you feel this was the same as similar families to your own?

What was speaking like for you at school—primary/secondary level, further education? Were there rules about asking questions, offering opinions, agreeing, disagreeing, or interrupting in these settings?

How have you found speaking in adult learning? Is it similar to your school experience or different?

How do you find speaking at work? What enables/constrains you in this context?

Are you usually like this in groups, with family, friends or to authority? What influences how much you contribute in various settings?

Is it different for you asking a question rather than making a statement? If so, in what way? Do you think you offer opinions more than ask questions in supervision or vice versa? Would this be true in other contexts, for example, home, work, socially?

Do you think you do justice to your ideas in terms of how you express yourself verbally? If this could be improved what could contribute to that change?

How do you find speaking in supervision? What could facilitate you taking more risks?

When working as a therapist do you notice yourself being different/the same as in other contexts, regarding speaking? What would your family of origin think of how you "do" talking in therapy? Would they be surprised, impressed, disapproving, unaffected?

Would you like to "do" talking differently in therapy? If so how?

How helpful/unhelpful/irrelevant would you say your culture of origin is in terms of how you make verbal contributions in therapy? Is this the same across contexts?

Are there other significant factors, such as gender, religion, or class, as examples, which have affected your verbal contributions in therapy?

Have you changed in relation to how you speak in different contexts? If so, what has been influential in this?

Can you describe a significant moment when you chose to speak despite feeling constrained? This might be in your family, at work, or in a learning context. What influenced you to speak and what was the effect? Do you often do this or is it unusual?

Can you identify a significant moment when you wanted to speak but decided against it? This could be in your family, at work, or in a learning context. What informed your decision? What do you think about it now?

If you could go back and change anything in your history regarding what you were taught about speaking would you want to? If so, what would it be?

Do you speak more than one language? If so, which ones?

What would you say the difference is for you speaking in a second language in supervision as opposed to if it was conducted in your first language? (Additional question for those with more than one language.)

If there were anything that could be changed, regarding the way we talk together, which would make supervision more helpful, what would it be?

How have you found this task?

Would you like to add anything?

Movement of "self" via language and culture

Language and cultural issues featured prominently in the life of the group. Although English was not their first language, both Safria and Maria stated their preference for speaking it in the supervision group (although there was no alternative available to them). Maria thought English was a "very polite language" and that if the group was conducted in German she "would shout more … it would bring out the negative things in me, being loud". However she also felt "it would be more me … I'm never as authentic in English as I would be in my language." Safria felt that with regards to English the "words are quite specific" and that there were differences between Gujarati and English that were cultural in origin. She felt her culture placed less emphasis on "feeling talk" and that Gujarati therefore had fewer words for different feelings.

Speaking English as a second language was an interesting aspect of exploring Maria's and Safria's narratives. For a time the impact of living with more than one language had not featured in the family therapy literature apart from De Zulueta (1990) and Burck (1997, 2004). Safria expressed a preference for speaking English in the group because of her view that Gujarati has fewer words for different emotions. Dwivedi (1996), however, highlights the richness of Asian languages in describing feelings, which challenges this idea. Other research shows that bilinguals experience a change of personality when using different languages (Grosjean, 1982) and suggest a concept of biculturalism, with different languages encompassing different world views. Safria talks about her family and culture not valuing "feeling talk" and I wonder whether speaking English allowed her to position herself differently without an overt rejection of this cultural value. "Languages can thus be viewed not only as being constitutive of meaning but also as contexts within which we position ourselves and are positioned" (Burck, 1997: 71). These ideas seem pertinent when considering Maria's preference for speaking English rather than German. Her reason was related to uncomfortable images associated with her German way of talking. She imagined that she might start shouting or being loud (something she works hard to restrain) and which is reminiscent of her early family life. Burck (1997) draws attention to adults using language to make boundaries between themselves and their family. She cites Casement (1982) who argues that Samuel Beckett (first language English) wrote in French to distance himself from his influential mother.

Bilingualism (or biculturalism) appears to provide opportunities for individuals to distance themselves from unwanted traits or ideas. It therefore offers possibilities for alternative "selves" which can be switched between. Safria and Maria both appeared to have encompassed different "selves" whilst retaining old ones. (Maria still describes returning home to Germany and being her loud self.) This suggests that supervisors could usefully pay attention to second language effects in this narrative form (in particular, exploring difference).

Cultural membership was implicated in self and identity issues for trainees. Maria's discomfort with aspects of her "Germaness" became apparent in her narrative. Her initial reticence to do her cultural genogram (Hardy and Laszloffy, 1995) in the supervision group seemed related to her rejection of negative images of her culture of origin. She expressed a sense of enduring shame connected to German aggression in the Second World War. Winawer and Wetzel (1996) draw attention to the little written about German families in the United States despite them being one of the largest and oldest immigrant groups there. They conclude that most Germans tend to suppress their Germaness in the face of negative imaging of the culture due to the holocaust and the Second World War. They view Germans as tending to blend with the dominant white culture (which their skin colour allows) rather than drawing attention to their origins. Maria describes her ethnic origin as white Caucasian, which could be an example of this. She prefers to use the description

Caucasian perhaps because it avoids being associated with Germaness, a painful reminder of cultural shame. Maria referred to herself as a more authentic therapist when using her first language (German) but preferred to speak English in the group. What was striking was her "giving up" of her authenticity in favour of speaking English because it removed the risk of her being loud. Maria's rejection of her "loud self" seems situated in her dilemmas around her culture of origin with the possible rejection of that too. The losses for Maria seem profound here. When writing about the effects of doing a cultural genogram, she reflected: "My perception of clients, my hypotheses, my prejudices, likes and dislikes are informed by my background … listening and learning from the genograms of co-students was an eye-opener. I think I will never be so blind again towards issues of cultural difference."

Last reflections

The fact that the supervision group was made up of women inevitably poses questions regarding what men's speaking histories may reveal. It would be interesting to explore men's voice entitlement narratives in a similar study as a follow-up to this work.

The construction of speaking narratives for the women inevitably invited reflections of my own history. I was reminded of exhilarating childhood memories of poetry reading in public where I was praised for the power to project my voice and, equally, of painful moments of silence when finding that a voice eluded me. In my early working life I can recall the fear when trying to contribute in professional meetings. I now think that that challenge was the beginning of a recognition of my own voice entitlement. The identification of my own dilemma in relation to being powerful/constrained has provided an important punctuation in my own self-reflexivity. I now find myself reflecting on this dilemma and experimenting in contexts previously characterized by one mode. The promotion of self-reflexivity both for me and the women in the group has been an important feature in the process. Initially, the challenge of supervising an ethnically diverse group with people at different stages in their training filled me with anxiety. However, it proved in the long run to be a significant learning experience. I am particularly grateful to the women in the supervision group for their enriching and moving contributions.

Acknowledgements

In addition to the women in the group I would also like to thank all those who supported me in the work, including Percy Aggett, David Campbell, Sara Barratt, and most notably Charlotte Burck.

References

Aggett, P. (2004). Learning Narratives in Group Supervision: Enhancing Collaborative Learning. *Journal of Systemic Therapies*. 23(3): 36–50.

Bakhtin, M. (1973/1929). *Problems of Dostoevsky's poetics* (2nd edn). Translated by R.W. Rotsel. MI, Ardis: Ann Arbor.

Baron-Cohen, S. (2003). *The Essential Difference*. Penguin Books.

Boyd-Franklin, N. (1989). *Black Families in Therapy: A Multi-systems Approach*. Guilford Press.

Brah, A. (1996). *Cartographies of Diaspora: Contesting Identities*. London/New York: Routledge.

Brown, L.M. (1998a). Voice and Ventriloquation in Girls Development. In: Henwood, K., Griffin, C. and Phoenix, A. (eds) *Standpoints and Differences: Essays in the practice of Feminist Psychology*. London: Sage. pp. 91–114.

Brown, L.M. (1998b). *Raising Their Voices: The Politics of Girls Anger*. Cambridge, MA: Harvard University Press.

Bruner, J. (1990). *Acts of Meaning*. Cambridge, MA: Harvard University Press.

Burck, C. (1997). Language and Narrative: Learning from Bilingualism. In: Papadopoulos, R.K. and Byng-Hall, J. (eds) *Multiple Voices: Narrative in Systemic Family Psychotherapy*. London: Duckworth. pp. 64–85.

Burck, C. (2004). Living in Several Languages: Implications for Therapy. *Journal of Family Therapy*. 26(Ps): 314–339.

Carter, R. (1998). *Mapping the Mind*. London: Weidenfeld and Nicolson.

Casement, P. (1982). Samuel's Beckett's Relationship to his Mother Tongue. *International Review of Psychoanalysis*. 9: 35–44.

Chodorow, N. (1974). Family Structure and Feminine Personality. In: Rosaldo, M.Z. and Lamphere, L. (eds) *Woman, Culture and Society*. Stamford University Press.

De Zulueta, F. (1990). Bilingualism and Family Therapy. *Journal of Family Therapy*. 12: 255–265.

Down, G. (2000). Supervision in a Multicultural Context. In: Barnes, G.G et al. (eds) *Systemic Supervision: A Portable Guide to Supervision Training*. Philadelphia: Jessica Kingsley. pp. 61–77.

Dwivedi, K. (1996). Race and the Child's Perspective. In: Davies, R., Upton, G. and Varma, V. (eds) *The Voice of the Child: A Handbook for Professionals*. London: Falmer Press. pp. 153–169.

Feingold, A. (1988). Cognitive Gender Differences are Disappearing. *American Psychologist*. 43(2): 95–103.

Foucault, M. (1980). *Power/Knowledge: Selected Interviews and other Writings: 1972–1977*. Gordon, C. (ed.) Translated by Gordon, C., Marshall, L., Mepham, J., and Soper, K. New York: Pantheon.

Frackowiak, R.S.J., Ashburner, J.T., Penny, W.D., Zeki, S., Friston, K.J., Frith, C.D., Dolan, R.J. and Price, C.J. (2004). *Human Brain Function*. London: Academic Press.

Gilligan, C. (1982). *In a Different Voice: Psychological Theory and Women's Development*. Cambridge, MA/London: Harvard University Press.

Gilligan, C. (1993). Letter to readers (in preface to second edition). *In a Different Voice: Psychological Theory and Women's Development*. Cambridge, MA/London: Harvard University Press. p. ix–xxvii.

Gorell-Barnes, G. (2002). Getting it Right, Getting it Wrong: Developing an Internal Discourse about Ethnicity and Difference. In: Mason, B. and Sawyer, A. (eds) *Exploring the Unsaid*. Karnac Books. pp. 133–147.

Greenfield, S. (1996). *The Human Mind Explained: The Control Centre of the Living Machine*. London: Cassell.

Grosjean, F. (1982). *Life with Two Languages*. Cambridge, Mass: Harvard University Press.

Hardy, K.V. and Laszloffy, T.A. (1995). The Cultural Genogram: Key to Training Culturally Competent Family Therapists. *Journal of Marital and Family Therapy*. 21(3): 227–237.

Harvey, E. (1992). *Ventriloquized Voices*. New York: Routledge.

Hermans, H.J.M. and Kempen, H.J. (1993). *The Dialogical Self: Meaning as Movement*. London: Academic Press Inc.

Hines, M., Allen, L. and Gorski, R. (1992) Sex Differences in Sub Regions of the Medial Nucleus of the Amygdale and the Bed Nucleus of the Stria Terminals of the Rat. *Brain Research*. 579: 321–326.

Kimura, D. (1987). Are Men's and Women's Brains Really Different? *Canadian Psychology*. 28: 133–147.

Kitzinger, C. and Wilkinson, S. (1996). Theorizing Representing the Other. In: Wilkinson, S. and Kitzinger, C. (eds) *Representing the Other*. London: Sage. pp. 1–32.

Krause, I-B. (2002). *Culture and System in Family Therapy*. London/New York: Karnac Books.

Kroeber, A.L. and Kluckhohn, C. (1952). Cultures: A Critical Review of Concepts and Definitions. *Peabody Museum Papers*. 47.

Laird, J. (1998). Theorizing Culture, Narrative Ideas and Practice Principles. In: McGoldrick, M. (ed.) *Re-Visioning Family Therapy*. The Guilford Press.

Linell, P. (1990). The Power of Dialogue Dynamics. In: Markova, I. and Froppa, K. (eds) *The Dynamics of Dialogue*. New York: Harvester Wheatsheaf. pp. 147–177.

Newson, J. (1977). An Intersubjective Approach to the Systematic Description of Mother–Infant Interaction. In: Schaffer, H.R. (ed.) *Studies in Mother–Infant Interactions*. London: Academic Press.

Parekh, B. (2000) *Rethinking Multiculturalism: Cultural Diversity and Political Theory*. Palgrave.

Piaget, J. (1965/1932). *The Moral Judgement of the Child*. New York: The Free Press.

Pinker, S. (1994). *The Language Instinct*. London: Penguin.

Shaywitz, B., Shaywitz, S., Pugh, K., Constables, R., Skudlarski, P., Fulbright, R., Bronan, R., Flekher, J., Shankweiler, D., Katz, L. and Gore, J. (1995). Sex Differences in the Functional Organization of the Brain for Language. *Nature*. 373: 607–609.

Smith, J.A., Jarman, M, and Osborn, M. (1999). Doing Interpretative Phenomenological Analysis. In: Murray, M. and Chamberlain, K. (eds) *Qualitative Health Psychology Theories*. London: Sage Publications. Chapter 14.

Stern, D.N. (1977). *The First Relationship: Infant and Mother*. Cambridge, MA: Harvard University Press.

White, M. and Epston, D. (1990). *Narrative Means to Therapeutic Ends*. New York: Norton.

Winawer, H. and Wetzel, N.A. (1996). German Families. In: McGoldrick, M., Pearce, J.K. and Giordano, J. (eds) *Ethnicity and Family Therapy*. New York/London: Guilford Press. pp. 555–572.

CHAPTER ELEVEN

Addressing issues of race and culture in supervision

Yvonne Ayo

I recently had an interesting conversation with a white colleague about the film Slumdog Millionaire (2008), *a story of a young Indian man who grew up in the slums of Mumbai and enters the competition* Who Wants to Be a Millionaire? *I had queried whether the term "slumdog" was an appropriate term to use and my colleague had responded with an assurance that the director had been sufficiently culturally sensitive. A couple of weeks later, she returned to the earlier discussion and noted how, as a white woman, she had quickly ended any further talk of a possibly controversial issue in which we may have different ideas and opinions and give different meanings to the term "slumdog". This later conversation was particularly interesting because it made me aware of how, having initiated the discussion, I had not pursued it further at the time. It was also significant that my colleague chose to return to a difficult episode and reflect upon the meaning of her response to my query. We talked of white privilege and how this can impact upon conversations about race and culture between experienced colleagues who are racially and ethnically different.*

This episode connected me to my interest in how these conversations occur within the supervisory relationship, the subject of this chapter. Based on a small qualitative research project in which supervisors and supervisees were interviewed about their experience of how race and culture were addressed in their training and within their team, I draw upon ideas of racial sensitivity and racial awareness to explore the complexities of talking about race and culture in supervision groups. I consider ways in which questions of race, culture and ethnicity are raised in supervision and how these impact upon the therapist and supervisor and their relationship. I go on to discuss the implications for practitioners.

Terminology

It is crucial to discuss culture in relation to race and ethnicity. Karamat Ali (2003) suggests that culture is a concept that people are more familiar discussing than that of race and that this emphasis on culture has overshadowed thinking and talking about race as a separate and legitimate subject. Akamatsu (1998) argues that phrases such as "multiculturalism" and "cultural difference" often obscure the experience of inequality in our society and can prevent culturally sensitive practices. "Not having to notice" is a privilege and "noticing", not surprisingly, arouses much anxiety and defensiveness. This is a valid point, but my view is that the terminologies of "ethnicity", "race" and "culture" are so intertwined that each term connects to the other. The issue is how therapists, supervisors and training programmes connect these terms.

Such terms are subject to debate because they have socio-political consequences. I shall begin by offering a definition as a marker for further discussion.

Culture used to be considered as "something out there", a social concept, but is now often seen as being something which is "inside" a person, a psychological state (D'Andrade cited in Fernando, 1991: 9). More broadly, culture refers to distinctive ways of life, as well as the shared values and meanings common to different groups—nations, classes and sub-cultures—and historical periods. Culture is part of everyday social practices by which meanings are produced and exchanged within a group. These practices form part of everyday life, are deeply embedded in social relationships (Krause, 2002) and are constantly evolving processes. Brah considers these processes as "signifying practices" in which "social meaning is constituted, appropriated, contested and transformed" (1996: 234). Identities are developed within these practices and individuals are postioned or position themselves in relation to their racialization, ethnicity, class, gender, sexual orientation and disability.

Ethnicity applies to everyone and as a term lacks precision but refers to the definition of cultural and racial groups. The main feature of an ethnic group is the sense of belonging together with shared common attributes to do with cultural practices, shared history and language in which the construction of subjectivities and identity are located (Hall, 1992).

Although race is a social construct, the essentialist approach to this is socially significant. Race is frequently used to refer to "black" and "white", which have been regarded as opposites. Race is seen as inherited and evident in biological or physical differences or in culture. Skin colour, physiognomy, culture, or territory have been used as markers of the boundaries between races which overlap with notions of ethnicity. The term "racialization" emphasizes the idea that "racial meanings are not static but are social processes" (Tizard and Phoenix, 2002: 6). Racialization of identities intersects with ethnicities, culture, class and gender and as Brah (1996) points out, is the site of multiple contradictions.

Race, culture and family therapy

Within the past ten years family therapy theory has broadened to include issues of class, culture, race, gender and sexual orientation and is reflected in training programmes and in the elaboration of culturally competent practices.

The thinking about culture and race in family therapy is informed by social constructionism, considering knowledge to be context-bound, not fixed or universal; there are multiple "knowledges". There is no objective reality and what we know as "truth" is considered to be part of power relations. Postmodern ideas of the self, created and re-created through language, have challenged essentialist ideology within systemic therapy. Identities are viewed as socially produced, multiple and multi-positioned in different contexts. Each individual is located in and opts for differing and at times conflicting identities, depending on the social, political, economic and ideological aspects of their situation which change over time. Contextual variables such as race, gender, class and religion are a few of the dimensions of self that shape identity (Hardy and Lappin, 1997).

The concept of "othering", which was developed in anthropological literature in relation to representations of ethnicity and race, is a particularly useful idea. The process of othering considers dualities of power and powerlessness, inclusion and exclusion and representation. "The Other is a construction or a set of discourses through which the dominant group defines itself ... the Other is silenced or delegitimized" and not accorded expert status on their own life or on that of the dominant group (Wilkinson and Kitzinger, 1996: 9). This concept is particularly helpful in relation to how cultural narratives of supervisees are addressed in supervision.

Supervision and training issues

Increasingly, family therapy theory has been developed to locate culture at its theoretical core (see Falicov's [1995] multi-dimensional ecological comparative approach and Almeida et al.'s [1998] cultural context model). Burnham and Harris (2002) coined the acronym SOCIAL GRRAACCES to raise therapists' awareness of gender, race, religion, age, ability, class, culture, ethnicity and sexuality. Others have applied a cultural lens to family structures, for example, the cultural genogram (Hardy and Laszloffy, 1995) and the African-American genogram (Watts-Jones, 1997) and guidelines for multicultural training (Green, 1998) have been produced. Hardy and Laszloffy (2000) have also provided strategies for addressing race and racism in family therapy training. They have distinguished between racial awareness (the recognition of race and that it shapes realities) and racial sensitivity (the ability to translate racial awareness into action).

Use of self has become increasingly important in systemic therapy and training when working with cultural/racial differences. Some training programmes are based on cultural knowledge, awareness raising, skills training and contact with minority groups or clients (Green, 1998). Ladany et al.'s (1997) research into supervisees' cultural competence and racial identity found that the supervisor's instruction to focus on multicultural issues was a significant factor in trainees' development as clinicians. Boyd-Franklin (1989, 2000),

McGoldrick (1998) and Owusu-Bempah (2002) addressed ways to develop therapists' abilities to work with culturally diverse groups. This questioned the cultural value systems of Western trained professionals whose focus is predominantly upon the individual and how they conceptualize working with collectivist cultures (Owusu-Bempah, 2002; Triandis, 1994 cited in Owusu-Bempah, 2002). Embedded within some of the trainings is the implication that it is for the white majority students to inform themselves of the minority cultural groups. McGoldrick (1982) and others have pointed out the diversity of white American ethnicities which also need to be explored within the context of training and that can disrupt "othering" (Nolte, 2007; Santin, 2008).

Fine and Turner (1997) addressed the important issues of how power relations are constructed and played out in collaborative supervision relationships. The first level of practice is the "interpersonally situated realities" which are developed from the on-going conversations between the supervisor and supervisee in which they can mutually understand and influence each other. The second level is the "personally situated realities" which arise from internal conversations of the individual therapist and supervisor which shape personal and ethical meanings and practices. Gender, race, culture and religion are personally situated realities concerning which collaborative supervision can provide a space for circulation of ideas and beliefs. But the authors note that the "preferred patterns" of some supervision do not always take particular needs of supervisees into account. This has significance for supervisees of ethnic and minority cultures within predominantly white supervision groups.

Holloway's (1995) research of the supervisory relationship echoed some of these constraints in supervision regarding race and culture. Holloway found that supervisors and supervisees, particularly in cross-cultural contexts, did not speak directly about cross-cultural issues and that many of the issues of power and race are undetectably subtle in such contexts or remain only "inside the head of the participant" (p. 76).

There is also the issue that when race and culture are raised in training contexts, a pattern can develop of the group's expectation of a member, who is perceived as having a particular cultural heritage and expertise, to act as the "native informant" (Bell Hook, 1994: 43). This can cause constraints for the individual if they wish to talk from another position and raises questions for the supervisor as to how to manage the dilemma for the individual and encourage the team to broaden their thinking about culture and race.

The study

The literature both conveys the importance of addressing race and culture in family therapy training and the constraints of talking about it within the supervisory relationship. It also highlights the dilemmas created for all by the ways in which black and ethnic minority supervisees are sometimes positioned. I wanted to explore in more depth how questions of race, culture and ethnicity are actually raised in supervision and its effects.

Six participants; three supervisors and three supervisees, were selected from various cultural backgrounds and were interviewed using a semi-structured interview. Discourse analysis, which poses questions about the use and meanings of language to analyse ways in which individuals give accounts of themselves in interaction with others, how these accounts are context-dependent and the consequences of particular discourses, was chosen as particularly relevant. Discourse here refers to a set of meanings, statements, metaphors, images, stories and representations that produce particular versions of events in particular ways (Potter and Wetherell, 1987). Discourses are drawn on and developed from individual experiences, but also represent meanings in the wider society which are constantly changing. Harré and Gillett (1994) note how we live in many different discourses, some of which will conflict; that we develop a complex subjectivity from participation in these discourses, some of which are more dominant than others. Within discourses we choose to take up a position, or are positioned by others, on the basis of what we say and do (Campbell and Groenbaek, 2006). In conversation a person's moral beliefs and personal attributes as a speaker are collected and different types of discourses influence the position taken up by individuals. It is a fluid process used by individuals to make sense of a conversation, speech act, or action. Examining the discourses that systemic supervisors and supervisees draw upon may help reveal contradictions and assumptions.

Three supervisors—Jane and Sheila (white English) and Josie (African Caribbean)—and three supervisees—Emma (white Welsh),

Bella (mixed heritage) and Evelyn (Asian)—took part in the study. They all shared the view that it was the supervisor's responsibility to raise issues of culture and race within the supervisory relationship. I was interested in exploring with them the different ways in which the discussion was raised and the effects upon the supervisors, supervisees and the supervisory relationship. This first section focuses on the supervisors' accounts and the second on the supervisees' perspectives.

Supervisors' discourses

The three supervisors talked of race and culture within different contexts: a team of mental health and educational professionals; a training context; and a clinical supervision group. The first extract is from Jane, a white English manager of a mental health team.

Extract one

Y: "Do you think that discussions on race, ethnicity and culture should be initiated by the supervisor?"

Jane: "Yes, no question about it, you know, when ... when I took over the supervision of the team and I increased the people ... I talked to them and I said have you had white supervision, black supervision, what might I be missing as a white worker, how am I going to know I'm missing it and how can we create a safe enough context for you to be able to say to me 'look, it's rubbish,' my experience as a black worker, you can't say that, how can we create that context, yes I think it has to be raised by the supervisor. I think it's an ethical responsibility."

The text shows how Jane develops her team and enquires about collaborative practices to the point where staff are invited to declare her perspective as "rubbish". There is the recognition, acknowledgement and articulation of racial and cultural diversity in the way in which Jane initiates the naming of her whiteness, thus centrally locating race within the supervisory and managerial relationship. Jane recognizes her powerful position as manager and demonstrates a way of working towards a collaborative model of supervision. Her discursive use of "I" here demonstrates her sense of agency in the organizational context, in that she "took over the team" and "increased the people" and draws upon her use of power and demonstrates her effectiveness in organizational practices. In her supervisory/managerial role, Jane positions herself as responsible, moral and reflective by initiating talk on racialization in the supervisory relationship. Her racially and ethnically diverse team are invited to collaborate in the development of safe practices when talking of race and can express their expertise in this inclusive style of management. In order for these conversations to take place a shared understanding of a safe context is to be created between the supervisor and her team.

Josie, an African Caribbean supervisor, described a training context in which she addressed race and culture with her students. Using a chapter from Fernando's (1995) book, *Mental Health in a Multi-Ethnic Society*, the trainees were invited to offer their comments and ideas.

Extract two

Y: "It sounds like you also had to manage a level of discomfort that people experience."

Josie: "Fairly recent umm ... I think it comes up every year, every year it is there and it is this year in a different way because I gave them a different task ... to do ... I gave them a paper to read and to select whether it was the kind of thing that was new to them, the Fernando paper, you might know it, yeah and ... some people say 'Well oh God there we go again, whingeing, these people are always whingeing' and some say 'He's got it on the button, that is exactly what we should be thinking and the way we should be thinking ...' and some people say 'Oh whatever, I don't care, it doesn't bother me', so I got them to go into three groups to pick which group suited them and then to talk out to each other about why they were in that group and so on and then fed that back and that was really interesting umm to begin to understand how some people might think I have been talking about this, I think a lot of people were interested where it was found that a black person might go into the group that had said 'oh whatever' you know and so so it's getting people to think about it and not to judge each other about it and have a dialogue which is difficult."

Josie directly addresses race and culture with trainees who are at the early stage of their systemic practice. Here, the training context is the highest context marker for Josie, who facilitates the trainees' differences of experiences and understanding of race and culture and relevant literature. Use of reading material from a black clinician's perspective creates a range of responses which are further explored in self-selected smaller groups. Some surprise emerged from trainees that black trainees chose to go into a group which appeared less concerned about the issues raised in the article. Three discourses are presented, that of denial ("these people" who "are always whingeing"); recognition ("that is exactly what we should be thinking") and imperviousness ("it doesn't bother me") and trainees then give account of their own position in relation to the literature and their choice of membership of a particular group. The discourse of group membership is privileged—of sharing the same responses to the issue of race and culture, of being of like minds— rights of membership thus creating the possibility of open dialogue between groups. However, also demonstrated are assumptions of students to black membership of a group who are less focused on race and culture. The discourse of training, of challenging trainees' ideas and assumptions, of generating new ideas through experiential methods, is part of Josie's intention and an established part of her practice. This approach, through the facilitation of inter-group discussions forms part of Josie's way of her discovering how her trainees had understood her presentation of the topic; it also links the issue of race and culture, Josie's own position, the students' response and their abilities to give a moral account of their individual choice to join a particular group. The supervisor seeks to open a dialogical space for different belief systems to be discussed.

Sheila, a white, English supervisor of a clinical group discussed her thoughts about race and culture in her practice.

Extract three

Y: *"So do you think that the discussions on race, ethnicity and culture should be initiated by the supervisor?"*

Sheila: *"Well I think it ... obviously the supervisor has the responsibility to cover, try and cover everything and keep the thinking ... and I, it is I mean it is something I have struggled with a bit with*

>   *the ... course of how to do it when the yes, when the conversation hasn't wanted to go there, do I, how much do I bring it back and how skilled am I at doing that."*
> Y: "Umm."
> **Sheila:** *"... because maybe I have a tendency to not want to think about it either."*

This text demonstrates the discourse of professional obligation which Sheila draws on to "cover everything" including the trainees' abilities to think and talk about race and culture and the effects upon her ("I have struggled ...") in relation to the issue, her trainees and their learning context. The supervisor's "obvious" responsibility represents the moral and professional obligation in which supervisors take on sole responsibility for "keeping the thinking". The juxtaposition of the professional expectations of supervisory practice and the personal experiences of undertaking the supervisory role suggests a "struggle" in achieving this. Is this a personal expectation of the supervisor or of the clinical supervision context or both?

The conversation on race is reported as separate, independent, active and determinant ("when the conversation hasn't wanted to go there") which the supervisor struggles to organize ("to bring it back") and queries the extent to which she has the right to do so and whether she is sufficiently skilled to do so. "Skill" in managing talk on race is presented as a key component in supervision when race talk occurs and raises a moral dilemma for Sheila who queries her right to facilitate the talk and her skill in doing so. However, "skill" could also signify a technique which is acquired through learning or experience and the determinant nature of talk on race and culture de-skills the supervisor. The text informs us of ways in which such talk can be discomforting for supervisors and trainees. Sheila's reflection that she may have "a tendency to not want to think about it either" further compounds her dilemma. As a white supervisor there are professional obligations to include race talk in supervision groups yet Sheila notes her "tendency" not to engage with race talk. Simpson notes how "the silencing of whiteness has led to de-racialization of identity enabling those categorized as white to ignore, deny, avoid or forget their racialized subjectivity and social positionings" (cited in Guneratnam 2005: 112). Sheila's tendency not to talk of race is an aspect of the avoidance of racialization and is in opposition to her professional supervisory obligations thus contributing to her discomfort.

Discussion: Supervisors' discourses

The supervisors' discourses include their power in the production of meanings in the interpersonally situated realities when race and culture are centrally located. In the three extracts, the supervisors' discourse is of acceptance of responsibility for initiating and maintaining talk of race in terms of: declaration of whiteness; power and mutuality (Jane); facilitation of different positions (Josie); and of dilemmas of practice (Sheila). Both Jane's and Sheila's extracts show how the direct relationship between the supervisor, the supervisees and race/culture talk is managed, whereas Josie's extract demonstrates the use of group process to facilitate ideas. The chosen exercise permits black supervisees to join the "denial" group and indicates their differences from the writer and/or the subjects of the article selected for discussion. This process enables the trainees to position themselves in relation to the training context, the literature and the different meanings that emerged during discussions.

The complex topic of race and culture and the complexities of supervision are demonstrated by these supervisors who use their positions of power to facilitate race talk, informed by their personal and professional experiences. Jane, for example, recalled her earlier experiences of being a white minority member of predominantly black and non-European groups and how these exposures to cultural difference and othering have contributed significantly to her professional practice of naming racial and cultural differences early in the supervisory relationship. Josie's practice as a supervisor adheres to "contextual markers" (Lawless et al. 2001: 188), those aspects of a conversation which include either a subtle or direct reference to race, ethnicity, or culture which Josie identifies and discusses further with all her supervisees. Josie's racially and ethnically mixed trainees talk of their subject positions in relation to literature from a black perspective, similar to that of McDowell et al. (2002) who discussed ways of creating a space for racial dialogue. Sheila talks of her own reluctance to talk of race.

These supervisors' talk demonstrates different levels of racial awareness and sensitivity (Hardy and Laszloffy, 2000). Jane draws on discourses of whiteness, power, race and culture. She names her whiteness in relation to the racial differences within her team and presents positions of hierarchy and equality. Her team are invited to inform, correct and adjust her ideas about race, thus placing them in a position of expertise but it remains ambiguous whether they talk from their own personal position or that of the native informant. Power is re-negotiated between the supervisor and the team as their cultural expertise is privileged. Josie facilitates the positioning of trainees in relation to literature which opened dialogue. Sheila positions herself in the discourse of supervisors' responsibilities and dilemmas when talking of race and culture, the reliance on technique and her discomfort in facilitating talk on race. The extract concerns constraint in having to include "everything" and the experience, as a white supervisor, in managing a discomforting topic. The tensions indicate the reflexive relationship between the culture of supervisory practice and the culture within the supervisory relationship (Burnham and Harris, 2002). They highlight the levels of tension that occur, for example, the reluctance and the professional obligation to ensure that race and culture is addressed and the effect on trainees when they are obliged to engage with issues of race and culture.

Both Jane and Josie have developed a level of comfort within themselves and draw upon personal and professional experiences in their managerial and training contexts. The supervisor's abilities in raising these discussions model a sense of "comfort in themselves" (Boyd-Franklin, 2000: 208) which allows the trainees to develop their own skills and confidence to talk within the team and to their clients about race and culture. But how do supervisors develop skills to facilitate these discussions with trainees?

Supervisees' discourses

Three supervisees, Bella (English/Jamaican), Emma (white (Welsh) and Evelyn, (Pakistani) thought it was important that the supervisor takes responsibility to raise race and culture but that it was also a shared responsibility.

The first supervisee, Bella, is of mixed heritage in a culturally diverse team with a white supervisor.

Extract four

Bella: *"I think it is important ... I mean my team, we are from everywhere, we are from all over the world, it's amazing ... and the issue of culture, it doesn't ... does it come up ... it must come up ... it ... it comes up in a sense that we speak from different positions and we are all heard so that is how it comes up and obviously my team is managed by Iris and she does that really, really well and acknowledges different experiences in regards to culture, ethnicity, class, educational and ... and ... and ... it's all valid."*

Bella describes a multicultural mental health team whose international make up is valued, an indication of how unusual this may be. The discourse is of validation of cultural and racial differences. The descriptions of being from "everywhere" and "all over the world" suggests the team's global nature and how they occupy, represent and articulate different cultural and racialized positions. Their appointment as a team informs us of the significance of cultural differences and the multicultural population from whom they draw their clients within the discourses of management. Differences are acknowledged within the team whose individual voices are "heard" and the facilitation of the manager demonstrates her recognition of the intersection of "culture, ethnicity, class and education" of her team members' experiences. This approach fits with Falicov's (1995) and Brah's (1996) critique of "ethnicism" which posits ethnic difference as the primary modality around which social life is constituted and experienced and such groups are assumed to be internally homogeneous. This approach contests stereotypes and acknowledges the social experiences of individuals. Although team members are "native informants", a collaborative context is created in which talking and listening to experiences of difference are significant and valued.

The next participant, Emma, White, Welsh-speaking, is part of an all white clinical training group with a white supervisor.

Extract five:

Emma: *"Yes, they are but ... sorry ... I am hesitating here because I also think that there's a danger of it becoming ... I'm trying to think*

> *what the word is, where it becomes like tokenism, let's be aware and the supervisor takes the responsibility for that and we don't, so ... yes it is important that it is raised but I also think that responsibility is shared 'cos otherwise it can, as it has done in the past, appear like it's ticking the race/culture box.*

Emma tells us about the pitfalls of possible "tokenism" or "ticking the race/culture box" in discussions of race and culture within supervision groups. Within the collaborative relationship, Emma refers to the transparency of the power relations—"the supervisor takes responsibility for that and we don't", draws upon the supervisory contract and the ethical and professional responsibilities of the supervisor for what occurs in supervision (Fine and Turner, 1997). Emma's statement suggests that the supervisor takes responsibility for ensuring that talk on race and culture does not become tokenistic and that the supervisor has the ability to facilitate conversations on race and culture. Yet Emma makes two claims: that the responsibility of race talk lies with the supervisor; and that "responsibility is shared", suggesting that supervisees also participate in the initiation of race talk. Collaborative practice and the personal agency of the supervisees are developed in the group who feel able to initiate talk on race and culture if the supervisor does not do so. This may also be the supervisor's way of finding out the extent to which race talk is embedded in her group or whether supervisees are sufficiently comfortable and confident to demonstrate racial and cultural awareness.

Emma's reference to "ticking the race/culture box" draws from her previous experiences of how such talk has been done in professional contexts and forms part of white privilege and the constraints in talking of race and culture. Nolte (2007: 82) writes of white therapists taking a normative position, thus finding "any exploration of their own ethnic and cultural differences, privilege and power, a risky encounter which could be counter-productive". Emma also referred to her childhood experience of being a member of a minority linguistic group and her deep sense of marginalization, particularly in her early years. This sense of difference has enabled Emma to identify with those who are disadvantaged and powerless and she has often chosen to learn about race and culture from her clients and colleagues using cultural naiveté and curiosity (Dyche and Zayas, 1995).

Evelyn (Asian) talked of an episode in an all white supervision group with a white supervisor as follows:

Extract six

Evelyn: "I felt very aware of the difference, my difference, so there's the couple and the white team coming in ... I felt undermined ... slightly."

Y: "So is that something that has been talked about in your team before about differences, as sense of difference?"

Evelyn: "No actually ... It was only that incident highlighted it and then I was able to talk about it, saying this really made me feel this way."

Y: "Do you think if it had been raised before, it had been brought up before ... if your team had discussed differences before, do you think that it might have been more helpful?"

Evelyn: "Yeah, I think it would have helped if we had talked about it beforehand umm to be aware of it, so it did not catch me by surprise, you know, hold on, I'm feeling like ... the couple would respond to the team and not to me umm so if we talked about the differences we might have talked about the technique a little bit more ... all the things that I might have felt might have come up and we could have tackled it before we actually did."

Evelyn talks of the dilemmas created for her when talk of race and culture had not been previously discussed in her group and her individual responsibility in having to raise this in her team. However, Evelyn was the only member of the group who was visibly culturally and racially different and describes a double experience of marginalization. Franklin (1999: 122) writes of this discourse and names it the "invisibility syndrome" which refers to the "small social slights" experienced by African American men in which they are rendered invisible by white people and not perceived of "as ourselves". This wider discourse is also shared by black and ethnic minority people in Britain. Evelyn's first experience is of awareness of difference—"I felt very aware of the difference"—followed by being "undermined" or made invisible, marginalized by the white clients who acknowledged her white team members. The second part of the marginalization process is her dilemma in raising the issue with her white team members and supervisor, an experience echoed by Santin (2008) and Khan (2002). Evelyn was aware of how she could be perceived by her colleagues and supervisor, the effect upon their group relationships and of her relationship with her supervisor and a "fear of not being heard or understood" (Santin, 2008: 14). In order to make sense of the clinical episode, Evelyn adopts the position of initiator of the team discussion thus taking a risk with her group. Evelyn processes ways of managing racism and selects a personal, direct statement of "saying this really made me feel this way". She demonstrates self-management in terms of controlling her emotions, "feeling undermined", observation of the couple's response to her white team members and formulation of her response—"that incident highlighted it and then I was able to talk about it".

Evelyn's statement suggests that the incident created an opportunity to raise issues of difference, race and culture which had been previously silenced—"no actually … it was only that incident …" Talk on race and culture occurred from an episode, which suggests that if this had not occurred Evelyn's experiences and ideas would have remained "inside her head" (Holloway, 1995: 76). Evelyn's discourse of being "caught by surprise" draws from the black trainee discourse of expectation that race and culture will be raised but uncertainty as to when this will occur and how it will be discussed. She occupied a visible racial and cultural difference from her group which was silenced and experienced a dilemma; a sense of not being prepared in relation to the group, the clients and the supervisor, resulting in being othered.

Discussion: supervisees' discourses

Bella's (of mixed heritage), Emma's (white, Welsh) and Evelyn's (Asian) extracts demonstrate the different positions and effects upon supervisees when issues of race and culture are discussed in supervision groups.

All three representations show us the different racialized subject positions that the supervisees occupy and speak from in their supervision groups. Bella's representation is of acknowledgement of race/culture and the intersections of culture, class, ethnicity and class which enable the supervisees to talk from their own subject positions within her team. This description draws upon the discourse of naming difference, culture and race and the effects upon the team members of validation of their experiences. Emma's talk represents the sharing of responsibility between supervisor and supervisees of race talk within supervision groups. Emma draws upon her membership of a minority language group which has particular experiences of historical, political and cultural marginalization. Her description of "tokenism" and "ticking the race/culture box" refers to her view of the importance of centrally locating race talk which creates further understandings in supervision groups thus avoiding practices of tokenism.

Evelyn's text represents the effects of black and ethnic minority individuals placed in a culturally mixed supervision group where race and culture are silenced topics. An episode with clients triggers Evelyn to draw from the discourse of black professionals, to take a position and to name the effects of the clients' behaviour towards her.

Researcher and participant relationships

I am mindful of the impact of the identity and the power of the researcher upon participants and the extent to which the subject of race, the racialized identities of the participants and myself influenced the responses to the questions. Bella's extract almost disclaims talk of race by referring to "different positions" which may have been co-created between us, as women of mixed heritage. I note the contrast to the justificatory rhetoric of Jane and Emma, supervisor and supervisee, who use terms of "tokenism" and "ethical responsibility" to announce their moral position. Was my racial difference a constraint in how to talk in a particular way about race? One of my assumptions of the research was that those who volunteered would find it easier to talk about race but now wonder about the extent to which the intersection of topic, our different positions and our racialized identities created particular meanings, unease and discomfort which I had not explored. Gunaratnam (2005: 114) questions "the hidden assumptions through which we routinely attempt to understand and read the meanings of 'race' and 'ethnicity' in people's lives".

Implications for practice

Both the supervisors and supervisees in this small study present a range of practices, dilemmas and tensions around the subjects of race and culture. Three themes have emerged which are important for practice.

The first is that direct, open talk of racialization and an acknowledgement of the supervisor's power enabled race and culture to be normalized and be central in the supervisory and therapeutic relationships. Ideas can be embedded in practice if there is an open space for curiosity or uncertainty about cultural knowledge. Lawless et al. (2001: 191) note that race talk is not "a neat and tidy conversation", that the talk can be "ambiguous and meander through and around other topical areas" and, if the supervisor's attention is insufficient, can be missed. They described ways in which markers such as "values, immigration and language" were interwoven into other aspects of the conversation and the supervisors' recognition enabled race talk to become more explicit. In my study, participants talked of their varied experiences of race talk which ranged from descriptions of episodic experiences to everyday accounts of differences. There was a notable difference between those who experienced race talk regularly, as part of their everyday conversations and those who had more episodic talks on race. Regular race talk enabled participants to discuss race and culture from different positions and to share responsibility in initiating race talk which echoes Boyd-Franklin's (1989) idea of the developing comfort in race talk. Hardy and Laszloffy (2000) recommends that white professionals should experience being a member of a minority exposed to another culture to question white privilege and increase racial awareness.

A second important theme to emerge in this research is that of the timing of talk of race and culture in supervision groups. There is a marked difference between those supervisees whose teams had begun to talk of race and culture and the one whose team had not yet done so. Whilst it may have been the supervisor's intention to discuss race and culture in the group, the clinical episode became more significant because of the apparent silencing of race which created the supervisee's obligation to raise the issue with her team.

The third issue is that the research raised some questions about the assumptions that supervisors may make about trainees' levels of cultural competence before their attendance in the group. The cultural competency models that are used in the early stages of training can be re-visited to further develop supervisees' ideas about race and culture. This would enable race and culture to be embedded in practice and normalized within supervision groups.

In my own practice as a supervisor, I am developing methods and techniques for centralizing race and culture within the supervision context which include initial enquiries about whether supervisees have any experiences of difference, whether they have had supervisors of different ethnicities and whether they worked clinically with clients of difference. The cultural genogram is then completed and supervisees are requested to bring their genograms to the clinical sessions to discuss any personal resonances and other issues from the clinical work. Reading material is provided for further discussion and I consider the importance of balancing my attention to race and culture versus the academic requirements of formally assessed clinical supervision.

In some of my conversations with other supervisors we have shared ideas about how to keep ideas of cultural and racial differences alive in, for example, an all white supervision group or a group who did not openly acknowledge their differences. Peer groups for supervisors can provide an opportunity for supervisors to share practice and discuss dilemmas. I have been a member of a support group of systemic practitioners (African Caribbean, European, white English) who meet together regularly to discuss issues of race and culture. It provides a forum for us to share our experiences of racism, white privilege and marginalization and for us to further develop our professional expertise.

Conclusion

The six supervisors and supervisees who have participated in this small project have shared their experiences and dilemmas of practice in relation to talking of race and culture within the supervisory relationship. Within the discourse of supervision, supervisors have taken positions of naming whiteness, power and racial and cultural diversity, facilitated discussions in which black and ethnic minority group members can take up their subject positions in relation to the discussion of race and culture and represented reluctance, discomfort and dilemmas regarding the supervisor's responsibilities and obligations.

The supervisees have talked of the contrasting effects of opening dialogue on race and culture and the silencing of race/culture talk within teams. The silencing of race talk, broken by a clinical episode, caused the supervisee to take a position with her team and initiate a discussion. It is clear from this small project that significant differences were experienced between Bella and Emma who understood race/culture talk as part of collaborative practices and Evelyn who experienced race/culture talk within a context of silence. In order for these conversations to take place a context of safety, trust, collaboration and transparency is required for supervisees to avoid experiences remaining "inside their head". The challenge for supervisors and supervisees is to create a relationship in which differences can be identified and regularly articulated.

References

Aggett, P. (2004). Learning Narratives in a Group Supervision: Enhancing Collaborative Learning. *Journal of Systemic Therapies*. 23(3): 36–45.

Akamatsu, N. (1998). The Talking Oppression Blues. In: McGoldrick, M. (ed.) *Re-Visioning Family Therapy*. New York: Guilford Press. pp. 129–144.

Almeida, R. Woods, R., Messineo, T. and Font, R. (1998). The Cultural Context Model. In: McGoldrick, M. (ed.) *Re-Visioning Family Therapy*. New York: Guilford Press. pp. 414–431.

Ariel, S. (1999). *Culturally Competent Family Therapy: A General Model (Contributions in Psychology)*. Connecticut: Praeger Publishers.

Beaty, E., Dall'Alba, G. and Marton, F. (1997). The Personal Experience of Learning in Higher Education. In: Sutherland, P. (ed.) *Adult Learning: A Reader*. Sterling, VA: Kogan Page Ltd. pp. 150–165.

Bobele, M., Gardiner, G. and Biever, J. (1995) Supervision as Social Construction. *Journal of Systemic Therapies*. 14(2): 14–25.

Boyd-Franklin, N. (1989). *Black Families in Therapy: A Multisystems Approach*. London/New York: Guilford Press.

Boyd-Franklin, N. and Hafer-Bry, B. (2000). *Reaching Out in Family Therapy*. London/New York: Guilford Press.

Brah, A. (1996). *Cartographies of Diaspora*. London: Routledge.

Buhl, K. Christie, Y. and Bhugra, D. (1995). The Essential Elements of Culturally Sensitive Psychiatric Services. *International Journal of Social Psychiatry*. 41(4): 242–256.

Burnham, J. and Harris, Q. (2002). Cultural Issues in Supervision. In: Campbell, D. and Mason, B. (eds) *Perspectives in Supervision*. London: Karnac. pp. 21–44.

Campbell, D. and Groenbaek, M. (2006). *Taking Positions in the Organization*. London: Karnac.

Coale, H.W. (1994). Using Cultural and Contextual Frames to Expand Possibilities. *Journal of Systemic Therapies*. 13(2): 5–23.

CONFETTI Report (1999). Sowing the Seeds of Cultural Competence. *Context*. 44.

Congress, E. (1994). The Use of Culturegrams to Assess and Empower Culturally Diverse Families. *Families in Society: The Journal of Contemporary Human Services*. 531–540.

Divac, A. and Heaphy, G. (2005). Space for GRRAACCES: Training for Culturally Competence in Supervision. *Journal of Family Therapy*. 27(3): 280–284.

Down, G. (2000). Supervision in a Multicultural Context. In: Barnes, G., Down, G. and McCann, D. (eds) *Systemic Supervision: A Portable Guide for Supervision Training*. London/Philadelphia: Jessica Kingsley. pp. 61–79.

Dyche, L. and Zayas, L. (1995). The Value of Curiosity and Naivete for the Cross-cultural Psychotherapist. *Family Process*. 34(4): 389–399.

Emerson, S. (1996). Creating a Safe Place for Growth in Supervision. *Contemporary Family Therapy*. 18(3): 393–403.

Falicov, C. (1995). Training to Think Culturally: A Multidimensional Comparative Framework. *Family Process*. 34: 373–389.

Fernando, S. (1991). *Mental Health, Race and Culture*. Basingstoke: Macmillan in association with Mind publications.

Fernando, S. (1995). *Mental Health in a Multi-Ethnic Society: A Multi-Disciplinary Handbook*. London: Routledge.

Fine, M. and Turner, J. (1997). Collaborative Supervision. In: Todd, T.C. and Storm, C.L. (eds) *The Complete Systemic Supervisor: Context, Philosophy and Pragmatics*. Boston: Allyn and Bacon. pp. 229–240.

Franklin, A.J. (1999). Invisibility Syndrome and Racial Identity Development in Psychotherapy and Counselling African American Men. *The Counseling Psychologist*. 27(6): 794–801.

Fruggeri, L. (2002). Different Levels of Analysis in the Supervisory Process. In: Campbell, D. and Mason, B. (eds) *Perspectives in Systemic Supervision*. London: Karnac. pp. 3–20.

Green, R. (1998). Training Programs: Guidelines for Multicultural Transformation. In: McGoldrick, M. (ed.) *Re-Visioning Family Therapy*. New York: Guilford Press. pp. 111–117.

Gunaratnam, Y. (2003). *Researching "Race" and Ethnicity: Methods, Knowledge and Power*. London: Sage.

Hall, S. (1992). New Ethnicities. In: Rattansi, A. and Donald, J. (eds) Race, Culture and Difference. London: Sage. Chapter 11.

Hardy, K. (2005). *Race, Reality and Relationships: Implications for Family Therapists*. Paper presented at conference: Race, Reality and Relationships: Implications for Family Therapist. Institute for Family Therapy.

Hardy, K. and Lappin, J. (1997). Keeping Context in View. In Todd, T.C. and Storm C.L. *The Complete Systemic Supervisor: Context, Philosophy and Pragmatics*. Boston: Pearson, Allyn and Bacon. pp. 41–58.

Hardy, K. and Laszloffy, T. (1992). Training Racially Sensitive Therapists: Contexts, Content and Contact. *Journal of Contemporary Human Sciences*. 73: 364–370.

Hardy, K. and Laszloffy, T. (1995). The Cultural Genogram. *Journal of Marital and Family Therapy*. 21(3): 227–237.

Hardy, K. and Laszloffy, T. (2000). Uncommon Strategies for a Common Problem: Addressing Racism in Family Therapy. *Family Process*. 39(1): 5–50.

Harré, R. and Gillett, G. (1994). *The Discursive Mind*. London: Sage.

Holloway, E.L. (1995). *Clinical Supervision: A Systems Approach*. London: Sage.

hooks, bell. (1994). *Teaching to Transgress*. London: Routledge.

Karamat-Ali, R. (2003). *Talking About Race: To Talk or Not to Talk? A Training Video*. For Masters in Systemic Psychotherapy at Tavistock Centre. London.

Khan, S. (2002). Visible Differences: Individual and Collective Risk-taking in Working Cross-culturally. In: Sawyerr, A. and Mason, B. (eds) *Exploring the Unsaid*. London: Karnac. pp. 95–110.

Knowles, M. (1989). *The Adult Learner*. Houston: Gulf Publishing.

Kolb, D.A. (1984). The Process of Experiential Learning. In: Kolb, D.A. (ed.) *Experiential Learning*. Englewood Cliffs, N.J.: Prentice-Hall.

Krause, B. (1995). Personhood, Culture and Family Therapy. *Journal of Family Therapy*. 17(4): 363–382.

Krause, B. (2002). *Culture and System in Family Therapy*. London: Karnac.

Ladany, N., Inman, A.G., Constantine, M. and Hofheinz, E. (1997). Supervisee Multicultural Case Conceptualization Ability and Self-Reported Multicultural Competence as Functions of Supervisee Racial Identity and Supervisor Focus. *Journal of Counselling Psychology.* 44(3): 284–293.

Lawless, J., Gale, J. and Bacigalupe, G. (2001). The Discourse of Race and Culture in Family Therapy Supervision: A Conversation Analysis. *Contemporary Family Therapy.* 23(2): 181–197.

Malek, M. and Joughin, C. (2002). (eds) *Mental Health Services for Minority Ethnic Children and Adolescents.* London: Jessica Kingsley Publishers Ltd.

Malik, R. and Krause, B. (2005). Before and Beyond Words: Embodiment and Intercultural Therapeutic Relationships in Family Therapy. In: Flaskas, C. Mason, B. and Perlesz, A. (eds) *The Space Between: Experience, Context and Process in the Therapeutic Relationship.* London: Karnac Books. Chapter 7.

McDowell, T., Fang, S., Brownlee, K., Young, C. and Khanna, A. (2002). Transforming an MFT Program: A Model for Enhancing Diversity. *Journal of Marital and Family Therapy.* 28(2): 179–191.

McIntosh, P. (1998). White Privilege: Unpacking the Invisible Knapsack. In: McGoldrick, M. (ed.) *Re-Visioning Family Therapy.* New York: Guilford Press. Chapter 11.

Nolte, L. (2007). White is a Colour Too: Engaging Actively with the Risks, Challenge and Rewards of Cross-cultural Therapy Training and Practice. *Journal of Family Therapy.* 29(4): 378–388.

Owusu-Bempah, K. (2002). Culture, Self and Cross-Ethnic Therapy. In: Mason, B. and Sawyer, A. (eds) *Exploring the Unsaid.* London: Karnac Books.

Potter, J. and Wetherell, M. (1987). *Discourse and Social Psychology: Beyond Attitudes and Behaviour.* London: Sage.

Potter, J. and Wetherell, M. (2001). *Discourse and Social Psychology.* Sage.

Ramondo, N. (1991). Cultural Issues in Therapy: On the Fringe. *Australia and New Zealand Journal of Family Therapy.* 12(2): 69–78.

Richardson, J.T.E. (1996). (ed.) *Handbook of Qualitative Research Methods.* Leicester: The British Psychological Society.

Santin, C. (2007). Muddles and Struggles of a Trainee Researching Race and Culture: Implications for Family Therapy Training. *Context.* 98: 13–15.

Schön, D. (1983). From Technical Rationality to Reflection in Action. In: Schon, D. (ed.) *The Reflective Practitioner.* London: Temple-Smith. Chapter 2.

Sincere-Wong, Y-L. (1997). Live Supervision in Family Therapy: Trainee Perspectives. In: *The Clinical Supervisor*, 15(1): 145–157.

Singh, R. (2004). Exploring Culture in Practice: A Few Facets of a Training Course. In: Nichols, W.C. (ed.) *Family Therapy Around the World: A Festschrift for Florence W. Kaslow.* Haworth Press. pp. 87–104.

Smith, J., Jarman, M. and Osborn, M. (1999). Doing Interpretative Phenomenological Analysis. In: Murray, M. and Chamberlain, K. (eds) *Qualitative Health Psychology: Theories and Methods.* London: Sage. Chapter 14.

Sprenkle, D. and Moon, S. (1996). *Research Methods in Family Therapy.* New York: Guilford Press.

Sue, S. and Zane, N. (1987). The Role of Culture and Cultural Techniques in Psychotherapy. *American Psychologist.* 42: 37–45.

Storm, C.L. and Todd, T.C (1997). *The Reasonably Complete Systemic Supervisor.* Boston: Allyn and Bacon.

Stratton, P. (1998). (ed.) Culture. Special Issue. *Human Systems.* 9(3–4): 155–158.

Tizard, B. and Phoenix, A. (2002). *Black, White or Mixed Race.* London: Routledge.

Triandis, H.C. (1994). *Culture and Social Behavior.* New York: McGraw-Hill, Inc.

Watts-Jones, D. (1997). Toward an African-American Genogram. *Family Process.* 36: 375–383.

Wilkinson, S. and Kitzinger, C. (1996). *Representing the Other.* London: Sage.

Woodcock, J. (2001). Threads from the Labrynth: Therapy with Survivors of War and Political Oppression. *Journal of Family Therapy.* 23(2): 136–154.

Wong, M.L. (1994). Di(s)-secting and Dis(s)-closing "Whiteness": Two Tales about Psychology. In: Bhavnan, K.K and Phoenix, A. (eds) *Shifting Identities and Shifting Racisms.* London: Sage. pp. 133–154.

Yutrzenka, B. (1995). Making a Case for Training in Ethnic and Cultural Diversity in Increasing Treatment Efficacy. *Journal of Consulting and Clinical Psychology.* 63(2): 197–206.

CHAPTER TWELVE

Putting a face to institutionalized racism: The challenge of introducing a live-supervised training programme for black social workers in a predominantly white institution

Sharon Bond

Introduction

I have taken the bold step of entitling this chapter "Putting a face to Institutionalized Racism". Bold because talking about racism in any form is often a sure way of losing people's interest. Racism is a word that can evoke powerful feelings of guilt, blame, shame, and anger, leading people to withdraw from conversations that they fear might be discomfiting and/or distressing. In Ruth Erskine's words it is a "conversation stopper" (Erskine, 1994: 30). I think the step I have taken is also bold because writing about a training programme designed solely for black social workers may be perceived by some as a challenge to an unspoken belief that training and therapy—in their delivery and consumption—are colour blind activities.

In a book in which attention is mainly focused on the relationships between supervisees and supervisors, this chapter takes a wider-angled lens to look beyond the supervisor–supervisee relationship to foreground the tensions and challenges of being a black social work manager setting up a live-supervision programme for black social workers in a predominately white institutional setting. I justify this deviation on my part by arguing that there is isomorphism between the supervisor–supervisee relationship and that of a black manager in a predominantly white institution.

Isomorphism, a concept borrowed from the field of mathematics, "is a systemic reworking of the notion of parallel process" (White and Russell, 1997: 316). In a journal article looking at the relationship between training and therapy, Liddle and Saba (1983) highlight Hofstadter's definition of the concept isomorphic as referring to two complex structures that can be mapped onto each other in such a way that they correspond with each other; that is to say the corresponding parts play similar roles in their respective structures. The point both these writers are making—and central to my argument—is that isomorphism, as a conceptual framework, enables the exploration of the complex patterns of relationships that connect the seemingly unrelated social worlds of the supervisor–supervisee and the black manager in a predominantly white institution. In my view, it offers a way of understanding how the concept of "power"—in the form of rights, duties, and responsibilities—is enacted in interpersonal relationships. I want to make the argument that these rights, duties, and responsibilities are "played out" in acts of entitlement, obligation, permission giving and withholding and that these ways of acting are legitimated in the discourses we call on when giving accounts to ourselves and others for our actions (Lang and McAdam, 1995; Pearce, 1994, 2007).

I will first of all define the concept of "institutionalized racism" before going on to give an account of the rationale for introducing a programme designed solely for black practitioners. The issues and dilemmas that presented themselves in the process of implementing the programme will be examined and I will conclude with my observations and learning from this experience.

The concept of institutionalized racism

The term "institutional racism" was coined in the 1960s in America and came into widespread usage after the publication of the book *Black Power: The Politics of Liberation in America* (1967) by Stokely Carmichael and Charles Hamilton.

Carmichael and Hamilton were prominent activists for civil rights in America. Richardson and Wood (1999) comment that their use of the term "institutional racism" was a deliberately provocative way of saying that major changes were still required throughout American society even though racism was no longer enshrined in the legal system. They were intent on making the point that, although racism was no longer institutionalized, racist attitudes, assumptions, and beliefs were still embedded in American institutions and in white American culture. They argued that institutions can act with racist effects even when individuals in those institutions neither realize that this is the case nor intend it to be so.

The British experience of race and racism differed from the American in that the "apartheid" or "Jim Crow" system was not a part of the British experience. The phrase "institutional racism" in the British context has generated a great deal of debate and a range of definitions. Madan Sarup, writing about the politics of multiracial education, defined "institutional racism" as existing in "the policies and practices of agencies and organisations" (Sarup, 1986: 11). The Commission for Racial Equality (CRE) in its evidence to the Stephen Lawrence Inquiry also focused on practice within agencies. They defined it as "organisational structures, policies, processes and practices which result in ethnic minorities being treated unfairly and less equally, often without intention or knowledge" (Macpherson Report, 1999 para. 6.30).

These definitions fit within a powerful discourse of custom and practice. It is a discourse that often serves as a backdrop to give meaning to the lived experience of our day-to-day working lives. It provides us with the "common-sense" reasons for our behaviours, the sense of knowing what to expect from ourselves, and others in our relationships and the confidence that gives legitimacy to our actions. Our dependency on custom and practice often goes unnoticed until changes to our familiar patterns of behaviour give rise to feelings of uncertainty and anxiety linked to fears about the unknown.

It is those, often informal, practices, developed over time, and increasingly embedded in the habits and customs of an organization, that I want to highlight. I shall argue later in the chapter that discourse theory (Foucault, 1972; Burr, 1995) and positioning theory (Harré and van Langenhove, 1999; Campbell and Groenbaek, 2006; Partridge, 2007) offer us ways of understanding how these habits and customs can become racialized in practice.

First, I will describe the agency, its staff composition, geographical location, and the make-up of the client groups using its services, as a way of providing a rationale for my development of a training programme for black social workers.

The rationale for the development of a programme for black social workers

The agency is situated in an inner city London borough that is diverse in terms of race, religion, ethnicity, and culture. The multi-disciplinary staff group comprised psychiatrists, psychologists, child psychotherapists, and psychiatric social workers who were also qualified family therapists. I am a qualified social worker, family therapist and supervisor. I worked in the agency as a senior member of the psychiatric social work team and was the only black member of the professional staff group, which numbered thirteen in total.

The clinic received referrals from general practitioners (GPs), social services, schools and a sizeable proportion of self-referrals. Approximately two-thirds of all referrals were for children and families from black and minority ethnic communities. Many of the children and families referred to the clinic via social services and schools were of African heritage (that is, African, African Caribbean, and mixed- race). School referrals were often made by parents at the suggestion of schools, and to that extent they were treated by the clinic as self-referrals. The families, however, perceived themselves as attending the clinic through "compulsion" rather than choice.

A few black parents telephoned the clinic to ask whether they could be seen by a black worker. However, the request for a black worker for black families generally came from social workers, both black and white.

As a staff team, we subscribed to the principle that we needed to be more representative of the community in which we were situated. However, the reasons often cited as stumbling blocks to achieving this objective were lack of finance and the dearth of suitably qualified professional staff from black or minority ethnic backgrounds.

The idea of setting up a training programme grew from conversations with referring social workers. I spoke to colleagues in my agency and wrote a discussion paper in which I proposed that the clinic offered a "clinical practicum" for black social workers. The "clinical practicum" as a method for enabling practitioners to develop their therapeutic abilities while being live-supervised by a qualified family therapist is an established training model used in a number of family therapy training institutions. It offered a way to introduce social workers to systemic concepts, techniques, and skills which they could then transfer to their own work environments.

The proposal drew heavily on The Just Therapy team's approach which acknowledged and validated the importance of community experience and cultural knowledge in working with particular cultural/racial groups (Waldegrave, 1990).

The proposal

The proposal was for six qualified and experienced Black social workers, mixed in gender, to be seconded to the clinic for one day a fortnight over a period of 9–12 months.

The structure for delivering the programme offered social workers:

- morning seminars comprising teaching from the family therapist, child psychiatrist, and child psychotherapist in the multi-disciplinary team.
- afternoon live-supervised sessions with black families referred to the clinic
- attendance at a referral panel meeting in the role of observer
- attendance at a multi-disciplinary clinic team discussion meeting; and
- an opportunity to undertake a piece of joint work with a member of the multi-disciplinary team.

The objective of the programme was four-fold:

1. to enable the agency to add to its existing range of therapeutic provision by offering families from black communities the opportunity to work with a team of professionals from backgrounds similar to their own
2. to make available to the clinic many more perspectives and expertise to draw on when thinking about its work with families from different races and cultures
3. to provide a way for the agency to give practical expression to the principle in its handbook which stated that it would endeavour

to provide a service that was sensitive to the culture, race, and gender of service users
4. to provide social workers with practical experience of working in a child and adolescent mental health setting and gave them an "insider" understanding of the agency to which they were referring clients.

Dilemmas and concerns voiced by the clinic team

Introducing changes and new ideas in an established system will often bring to the fore a range of feelings and emotions (Miller and Thomas, 1994). For those already in the system it is likely to raise anxieties about changes in expectations and patterns of relating as adaptations are made to usual routines to make space for new relationships and tasks.

Team conversations brought forth dilemmas and concerns about the difference the introduction of a group of secondees would make to the agency. I have separated them into concerns in relation to the secondees and clients, the agency, and team members.

Concerns for secondees and clients were, in the main, framed in terms of equity and ability. For example, team members questioned whether black social workers participating in the programme were being exploited. The thought expressed was that they were, potentially, being used as a cheap source of labour. The basis for their concern about the secondees' abilities lay in assumptions held that the social workers did not have the theoretical knowledge and therapeutic experience to draw on when working with the complex and difficult client group seen in the clinic. The concern for clients focused on their right to see a qualified staff member. The question posed was what would happen if the client did not want to be seen by the black social worker secondees.

The concerns about secondees and clients were closely linked to those about agency duty, responsibility, and obligation. Conversations centered on whether the agency had a duty to be more proactive in employing qualified, black, therapeutically trained, professionals and pay them according to their professional status and abilities. Also raised in discussion was where and with whom responsibility would be held for supervising the seconded social workers and how their role would be explained to clients.

Continuing professional development (CPD) was another area that provoked disquiet as some team members voiced their concern that the secondees might be seen as the "experts" to which all black service users would be referred. They thought that this would have the effect of invalidating the skills, experience, and knowledge of white professionals working trans-racially and trans-culturally and diminish opportunities for their future development.

These are without doubt important and relevant issues for discussion. Conversations about recruitment of clinical staff that would more closely reflect the demographics of the population the clinic served had been on-going for years: this had, however, not resulted in a change in the composition of the staff group.

The agency, in common with most agencies providing a child and adult mental health service, has a history of offering training placements to student social workers, clinical psychology, art therapy, child psychotherapy and family therapy trainees, child and adolescent psychiatrists on rotation as part of their training, and counsellors. It has a structure, which is discipline-led, for managing the induction, supervision, and training of professionals wishing to develop their therapeutic skills working with children, young people, and families. I, therefore, found myself challenged, and sometimes confused, by the conversations taking place around, what was, from my perspective, the creation of additional training places in the agency.

Reflecting on these conversations several years later, I find it useful to draw on ideas from discourse theory (Foucault, 1972; Burr, 1995) and positioning theory (Harre and van Langanhove, 1999) to give meaning to an experience that I would describe as a racializing process. I will say something about my understanding of discourse and positioning theories before going on to discuss the way in which I have used them to identify the process of racialization.

Discourse theory, positioning theory, and the racializing process

Discourse theory and positioning theory are embedded in the wider philosophical framework of social constructionism (Burr, 1995; Pearce, 1994; Gergen, 1992). The belief that underpins a social constructionist world view is that there is no objective reality. One way of putting this is to say that "our experiences of reality are based in part on the physical world that we inhabit and the things that we literally and metaphorically bump up against (for example, people, objects and our interaction with them)" (Ekdawi et al. 2001: 7). In this way of thinking we shape our social worlds in language (verbal and non-verbal) and interaction with others and, in turn, we are shaped by those events and people who make up our social worlds. Who we are (our identity), what we can and cannot do, and what we can or cannot say are social constructions "made" in conversations with others (Pearce 1994). This way of thinking positions us as "actors" and, therefore, moral beings in the making of our social worlds (Pearce, 1994, 2007).

Foucault's contribution to social constructionism helps us understand the power of language in shaping reality. Foucault defined discourse as "practices which form the objects of which they speak" (Foucault, 1972: 49). From his perspective, "discourse" could be understood as a system of representation. Foucault's interest lay in "the rules and practices that produced meaningful statements and regulated discourse in different historical periods" (Hall, 2001: 72). The hypotheses he pursued were rooted in the belief that language, structured in discourses, has the power, in practice, to determine the "rules" that govern what a society thinks are acceptable and less acceptable ways of "being" and "doing" any particular time in its history.

The proposal for a training programme for black social workers and the agency's agreement to run the programme can be understood in the context of an equal opportunities discourse. Edwards (1990) locates the concept of equal opportunities in two competing discourses:

i. the discourse of equal opportunities as access to the "glittering prize" (1990: 22); foregrounding competition and reward and;
ii. the discourse of equal opportunities as a means of self-development; foregrounding social justice.

Fishkin (1990) introduces the ideas of compensatory justice between generations to the discourse of social justice foregrounding the argument for compensation as a means of creating a more "level playing field". I would argue that these discourses are interdependent rather than competing. However, when we make the kinds of distinctions that Fishkin and Edwards make, it allows us to frame and validate some actions as legitimate and others as not. Missing from discussions of this nature is, invariably, an analysis of the power structure engaged in determining which of the discourses become more dominant in society at any given period in time.

Discourses are multilayered (made up of discourses within discourses). The discourse I privileged when I proposed the training programme was informed by my knowledge of the agency as a promoter of training and professional development in the therapeutic disciplines. Located within an equal opportunities discourse, it foregrounds equal opportunities as self-development. At the same time, when taking into account that the social workers on the programme are black, it can also be seen as being located in an equal opportunity discourse which argues for "compensatory justice between generations" (Fishkin, 1990: 41).

The questions raised by the team illustrating their concerns, suggests that within the wider equality of opportunities debate, they too could have been foregrounding a discourse of self-development. However, it seemed to me that their higher context marker (Cronen and Pearce, 1986) was one which foregrounded differences made visible in terms of race and colour and with it models of deficiency in which much of the discourse on race in Western society is embedded.

Discursive Psychologists also talk about discourses. When they use the concept they are drawing attention to the performative qualities of discourse. That is to say how people position themselves and others with their talk. Harré and van Langenhove (1999: 22) define positioning as "a discursive practice in which people position themselves, position others and are positioned by them". Discourses make available positions for persons to take up which provide them with a way of being in relation to others. So, for example, a gender discourse which assigns the task of caring and nurturing to women and competing and rational/analytical thinking to men, ascribes each gender acceptable identities and "rules" for behaving within that society, its communities, and family structures. We can say that positioning gives each of us an identity in a storyline (episode) that confers a set of rights, responsibilities, and obligations which are legitimated by dominant societal discourses. The act of positioning is, therefore, both relational (Holloway, 1995) and moral (Harré and van Langenhove, 1999; Pearce, 1994, 2007).

A major aim of the training programme was to enable the agency to have additional resources to draw on in its objective of providing a more racially diverse and culturally sensitive service. Training black social workers from locality teams, who were already linked to one of the agency's significant referral sources, presented itself as an ideal opportunity. However, with hindsight, this proposal could also have been experienced as a "challenge" to the agency's usual practice for allocating training places.

The agency's usual custom and practice was to recruit trainees already in training in a host training institution. The "challenge" can be articulated in the question: Who has the authority to change the rules that govern how invitations are made as well as who gets onto the invitation list? In designing and delivering a therapeutic programme for black social workers, I had positioned myself as someone moving outside of the established way of doing things.

The training placements being provided were different in that:

1. The trainees were all seconded workers from the local authority social services departments in the borough.
2. They were a group of six.
3. They were all black.
4. They worked only with black families.
5. They did not belong to a training institution.

One way in which my breach of protocol was fed back to me was in comments like "it's not so noisy today" made within my hearing on the days the seconded social workers were not present in the clinic.

Wetherell and Potter (1992) remind us that the language we use is not neutral. On the face of it a comment like "it's not so noisy today" could be about levels of noise. However, when said in the context of a societal discourse that describes the arrival of black people in any number as "an influx" or as "an invasion" and the effect of their presence as "swamping" the host population, the phrase can take on the meaning of unwanted or uninvited guests. This sense of being an unwanted or uninvited presence was further highlighted by the reservations expressed about the secondees being present while the team conducted its usual business (that is, referral meetings and case discussions). The point that I am making here is that a racializing process that lends itself to the charge made by Macpherson (1999) of institutional racism is subtle and can be seen as residing in the way comments may be made by members of the majority white group with no understanding of the effect hearing what is said could have on members of the minority black group.

If I were to hypothesize (Palazzoli et al. 1980) about the performative function of the communications referred to above, using the "lens" (Hoffman 1990: 1) of positioning theory I would have to consider how congruent my positioning of myself was with the expectation of my team. Harré and van Langenhove (1999) talk about the place of "gossiping" in the process of positioning as a way of showing trust but also as a form of moral reproach. This makes sense to me in that by "gossiping" within my hearing about the difference that the presence of the secondees made to the life of the clinic, team members may also have been letting me know that they were unsure where my loyalties were.

Interpersonal relationships in a multi-disciplinary agency are complex. This complexity encompasses differences in professional training, class, culture, race, and gender differences to name a few. I have been arguing above that such differences have implications for how people are positioned and position themselves in their relationships with each other. It can also become the site for "status contradiction" (Littlewood and Lipsedge, 1989: 58; Downs, 2000: 62). This phrase succinctly describes the situation where status from one level of context creates incoherence with status at another level. For example, in a wider societal context being black and being female translates as being less authoritative than being white and being male. In relational terms this places white men at the top end and black women at the lower end of the social pecking order

In the context of my agency, my professional identity as a senior member of staff with decision-making responsibilities for the staff group that I managed conferred on me a status that was at the higher end of the agency's hierarchical structure; a position not compatible with the status accorded me as a black woman in the wider societal context. In my view, the concept of "status contradictions" gets to the heart of the difficulties experienced in many of the interpersonal relationships that are described and rationalized in acts of institutionalized racism.

Suman Fernando (1996) touches on this in an article entitled "Black people working in white institutions: lessons from personal experience", in which he describes how his position as chair for the national standing committee on race and culture in the Mental Health Act Commission was questioned on the basis that he, as a black man, could not be as effective as a white chair. While Fernando's experience would not be unfamiliar to many black people who find themselves in positions of authority in predominantly white institutions, it is, nevertheless, one that is little addressed in either organizational or therapy literature.

Discussion

At this point I want to comment on the link I made between the supervisor–supervisee relationship and that of a black manager in a predominantly white institution and how I see this as isomorphic. To do this I need to say something of my experience of joining the agency as a Senior Psychiatric Social Worker.

The Psychiatric Social Work Service, like the Education Social Work Service where I worked before joining the agency, were both run by the Inner London Education Authority (ILEA). Prior to joining the agency, I worked as a Deputy Divisional Officer in the Education Social Work Service. I was recruited to my post as Senior Psychiatric Social worker under a policy known in employment law as "Genuine Occupational Qualification" (GOQ). This meant that in addition to my academic and professional qualifications, managerial experience, and skills in social work, being black was a qualification that made me suitable for the post. Promotion to senior posts within the Psychiatric Social Work Service was usually made from within. I, as an "outsider" had no experience of working in a clinic environment and, so the thinking went, would have difficulty in taking on a management role.

I learned that there had been fierce discussions in the team about employing me at a senior level; that there were strongly held views that customary recruitment practices were being set aside in favour of positive discrimination; and that there were concerns that my appointment smacked of tokenism and sufficient thought had not been given to the implications of this action and possible consequences that might follow in its wake.

From my perspective, I had been positioned as an intruder; an unwanted guest with very few rights or entitlements. What I recognize—although not at the time—is the similarity in the pattern of behaviour repeated some ten years later when I proposed the live-supervision programme for black social workers. In both episodes the pattern of relationship foregrounded is that of wariness, tension, and resistance. It seemed to me that there was no space in the first episode and only heavily circumscribed space in the second, to discuss and explore the fit between my own aspirations, hopes, and expectations and those of the team.

In systemic family therapy training, the supervisory relationship calls for a fit between supervisor and supervisee in order that each person is able to fulfill his/her tasks in the partnership. Schwartz says:

> "The degree of fit between the expectations that the trainer and trainees have for the training experience will often determine the degree of initial difficulty in their relationship. For example, if the trainer subscribes to the ethic that successful family therapy training involves total transformation of epistemology, but the trainee simply wants to add some techniques to his or her treatment armamentarium, the potential for a resistant relationship is high."
>
> (Schwartz, 1988: 173)

Scaife makes a similar argument. She says:

> "Failure to take account of the learning process and its relationship to the interaction between supervisor and trainee may lead to difficulties in the relationship arising from a mismatch of expectations, values or models of work which are likely to be more difficult to resolve as they become entrenched and consolidated."
>
> (Scaife, 1993: 162).

It is easy when reading statements such as these to "not see" or to be unaware of the power relationship being commented on as this is implicit and invisible. Talking about "fit" implies an ease and equality in negotiation leading to a mutual co-ordination of meaning and action. Another way to look at what is being said is by being curious about the relationships in focus in the context of entitlements. By this I mean asking questions such as, "Who is entitled to say what is acceptable/not acceptable?" "Where is his/her authority located?" "Is the authority legitimated through gender/race/professional status/age?" "What are the obligations of each person in the relationship?" "Who or what are their obligations to?" "What does it allow them to do?" "What does it disallow or prohibit them from doing?" "What are the values and beliefs that support each of their ways of thinking at societal level?"

In my supervisory relationships, I am ever mindful of my obligations to those I am supervising. This informs how I position myself and them. These positionings are informed by discourses embedded in the professional code of conduct to which I subscribe, as well as gender, cultural, ethnic, racial, and other stories that influence my perception of myself and my supervisee(s) and, in turn, their perception and positioning of me. This process is also "acted out" in relationships with clients, with colleagues who I manage, and with who manages me. When race is a pertinent or key factor in the conduct of those relationships, it is important to be aware of the many discourses at a macro level of context (for example, societal, economic, political, and legal) that informs and influences actions at the micro level.

At the beginning of this chapter I gave a definition of isomorphism that can be summarized as "mirroring". What makes it a useful conceptual framework, in my opinion, is that it encourages us to look for "patterns that connect" (Bateson, 1972: 8). This provides a way to think of issues of power and how they show themselves in interpersonal relationships; in acts of entitlement, obligation, prohibition, and validation.

The point I am making here is that highlighting patterns helps to move the focus from the content of individual episodes and foreground connections between and across episodes and relationships (Bateson, 1972). This, in turn, offers a way to appreciate and understand how our values and beliefs give meaning to and inform what we do and say in the many interpersonal relationships that make up our day-to-day experiences of life.

Conclusion

I am aware that this is a highly personal account of my experience as a black social work manager and family therapist supervisor working in a child and adolescent mental health setting that was predominantly white. In giving it, I have described some of the dilemmas I encountered when I set out to design and deliver a practice-based training programme for black social workers from the local authority area offices that were a source of many of our referrals.

The programme was successful on many levels. The social workers who took part in it commented that the theoretical ideas they learned help them to think differently about their practice and helped to raise their self-confidence and self-esteem. Three of the four adults seen during the life of the programme took part in a qualitative research study which evaluated their experience of the service they received. They commented on their sense of relief at being in conversation with people with whom they shared similar world views and the effect that that had on helping them find new ways of thinking about and approaching the difficulties and concerns that had initially brought them to the clinic (Bond, 1997). Colleagues who participated in running seminars expressed satisfaction and enjoyment at being involved. Perhaps the best tribute and validation to the programme's success was the number of enquiries from social workers wanting a place on the next programme. Disappointingly, the programme was not repeated and my sense of having failed in what I had set out to do, that is, develop a resource that would benefit the clinic as well as the community it served, was great at the time.

I have argued that my experiences can be understood in the context of a process whereby customary practices can become institutionalized and enacted in relationships that are racializing and marginalizing in their effect. I have articulated the episode of designing and delivering a training programme for black social workers as a challenge to custom and practice. In so doing I have brought to the fore the issue of power and invited an exploration of acts of entitlements and obligations and the discourses in which these are legitimated. I have commented on my understanding of this using both discourse and positioning theories.

I still struggle to articulate my learning from this experience. In part this is because it was not a unique experience for me. Reflecting on it, it occurred to me that it has resonances with many points in my professional life and development including my arrival into the team under an equal opportunities initiative. The most positive and hopeful learning from the experience that I see is an awareness and acknowledgement that recurring experiences bring with them opportunities for taking small steps in the evolutionary process of change.

I have no doubt that my experience will also have resonance for people who are not black or female as the effects of exclusion and marginalization are not limited to any one group. I have written from a perspective that fits with who I am with the hope that my contribution will encourage more personal and public debate and discussion about the interactional aspects of institutionalized practices—one of which is racism.

References

Andersen, T. (1987). The Reflecting Team: Dialogue and Meta-dialogue in Clinical Work. *Family Process*. 26(4): 415–428.

Bateson, G. (1972). *Steps to an Ecology of Mind*. New York: Balantine.

Bateson, G. (1979). *Mind and Nature: A Necessary Unity*. New Jersey: Hampton Press.

Bond, S. (1997). *Black Families with Black Therapists: A discussion on Colour Matching in Family Therapy Practice*. MSc dissertation (unpublished). London: KCCF.

Burr, V. (1995). *Introduction to Social Constructionism*. London: Routledge.

Campbell, D. and Groenbaek, M. (2006). *Taking Positions in the Organization*. London: Karnac Books.

Carmichael, S. and Hamilton, C.V. (1967). *Black Power: The Politics of Liberation in America*. New York: Vintage Books.

Cronen, V.E. and Pearce, W.B. (1986). Towards an Explanation of How the Milan Method Words: An Invitation to a Systemic Epistemology and the Evolution of Family Systems. In: Campbell, D. and Draper, R. (eds) *Applications of Systemic Family Therapy: The Milan Approach*. London: Grune & Stratton. pp. 69–86.

Downs, G. (2000). Supervision in a Multicultural Context. In: Gorrell-Barnes, G., Downs, G., and McCann, D. (eds) *Systemic Supervision: A Portable Guide for Supervision Training.* London: Jessica Kingsley.

Edwards, J. (1990). What Purpose does Equality of Opportunity Serve? *New Community: A Journal of Research Policy on Ethnic Relations,* 17(1): 19–35.

Ekdawi, I., Hathaway, J., and Sheppard, T. (2001). *Whose Reality is it Anyway? Putting Social Constructionist Philosophy into Everyday Clinical Practice.* Brighton: Pavillion.

Erskine, R. (1994). Therapy Teams. *Context.* 20: 29–31.

Fernando, S. (1996). Black People Working in "White Institutions": Lessons from Personal Experience. *The Journal of Systemic Consultation and Management.* 7(2–3): 143–154.

Fishkin, J. (1990). Equal Opportunity and Justice between Generations. *New Community: A Journal of Research and Policy on Ethnic Relations.* 17(1): 37–48.

Foucault, M. (1972). *The Archeology of Knowledge.* London: Tavistock.

Gergen, K.J. (1992). Social Constructionism in Question. *The Journal of Systemic Consultation and Management.* 3(3–4): 163–182.

Hall, S. (2001). Foucault: Power, Knowledge and Discourse. In: Wetherell, M., Taylor, S. and Yates, S.J. (eds) *Discourse Theory and Practice: A Reader.* Milton Keynes: OUP.

Harré R. and van Langenhove, L. (1999). The Dynamics of Episodes. In: Harré, R. and van Langenhove, L. (eds) *Positioning Theory: Moral Contexts of Intentional Action.* Oxford: Blackwell.

Hoffman. L. (1990). Constructing Realities: An Art of Lenses. *Family Process.* 29(1): 1–12.

Holloway, E. (1995). *Clinical Supervision: A Systems Approach.* London: Sage.

Lang, P. and McAdam E. (1995). Stories, Giving Accounts and Systemic Descriptions. *Human Systems: The Journal of Systemic Consultation & Management.* 6(2): 71–103.

Liddle, G. and Saba, A. (1983). On Context Replication: The Isomorphic Relationship of Training and Therapy. *Journal of Strategic & Systemic Family Therapies.* 2(2): 3–11.

Littlewood R. and Lipsedge, M. (1989). *Aliens and Alienists: Ethnic Minorities and Psychiatry* (2nd edn). London: Unwin Hyman.

MacPherson. Sir W. (1999). *The Stephen Lawrence Inquiry.* London: HMSO.

Miller, A. and Thomas, L. (1994). Introducing Ideas about Racism and

Culture into Family Therapy Training. *Context.* 20: 25–29.

Palazzoli M., Boscolo, L., Cecchin, G., and Prata, G. (1980). Hypothesizing, Circularity and Neutrality: Three Guidelines for the Conductor of the Session. *Family Process.* 19: 3–12.

Partridge, K. (2007). The Positioning Compass: A Tool to Facilitate Reflexive Positioning. *Human Systems: The Journal of Systemic Consultation & Management.* 18: 96–111.

Pearce W.B. (1994). *Interpersonal Communication: Making Social Worlds.* New York: HarperCollins.

Pearce W.B. (2007). *Making Social Worlds: A Communication Perspective.* Oxford: Blackwell.

Richardson, R. and Wood, A. (1999). *Inclusive Schools, Inclusive Society: Race and Identity on the Agenda.* Stoke-on-Trent: Trentham Books.

Sarap, M. (1986). *The Politics of Multiracial Education.* London: Routledge & Kegan Paul.

Scaife, J. (1993). Setting the Scene for Supervision: The Application of a Systems Framework to an Initial Consultation Interview. *Human Systems: The Journal of Systemic & Management.* 4(3–4): 161–172.

Schwartz, R.C. (1988). The Trainer–Trainee Relationship in Family Therapy Training. In: Liddle, H.A., Breulin, D.C., and Schwartz, R.C. (eds) *Handbook of Family Therapy Training & Supervision.* New York: Guilford Press.

Waldegrave, C. (1990). Social Justice and Family Therapy. *Dulwich Centre Newsletter.* No.1. Adelaide: Dulwick Centre Publications.

Wetherell M. and Potter J. (1992). *Mapping The Language of Racism: Discourse and the Legitimation of Exploitation.* London: Harvester Wheatsheaf.

White M. and Russell., C.S. (1997). Examining the Multi-faceted Notion of Isomorphism in Supervision. *Journal of Marital & Family Therapy.* 23(3): 315–333.

CHAPTER THIRTEEN

The power of delegated authority and how to deal with it

Mojca Brecelj-Kobe and Dubravka Trampuz

Introduction

Supervision can be seen as the cornerstone of psychotherapy training, enabling future practitioners to learn the art of psychotherapy. In our experience, this process involves a dialectical interplay between the urge to learn, to adopt new ideas and different ways of thinking, bringing changes to practice, and the opposing urge to resist the learning process and remain safely anchored in the stale waters of certainty provided by previously acquired knowledge. In the process of dealing with these "resistances to learning", supervision can be seen to straddle the boundary between the process of teaching and the experiential, personal process of therapy.

Different psychotherapies approach supervision differently. Psychodynamic and psychoanalytic supervision work through uncovering the supervisee's blind spots that are seen as rooted in irrational, unconscious processes, as well as by analysing parallel process, that is, the way the analytic relationship is reflected in the process of supervision (Doehrman, 1976). Systemic supervision deals with unpacking the dominant stories that organize and position the supervisee in his/her habitual ways of thinking and acting as well as addressing the isomorphic relationship between the processes of therapy and supervision (Liddle and Saba, 1983).

The power delegated to the supervisor is multi-layered and masked by the different, often contradictory, tasks assigned to the supervisor by a number of systems: the training institution that sets the goals of teaching and standards of evaluation; the professional community that sets the ethical and professional standards; and the supervisees that expect the supervisor to provide a safe and creative context for their professional development. The influence of post-modernism, that has swept the family therapy field, challenges the power delegated to the supervisor and promotes creativity in the process of resolving the contradictory positions of the supervisor. This chapter illustrates how, in the setting of our training and supervisory practice, we attempted to resolve this dilemma.

The inherent paradox of postmodernism

The postmodern practices of therapy and supervision define those therapist and supervisory practices that are not postmodern, but offer few clear answers as to how to deal with the power delegated to therapists and supervisors to use their expertise to treat and to teach, activities they can only abdicate by giving up their roles (Epstein and Loos 1989). Attempts to dissolve the inherent paradox in the notion of collaborative supervision (Atkinson and Heath, 1990) and in the presence of the "normalizing gaze" (Foucault, 1975: 190) have turned to ethics (Flemons, Green, and Rambo, 1996) and its relational dimensions, transcending the subject–object dichotomy (Keeney, 1983), making the power imbalance transparent by deconstructing the power relationship (Turner and Fine, 1996) and levelling the hierarchy within the supervisory relationship (Golann, 1988).

Postmodernism has had a major influence on both systemic psychotherapy and psychoanalysis, paradoxically bringing these two, traditionally opposing, psychotherapy practices to a closer intersection (Morris, 1993; Daniel, 1998; Flaskas, 2002). Systemic psychotherapy has moved away from cybernetics towards the contextual and relational search for multiple meanings in the therapeutic and supervisory systems, entering the domain of inter-subjectivity, now also occupied by psychoanalysis and psychodynamic psychotherapies. For psychoanalysis, in the words of Flax, the most important lesson of both postmodernism and feminism was "that clinical treatment cannot be politically or socially neutral" (Flax, 1994: 15). Ogden views the analytic supervisory relationship as a form of "guided dreaming", a creative process that "generates fresh perspectives on what the supervisor and analyst felt they already knew" (Ogden, 2005: 1,278) which is in large part determined by the "fluid history of (both supervisors and supervisees) storied over time" (p. 1,271). The patient, that the supervisee brings to life in the process of supervision, is a dream, or fiction created in "the medium of words, voice and physical movements" (p. 1,267).

The inclusion of postmodern concepts and ideas into the field of systemic practice and supervision has sensitized therapists and supervisors to the influence of their relational selves (Fishbane, 2001) and the way they position themselves as therapists and supervisors. It has helped systemic therapists recognize the inherent potential for healing and change in the process of developing a coherent story of one's experience (McFadyen, 1997). Systemic therapists and supervisors have been encouraged to develop awareness of the power dynamic inherent in every relationship and have been sensitized to the many faces of power or abuse that they themselves might be perpetrating (Goldner, 1993; Trampuž and Brecelj-Kobe, 2003). They have realized that listening (Weingarten 1995) is at times more important than talking and acting and that only if we know how to listen can we hear the different voices and discourses previously concealed by the dominant discourse (Anderson and Goolishian, 1988). Most of all, postmodern ideas have encouraged us to question our certainties, our theoretical concepts, and our preferred ways of conceptualizing our roles as therapists and supervisors. They pose a challenge to the Western mind that has constructed a world of dogmas that can undermine personal growth, so that their appeal to psychotherapists may be rooted in their search for liberation from the ties of indoctrination. On the other hand, the fascination of systemic practitioners with postmodern ideas might be seen to "represent a failure in our ability to stay with what we know" (Frosh, 1995: 189).

Therefore the enthusiasm for postmodern ideas may create a paradox (Watzlawick, Beavin Bavelas, and Jackson, 1967). Postmodern systemic practices do not make use of paradox as a therapeutic technique but are themselves embedded in it. The very nature of postmodern systemic therapy and supervision is in its essence paradoxical because in practice we are not doing what we are claiming we do (Hayward, 1996). The enthusiasm with which systemic practitioners have embraced postmodern ideas might be connected to this inherent paradox and may, in itself, be a promoter of change in the consulting room.

Postmodernism seems to be incompatible with the practice of psychotherapy for two reasons. The first is embedded in its philosophy which searches for the irrational that surfaces when symbolization and language, the main tools of psychotherapy, break down (Žižek, 1991; Frosh, 1995). The second might be attributed to the structure of the human living system which according to Maturana and Varella (1973) is structurally determined, which means that our internal structure determines and limits our responses. We live in a dialectical world in which we constantly make choices about the more or less good story, the more or less useful idea, and make judgements about the more or less moral and ethical practice. As much as we try, we cannot have a therapy and supervision practice congruent with the proclaimed theoretical concepts without being first grounded in a frame of certainties that enable us to make these choices. As therapists and supervisors we will probably have to accept that we are determined by the humanity that organizes our world of struggles and doubts. We can search for ways to transcend the limits of our nature by striving towards some of the goals set by postmodern theoretical concepts of deconstruction introduced by Derrida (1987), social constructionism, and second order change, but we will probably never run the risk of reaching the impossible and becoming the ideal postmodern therapist or supervisor which, in Keeney's opinion, should never even be imagined (Keeney, 1994).

Postmodern ideas challenge our ways of knowing and doing and thus invoke our creativity. We share some of the dilemmas and creative tensions embodied in our training programme and our attempts to resolve these challenges and extend our practice.

Implementing postmodern concepts in supervision in the context of systemic training in Slovenia

The first generation of systemic family therapists in Slovenia, to which both authors belong, was trained by teachers and supervisors from The Institute for Family Therapy, London and our mutual experience of both resisting and replicating colonizing practices was described from the position of both trainees and trainers (Borštnar et al. 2005). As we developed as teachers and supervisors with the encouragement of our original trainers, we decided to organize our first independent training course in the university context, the Faculty of Medicine of the University of Ljubljana. We were confronted by a number of dilemmas. These involved, in particular, the hierarchical structure of the University context with its strict set of rules and demands and the medical-psychiatric context with its current views and understandings of mental illness and psychological problems, as well as medical ethics and professional responsibility. As teachers and supervisors we were aware that in such a training context we would be expected to provide teaching that guaranteed quality and well defined standards for evaluation. We also knew that candidates joining the course would expect a traditional teacher role with extensive theoretical input and little personal and interactive involvement.

The group of teachers and supervisors are women, all professionally working in the medical-psychiatric context as psychiatrists and clinical psychologists. We were aware that our work as trainers and supervisors, who both teach and evaluate, will be evaluated on many levels: by the University administration, the candidates, our professional setting, and the English consultants. We were caught in a paradox. We were starting a course within a highly traditional teaching context, yet equipped with postmodern ideas and aspirations. Being aware of the inherent paradox of our postmodern aspirations we wondered if we could set the stage in order to, in Shakespearian tradition, dissolve the boundary between spectator and actor. We were to teach and be taught, evaluate and be evaluated. This last but not least was the dilemma of how to accomplish our task so as to promote the interplay of different roles on many levels. In order to be able to step in and out of different roles we needed to create a course structure that would be strong enough to enable us to use the power of delegated authority whilst being sufficiently flexible to allow us to join with our trainees and supervisees in order to deconstruct it.

The beliefs and prejudices that organize our work as supervisors

As supervisors we became aware of an increasing uneasiness about our own input in the supervisory relationship. It was as if the postmodern paradigm, which shattered the foundations of reality, hierarchy, power, empowerment, morality, and ethics, was positioning us in a paralysing uncertainty that constrained our thoughts and creativity. We realized that we needed to hold to a set of beliefs and prejudices (Cecchin et al. 1994) in order to develop a level of uncertainty that felt safe enough to allow us to free up our creativity. We had to have our feet well grounded in modernism and first order cybernetics to allow our thoughts to drift freely in the narrative world of the social mind (Bateson, 1972) in search of new meanings and meta-positions that would widen our own and our supervisees' perspectives.

Sharing our internal dialogues, we recognized that the beliefs and prejudices that organize us as supervisors are closely connected to our clinical work which inclines us towards a pragmatic stance. We all work in the medical-psychiatric context, often with difficult patients whose problems and diagnostic labels cannot be dismissed as a linguistically constructed problem system that will dissolve in the process of therapeutic conversation. We have outgrown the belief that there is a therapeutic practice that will solve all and every problem. On the contrary, we believe in the uniqueness of every system we work with and in the need to search for those theoretical concepts and practices that reflect best the specific needs of each particular system. In order to do this we believe we have to rely on practical wisdom (Grunebaum, 2006) which we understand in a pragmatic way, as a choice we make at a given time and in a given system that seems to make the best fit, keeping in mind that there could always have been an even better fit. We believe that the requirements for making this choice, as best and wisely as possible, reside in extensive theoretical knowledge, practical skills, and experience as well as high moral and ethical standards.

We believe that problems and states of distress have their own separate existence and that language, through therapeutic dialogue, helps explore and resolve them. In our clinical practice we often see that the naming of the problem or uncomfortable state of being does not construct the problem but rather helps alleviate the accompanying distress and facilitates the process of its dissolution. The victims of trauma often show their uneasiness and discomfort in non-verbal ways and need time and patience before feeling safe enough to venture to find words for their state of distress and start creating a story that, with the further passage of time, may or may not develop into a coherent narrative. At times, creating a safe context to be and to feel, sitting with and sharing the pain, is sufficient for distress to begin to dissolve.

We came to accept that, in order to function in our professional roles as therapists and supervisors, we needed to hold onto the belief that our knowledge, expertise, experience, and practical wisdom can promote the dissolution of discomfort. We are aware that in our respective roles of therapist, trainer, and supervisor we become part of the system we work with and both influence and are being influenced by it, but we have to hold to the belief that we can, through our knowledge and professional training, take different positions that allow us to intervene and promote change. As clinicians we are particularly aware that the healing process needs time, patience, and, above all, the preservation of hope. We believe that it is the therapist's role to be a step ahead and to help the client system prevent the light of hope from fading out.

Our historical, political, and social discourses have sensitized us to the role of language in promoting relational imbalance. Language played a prominent role in organizing and promoting the Slovenian national identity. It helped connect and provide a secure sense of belonging and at the same time helped separate and draw a clear line between "us" and "them". Slovenia did not have an independent state until 1991, but throughout its history the power of its language secured a sense of national uniqueness and separateness and kept the dream of an independent state alive through the centuries. We witnessed the powerful role language played in the process of acculturation of immigrants from other parts of the former state of Yugoslavia and its role in the promotion of different cultural values. It made us aware of the prominent role language has as the context that positions us and in which we position ourselves in relation to different social and cultural discourses (Burck, 1997) as well as in relation to different professional discourses (Borštnar et al. 2005).

Our social and political heritage is embedded in myths about power and equality. Collective action and collaboration was politically institutionalized as self-government, which promoted the notion of shared power and collective responsibility. Power relationships and power struggles among those proclaimed as equals were therefore masked. Brotherhood among different nationalities and gender equality were idealized. As our former joint state collapsed we were left with deeply rooted prejudices and a distrust of the power of dialogue to resolve problems and to promote change.

Incorporating these beliefs and prejudices into our narratives about our professional selves, enabled us to venture on the quest of how to deal with the authority delegated to the supervisor by the training institution and the trainee supervisees.

The process of supervision in the context of multiple relationships

In a small professional community such as ours, supervision is just one of the relational contexts in which supervisors and supervisees engage. Different relational contexts create a number of relational and personal narratives and stories that organize the supervisor–supervisee relationship and influence the supervision process. The personal and professional narratives of supervisors and supervisees are exchanged in the inter-subjective space created through dialogue that organizes the learning processes of both supervisors and supervisees. The context of multiple relationships enhances the development of a collaborative teaching and learning system both in the process of supervision and teaching. Issues concerning the trainees' and supervisees' delegation of the power of authority to the trainers and supervisors have to be closely monitored, by listening to different voices and discourses, and appropriately renegotiated as the process of teaching and learning progress.

Sharing our internal dialogues helped us, as trainers and supervisors, to deconstruct our stories and challenge our beliefs and prejudices about authority, equality, and responsibility. We shared our feelings of lack of authority on account of our gender, inexperience, and the negative connotations of power positions particularly in regard to colleagues we see as our equals. As clinicians we often tend to feel over-responsible towards our patients and we had to look at the different meanings of responsibility in the context of teaching and supervision. This enabled us to experiment with taking different positions in our negotiations with our supervisees, particularly regarding the use of authority in the process of teaching and evaluation.

THE POWER OF DELEGATED AUTHORITY

In the process of supervision itself, narratives developed about the supervisor and her preferred style of supervising, the supervisor–supervisee relationship, the supervisee in his/her role of therapist, team member, and supervisee. Some narratives predominated and were spoken more often than others which remained in the shadows and were rarely or never voiced. In our quest for a way to engage both supervisors and supervisees in exploring these many narratives, we developed a multi-level context that reflected the context of multiple relationships in our systemic family training programme. We will describe the structures we set up for live supervision, for group supervision for supervisors, and the reflective hand-over we devised.

The context of live supervision

In the context of live supervision, two supervisors are allocated to two supervisees. During live supervision, one of the supervisees takes the role of therapist while the other remains behind the screen with the two supervisors. This setting offers numerous possibilities for experimenting with second order ideas and the ways that they can be implemented in the process of supervision. One of the supervisors assuming a meta-position to the process of supervision offers valuable feedback on the process of supervision. The observing supervisor can have a discussion with the working supervisor with both trainees listening and then reflecting on the dialogue. As novice supervisors with no prior experience in systemic supervision but the one we acquired during our training, we found that working in pairs enabled us to organize our thinking and our discussions in a way that enhanced our learning and the development of our supervisory skills and made our learning process visible to the supervisees.

We have all had experience in psychodynamic psychotherapy and some have worked as supervisors in other contexts. Working in a pair helped us explore the influences and practices we were implementing from other psychotherapy contexts and encouraged us to discuss the advantages and disadvantages of doing so. Working in pairs made the process of evaluation a shared task. It enabled the supervisors to explore the prejudices that underlay stories created about the supervisee in the relational context of therapy and supervision, as well as their own role in the supervisee's development of certain therapeutic skills and/or lack of development of others.

The supervisors' supervision group

Our all women's group of trainers and supervisors struggled with issues of power and authority. It functioned as a leaderless group of equals that seemed to be in a constant search for a leader but with every potential one having their authority challenged and disqualified. It seemed as if a shared myth about the power of authority constrained our group from delegating authority to one of its own members. In our professional context we described ourselves as "mist". The "mist" metaphor brings to mind Christian Anderson's Little Mermaid who was turned into sea foam for being unsuccessful in her attempts to capture and hold the love of a man. Similar to the Little Mermaid, our group had been "unsuccessful" in holding onto men in training. With no males to take over the power struggle, we had to deal with it ourselves. It took a few years before we resolved the issue by redefining the position of leader from one who has "power over" into one who has "power with" and helps contain the group, strengthening feelings of belonging and promoting the group's potential for creativity. Our redefinition of leader as container evokes a vessel which is the Jungian female archetype. It seems as if being a female group we first had to challenge the myth of authority being invested in maleness in order to find a new meaning that would connect with our femaleness. We were finally able to delegate authority to two senior group members to supervise our work as supervisors. We were able to develop trust in the group by experiencing it as a holding environment and a source of empowerment.

Responding to challenging feedback

Towards the end of the first year of training, we received a letter from the trainees that was critical of the organization of the training course and of our input as teachers and supervisors. It was a test of the newly acquired cohesiveness of our group and its ability to deal with critical events. We discussed the letter at length and decided to ask the group to formulate questions for the course coordinators (the authors of this paper) who would read and answer them in the presence of the trainees. The group formulated a number of questions that enabled the course coordinators to openly discuss their dilemmas and enter into a dialogue with the trainee group. This helped challenge social and cultural beliefs about authority and responsibility in a traditional teaching setting.

Vignette 1

Question: In the interactive process of teaching and learning during the past year, which processes, in your opinion, had the main impact on the content of the letter you received?

Answer: Well it is difficult to know, but I was thinking of our own uncertainties of how to organize this course, in particular this first year and I remember that our major concern was how to get the group organized into working teams that would enable them to start working with families so they have the opportunity to put into practice the theoretical knowledge they already acquired. Now this group I see as having a very strong theoretical background. It is a group that is very eager to learn and very capable so maybe we underestimated their abilities and maybe we were too protective, trying to make it easier for them by not pushing them too much with theory and making more space for organizing their therapeutic work in teams and with families. What would you say?

....

Question: What in your opinion has been your input or lack of input as course coordinators during this year so that the candidates understood as a message from you that words cannot be spoken but have to be written in order that you and we can hear them?

Answer: There was a substantial change in the process of teaching this year brought in by the start of the supervision process and the work in teams. In our trainers' group we were very much engaged with this. I am thinking if we might have been too busy dealing with our own dilemmas, developing our own story, so we were missing the story the candidates were developing about their process of learning. It makes me think of the couple where each partner constructs his/her own story that they never share. I would say it is a good thing that this letter was written. It gives us the opportunity to share our stories and maybe start rewriting them together into a new story we will all share.

When the course coordinators finished their responses to the questions from the trainees, the trainees were invited to comment. Further clarifications were made and a conversation developed about ways to share responsibility for the learning process. Trainees felt that, from their point of view, things were changing. They experienced this different style of teaching and learning as helpful in expanding their knowledge and therapeutic skills and they acknowledged that it is a process that takes time.

This critical event strengthened the trainers' group. The challenge to our roles as teachers and supervisors prompted us to reconsider our positions and the ways that we share in the responsibility of this mutual project. As we thus started to own authority, the trainees' group also seemed to be able to look at the idea of having their own responsibility for learning.

The reflective hand-over

In the middle of the three-years advanced training course, the trainee supervisees are allocated to a new supervisor pair. Our decision to do this was embedded in the belief that a supervisory system similar to a family system develops certain habitual interactions and behaviours (Bateson, 1972) that might constrain the supervisees from fully developing their therapeutic potential. With a new pair of supervisors, a new network of beliefs, values and expectations is formed that triggers the supervisee's curiosity and enhances the learning process.

We used Tom Andersen's (1991) ideas and use of the reflecting team and developed a reflective hand-over of supervisees from one pair of supervisors to the next. Our belief was embedded in our prejudice that our professional culture does not encourage openness in discussing the work of colleagues. Professional performance is highly valued and professionals are driven by the wish to be perfect. Any hint that their accomplishment is not as perfect as they would wish it to be is taken as criticism with a negative connotation. In the context of multiple relationships, where trainers and trainees meet outside the training context in different roles and relationships, from horizontal to vertical, we anticipated an even greater pressure to perform well, and an increased sensitivity to feedback that might be heard as critical. Our concern was that the supervisors might feel the pressure to underline the trainee's strengths and achievements and give hazy information as to what in the trainee's work needs further development. The setting of the hand-over invites both supervisors and supervisees to take a meta-position on their respective roles and accomplishments in the process of supervision so far.

In the hand-over the supervisee pair is behind the screen and listens to the discussion unfolding between the old and new pairs of supervisors. The new pair of supervisors is particularly interested in the observations of the old pair regarding the accomplishments of the supervisees within supervision, how they have used the supervision process, what theoretical concepts and skills they show familiarity with, and what theoretical concepts and skill they should develop further. The old pair of supervisors tells their story of the supervision process, their own role in it, and their view of the relationship with the supervisees.

When the new pair of supervisors feels that they have enough information about the supervisees they invite them to change places with the old supervisory pair. The supervisees are invited to reflect on what they have heard and how well this fits with their own views on their learning and achievements so far. They are encouraged to tell their own story of the supervision process, what they found helpful for their learning, and what they would have wished to be different. They proceed to negotiate how they will organize their joint work. The new supervisors encourage the supervisees to define the abilities they need and want to develop further and how the continuing process of supervision will help them achieve this.

Vignette 2

The trainees are behind the screen, listening to the conversation that unfolds between the new and old pair of supervisors.
New supervisor 1: How do you think the supervisees will describe you as supervisors? What strengths and weaknesses do you think they have observed in your style of supervision?
Old supervisor 1: In my opinion I think they saw us a complementary pair, something of the good cop/bad cop pair. I tend to be more challenging, underlying moments in therapy that could have been handled differently, while she underlined strengths and therapy that went well. I would say that in this I see our strength, that the difference in

our personal styles provides a rather good balance for the supervisees' feelings of security versus insecurity. As to our main weakness I would expect them to have observed that we get so carried away with different ideas that we flood them and leave too little space for them to develop their own ideas.

New supervisor 2: What was the greatest challenge for you as supervisors?

Old supervisor 2: Finding ways to promote their professional development so they wouldn't feel criticized or uneasy about developing their ideas. They were bringing many ideas and it was often a dilemma to know how much input to give, how to encourage them to master the necessary skills and at the same time not undermine their own creativity

....

New supervisor 1: Before we finish this conversation and invite the supervisees to join us I would like to put just one more question. Have you by any chance observed any kind of orthodoxies developing in this particular team?

Supervisor 2: Well it seems as if this group was getting organized by the dominant social construct of gender roles. The two women seem to have been promoting a holding environment for the male member. The women seem to have been adapting more to the needs of their male member. It seems that they tended to be less challenging of him...

Vignette 3

The old pair of supervisors has moved behind the screen and the new pair of supervisors invited the supervisees to reflect on what they have heard.

New supervisor 2: While you were listening to our conversation with your old supervisors were there any thoughts you could identify with, any that you would strongly disagree with or find alien to your own experience of the supervision process so far?

Supervisee 1: This was a really new experience for me to hear so many good things about my work. I was expecting to hear more critical remarks. I realize I have to do more work on my clinical skills and I think that I have to do some more work in connecting what I do with theory.

Supervisee 2: I am thinking about that last thing that was said about our group. I really don t see myself as a woman adapting to the needs of a man. It is true though that at one point it seemed that Nick will leave us and the course, and that did affect us so we were more tolerant and

I guess it might have looked as if we were adapting more to his needs than ours. But now I think things have changed and I think I can be challenging of him. I do though wonder at times how he will take it so at times I rather hold back.
Supervisee 3: *I did have a difficult time at the beginning. I felt I was not allowed to develop my own line of thoughts. I have so many ideas I find it difficult to focus ... I find it more difficult to be challenging when I myself feel insecure ... I still find it hard to follow the feedback from my team and the supervisors.*
New supervisor 2 turning to the first supervisee: *You mentioned you were expecting more critical remarks from your old supervisors. I wonder what in the supervision process made you think that the supervisors will be more critical of your work.*
Supervisee1: *Well, nothing in particular, but I did get the feeling at times they expect something else, like a better systemic formulation of the problem or better use of skills and I saw they are not quite satisfied. It may be that I myself was not quite satisfied with my own work...*

The reflective hand-over made the power of our delegated authority in the process of evaluation more transparent. It gave us, the supervisors, the space and time to voice dilemmas and the responsibilities we feel in our roles as supervisors. In the reflective hand-over, using language that is not pejorative or negatively connoted, we are able to point out the strengths and weaknesses we see in our supervisees. We try to underlie the skills and abilities we see the supervisee has to work on and point to the theoretical concepts that they still find difficult to apply in practice.

The supervisees, behind the screen, feel safe enough to let go of their defences and attend to the stories their supervisors have created about their joint venture. They are given time and space to reflect on the stories that they have heard and are invited to tell their own stories. They are invited to make their own evaluations of the supervision process, their own work as therapists and supervisees, and the work of the supervisors. From their experience with the first pair of supervisors, they can negotiate different ways of relating and working that they might see as more useful to their learning process. They are encouraged to formulate clear goals for their further learning and are invited to consider how they and their new supervisors will know that they have attained them.

The process of communication in the reflective hand-over is horizontal and each participant has equal opportunity to share ideas and experiences in the supervision process. The power relationship in the supervision–supervisee relationship is unmasked and openly discussed. The responsibilities are clearly delineated. The supervisees share the responsibility with their supervisors for their process of learning. The supervisors, on account of the power of authority delegated to them, have the responsibility to ensure that the professional and ethical standards are met and that future patients will receive the expert help they expect.

Concluding dilemmas

In the context of a small professional community with multiple relationships and a history of myths about power, the power of language, equality and gender, collaboration and responsibility, we searched for ways to deal with the ways that these issues intersected with the authority delegated to supervisors. To this end, we interwove postmodern concepts and practices into the multi-levelled processes of teaching and appraisal. Postmodern ideas introduced uncertainties into our ways of thinking and acting and prompted us to question the certainties of theories and knowledges constructed under the influence of dominant social, political, and religious discourses.

In line with these postmodern discourses we have found a position from which to question and challenge the usefulness of these very same concepts in clinical practice and supervision so that we continue to be aware of their paradoxes. Recursive reflexivity, or the discussion that folds back on itself (Hoffmann, 1993), is intended to minimize expertise and enhance the collaborative co-creation of new meanings and narratives. Using reflecting conversations (Andersen, 1991) involving a team of up to four professionals adopting a non-expert position is nevertheless likely to be perceived by a family as an expert authority. Their ideas and observations are listened to and processed as expert opinions and listening to four experts discussing one's family has a greater impact, one which may even be overwhelming, than listening to only one. Similarly, listening to four supervisors evolving narratives about the supervision process has a much greater impact than hearing the narrative of only one.

Even if intended to minimize the power imbalance, it might actually enhance it.

It is therefore important to be aware of the limitations of reflective conversations as a means of generating new ideas and meanings. An on-going process of recursive reflexivity could eventually, due to a temporary exhaustion of thoughtful creativity, lead to the breakdown of language and conversation. This would enable a postmodernist exploration of the gap that opens up when words cease.

In our dialectical world we are always left with a choice between good and bad, better and worse, useful and harmful. In the consulting room the good enough therapist can help the clients develop new stories that will help them move on, but a therapist who has not been trained well enough can urge the clients to develop stories that will not help the resolution of their problems and their personal development. In the social, political, and psychological contexts we are witnessing positive effects in the deconstruction of gender stereotypes and the development of new stories about gender that are liberating to both men and women. However living in a part of the world where stories have played such a crucial part in recent conflicts, we need to hold the tension between "stories" and "reality". Just as the toxic effects of restorying would be seen in any attempt to "restory" the holocaust, we are also alert in our country to ways that the story of the birth of our independent nation could also have the potential for instigating or reigniting hatred and segregation.

Postmodern therapists and supervisors are like tightrope walkers, balancing their practice on the edge where the objectivism of modernism meets the (inter)subjectivity of postmodernism. As therapists and supervisors we have to keep our balance among the multitude of different, often contradictory and opposing ideas. In the narratives of our professional and personal selves we have to include moral and ethical values to support our sense of responsibility that will, in the process of re-storying, alert us from stepping over the edge, as do those who try to re-story the past, serving as a warning that in our dialectically structured world the co-construction of stories can trigger both the potential for growth and development and the potential for decay and destruction.

References

Andersen, T. (1991). *The Reflecting Team: Dialogue and Dialogues about the Dialogues.* New York: W.W. Norton & Company.

Anderson, H. and Goolishian, H. (1988). Human Systems as Linguistic Systems: Evolving Ideas about the Implications for Theory and Practice. *Family Process.* 27(4): 371–393.

Atkinson, B.J. and Heath, A.W. (1990). The Limits of Explanation and Evaluation. *Family Process.* 29(2): 164–167.

Bateson, G. (1972). *Steps to an Ecology of Mind.* New York: Ballantine Books.

Borštnar, J., Močnik-Bučar, M., Rus-Makovec, M., Burck, C. and Daniel, G. (2005). Co-constructing a Cross-cultural Course: Replicating Colonizing Practices. *Family Process.* 44(1): 121–131.

Burck, C. (1997). Language and Narrative: Learning from Bilingualism. In: Papdopoulis, R.K. and Byng-Hall, J. (eds) *Multiple Voices: Narrative in Systemic Family Psychotherapy.* London: Duckworth. pp. 64–85.

Cecchin, G., Lane, G. and Ray, W. (1994). *The Cybernetics of Prejudices in the Practice of Psychotherapy.* London: Karnac Books.

Daniel, G. (1998). Broadening the Gap or Narrowing the Vision. *Journal of Family Therapy.* 20: 211–218.

Derrida, J. (1987). *The Post Card: From Socrates to Freud and Beyond.* Translator: Bass, A. Chicago: Univ. Chicago Press.

Doehrman, M.J. (1976). Parallel Processes in Supervision and Psychotherapy. *Bull. Menninger Clin.* 40: 3–104.

Epstein, E.S. and Loos, V.E. (1989). Some Irreverent Thoughts on the Limits of Family Therapy: Towards a Language-based Explanation of Human Systems. *Journal of Family Psychology.* 2: 405–421.

Fishbane, M.K. (2001). Relational Narratives of the Self. *Family Process.* 40: 273–291.

Flaskas, C. (2002). *Family Therapy beyond Postmodernism: Practice Challenges Theory.* Hove/New York: Brunner-Routledge.

Flax, J. (1994). Final Analysis? Psychoanalysis in the Postmodern West. *The Annual of Psychoanalysis.* XXII: 1–20.

Flemons, D.G., Green, S.K. and Rambo, A.H. (1996). Evaluating Therapists' Practices in a Postmodern World: A Discussion and a Scheme. *Family Process.* 35: 43–56.

Foucault, M. (1975). *Discipline and Punishment: The Birth of the Prison.* New York: Random House.

Frosh, S. (1995). Postmodernism versus Psychotherapy. *Journal of Family Therapy.* 17: 175–190.

Golann, S. (1988). On Second Order Family Therapy. *Family Process.* 27: 51–65.

Goldner, V. (1993) Power and Hierarchy: Let's Talk About It. *Family Process.* 32: 157–162.

Grunebaum, H. (2006). On Wisdom. *Family Process.* 45: 117–132.

Hayward, M. (1996). Is Second Order Practice Possible? *Journal of Family Therapy.* 18(3): 219–242.

Hoffman, L. (1993). *Exchanging Voices: A Collaborative Approach to Family Therapy.* London: Karnac Books.

Liddle, H. and Saba, G. (1983). On Context Replication: The Isomorphic Relationship of Training and Therapy. *Journal of Strategic and Systemic Therapies.* 2: 3–11.

Keeney, B. (1983). *The Aesthetics of Change.* New York: Guilford Press.

Keeney, B. (1994). Foreword. In: Cecchin, Lane, G. and Ray, W. (eds) *The Cybernetics of Prejudices in the Practice of Psychotherapy.* London: Karnac Books.

Maturana, H. and Varela, F. (1973). *Autopoeisis and Cognition: The Realization of the Living.* Dordrecht: Reidel.

McFadyen, A. (1997). Rapprochement in Sight? Postmodern Family Therapy and Psychoanalysis. *Journal of Family Therapy.* 19: 241–262.

Morris, H. (1993). Narrative Representation, Narrative Enactment and the Psychoanalytic Construction of History. *Int. J. Psycho-Anal.* 74: 33–54.

Ogden, T.H. (2005). On Psychoanalytic Supervision. *Int. J. Psychoanal.* 86: 1265–80.

Trampuž, D. and Brecelj-Kobe, M. (2003). Uses and Misuses of Systemic Theories: The Double Bind of the Systemic Psychotherapist. In: Trampuž, D. and Rus-Makovec, M. (eds) *Resisting Abuse: Papers and Proceedings from International Conference on Family Therapy*, Bled 8–10 May 2003, pp. 219–226. Ljubljana: Univ. Psychiatry Hospital & Slovene Society for Family Therapy.

Turner, J. and Fine, M. (1996). Postmodern Evaluation in Family Therapy supervision. *J. of Systemic Therapies.* 14: 57–69.

Watzlawick, P., Beavin Bavelas, J. and Jackson, D. (1967). *Pragmatics of Human Communication.* New York: W.W. Norton & Company.

Weingarten, K. (1995). Radical Listening: Challenging Cultural Beliefs for and about Mothers. *J. of Feminist Family Therapy.* 7: 7–22.

Žižek, S. (1991). *For They Know Not What They Do: Enjoyment as a Political Factor.* London: Verso.

SECTION IV

AGENCY AND PROFESSIONAL CONTEXTS

CHAPTER FOURTEEN

Managing multiple relationships in supervision: Dealing with the complexity

Angela Abela and Clarissa Sammut Scerri

Introduction

As we discovered at first hand when we gave our workshop on multiple relationships in a supervision conference held at the Tavistock Clinic in 2005, multiple relationships in supervision practice can and do happen, not only in small communities such as ours, but also in big cities in other parts of the world. When we were planning our presentation, we were cautious about sharing our experience of multiple relationships lest the practitioners present would perceive us as unprofessional! Our caution soon dissolved when we started to listen to their stories though. One member of the workshop told us how she and her supervisee had developed a romantic relationship. Another married couple, who were also colleagues at work, shared that they often supervised each other. Very quickly we were all deeply immersed in discussing the ethical dilemmas of such situations.

Living in a very small country such as Malta, we cannot avoid crossing each other's paths, playing different roles in different circumstances over time. Multiple relationships are part and parcel of the fabric of our relationships and managing them is indeed part of our *savoir-être*. But it is not always easy. We are often bound to tackle the "slippery slopes" (Gutheil and Gubbard cited in Gottlieb, Younggren, and Robinson, 2007: 241).

In the supervisory context, it is not out of the ordinary to have to face a supervisee whose family background we might know about from other contexts. What does the supervisor do with that information in a context where the supervisee may not know that the supervisor knows about his or her family background? Multiple relationships are complex. They do not always develop smoothly and a number of tensions and dilemmas may arise. In the best of circumstances, multiple relationships move in stages (Pearson and Piazza, 1997) but sometimes they come to a halt, move backward and then again forward. Some situations may even give rise to unethical practice.

Locating our supervisory practice in the Maltese cultural context

Before embarking on our discussion of the complexities of this topic, we would like to introduce our supervisory context to the reader. Malta is a small country where there is a high degree of social visibility (Sultana and Baldacchino, 1994), which means that knowledge which elsewhere is either private or unavailable is quickly acquired, giving rise to multiple contexts and relationships. With a population of just over 400,000 inhabitants spread over an area of 316 square kilometres, the island of Malta is the sixth most densely populated country in the world, following countries such as Monaco (first) and Singapore (second). This has a huge psychological impact on the Maltese psyche, pushing us to fiercely guard our privacy, given that one cannot help getting to know about other people's business. In this context, the confidential nature of the supervisory context is highly valued.

Furthermore, in Malta, the psychology and psychotherapy professions are still in their infancy. The founding members of these professions are the most senior practitioners on the Island and hence supervisors. In the case of systemic psychotherapy, professional training started in the late nineties. To date, there are only 12 such therapists, three of whom are trained systemic supervisors. Thus, practitioners have had to take on multiple roles in the profession and have had to become increasingly mindful of (non-sexual) multiple relationships and the need for creativity in the pursuit of ethical practice.

By "multiple relationships", we are here referring to the situation where a systemic supervisor is in a supervisory role with a person and at the same time fulfils another role which leads them to come into contact with the same person. In our context, due to the lack of numbers, supervisors and supervisees often would lecture in the same course, do research together, sit on government boards and have roles in organizations that invariably create multiple relationships (Mifsud, 2004). Several authors in the Anglo-American literature (Goodyear and Sinnett, 1984; Ryder and Hepworth, 1990; Schindler and Talen, 1996; Storm, Peterson, and Tomm, 1997; Syme, 2003; Davidson, 2006; Gottlieb, Robinson, and Younggren, 2007) also recount that supervision very often involves a multiple relationship including collegiate relationships at faculty level, personal and professional development of the supervisee, and assessment of performance. In our context, such constraints are often compounded for those supervisors who may have had a previous therapeutic relationship with a supervisee or by possible family relationships and long-standing friendships.

Our multiple relationship

We first came to know each other at University in our respective roles as lecturer (Angela) and psychology student (Clarissa). Angela had the opportunity to establish a personal relationship with the students as they were only a small group of nine at the time.

Soon afterwards we both left Malta to pursue postgraduate studies abroad. Upon our return to Malta, Angela was asked to act as external consultant to the Family Therapy Service, while Clarissa was asked to supervise the family workers at the same agency. Finding ourselves in the same work place, our professional relationship was able to develop. As an external consultant to the service, Angela supervised Clarissa. We also worked together, and with the family workers at the agency as well as with a number of consultants from the Tavistock Clinic, to develop and deliver systemic training to other professionals. We formed part of the team of three supervisors in the Service who embarked on the systemic supervision course offered by the Tavistock Clinic. Here, as students on the same course, our relationship took another shift. Our experience of managing power in multiple relationships was further explored in the context of our professional practice. In fact, one of us (Angela) struggled with managing multiple relationships from her perspective as a senior practitioner and as a founding member of the profession. The other (Clarissa) invested energy into thinking about owning her authority as a supervisor in a context where she felt catapulted into taking a supervisory role at a young age, acquiring in the meantime competence and experience and developing confidence over time. In supervising Angela, as part of the course, Clarissa felt ill at ease supervising someone who was her senior and it was only gradually that she let herself go and expressed her thinking freely.

In this context, Angela became increasingly aware of, and somewhat uncomfortable about, the power she carried in these relationships. This provided a learning context for her professional growth and urged her to maximize her collaborative approach to supervision (Anderson and Swim, 1995).

Over time and since we continued working in the same context, our relationship transformed in many ways. The relationship developed into that of a mentor–supervisee one. This implied a deeper kind of relationship where Angela felt that she now knew Clarissa in a more holistic manner and could give more pertinent feedback regarding the personal and career aspects of her development. Clarissa connected with this feedback and found it helpful to the extent that she sought more of it.

Nevertheless, there was also space for Angela to seek peer supervision from Clarissa. Becoming increasingly comfortable with a collaborative stance enabled Angela to seek feedback about her clinical work more readily from Clarissa and also from other sources including those of her trainees at university. On her side, Clarissa felt increasingly empowered to make her contribution. At the same time she still appreciated the supervisory relationship with Angela and was keen that the supervisory hour was kept intact. She felt that she needed that space to reflect on her clinical work and her personal and professional development. In the meantime, Clarissa was promoted to Head of the Family Therapy Unit and the Psychological Services in her agency. Our relationship continued to evolve and mature. We also continued to work together in other contexts: we were both on the executive council of the Maltese Psychological Association. At a particular meeting with a foreign consultant, Clarissa made a timely intervention by kicking Angela under the table! For us this illustrates the multiple facets of our relationship and its development. In one context, our relationship was that of a supervisor-supervisee/mentor-mentee. In other contexts, we positioned ourselves as peers. Eventually we became colleagues at university and this further transformed our relationship into a more collegiate one.

In our supervision of supervision, we have often found ourselves talking about the complexities of multiple relationships, including our own relationship. In this chapter we share our reflections and conversations including those with other supervisors and supervisees on this aspect in the supervisory relationship. We also draw on some ideas from the literature. We hope this chapter will serve as an opportunity for more conversations, ideas, and different points of view between supervisors and supervisees.

Disentangling the complexity of multiple relationships

The dominant discourse informed by the profession's ethical code of practice is that multiple relationships can be problematic. The Association of Family Therapy and Systemic Practice (AFT) code of ethics and practice (2008) discourages multiple relationships whereas the British Psychology Society (BPS)'s code of ethics and conduct (2006) specifically highlights the dangers of multiple relationships in the therapeutic, teaching, and supervisory contexts. Gottlieb, Robinson, and Younggren (2007) on the other hand, state that in 2003 the American Psychological Association considered sexual relationships unethical but pointed out that other non-sexual types of multiple relationships are not necessarily harmful or unethical per se.

In trying to understand multiple relationships in more depth, we were curious as to how the Anglo-American literature discusses situations where supervisor and supervisee have multiple relationships and interact according to these roles in different settings. According to Bograd (1993), the literature speaks of two positions regarding multiple relationships. One position is that supervisors should avoid multiple relationships whenever possible. The other position believes that multiple relationships are mutually rewarding for the parties involved. As we have highlighted above, multiple relationships in supervision are inevitable and they need to be managed. As one senior Maltese supervisor pointed out: "I have been in these situations [supervising a friend] and it never occurred to me to say, 'This is unhealthy, I don't want it.' I kind of, accept it as a fact of life and that I have to face these things" (Mifsud, 2004: 60).

These experiences have moulded our belief that multiple relationships have the possibility to both enhance and/or harm the supervisory relationship. We will elaborate on this later in the chapter.

In our experience of dealing with multiple relationships, we had to engage in an on-going reflexive process that would help us manage such relationships in an ethical and helpful manner. Storm, Peterson, and Tomm (1997) propose three different ways in looking at multiple relationships.

a) The mentoring relationship: in addition to functioning as supervisors, practitioners may also be collaborators of their supervisees, discussing professional issues, engaging in writing and publishing, and hence extending their contact beyond their supervision hour. This relationship would effectively act as a medium for the professional socialization of the less experienced systemic practitioner into a fully participating colleague of the profession.

b) Personal and professional relationships: by combining a mixture of social, business, or other personal connections with the supervisory role.

c) Where there is a combination of supervision and therapy: this would evolve when supervisors believe that focusing on a supervisee's personal issues is critical to the therapist's development and competency as a clinician.

These three different categories resonated with our thinking about how to keep in mind different relationships and contexts. Protinsky and Coward (2001: 78) state that, as practitioners matured and developed, there is a "flexing of the lines between friendship, mentorship, support and supervision and in some cases, even therapy. There were associations with clients, supervisors, mentors in a number of roles, all of which appeared to be in the interest of those involved rather than being detrimental. For example: supervisors and supervisees often become friends and colleagues even when a supervisory relationship still existed."

In our experience, this kind of relationship develops in stages. Progress from one stage to another is dependent on the successful management of multiple roles, keeping ethical practice as the highest context for evaluating the relationship. One can understand the progression from one stage to another as a process whereby boundaries are drawn (and re-drawn) differently by the people involved in the relationship.

Managing boundaries

By boundaries we are referring to "rules of the professional relationship that set it apart from other relationships" (Knapp and VandeCreek 2006: 75). In the context of multiple relationships, boundary crossings (Gutheil and Gabbard 1993) as opposed to boundary violations, occur frequently. For example, at a point in time a supervisee and her partner may be invited to a social event involving training staff at the supervisor's home. The fact that the supervisor and the supervisee are also collaborating on a training programme creates a context where such a social event can take place. However, what would happen if the supervisee becomes tipsy and flirts inappropriately with one of her colleagues? In such a situation, how is the supervisory relationship affected? And to what extent do gossip and/or the non-verbal reactions of the guests present impact upon how the supervisory relationship is managed? Can the social event be considered just as a social context or does the training context remain the higher context?

One of our supervisees thought of inviting her supervisor to drinks at her house over Christmas but did not do so as she felt that she would not have been able to relax in the company of her supervisor. Having the supervisor at home would have implied exposing further the relationship dynamics within her family at a time where she would have had to play the role of hostess. Presumably this would have made the supervisee more self-conscious. What if something went wrong? In this sense, the supervisee preferred the supervision context to remain the primary context determining the relationship. Her wish for the relationship or friendship was "constrained" by the supervision context.

Furthermore, how does one reconcile the wish of a supervisor and a supervisee to get closer to each other without impinging on the necessary space needed for the reflexive nature of the supervisory relationship? Could it be that too close a relationship would prevent the supervisor and supervisee from keeping the clients' needs in the foreground and would put too much focus on their own relationship? When things do not go smoothly in a social context, does this also have to be processed in supervision, adding to the complexity? Gottlieb, Robinson, and Younggren (2007: 245) point out that, with time, supervisory relationships may become more complex than one could have anticipated and recommend that if a role is to be added to the supervisory relationship, "it is safer to add only those that are compatible with the supervisory one".

Socializing with a supervisor does not therefore simply occur naturally. Were the supervisor and supervisee to socialize regularly at the weekends, the boundaries of the multiple relationships could become blurred and in this sense a boundary violation may occur. Gottlieb, Robinson, and Younggren (2007: 242) argue that "boundary crossings do not become violations unless they reflect exploitation of the supervisee, a supervisor's loss of objectivity, disruption of the supervisory relationship, or the reasonable foreseeability of harm". One supervisor described how uncomfortable he felt when some of his supervisees clearly expected him to appoint them to current posts that had become available in his organization. When this happened, he found it hard to raise the matter with them even though he was upset by what happened, especially with those supervisees with whom he had developed a friendship. He preferred to redress the boundaries of the supervisory relationship, moving back and starting to let go of the friendship. His reflection made us more aware of how, in some contexts, it may be difficult to have conversations about such sensitive matters. We wonder whether some situations call for a response by "doing" rather than by "talking". As discussed earlier, friendships within the context of a supervisory relationship can be problematic and in this case ethical considerations may become blurred.

A close relationship between supervisor and supervisee may also lead to favouritism or be perceived as such. Living in a society that is based on the "patron–client relationship" (Boissevain, 1993), we have often heard indignant remarks made by colleagues and students that some of their peers may have "made it" because their mentor had "smoothed the path" for them. Others complained that some succeed because they are part of the "old boys' network". Managing multiple relationships, particularly mentoring relationships, implies attending to the external implications of the relationship to avoid "loss of credibility in the eyes of others ... or charges of protégé favouritism" (Hopkins, O'Neil, Passarelli, and Bilimoria 2008: 356). For example, in the case of faculty appointments or significant posts in other organizations, the perception of favouritism loses its hold because of the formal selection process which creates a consensus that the person selected merits it, based on his or her track record, competence, and experience. In cases where the supervisor may have an influence on whether or not a supervisee may get a job promotion, the supervisor needs to reflect on his or her position and the kind of feedback that she or he gives. In stating their opinion of the supervisee, supervisors need to make explicit the fact that they know the supervisee extensively but take the ethical position of not becoming the champion of the supervisee. The onus is on the supervisor not only to act ethically but also to be seen as acting ethically by his or her professional community.

In a country like ours such appointments can give rise to gossip in situations where the supervisee might be seen as climbing up the career ladder on the basis of his or her supervisory relationship. This can also occur within professional communities anywhere in the world. Such gossip may escalate into character assassination and can be very detrimental for both supervisee and supervisor. On the other hand, when faculty staff socialize with students, it becomes more complicated to dispel the perception by other students or faculty that such a relationship is susceptible to favouritism (Pearson and Piazza 1997; Murphy and Wright, 2005).

We believe that such examples illustrate how important it is for supervisors not to lose manoeuvrability but to keep a systemic perspective that facilitates attention to multiple contexts. Ultimately the responsibility for drawing boundaries rests with the supervisor because of the power that he or she carries.

When the supervisory relationship endures over time, then it is inevitable that boundaries will be redrawn. As Johnson (2007: 263) points out, in such circumstances the supervisory relationship "must also evolve and mature to match the supervisee's changing professional needs ... however, supervisory practice must also remain fluid and responsive to the exigencies of the moment—always with an eye on the client's and supervisee's best interests".

Kral and Hines (1999) argue that it takes five to six years to mature into a fully fledged professional. Protinsky and Coward (2001) also point out that there needs to be an integration of personal and professional identities in order for professionals to feel that they can act out of their own "personhood". We believe that the supervisory experience that takes into account the three different relationships proposed by Storm, Peterson, and Tomm (1997) enhances this integration of personal and professional selves and hence helps the supervisee develop into a mature professional.

For multiple relationships to be sustained there must obviously be a comfortable fit between supervisor and supervisee in terms of mutual trust, common interests, and recognition of the value of the different roles and responsibilities of the supervisor and supervisee. One supervisee pointed out that, given the Maltese context (where everyone knows everybody else), the choice of supervisor is extremely important. His or her ability to keep confidentiality and to understand and empathize with the supervisee's position are essential attributes of the supervisor that help the supervisee take the risk of being vulnerable in the multiple relationships. This mutual trust develops over time and is not found within all supervisory relationships. Johnson (2007) refers to this development of mutual trust and willingness on the part of the supervisor to attend to the supervisee's development in a more holistic manner as transformational and argues that it marks the leap from a supervisory to a mentoring relationship.

Another dilemma of multiple relationships may include focusing on the supervisee's personal and professional development to the extent that the clinical work is ignored. One supervisee who was also undergoing personal development sessions with her supervisor on a particular family issue, remarked that one of her dilemmas during supervision was around making the best use of supervision without letting her personal issues take over the supervision sessions. At the same time, we have often felt that it was the particular journey of some supervisees to want to invest in sessions that focused on their personal development in an intensive way, at a point in time. Accompanying them in this journey seemed crucial for their growth as therapists. Given the quality of the supervisory relationship and its therapeutic dimension, asking supervisees to consult a therapist for individual work may be something that they would do reluctantly or not at all.

Since with multiple relationships there is more accessibility to the supervisor, tensions may arise such as supervisees wishing to push the boundary and receive more intensive mentoring when the supervisor may not consider it appropriate either because of fears of perceived favouritism with peers or because they consider it not to be in the best interest of the supervisory relationship. How can these tensions be managed? How can the supervisor prioritize the space to think and at the same time not give the message that he or she is aloof or unavailable to the supervisee? In this context we wonder whether female supervisors are expected to be more accessible, more caring, and friendlier because of their gender.

Gender and multiple relations in supervision

As practitioners we hold a feminist, postmodern, collaborative perspective that has developed over a number of years (Abela and Sammut Scerri, 2003). We believe that holding this stance makes sense in the context of the position of women in relation to authority and expertise in our culture. In as much as the expert position is still desirable where men and foreign consultants are concerned, women are still frowned upon if they adopt a dominant voice. As Schriha (1999: 46), who is a female Maltese academic, points out, if women are "unassuming about their achievements, no one will give credit for their work. On the other hand, if they learn to interact in the same style that males do, they are subjected to a lot of flak and snide remarks."

In this sense, women may be more socialized into adopting a collaborative approach informed by a feminist perspective. Hopkins et al. (2008: 349) cite a meta-analysis of more than 160 studies of sex-related differences in leadership and state that "women use a more participative or democratic style and a less autocratic or directive style than men do". These authors also quote other studies cited by Goleman that reveal that "women are more aware of their emotions, show more empathy, and are more adept interpersonally" (p. 350).

We believe that the collaborative approach also provides more flexibility in terms of managing different positions in the hierarchy.

In our experience, it is much easier to manage being a supervisor in one context and a member of a team led by the supervisee in another context when adopting this approach. By contrast, an expert approach is not particularly helpful as it may constrain the practitioner in a "one–up" position, irrespective of context. More research may be helpful to explore how gender construction and gender inequality intersect with multiple relationships in supervision.

Male and female supervisees might also behave differently in the context of multiple relationships. For example, one of us noted that her supervisees in the organization where she worked (all females) frequently asked her to socialize with them and in this context would relate to her as a peer. Interestingly, a male colleague of ours who is also a supervisor remarked how his male supervisees would invite him for a drink after supervision whereas female supervisees seemed to respect the boundaries more. We wondered whether this behaviour can be explained in terms of fear that relations outside of the workplace between a male supervisor and female supervisee would be perceived by others as being sexual.

Research on mentoring relationships (Johnson and Huwe, 2002: 48) explains that attraction is common given that successful mentorship typically involves "good matching ... of personality, career interest, scholarly interest, and commitment to the relationship". Furthermore, Lamb, Catanzaro, and Moorman (2004) report that attraction between supervisors and their supervisees occurs more often than it does with clients, and to an extent that they suggest that supervisors discuss attraction issues with their supervisees as they begin their work together. Personally we both question what the particular effects of highlighting this aspect would be. We agree with Haug's (1999) position that the more dissatisfied supervisors are with their sexual lives, the more they are likely to seek for the needs to be met from their supervisees. At the same time, we do not want to imply that such attractions, including same-sex attractions, cannot happen, or that if they do they should be "nursed in the dark" (Haug, 1999: 415) because of the shame and embarrassment that they may trigger. Lamb et al. (2004: 253) point out that supervisors need to be alert to the cues of attraction when they occur and "avoid reinforcing and reciprocating those cues; and be prepared to respond to such overtures in a clear, unequivocal and professional manner". Another way of addressing such issues is in the context of a safe supervision-of-supervision (SOS) relationship.

Dilemmas and challenges as the multiple relationship develops

As has already been pointed out, not all multiple supervisory relationships develop smoothly. A supervisee might decide to develop in ways that do not fit with this complex relationship. He or she may find it difficult to manage both the supervisory relationship and the other relationships that he or she has with the supervisor in other contexts including group supervision contexts. A supervisee may feel the need to compete with her peers in such a way that undermines team work. This competitive relationship may be exacerbated when these same peers compete for the same job or aspire to take on the same positions on various committees. While creating a context to talk about these issues is important, if supervisees are not ready to do this, it can be helpful just to tolerate the uncertainty and acknowledge that they can be "left to bake" and returned to at a later stage.

In so much as the supervisee needs to feel that her vulnerability is not exploited by the multiple relationship, the supervisor also needs to feel that he or she is allowed to keep his or her professional judgement both from a clinical and an ethical perspective. In this sense, both the supervisor and the supervisee need to value the supervisory relationship in order for it to be maintained. Attempts to capitalize on multiple relationships could sabotage or even destroy the supervisory relationship. The consolidation of the supervisor–supervisee relationship in the context of a multiple relationship implies a considerable amount of trust from the supervisor towards the supervisee and vice versa.

We would like to highlight how crucial trust is in this context, especially when knowledge about a supervisee can so easily be gained from other contexts to the point that this may be experienced as persecutory by the supervisee. In our experience, supervision in the context of multiple relationships can be indeed a very lonely job that involves holding and keeping to oneself information that cannot be shared in any circumstances.

It can be very tempting to want to consult with a colleague, to use him or her as a sounding board in order to be reassured that one is supporting good clinical practice and providing helpful supervision. Ethically this raises a number of dilemmas. What if in the course of the supervisory relationship the supervisor feels that the supervisee would feel increasingly vulnerable if the supervisor were to seek supervision of supervision? How explicit should the use of SOS be made; each and every time the supervisor feels the need to consult with her supervisor? Very often, in a community where multiple relationships are common, the supervisor of the supervisor would know the supervisee and possibly even her clients and this further adds to the dilemmas and the complexity! In this regard one of us has sometimes sought supervision of supervision outside of the country in order to be able to talk freely about some of her dilemmas during supervision. One other way to deal with this complexity is to make it explicit to supervisees from the start that the supervisor seeks regular supervision of supervision, naming the person concerned and asking the supervisee for consent. Before this practice was introduced, the multiple nature of supervision of supervision used to be left unspoken with supervisees. In spite of the fact that the anonymity of the supervisee is always safeguarded, there are many situations where it is easy to guess who the supervisee is and at times it may also add to the better understanding of the dynamics of the situation. In such circumstances we believe that confidentiality is nevertheless always paramount and sensitive information should not be divulged without the prior consent of the supervisee.

Another factor adding to the complexity of the supervisory relationship is that sometimes information about the supervisee is obtained from other contexts. When is it helpful to share this information with the supervisee? This dilemma becomes increasingly complex when the information about the supervisee concerns perceived professional shortcomings. Sometimes the situation becomes so difficult that as a supervisor you feel that you want to avoid bringing it up. In our experience this feeling is triggered mostly when the supervisor is concerned at the level of distress that the supervisee experiences when given feedback. The supervisor ends up having to process what needs to be prioritized: whether it is the quality of the supervisee's practice or his or her emotional well-being. On paper, it seems evident that the quality of practice comes first. However we have both experienced situations where we felt that we needed to consolidate our supervisory relationship further before entering into such vulnerable territory.

On the other hand, there may be times when the appointed clinical supervisor in an agency proves to be less talented than the supervisee, who in turn complains to the Head of service about the supervisor's shortcomings. How does the Head of service deal with this? The fact that the said supervisor and the Head of service are most likely to be colleagues adds to the sensitivity of this situation. It might be useful for the Head of service to meet the supervisor and supervisee individually and explore with them the possibility of a joint meeting to address the issues involved. If, following this meeting, the supervisee finds that the status quo remains, then what? Although the Head of service can provide some additional supervision to the supervisee, it is not as easy to remove the clinical supervisor from the picture. To what extent does the multiple relationship between the Head of service and the clinical supervisor hinder an adequate course of action?

From our experience in these circumstances it can become problematic for the supervisee to even dare report her supervisor. As Sultana and Baldacchino (1994: 17) point out we live in a society where we are "adapted at muting hostility, containing disagreement and avoiding disputes, a sophisticated mode of accommodation". In a society where we are confronted with multiple relationships all the time, burning bridges may prove to be painful and very unwise. The supervisee may also have access to information about the supervisor. Even though sought-after supervisors (especially those external to the organization and recruited for this purpose) would normally have earned their good reputation on the basis of past professional practice, and, additionally in a small society are more likely to be carefully scrutinized and perhaps less likely to "get away" with poor practice, this remains a powerful dilemma. The risk could be that, instead of overtly claiming their right to good supervision, supervisees who find themselves in this situation may prefer to leak information about the supervisor to people with whom they feel safe. Such a situation unfortunately is not very constructive either for the supervisor or for the supervisee. Gottlieb, Robinson, and Younggren, (2007) report that in a study by Ladany, Lehrman-Waterman, Molinaro, and Wolgast only 35% of supervisees discussed ethical violation directly with their supervisor whereas 54% discussed it with someone else.

In 14% of the cases, another person in a position of responsibility knew about the situation and did nothing about it.

We are also familiar, however, with situations where the supervisor was humble enough to take on ideas from a clearly more talented supervisee (who was also very skilful at imparting her knowledge) and as a result both became enriched by the process. Gabriel (2001) reports that those who had difficulties in sustaining self in various relationship roles and were unable to say no to the supervisor suffered, whereas those who gained from the multiple relationship were sufficiently able to intervene and deal with the overlapping roles.

Transformational possibilities

In a context where job opportunities are limited and professional jealousies and rivalries easily provoked, a supervisor and a supervisee may find themselves in a situation where they are competing for the same job. In such situations, the benign position of the supervisor may be very challenging to maintain! One wonders whether such a supervisory relationship can be sustained. If the supervisee succeeds in getting the job, then hierarchies would need to be renegotiated. This might be a challenging process and resolution may be painful even in the best of circumstances. However, a supervisor can also take huge pride in seeing how they have helped a supervisee develop in ways that they might have only dreamt of achieving themselves. We are sure that Maestro Paul Asciak swells with pride every time he hears about the success of his pupil and now world-renowned Maltese tenor Joseph Calleja!

Although multiple relationships do present complex dilemmas, our experience and that of other supervisors have shown that multiple relationships can benefit both the supervisor and supervisees. As two of our supervisees have told us, they believe that their supervision sessions have benefited from the multiple relationship in that the supervisor knows the supervisee intimately and within different contexts and can thus provide richer feedback: "I knew that you would integrate your knowledge of me in other contexts for a better outcome on supervision issues."

Ryder and Hepworth (1990: 130) state that multiple relationships "move away from exploitation, not toward it, to the extent that they are moving genuinely toward collegiality and equality". The Committee on Racial and Ethnic Diversity as cited in Storm, Peterson, and Tomm (1997), points out that multiple relationships are essential for minority therapists, in that they help them access mentors within the field. In one of the author's experience, the fact that her foreign tutors were willing to foster a collegiate relationship following her training, enhanced her professional development and provided her with an opportunity through which she could broaden her thinking and not be constrained by the limitations of living on a small island with very few senior professionals in the same field. Bograd (1992) also points out that supervisees who relate to their supervisors in multiple roles and contexts have more information about their supervisors, demystifying them in the process. This empowers supervisees to take on more challenging professional responsibilities.

This mentoring relationship adopted by the supervisor towards his or her supervisee is an important rite of passage for the supervisor who comes to a stage where he or she particularly enjoys sharing their knowledge and passing it on to a younger generation. Learning how to go about this in a collaborative manner is a challenge in itself and can be very exciting. Moreover the younger supervisees (at least in terms of their experience) offer the supervisor an enticing invitation to learn by revisiting and questioning their knowledge and keeping abreast of the latest developments in the field.

Conclusion

When living in multiply connected network such as ours, we find that we continually need to strive to manage the subtle nuances of multiple relationships. Practitioners have to continually grapple with the ethical dilemmas that such complex relationships demand, even in situations where it seems very easy to slip into comfortable arrangements. Unfortunately such situations can ultimately backfire and be detrimental to both supervisors and supervisees. To tackle such multiple relationships calls for increased reflexivity and for therapeutic acumen. When the relationship goes wrong it can be very taxing on those involved, and more than they would have bargained for. The upside of the story is that such relationships can be transformational, can contribute to the transmission of knowledge from one generation of professionals to another, and can introduce more equality and collaborative practice.

References

Abela, A. and Sammut Scerri, C. (2003). Collaborative Inquiry Versus Didacric Training with Organizations: A Case Study. *Human Systems*. 14(1): 1–14.

Anderson, H. and Swim, S. (1995). Supervision as Collaborative Conversation: Connecting the Voices of Supervisor and Supervisee. *Journal of Systemic Therapies*. 14(2): 1–13.

Association for Family Therapy and Systemic Practice. *Code of Ethics and Practice* (2008). Retrieved from: http://www.aft.org.uk/about/documents/CodeofEthicsAugust2008.pdf (accessed January 2009).

Bograd, M. (1993). The duel over dual relationships. *The California Therapist*. 5(1): 7–16.

Boissevain, J. (1993). *Saints and Fireworks: Religion and Politics in Rural Malta* (3rd edn). Valletta, Malta: Progress Press.

British Psychological Society. *Code of Ethics and Conduct* (2006). Retrieved from: http://www.bps.org.uk/document-download-area/document-download$.cfm?file_uuid=5084A882–1143-DFD0–7E6C-F1938 A65C242&ext=pdf (accessed January 2009).

Davidson, L. (2006). Supervision and Mentorship. The Use of the Real in Teaching. *Journal of the American Academy of Psychoanalysis and Dynamic Psychiatry*. 34(1): 189–195.

Gabriel, L. (2001). *Speaking the Unspeakable: Dual Relationships in Counselling and Psychotherapy*. York St John, University of Leeds: Unpublished Doctoral Thesis.

Goodyear, R. and Sinnett, E. (1984). Current and Emerging Ethical Issues for Counselling Psychologists. *Counseling Psychologist*. 12(3–4): 87–98.

Gottlieb, M.C., Robinson, K. and Younggren, J.N. (2007). Multiple Relations in Supervision: Guidance for Administrators, Supervisors, and Students. *Professional Psychology: Research and Practice*. 34(3): 241–247.

Gutheil, T.G. and Gubbard, G.O. (1993). The Concept of Boundaries in Clinical Practice: Theoretical and Risk Management Dimensions. *American Journal of Psychiatry*. 150(2): 188–196.

Haug, I.E. (1999). Boundaries and the Use of Misuse of Power and Authority. Ethical Complexities for Clergy Psychotherapists. *Journal of Counseling and Development*. 77(4): 411–417.

Hopkins, M.M., O'Neil, D.A., Passarelli, A. and Bilimoria, D. (2008). Women's Leadership Development Strategic Practices for Women and Organizations. *Consulting Psychology Journal: Practice and Research.* 60(4): 348–365.

Johnson, W.B. (2007). Transformational Supervision: When Supervisors Mentor. *Professional Psychology: Research and Practice.* 39(1): 44–55.

Johnson, W.B. and Huwe, J.M. (2002). Towards a Typology of Mentorship Dysfunction in Graduate School. *Psychotherapy: Theory/Research/Practice/Training.* 39(1): 44–55.

Knapp, S.J. and VandeCreek, L.D. (2006). *Practical Ethics for Psychologists.* Washington, DC: American Psychological Association

Kral, R. and Himes, M. (1999). A Survey Study on Developmental Stages in Achieving a Competent Sense of Self as a Family therapist. *The Family Journal: Counselling and therapy for Couples and Families.* 7(2): 102–111.

Lamb, D.H., Catanzaro, S.J. and Moorman, A.S. (2004). A Preliminary Look at how Psychologists Identify, Evaluate, and Proceed when Faced with Possible Multiple Relationship Dilemmas. *Professional Psychology: Research and Practice.* 35(3): 248–254.

Lawton, B. (2000). A Very Exposing Affair: Exploration in Counsellors' Supervisory Relationships. In: Lawton, B. and Feltham, C. (eds) *Taking Supervision Forward: Enquiries and Trends in Counselling and Psychotherapy.* London: Sage Publications. pp. 25–41.

Mifsud, D. (2004). *Inside the Oracle's Chamber: The Experience of Counselling Supervision in a Maltese Context.* University of Bristol: Unpublished MSc thesis.

Murphy, M.J. and Wright, D.W. (2005). Supervisees' Perspectives of Power us in Supervision. *Journal of Marital and Family Therapy.* 31(3): 283–295.

Pearson, B. and Piazza, N. (1997). Counselor Preparation: Classification of Dual Relationships in the helping Relationship. *Counselor Education and Supervision.* 37(2): 89–99.

Protinsky, H. and Coward, L. (2001). Developmental Lessons of Seasoned Marital and Family Therapists: A Qualitative Investigation. *Journal of Marital and Family Therapy.* 27(3): 375–381.

Ryder, R. and Hepworth, J. (1990). AAMFT ethical code: "Dual relationships". *Journal of Marital and Family Therapy.* 16(2): 127–132.

Schindler, N.J. and Talen, M.R. (1996). Supervision 101: The Basic Elements for Teaching Beginning Supervisors. *Clinical Supervisor.* 14(2): 109–118.

Schriha, L. (1999). The Glass Ceiling: Maltese Women in Academia. *Humanitas, Journal of the Faculty of Arts.* 1(1): 37–51.

Storm, C.L., Peterson, M. and Tomm, K. (1997). Multiple Relationships in Supervision: Stepping up to Complexity. In: Todd, T.C. and

Storm, C.L. (eds) *The Complete Systemic Supervisor: Context, Philosophy and Pragmatics*. US: Allyn & Bacon. pp. 253–271.

Sultana, R. G. and Baldacchino, G. (1994). *Maltese Society. A Sociological Inquiry*. Malta: Mireva.

Syme, G. (2003). *Dual Relationships in Counselling and Psychotherapy: Exploring the Limits*. London: Sage.

Tomm, K. (1991). The Ethics of Dual Relationships. *The Calgary Participator: A Family Therapy Newsletter.* 1: 11–15.

CHAPTER FIFTEEN

Systemic supervision in agency contexts: An evolving conversation with clinical psychologists in a mental health trust

Karen Partridge

Introduction

I work as a Consultant Clinical Psychologist in Systemic Psychotherapy in a Mental Health Foundation Trust. The key dilemma of my role is enshrined in my title; I am employed as a Clinical Psychologist and also as a Systemic Psychotherapist, and I see it as part of my remit to remain loyal to both descriptions. I am employed to provide systemic supervision and teaching for Clinical Psychologists across the trust and to carry out clinical work in the Adult Mental Health Service. The psychologists and other staff that I work with are employed in all major specialities in the trust, including Adult, Child, Older Adults, HIV and AIDS, Psychological Medicine, Forensic, Special Needs and Paediatric Psychology.

In this chapter I share perspectives on agency-based supervision illustrated by case examples taken from my supervisory practice with Clinical Psychologists. First I explore contributions from the literature that I have found helpful in constructing a position for agency-based supervision. The rest of the chapter describes my systemic interventions, which shift between different kinds of conversational patterns, but are presented in a linear fashion for ease of presentation. The process of arriving at this description of systemic work has been an essential aspect of the work itself and is not an end point, but rather a beginning in an on-going conversation.

Towards a position for agency-based supervision

In my supervisory practice I have been influenced by four potential constructions of supervision. First, I explore the idea of agency-based supervision as organizational development. This construction of supervision can be important in creating a distinction between agency-based supervision and supervision that takes place as part of more formal systemic training.

Supervision as organizational development

Over the past thirty years of working in the National Health Service (NHS) the pace of organizational change has increased exponentially, with governmental reforms resulting in trust mergers and multiple reorganizations. Schön (1973) talks about the state losing its stability in the resulting society and its institutions being in a continuous process of transformation. He argues that this has significance for learning, and consequently for supervisory practice, in that we need to invent and develop institutions which are learning systems, capable of bringing about their own continuous transformation. Schön proposes reflexive practice through double loop learning, where feedback enables a shift in the way that strategies and consequences for learning are understood (Argyris and Schön, 1978). His distinction between reflection-in-action and reflection-on-action has become an important idea in the training of systemic supervisors (Schön, 1987). From this perspective, agency-based supervision can be thought of as organizational development where the aim is to help staff to articulate their practice, become reflexive to it, and develop moral and aesthetic judgements which inform future directions. In agency-based supervision I am commissioned by the organization to facilitate these developments through formal supervision in systemic therapy and by supporting and facilitating informal "communities of practice" (Wenger and Snyder, 2000: 139).

Supervision as primary participative research

This construction appeals to me as it connects to organizational development and is also congruent with the idea of therapeutic conversations as interventions (McNamee, 2000). Penman (1996) outlines developments in communication theory and research that relate to the reformulation of knowledge and the nature of research. First she goes back to the Latin source meaning of context as "to weave together". This makes the concept of context more complex than a focus on surrounds, so that text and context mutually inform each other and meaning arises in the interplay. Second, social knowledge is reformulated as being contextually bound and constructed in the process of communicating. Informed by Wittgenstein (1953), Penman argues that we need to bring "communicating" into the foreground rather than focusing on "communication". This means that, as we research, we are participating in the processes we create and this process creates the social world. Penman argues that all inquiries into the nature of relationships are interventions; she introduces the term "primary research", which involves direct participation in the conversation, in contrast to "secondary research", which takes place from the removed position of the conventional researcher. From this perspective, all agency-based supervision could be described as primary participative research.

Primary participative research takes a forward-looking focus, building on possibilities. Within this generative, dynamic view of participation, there is a different way of knowing, what Shotter (1993) calls, "knowing of the third kind", a knowing from within. Penman talks about the ethics of participation, and the importance of mutuality between contributors. She quotes Krippendorff (1989) that we have a moral imperative to maintain or expand the range of choices that are available to people. In this way supervision could be seen as a way to increase the possibilities available both for individuals seeking supervision and for the organization.

The process of communicating is fluid and dynamic but the process of understanding needs closure, if only momentarily. Shotter (1993) states that when we talk about understanding we shift from a participatory position into an authoritative one. In this narrative frame we make aesthetic judgements about what is good and right and useful. As primary researchers we take these judgements back to the process of communicating, so we are continually shifting between participating and reflecting. The work we do inside the process has a moral dimension, while judgements from outside are aesthetic. The process of supervision can be seen as a conversational process of primary research where the supervisor is enabling moral action in supervisees and making aesthetic judgements to feed back into the process.

Supervision as learning to transgress

Supervision as organizational development and as primary research sets an interventive and contextualized frame for supervision in which knowledge is socially constructed and a moral and aesthetic dimension is intrinsic to the process. bell hooks (1994) addresses this dimension in her approach to training as learning to transgress. From this perspective we are training our supervisees to deconstruct the taken-for-granted and to challenge the "natural order of things". It becomes a moral imperative throughout the training process to expose and challenge imperialist assumptions which silence clients, supervisees, and colleagues who experience the debilitating effects of differential power. Burnham and Harris (2002) have termed this kind of ethical practice attention to the "social GRRAAACCEEESS" of gender, race, religion, age, ability, appearance, culture, class, ethnicity, education, economics, sexuality and spirituality.

Supervision as adult learning

Finally, supervision can be constructed as adult learning. The literature on adult learning has become an increasingly strong influence in systemic supervision (Burnham, this volume). Ideas from adult education are being incorporated into systemic training, including: a learning spiral proposed by Stratton (2005), information about students' learning styles (Kolb, 1983), Schön's (1987) elaboration of the reflective practitioner, and Anderson's (1982) distinction between declarative knowledge, "knowing that" which is conscious, and procedural knowledge, "knowing how to", which may not be conscious. In helping students become reflective practitioners, we invite them to become conscious of their own processes in a way that enables them to adapt and change as they go along. Supervision as adult learning thus connects with Guba and Lincoln's (1989) construction of organizational development as a system's ability to describe and account for its own processes in increasingly detailed and sophisticated ways.

The three examples that follow weave in and out of these four different constructions of supervision, privileging different versions at different times according to the context and the commission. The first two examples describe communities of practice that have evolved within the child and special needs service; the third describes more formal supervision of a systemic team in the adult service.

I will start by outlining some of the issues around managing the gap between clinical psychology and systemic therapy.

Mind the gap: Clinical Psychology and systemic therapy

The commissioners for my post, which was created to make training available for Clinical Psychologists, are the Clinical Psychology managers within the trust, spanning different specialities. Clinical Psychology training usually, but not always, promotes a scientist practitioner model, where the practitioner is a scientist in action, gathering information, making hypotheses, formulating problems, intervening, and evaluating effectiveness. At first glance this seems similar to a systemic approach but it is based on different assumptions about the nature of reality and knowledge and is more closely allied to the medical model and to other dominant discourses about treatment and effectiveness prevalent in the NHS. The assumptions of this way of thinking can create questions and dilemmas for Clinical Psychologists wanting to embrace systemic thinking. As systemic approaches have become more widespread in the health service and on Clinical Psychology training courses, supervisors and their trainees face the challenge of embracing both the rigour of psychology and the flexibility and evolutionary nature of current systemic thinking.

In my agency-based supervisory practice, I find that three shifts are often necessary to enable Clinical Psychologists to think systemically. The first relates to the nature of reality and construction of knowledge and the second to the use of self. In the same way that psychologists are usually trained to be objective observers of "reality", they are also typically trained to create a distinction, or clear "boundary", between their personal and professional lives while systemic thinkers often hope to harness personal resources and experiences in a way that might enhance the therapeutic relationship. The use of self (Jones, 2003) and issues of transparency (Roberts, 2005) are particularly pertinent where personal/professional consultations and a process of mapping the connections between professional and personal stories can be very helpful in making a shift into a systemic epistemology (Graff, Lund-Jacobsen and Wermer, 2003; Hedges and Lang, 1993). A third important difference between Clinical Psychology and Systemic Therapists employed within NHS Trusts is that Clinical Psychology tends to hold a more powerful position than that of Family Therapy. This may be due to the length of time that each profession has been established within the NHS but is also probably connected to the position that Clinical Psychology has taken in relation to the medical profession and to expert discourses about treatment and effectiveness. This means that an active awareness of the effects of differential power and exploration of dominant and subjugated discourses is a third important shift towards systemic thinking.

I have found that the shift from the third person positioning of traditional research to the first and second person positioning of primary participative research is central to the shifts in awareness that enable Clinical Psychologists to think systemically. In the following examples I have frequently used diagrams as a way to connect with Clinical Psychologists as conceptual learners, who often make connections from theory into practice. Diagrams fit with the grammar of Clinical Psychology training and help to create connections with theory and practice.

A spiral process for supervision as primary participative research

Systemic intervention could be described as an on-going conversation shifting between different conversational patterns, each defining a particular context and enabling a different kind of conversation to take place (Partridge, 2005). This kind of evolutionary conversation, in which meaning is constructed in the living moment (McNamee, 2003), fits with primary participative research. Systemic conversations create a shared reality in which incongruities in meaning and experience can be explored, evolving through feedback to enable participants to gradually clarify and refine their experiences. This process is described in Case Example 1, where senior psychologists explored and refined their definitions of supervision. In this approach to supervision the criteria for success are aesthetic, addressing what makes sense within the context of the organization, what is appropriate and timely, and what is morally and ethically desirable (Reason and Bradbury, 1994). For example, Whitehead and McNiff (2006), in their living theory approach, take life-affirming, energy-flowing values as their explanatory principles.

When an individual or group request supervision in an agency context, initial conversations need to address the position of the person making the request in the organization. So the first step is an awareness of the culture of the organization and the second an awareness of the supervisee's position within it. Only then can the particular learning needs that the professional brings for supervision be addressed. Initial conversations need to involve deconstructing the "system of concern" (Lang and McAdam, 1996a), that is, tracking all of the people in the organization who have an interest in the current request for supervision, mapping out the system of professionals and clarifying lines of accountability and authority. Exploring the culture of the organization and the department or work group requesting supervision involves unravelling all of the different and disparate stories about what needs to be done and why and exploring how this requests fits with the wider organization and its aims. This process was important in Case Example 2 where Clinical Psychologists working in Special Needs wanted to begin to work systemically.

The next step is to "warm the context" for change (Burnham, 2005: 9), opening out the presenting stories to negotiate a commission with all the actors in the system. The idea of commissioning and commissioners (Lang, Little and Cronen, 1990), that is, who wants who to do what for whom is important in keeping the systemic intervention coherent with the aims of the rest of the organization. These conversations transform a request for help within the domain of production into a piece of exploratory work within the domain of explanation (Mendez, Coudou and Maturana, 1988).

Within this exploratory domain, meaning can be further explored by investigating incongruities in people's stories, supporting "shy stories", addressing differential power, helping people to articulate their positions, and helping people build on strengths to construct enabling future visions. The third example with the systemic team in Adult Mental Health illustrates this kind of conversation. Here feedback enhances the system through reflexive positioning, enabling supervisor and supervisees to shift out of the primary research position to reflect on the action and make aesthetic choices about how to go on. Reflexive conversations foster relational responsibility by exploring the supervisor's position with respect to supervisees, clients, other professionals, and the work context. Reflexivity to theoretical ideas means that discourses privileged in the work context like evidence-based practice can also inform action. The final section, "A way forward for agency-based supervision" proposes an expansion of these conversations to construct evidence for different audiences in the organization.

Commissioning conversations: Mapping the system

One way of thinking about mapping and commissioning in agency settings is in terms of relational responsibility (McNamee and Gergen, 1999). The conversations that take place in setting up consultation or supervision could be seen as constructing and defining relational responsibility between participants who hold different positions and responsibilities in the organization. These commissioning conversations take on special significance within an organizational context because of the complexity of conversational patterning and multiple positions.

The three case examples all started as requests for systemic supervision but ended in different ways through the process of mapping, negotiating, and commissioning. In the first example a group of senior child psychologists wanted to use systemic ideas to inform and enhance their work as managers and supervisors of more junior psychologists. In the second example a group of psychologists from the Special Needs service wanted to set up live family sessions but discovered that it was a better fit with their service to apply a systemic approach to their work in multi-disciplinary teams. The third example of a group of psychologists working systemically in an Adult Mental Health centre challenges some of the traditional ideas held about boundaries between different models of therapy and in family relationships in different cultures. The subheadings describe what I as a supervisor am doing, the conversational strategies that I am using, and what my supervisees are learning through doing; the case examples are woven in and out of these learning aims.

Joining the conversation as a guest in the culture of the other

Lang and McAdam (1996b) talk about a request for help as a "gracious invitation" to enter into the culture of the other. As Ricoeur (2003) states, when you speak your language you live your culture and emotions. When I am invited to supervise, it is as a guest in the culture of that service. Each speciality within the NHS has its own unique culture, its own "grand narratives", practices, and moral integrity. I see my task as an anthropologist to explore and join with the cultural practices of the other to jointly find how systemic theory and practice might enhance their work. In these case examples I joined the culture of each group through exploring the dominant discourses that emerged in conversation about their service, deconstructing and discovering moral orders through the use of "Linguagrams" (Lang and McAdam, 1996c) and clarifying positions using the diamond representation of the Fifth province Approach (McCarthy, 2002).

Deconstructing "grand narratives"

Like all organizations, hospital systems are dominated by "grand narratives" which take on a life of their own and become defining of services, relationships, and people. In the NHS some of these grand narratives are enshrined in the medical model, including discourses of health and illness, diagnosis, treatment, experts and patients, effectiveness, efficiency and evidence-based practice. Deconstruction of a dominant discourse opens space for exploration, to challenge differential power and elaborate alternative subjugated stories, but it also allows you to join with a dominant discourse to explore its integrity. Nichterlein (2005) talks about the common misconception that deconstruction means destroying something and suggests that what should be spoken of is uncovering or elaborating the richness in an idea to be deconstructed.

Exploring moral orders

The theory of the Co-ordinated Management of Meaning (CMM) (Pearce and Cronen, 1980) sees every action as a moral action, with its own particular pattern of rights, duties, affordances, and constraints which can be acted into at any moment. These moral orders give integrity to action and are revealed in the "shoulds" and "oughts" of the way that people talk. Lang and McAdam (1996c) introduced "Linguagrams" as a way to talk with clients about the moral orders that govern action. A Linguagram is a like a brainstorm or a Mind Map™, starting with the word to be deconstructed in the centre, and, at each addition, the scribe checking with the client/s whether this new idea fits with the previous idea or is a departure; in this way a collaborative map of meaning is constructed. Fredman (2004: 30) describes this process as "walking into words", looking for the meaning within.

Case Example 1: Senior child psychologists
Exploring culture and moral orders using linguagrams

A group of senior child psychologists who held management roles with respect to their psychology teams requested a series of seminars to explore how systemic ideas might enhance the supervision they provided to more junior psychologists.

We started the process by exploring the psychologists' own experiences of supervision through examples of when supervision had gone well and when it had been difficult. This raised a number of issues about different organizational positions and boundaries between them. We discussed the potential for confusion between consultation, supervision, management, and leadership. Through questioning and discussion the psychologists began to explore the idea that when supervision went well relationships were clear and well defined in terms of rights, duties, and responsibilities. We decided to explore further distinctions between ideas by constructing four different Linguagrams, one each for leadership, management, consultation, and supervision.

One of the psychologists placed the word to be deconstructed in a central bubble and we began to generate all the ideas which linked to this dominant discourse. As we went along we grouped ideas into themes that connected with each other, revealing the moral orders, the integrity inherent in ideas about supervision, leadership, management, and consultation. This had the effect of constructing a common language between participants in the group and I was able to join their conversational grammar. In "physically moving ideas around", we were creating a ritual for the construction of a new grammar that encompasses the values of both the old and new. We were able to elaborate the meaning we were giving to the different organizational positions, of supervision, leadership, management, and consultation; clarifying the patterns of rights, duties, opportunities, and constraints that fit with each.

Constructing the Linguagrams made it clear that, like most NHS professionals, the senior psychologists held different positions at different times and within different parts of the organization. Clarity with respect to which role they were taking and when enabled the psychologists to develop what Oliver (1996) describes as "Systemic Eloquence", that is the ability to identify different contexts and to shift between different positions with elegance.

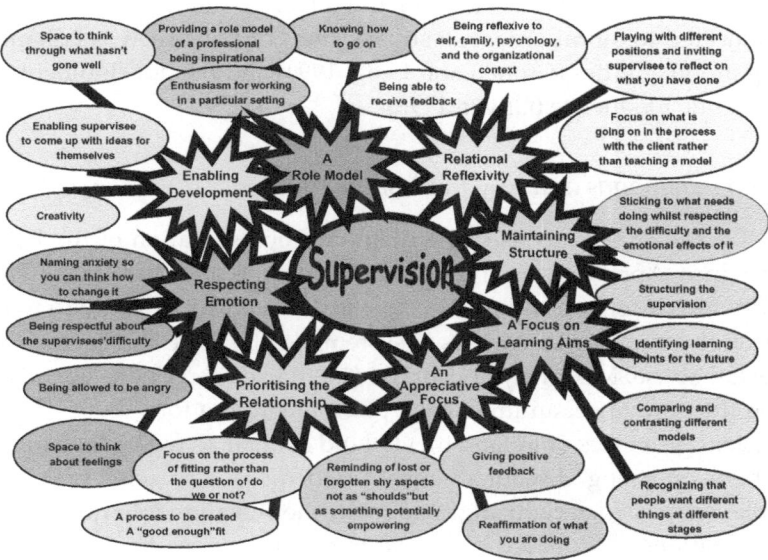

Figure 15.1. A Linguagram for supervision for senior psychologists.

Exploring different positions in the organization

Positioning theory offers a dynamic and relational way of thinking about the social construction of organizations (Campbell and Groenbaek, 2006). Davies and Harré (1990) introduce the idea of different person positions in relation to a discourse. First order positioning or the "I" position relates to the discourse set up by the first person in making an utterance which invites the other to enter the discourse in the "you" or second person position. Third order positioning occurs if the observer challenges the original discourse from a third discourse, or third person, "they" position. Moment by moment we are positioned and positioning each other in conversation. Each position has its own unique set of abilities, demands, and constraints.

First order positioning does not require the actor to be aware of their positioning but second and third order positioning requires awareness or reflexivity, in making the decision not to join, or to challenge, the current discourse. Supervision could be seen as a way to facilitate the learner's ability to become reflexive to their positioning and so enhance their ability to make choices about whether to join and accept the discourse or to shift into another. Choices are connected to moral orders so supervision could be seen as enhancing moral abilities (Cronen and Lang, 1994) and the development of Systemic Eloquence (Oliver, 1996).

Using diamonds as a way to illustrate positions

McCarthy (2002) has used the diamond representation of the Fifth Province Approach as a way to illustrate work dilemmas. The Fifth Province Approach was originally conceived as a way to map strongly opposing discourses in systems where there had been child sexual abuse. McCarthy and Bryne (1988) used the Celtic legend of the fifth province, an imaginary place where the four kings of the ancient provinces of Ireland met to hold council, to represent a place where opposing discourses meet. Two discourses with opposite poles are placed at right angles to each other, creating four quadrants or positions. A double line connects the discourses that are allied more closely to each other. These positions illustrate the dilemmas in which the system is caught. The Fifth Province is a fifth position at the centre from which all positions can be observed without entering into the dilemmas. This could be described as a reflexive position, a position with "insight" or "mindfulness".

Defining relationships and positions using diamonds

The senior psychologists were intrigued by the idea of the fifth province and we began to discuss distinctions between supervision and consultation, leadership and management, which had been illuminated in the Linguagrams. By identifying key discourses connected to these ideas we identified what seemed to be some crucial distinctions between these positions. We constructed these discourses as poles, and by drawing these at right angles we were able to come up with diamonds to illustrate these positions (Partridge, 2007). Distinctions between supervision and management focused on who takes the lead responsibility and whether the focus is on the content or the process of the session. For leadership and management we used the poles of "management versus leadership" and "pragmatic versus visionary". We felt that this second diamond felt uncomfortably polarized so experimented with "blunting the diamond" to create more both/and positions as in Figure 15.3.

Through this process we were able to talk about the way in which we would go on together in our supervisory group, clarifying my position as consultant to them as a group of senior clinicians, who held managerial responsibility for the psychologists they supervised. This led to further conversations about how the senior psychologists might explore and clarify

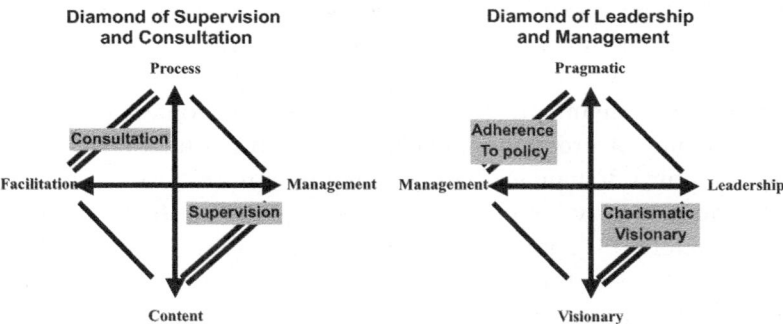

Figure 15.2. Diamonds to illustrate positions for the senior child psychologists.

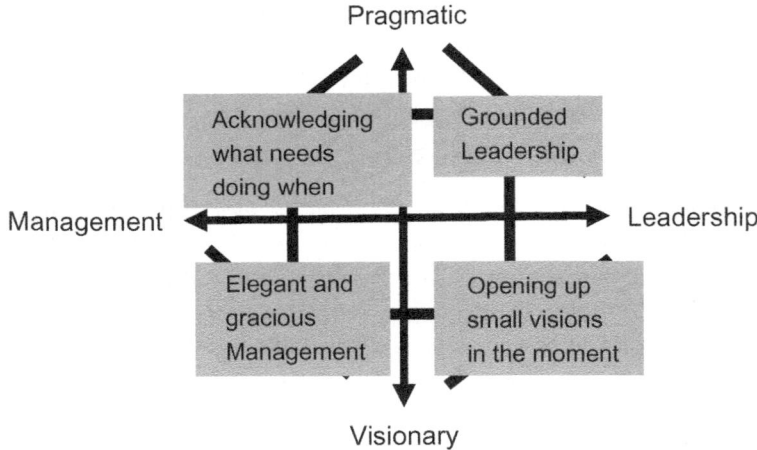

Figure 15.3. "Blunting" the diamond to create "both/and" positions.

relational responsibility with the more junior staff they supervised, as well as with their managers in their own supervision.

Exploring teamwork and professional identities

One of the specific issues of work in agency settings is that many of the staff I supervise are embedded in teams and yet have also their own professional allegiances. Multiple positions and multiple demands can lead to competing tasks and conflicting identities as well as dual lines of accountability. Maturana's (Mendez, Coudou and Maturana, 1988) domains of action and meaning can provide a helpful frame for professionals to sort out what tasks need to be done and by whom. Lang, Little, and Cronen (1990) describe the task of the systemic professional as elegantly negotiating between the domains of production, explanation, and aesthetics. A discussion of which domain staff are entering with respect to a particular task can be a very helpful way of freeing them up. In supervision we have found it helpful to talk about the activities of the team in terms of the triangle of actions presented in Figure 15.3. The request or "concern" arrives in the domain of production requiring action in the domain of production. Exploratory conversations, here called the "vision", require a shift into the domain of explanation, before shifting back into the domain of production in order to act. The way

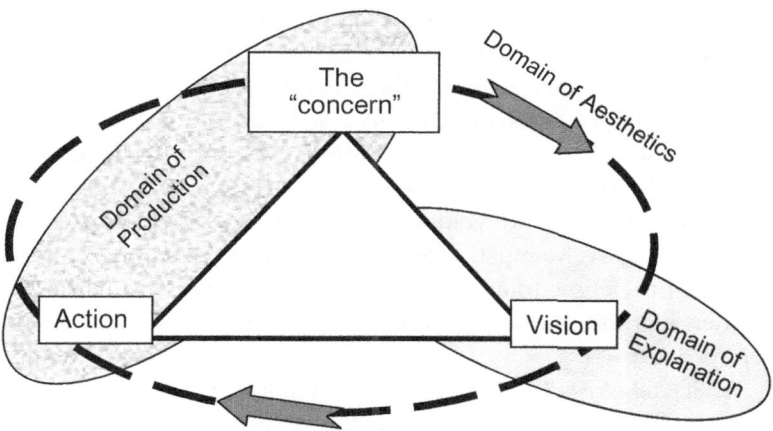

Figure 15.4. The tasks of the team.
Mapping domains of action and meaning

in which domains are negotiated is the domain of aesthetics. I have found that asking questions about what domain best describes the activities of a team is a helpful way to disentangle dilemmas and conflicts in teams.

Case Example 2: Special needs psychologists

In this example a group of Clinical Psychologists working in the Special Needs service of a large hospital requested an on-going monthly supervision group to explore how they might apply systemic ideas to their work. As is often the case, it was not clear from the start what kind of conversation might be most helpful. Part of the process of exploring the system of concern and clarifying the commission involved deciding together on the kind of work that would be most useful. This needs to take into account the learning needs of the group and different levels of expertise within it as well as their positions in the organization.

Mapping the system and exploring responsibilities, rights, and duties

In the initial sessions we mapped out on a large whiteboard who worked where and with whom and who was responsible for what. Through a process of questioning and exploring each individual's position and investigating similarities and differences between the teams I learned that the Special Needs service is highly specialized and that the primary focus of the work revolved around weekly multi-disciplinary assessment clinics that were borough-based. One psychologist was attached to each of these borough-based teams. One of the core responsibilities of the staff in each team was the assessment of children with developmental delay. A secondary responsibility for the psychologists was to meet with parents and children outside of the clinic to address concerns when this was requested, or when identified as an outcome of the multi-disciplinary assessment process.

The Special Needs Psychologists described the way in which they sometimes felt at odds with their teams regarding the issue of diagnosis. During multi-disciplinary team assessments the team met with a family with a child with developmental delay with the task of completing an assessment. The Consultant Paediatrician usually led the process and during the two-hour assessment different professionals would meet with family members and with the identified child to carry out assessments specific to their discipline. There would then be a break during which the professionals would pool information and come to a common view that would then be fed back to the family. Waiting lists were long and consequently the time allocated for completing the complex assessment was short but the psychologists became pre-occupied with what the experience was like for the family and how family members were processing the information about diagnosis.

We discussed the activities of the team in terms of the triangle of actions presented above. They noticed that questions about the way in which the family responded to the diagnosis could be described as an activity within the domain of explanation while the assessment clinic was completing a task of assessment in the domain of production. This clarification of domains enabled them to re-position themselves with respect to the assessment clinics. They began to create other opportunities, outside of the assessment clinic, to discuss with their colleagues the psychological effects of the assessment process on their clients.

Using diamonds to become reflexive about positioning

The psychologists began to explore the possibility of family work as a way to address the issues raised for families in the multi-disciplinary assessment process. They became curious that despite talking a lot about systemic ideas, they had not made the shift towards working directly with families, and that on the few occasions when they had managed to negotiate some family work it had been very difficult. This left the team feeling frustrated about lack of opportunities to "do therapy" and curious about the difficulty of carrying it out when an opportunity did arise.

This feeling of frustration let me to invite the group to become reflexive to the conversation that we were having. We noticed that we had been discussing the psychologists' role in the multi-disciplinary team, the demands of the organizational context, and the meaning given to the families' acceptance of the diagnosis. We began to wonder whether families tended to get referred for therapy when they did not accept the diagnosis that they had been given by the multi-disciplinary team. This idea opened up curiosity about the professional stories of the psychologists and other multi-disciplinary team members. Exploring this story enabled us to construct a diamond, which

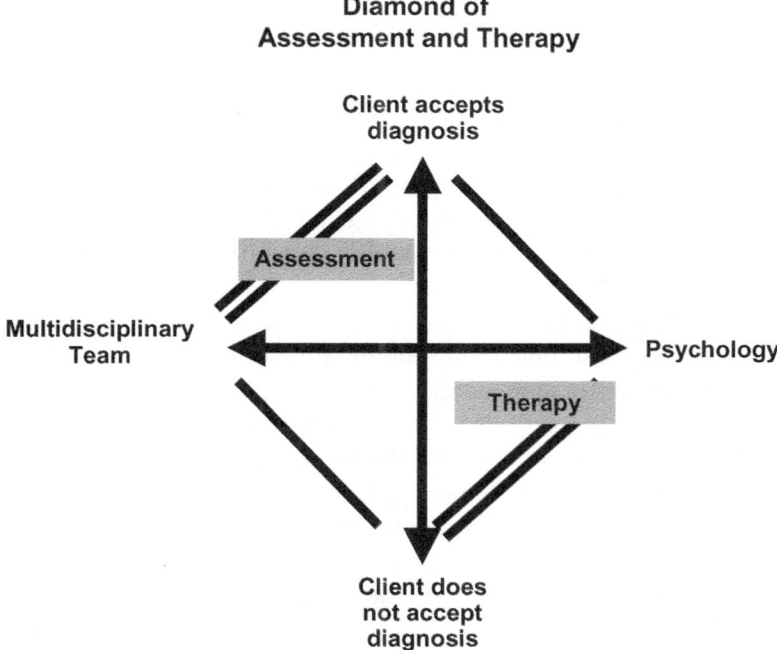

Figure 15.5. A diamond to illustrate positions for the Special Needs Psychologists.

seemed to capture the psychologists' dilemmas with respect to requests for assessment and therapy. Becoming reflexive to the work context and the role of the psychologist within it enabled individuals in the group to enter into discussions with each other and their team colleagues about the way in which they work together.

Feedback from one of the supervisees: "Personally I have found the diamonds really helpful to think with my team about a family's readiness to engage with psychology, the appropriateness of referrals and professional expectations. The diamonds have also opened up the possibility of having alternative conversations about families."

During the supervision sessions the psychologists were enthusiastic about learning more about systemic techniques and methods, but most of our conversation focused on systemic thinking about the system and the psychology team's position within it rather than privileging technique. In Burnham's (1992) terms, we were using systemic ideas at the level of approach rather than as method or technique, which was a better fit with their service.

Exploring dominant and subjugated discourses

One of the major challenges in working in the NHS is a difference between models; the above examples illustrate some of the contradictions and incongruities in meaning and experience. The medical model remains the dominant discourse within the NHS, which tends to subjugate alternative stories of what constitutes health, happiness, and a good quality of life. Working in the NHS means that professionals such as family therapists, social workers, and psychologists, whose primary training and predominant models are systemic and psychosocial rather than medical, need to negotiate with colleagues whose training and experience privilege the medical model.

The current context of the NHS means that every intervention needs to be justified in terms of what models are being used and how the work carried out fits with the research base. As a systemic supervisor working within this context it is a challenge to find ways to connect with predominant discourses and to find a position where both systemic approaches and evidence-based practice can be respected. I like Larner's (2005) description of a Para-modern perspective for systemic work, which encompasses both the traditional and the postmodern. The example below of working towards coherence between Systemic Therapy and Cognitive Behaviour Therapy (CBT) is an attempt towards this position.

Respecting different language games: Cognitive behaviour therapy (CBT) and systemic therapy

Case Example 3: Adult Mental Health psychologists

This work took place in an Adult Mental Health systemic team made up of psychologists at different stages in training. The team are trainees and qualified psychologists who have completed different levels of systemic training in the trust and I am supervisor to the team. This example fits with the construction of supervision as learning to transgress in that it challenges traditional ideas that different therapeutic approaches must be held as distinct and also challenges the Western construction of valuing horizontal over vertical alliances in families.

Developing coherence between CBT and systemic work

Don, a clinical psychologist experienced in CBT, was also a member of a systemic team that I supervise within the Psychology and Psychotherapy department. The department offers a range of psychological treatments from different theoretical orientations. Don assessed Ahmed, a young British man born in Pakistan, who had a diagnosis of Obsessive Compulsive Disorder (OCD). Ahmed had already received a series of sessions of CBT from a trainee psychologist, which had met with limited success. One of the difficulties of this work, as reported by the trainee, was that the young man's mother kept entering the sessions uninvited. The trainee psychologist had seen this as evidence of lack of boundaries between mother and son and referred them for family therapy. Another trainee clinical psychologist interviewed the family while I observed from behind a one-way screen with Don and another trainee.

The young man's parents had seen Professor Paul Salkovskis a proponent of CBT for OCD on television and felt strongly that they wanted individual CBT for their son. Given that CBT is the evidence-based treatment for OCD we decided to join this dominant discourse so Don began to work with Ahmed alongside the systemic sessions. We discussed how best to coordinate the individual CBT with the systemic work and I invited the team to reflect on the way in which race and culture might be informing the way that the family and the various therapists were experiencing individual and family sessions. This led to a discussion about responsibility, authority, and boundaries and the Western preoccupation with horizontal rather than vertical alignments in family structure (Falicov, 2000).

We began to explore ways in which we could include Ahmed's parents in the construction of the individual CBT sessions that was respectful to them whilst protecting the integrity of Don and Ahmed's relationship. Through discussion we decided that the lead therapist would invite Ahmed and Don to hold a reflecting discussion about their CBT work in the family session, in which Don would pose a number of questions to Ahmed about how he felt the work was going, and what he felt it would be important for his parents to know, so that the content and amount of information to be shared was in Ahmed's hands. The family welcomed the idea, and Ahmed's parents listened whilst he and Don discussed their work. In the reflecting conversation with Don, Ahmed confirmed that it was important for him that his parents received feedback about the individual sessions. He was able to say that he was finding the sessions useful but challenging and that something which was raised in the last session was particularly difficult for him (though he chose not to share the content of this), giving Don important feedback about their work together. The lead therapist then invited Ahmed's parents to reflect on what they had heard. They chose not to reflect on the content but on the quality of the relationship between Don and Ahmed, which they noted as being warm and respectful. It seemed that observing this relationship enabled them to step back and leave the individual work to Don and Ahmed. Everyone felt that the reflections had been useful and both sets of work were able to continue in a mutually reinforcing way.

The feedback from Don the CBT therapist was as follows: "It could have felt quite awkward for the family to observe Ahmed being interviewed by me as his CBT therapist, but as they were socialized into a systemic way of working, observing a conversation was nothing new to them. What was new was that Ahmed was participating in the conversation with his parents as observers. I think that being used to a systemic way of doing things meant that Ahmed felt comfortable and safe to have the conversation with me. It satisfied his wish to inform his parents of what was happening in the sessions with me and I wonder if doing it in this way was somehow easier for him and felt less intrusive than being asked questions by his parents at home afterwards. I also wonder whether observing our relationship had an effect on the way that the parents spoke to Ahmed about the therapy (and perhaps about other things) afterwards. Equally this might have then freed him up to talk in a more relaxed away to them. I think this approach was very respectful of my individual work with Ahmed and it added something to it that would have not been achievable in the one-to-one situation. This taught me that you can be quite playful and creative with the way you go about things as long as you have a theoretical link and are clear about the intention of your act. It also was very helpful to bring some curiosity and respect for the families' culture rather than aiming to try and 'correct' an 'intrusive parent'. I think I've learned to think more creatively about ways to join with the system."

The psychology trainee/lead therapist gave this feedback: "It was almost like a moment of enlightenment for me as I listened to their conversation—I really began to see the differences between the families' culture and my own. Up until that point I had been struggling to remain neutral towards some of the parent's actions. Without this session it would have taken me a lot longer to bring forth these different ideas about responsibility and concern for each other."

Holding the difference without trying to dissolve it

In this example I felt that it was important to maintain both the integrity of the systemic sessions and the CBT sessions without trying to integrate the two opposing perspectives; in Peter Lang's (2008) terms to "hold the difference without trying to resolve it". Using reflecting processes (Andersen, 1987) as an approach it was possible to respect the coherence of both a CBT model and a systemic epistemology without compromising either at the expense of the other. This idea originates in dialectical thinking and hermeneutics where the tension between ideas is the creative spur to new meanings. Maintaining the integrity of opposing positions enables a third discourse that encompasses the complexity of both. The resulting conversation adds to the richness of the description of selves in relation, rather than simplifying them and losing complexity. This has been important for me in terms of my supervisory work where I am interested in exploring differences and exposing the richness in distinctions rather than trying to mediate between opposing ideas to come to a common view. Many of the challenges and dilemmas which professionals bring for consultation or supervision could be described as being brought forth in incommensurate domains or realities, and as Pearce (1991) warns, it is an impossible task to try to make the incommensurate commensurate.

Ways forward in agency-based supervision

In the rapidly changing NHS, increasing expectations of the population in terms of health care are stretching limited budgets, and future directions are moving towards more cost-efficient ways of providing treatment. Layard's (2004) economically driven proposals employ graduate mental health workers to work in primary care settings, and guided self-help, packages of care, and manualized treatments are increasingly seen as the way forward in mental health. Systemic Therapists and Clinical Psychologists are costly to employ and increasingly the role of supervision of less highly qualified workers is likely to become a central aspect of our roles. The necessity of incorporating feedback and increasingly rigorous and robust measures into the practice of therapy and supervision has never been so important. In supervisory practice this needs to happen at two levels. Supervision could be evaluated according to the way in which it enables supervisees to account for their practice and provide outcome measures and evidence. In addition, supervision needs to account for itself in terms of the value-added benefit to the organization, the professionals who are being supervised, and the client group. With the implementation of the Agenda for Change continuing professional development (CPD) is the mechanism by which employees can move from one spine point to another within the Knowledge and Skills framework. This makes supervision and training an essential component of professional development in the NHS.

In this chapter I have framed supervision as primary research. The feedback from supervisees that I have included with the examples steps outside of the primary process to begin to make aesthetic judgements about the process. In order to join the grammar of the current NHS this feedback could be further refined and developed as secondary research to feed back into the organization and also into systemic training programmes. For the future I hope to further develop and refine the kind of feedback that supervision groups are presenting both in terms of their abilities to articulate their own practice and development and in terms of outcomes for clients. I am interested in continuing to try to articulate aesthetic judgements about moral processes in constructing different kinds of evidence for different audiences at different positions in the work context. These can be judged in terms of the choices available to clients whose voices are at risk of being least powerful in the process and to whom we are ultimately accountable as users of the service.

I want to emphasize that I have not been training Clinical Psychologists to become Systemic Therapists. I am employed to enable Clinical Psychologists and other staff in the NHS to use systemic ideas to enhance their core job descriptions. This does not detract from the need for more Systemic Therapists to be employed in the NHS especially in Adult settings where they are still sparse. Gross, McNab, Altschuler, and Ganda (2003) argue that connections with trainees' prior learning and their existing ways of working in their agency contexts have been relatively under-emphasized within existing Masters level training courses. This is an area rich for further development, as I have begun to explore. Articulating supervisory practice further will, I hope, also have a reflexive effect on training courses, highlighting the contexts in which qualified staff will practice and the skills they need to develop in order to connect creatively with different professionals and different discourses for the benefit of clients.

References

Andersen, T. (1987). The Reflecting Team: Dialogue and Meta-Dialogue in Clinical Work. *Family Process.* 26: 415–428.

Anderson, J.R. (1982). Acquisiton of Cognitive Skill. *Psychological Review.* 89: 369–406.

Argyris, C. and Schon, D. (1978). *Organizational Learning: A Theory of Action Perspective.* Reading, Mass: Addison Wesley.

Bateson, G. (1972/2000). *Steps to an Ecology of Mind: Collected Essays in Anthropology, Psychiatry, Evolution and Epistemology.* Chicago: University of Chicago Press.

Burnham, J. (2005). Relational Reflexivity: A Tool for Socially Constructing Therapeutic Relationships. In: Flaskas, C., Mason, B., and Perlesz, A. (eds) *The Space Between: Experience, Context and Process in the Therapeutic Relationship.* London: Karnac Books. Chapter 1.

Burnham, J. (1992). Approach, Method, Technique: Making Distinctions and Creating Connections. *Human Systems: The Journal of Systemic Consultation and Management.* 3: 3–26.

Burnham, J. and Harris, Q. (2002). Cultural Issues in Supervision. In: Campbell, D. and Mason, B. (eds) *Perspectives on Supervision.* London: Karnac Books. Chapter 2.

Campbell, D. and Groenbaek, M. (2006). *Taking Positions in the Organization.* London: Karnac Books.

Cecchin, G., Lane, G., and Ray, W.A. (1994). A Theory of the Cybernetics of Prejudices. In: Cecchin, G. and Ray, W.A. (eds) *The Cybernetics of Prejudices in the Practice of Psychotherapy.* London: Karnac Books. Chapter 2.

Champe J. and Kleist, D. (2003). Live Supervision: A Review of the Research. *The Family Journal.* 11: 268–275.

Cooperrider, D.L. (1990). Positive Image, Positive Action: The Affirmative Basis of Organizing. In: Srivatsva, S. and Cooperrider, D.L. (eds) *Appreciative Management and Leadership: The Power of Positive Thought and Action in Organizations.* Jossey Bass Business and Management Series. pp. 91–125.

Cronen, V.E. and Lang, P. (1994). Language and Action: Wittgenstein and Dewey in the Practice of Therapy and Consultation. *Human Systems,* 5: 5–43.

Davies, B. and Harré, R. (1990). Positioning, the Discursive Production of Selves. In: Wetherell, M. (ed.) *Discourse Theory and Practice.* London/Milton Keynes: Open University Sage. Chapter 19.

Falicov, C.J. (2000). The Cultural Meaning of Family Triangles. In: McGoldrick, M. (ed.) *Re-Visioning Family Therapy: Race, Culture and Gender in Clinical Practice.* New York: The Guilford Press. pp. 37–49.

Fredman, G. (2004) *Transforming Emotion, Conversations in Counselling and Psychotherapy.* London: Whurr.

Graff, J., Lund-Jacobsen, D. and Wermer, A. (2003). X-Files: The Power of Personal Stories in Private–Professional Consultation. *Human Systems.* 14(1): 17–32.

Gross, V., McNab, S., Altschuler, J., and Ganda, M. (2003). Agency Supervision: A New Module for Systemic Therapy Trainings. *Human Systems,* 14(1): 55–56.

Guba, E.G. and Lincoln, Y.S. (1989). *Fourth Generation Evaluation.* London: Sage Publications.

Hedges, F. and Lang, S. (1993). Mapping Personal and Professional Stories. *Human Systems: The Journal of Systemic Consultation and Management.* 4: 277–299.

hooks, b. (1994). *Teaching to Transgress: Education as the Practice of Freedom*. London: Routledge.

Jones, E. (2003). Working with the "Self" of the Therapist in Consultation. *Human Systems*. 14(1): 7–16.

Kolb, D. (1983). *Experiential Learning: Experience as the Source of Learning and Development*. Englewood Cliffs, NJ: Prentice-Hall.

Krippendorff, K. (1989). On the Ethics of Constructing Communication. In: Dervin, B., Grossberg, L., O'Kefe, B., and Wartella, E. (eds) *Rethinking Communication: Volume 1: Paradigm Issues*. Newbury Park, California: Sage. pp. 66–96.

Hedges, F. and Lang, S. (1993). Mapping Personal and Professional Stories. *Human Systems: The Journal of Systemic Consultation and Management*, 4: 277–299.

Lang, P. (2008). Personal communication.

Lang, P., Little, M., and Cronen, V. (1990). The Systemic Professional. Domains of Action and the Question of Neutrality. *Human Systems: The Journal of Systemic Consultation and Management*. 1: 32–47.

Lang, P. and McAdam, E. (1996a). *Referrals, Referrers and the System of Concern*. Pre-Publication manuscript.

Lang, P. and McAdam, E. (1996b). *The First Meeting*. Pre-publication manuscript.

Lang, P. and McAdam, E. (1996c). *Beyond Risk and Above Suspicion*. Pre-publication manuscript.

Larner, G. (2005). The Ethical Play of Irreverence in Deconstruction and Family Therapy. *Human Systems: The Journal of Systemic Consultation and Management*. 16: 31–44.

Layard Report. (2004). *Mental Health: Britain's Biggest Social Problem*. EMPHO2004.

McAdam, E. and Lang, P. (2008). *Appreciative Work in Schools*. Chichester: Kingsham Press.

McCarthy, I.C. and Bryne N.O'R. (1988). Mis-Taken Love: Conversations on the Problem of Incest in an Irish Context. *Family Process*. 27: 181–199.

McCarthy, I. (2002). *Diamonds are a Therapist's Best Friend: Bringing Hope to Child Protection*. Marlborough Day Hospital, London: One-Day.

McNamee, S. (2000). The Social Poetics of Relationally Engaged Research: Research as Conversation. Draft for: Deissler, K. and McNamee, S. (eds) *Philosophy in Therapy: The Social Poetics of Therapeutic Conversation*. Heidelberg, Germany: Carl-Auer-Systeme Verlag.

McNamee, S. (2003). Who is the Therapist? A Social Constructionist Exploration of the Therapeutic Relationship. *The Psychotherapy Section Newsletter*. 34.

McNamee, S. and Gergen, K.J. (1999). *Relational Responsibility, Resources for Sustainable Dialogue.* Sage.

Mendez, C.L., Coudou, F. and Maturana, H.R. (1988). The Bringing Forth of Pathology. *The Irish Journal of Psychology.* 9(1): 144–172.

Nichterlein, M. (2005). Systemic Fluidity: Therapeutic Knowledge and the Importance of Irreverence in Systemic Practice. *Human Systems: The Journal of Systemic Consultation and Management.* 16: 65–74.

Nieboer, R., Moss, D. and Partridge, K. (2000). A Great Servant but a Poor Master: A Critique of the Rhetoric of Evidence Based Practice. *Clinical Psychology Forum.* 136: 17–19.

Oliver, C. (1996). Systemic Eloquence. *Human Systems,* 7(4): 247–264.

Partridge, K. (2005). A Systemic Tale of Assessment and Formulation. *Clinical Psychology.* 46: 13–18.

Partridge, K. (2007). The Positioning Compass: A Tool to Facilitate Reflexive Positioning. *Human Systems: The Journal of Systemic Consultation & Management.* 18: 96–111.

Pearce, W.B. (1991). On Comparing Theories: Treating Theories as Commensurate or Incommensurate. *Communication Theory.* 1: 159–165.

Pearce, W.B. and Cronen, V. (1980). *Communication, Action and Meaning: The Creation of Social Realities.* New York: Praeger.

Penman, R. (1996). The Researcher in Communication: The Primary Research Position. In Owen, J. (ed.) *Context and Communication.* Reno, Nevada: Context Press.

Proctor, K. (1997). The Bells that Ring: A Process for Group Supervision. *ANZJT Family Therapy.* 18(4): 217–220.

Reason, P. and Bradbury, H. (1994). *Handbook of Action Research: Participative Inquiry and Practice.* London: Sage Publications.

Roberts, J. (2005). Transparency and Self-disclosure in Family Therapy: Dangers and Possibilities. *Family Process.* 44: 45–63.

Ricoeur, P. (2003). *The Rule of Metaphor: The Creation of Meaning in Language.* London: Routledge.

Schön, D. (1987). *Educating the Reflective Practitioner.* San Francisco: Josey Bass Publishers.

Schön, D.A. (1973). *Beyond the Stable State: Public and Private Learning in a Changing Society.* Harmondsworth: Penguin.

Shotter, J. (1993). *Cultural Politics of Everyday Life: Social Constructionism, Rhetoric, and Knowing of the Third Kind.* Milton Keynes: Open University Press.

Stratton, P. (2005). A Model to Co-ordinate Understanding of Active Autonomous Learning. *Journal of Family Therapy.* 27: 217–236.

Stratton, P. (2005). *Report On The Evidence Base Of Systemic Family Therapy.* Association for Family Therapy.

Wenger, E.C. and Snyder, W.M. (2000). Communities of Practice: The Organizational Frontier. *Harvard Business Review.* 78(1): 139–45.
Whitehead, J. and McNiff, J. (2006). *All You Need to Know About Action Research.* London: Sage.
Wittgenstein, L. (1953). *Philosophical Investigations.* Oxford: Blackwell.
Wittgenstein, L. (1965). *Philosophical Investigations.* New York: The Macmillan Company.
Winnicott, D.W. (2005). *Playing and Reality* (second rev. edn). Routledge Classics.

CHAPTER SIXTEEN

Competition, cosiness, collaboration? Peer relationships in family therapy teams

Jeanne Ziminski

Introduction

As family therapists we have the reputation among other professionals as the people who use "team and screen" and this approach to therapy has become part of our professional identity. In the process of my supervision training I learnt much about the live supervision contexts of training teams, but comparatively little about managing peer working arrangements as a member of a Child and Adolescent Mental Health Service (CAMHS) family therapy clinic, seeing families alongside other qualified systemic therapists. What I did encounter were a number of conversations with colleagues in the space between those "training conversations" where we would talk of the stresses and joys in our day-to-day relationships with our work-based family therapy teams. In what follows I want to review the place of the team in systemic therapy, to explore peer team relationships further through consideration of a small research project, and to discuss the implications for team practice.

I began working in family therapy teams before I qualified and learned that they already had an established format, a culture which, as a junior member, I joined rather than questioned. As a trainee I was "brought up" in the culture of the team, introduced to it within the pressured context of the training programme, and inducted into a process that involved complex professional and personal dynamics in a group to whom I looked for support as well as to provide an intervention to the family. Therefore, post-training, working in the "family therapy team/clinic" became an assumed part of my identity as a qualified family therapist, with a familiar pattern of "thinking family" rather than "thinking team".

When I came to read the available literature, it was clear that even to name what most therapists do week in week out when meeting together with families seemed rather confusing. Is it co-working, live peer supervision, live consultation? How equal is the relationship implied by "peer"? Live supervision is a highly valued part of working as a systemic therapist but seems often used as shorthand without clarifying the relationships operating within the team or the impact of these inter-relationships on the work with families.

A starting point is to remind ourselves why we work in family therapy teams. Overtly, the aim is to enhance therapeutic interventions with families and provide effective therapy. How much is the need for professional collegial support, finding a systemic haven of like-minded individuals, also a driver to working in this way? And do the teams we work in provide any of that? Or, alternatively, does practice involve a tense, uncomfortable afternoon of unspoken disagreements where family therapy happens despite group dynamics behind the screen? Clearly it is important to strive to make teams work as well as possible if we are to provide an effective service to the families we see.

Given the complexity of group process in therapy teams (for a recent discussion of this see Clarke and Rowan 2009; Burck, this volume; Granville, this volume), it is useful to consider how far team members see the need to become "meta" to their own process and, if so, what methods they use to do this.

I was therefore interested in pursuing further with team members themselves their experiences as part of a peer live consultation team. One way would have been for me to talk more about my own experiences but I wished to preserve the confidentiality of colleagues in my on-going team relationships. Using a small research project provided me with an alternative.

The development of peer consultation teams

Peer supervision and consultation, within a non–hierarchical, non-evaluative egalitarian relationship, is a well established form of reflective practice in the helping professions. However, systemic psychotherapy's tradition of peers working together within "live supervision" teams takes this collaborative relationship a stage further.

The use of live supervision teams in systemic psychotherapy appears to have two main traditions—the team as training context and the team as a therapeutic intervention. Both Montalvo (1973) and Minuchin and Fishman (1981) in particular promoted the training context of a team and screen, although all family therapy models appear to now use it as a basic training tool. In addition, the strategic school used it also as a tool for research and for designing tasks and offering intervention (Hoffman, 2002). These therapists, when working in the first order cybernetic paradigm of the 1970s, used the expert power of the invisible team to move the dynamics of what were seen as difficult, resistant families. "[The team] remains at a distance, an invisible eye, an anonymous voice, lending the impact of objectivity" (Minuchin and Fishman, 1981: 249). Besides the hierarchy in relation to the family, the power of the supervisor or teacher in relation to other team members was also generally taken for granted.

By contrast, the Milan group established a team process that aimed explicitly to be non-hierarchical, which as time went on moved away from its early paradoxical and ritual interventions and towards a second order cybernetic theory that incorporated the therapist position in their thinking. Boscolo et al. (1987) pointed out the downside of such teams as being, at times, self-absorbed and cliquish, exhibiting a missionary zeal that antagonized the host organization, and prone to splits. He saw dyads rather than larger groupings as a more stable team for on-going therapy.

Of particular importance to this paper in relation to non-supervisor led teams, and one which is still cited (for example, Vetere and Cooper, 2003), are Smith and Kingston's (1980) and Kingston and Smith's (1983) writings on live peer consultation (renamed from supervision). They described the therapy team as consisting of "professional peers", "in which the second person has some authority of expertise but no power to implement it without the invitation and permission of the therapist" (Smith and Kingston, 1983: 220). Their main emphasis was on in-the-room-working as a therapist plus consultant: they clearly distinguished live peer consultation from co-therapy because of the alternate and separate roles each person undertakes rather than each engaging directly with the family, and also from live supervision where there was an evaluative and accountability element to the relationship. They pointed out that in-the-room-working worked better with two experienced workers, with a prerequisite of personal and professional respect and a commitment to working at any difficulties that arose, in order to avoid "a situation of pseudo-unity and pretended congruence" (1983: 231).

In 1991 Selvini and Selvini-Palazzoli revisited the concept of the "team peer consultation" method (p. 33) of the Milan team, concerned that the bureaucratization of therapeutic services produced forced rather than spontaneous working relationships. Instead they promoted the rather idealistic concept of a team working in an independent research centre free from hierarchy. They reiterated the use of the team as offering binocular vision, as well as an ability to manage the family and therapist's emotional intensity and provide a "collective mind" (p. 35) in the service of the family, so increasing therapeutic efficacy. Selvini and Selvini-Palazzoli (1991: 43–46) set out criteria for increased collaboration in order to avoid the pitfalls of "competitive dysfunction", rigid hierarchies, or "make believe consultations": equality and a proper division of responsibilities, a safeguarding of psychological space so all members are valued, a defence of independent opinions and personal subjectivity, and the ownership of common objectives.

Throughout the 1990s the literature about team work was dominated by Andersen's papers on the reflecting team, and its enthusiastic take up (Andersen, 1990; Friedman, 1995). This fitted with the move in the field to second order, collaborative working, with the de-centering of the therapist and team as expert and an interest in social constructionist and linguistic rather than cybernetic processes (for example, Anderson and Goolishian, 1988; Hoffman, 1993; White, 1995). Andersen (1990, 1995) described this kind of team working as a joint conversation rather than an intervention, building on Anderson and Goolishian's (1988: 372) formulation of "the problem-organising, problem-dissolving system", rather than the team being separate from the family. He emphasized equalization between consultant and client, with friendly discussion replacing professional detachment. This therapeutic stance implied a similar equalization between team members—avoiding competitive hypothesis-making by multiple ideas being presented directly to the family via a reflecting team. As further innovations in the use of reflecting processes have continued, Shotter and Katz (2007: 32) speak about the meeting of team and the family as a place for "responsive reflective talk", where "transitional understandings" and "action guiding anticipations' inform the conversation".

A very different perspective on teams comes from the field of group dynamics and group relations. For Obholzer and Roberts, questions about authority, power, and leadership in a work group are fundamental to the ability of the group to carry out its tasks, while Roberts states that the question, "What is the primary task of the group?" is one which all groups need to clarify (Obholzer and Roberts, 1994: 38). Hawkins and Shohet (2000) point out that issues in group dynamics can become a preoccupation to the exclusion of the clients' interests, with the danger of a peer group falling into various "games" of scapegoating, competition, and collusive overvaluation of the group's abilities. Proctor and Inskipp's (2001) useful overview of group processes in non-live peer supervision groups compares supervisor-led and peer groups: they highlight the advantages and disadvantages of each, suggesting that higher level skills are needed for peer groups to run successfully, including negotiation about professional expectations and a working agreement. They indicate that peer groups can run the danger of becoming oppressive to less assertive group members, but also offer the possibility of serendipitous, improvisatory activity.

White (1995) pays particular attention to the potential power of the reflecting team to be expert and truth defining, and offers ways to create multiple views and definitions. White's comments are a useful corrective to a dominant assumption in the literature that in family therapy teams, particularly reflecting teams, there can be a dialogue about difference and collaboration without a consideration of power. Power issues are thought about much more in relation to the supervisor's position (for example, Fine and Turner's, [1997: 239] very useful exploration, exhorting supervisors to "mind the power") or in relation to the overt inequalities of the teacher/trainee positions.

Here the dilemmas between collaborative developments in systemic therapy and the needs of training and how to manage the necessary hierarchies involved in evaluating new therapists while maintaining a commitment to reducing power differentials between family, therapist, and team are more debated (see Biever and Gardner, 1995; Selicoff, 2006; Fine, 2003). In contrast, there is a tendency in peer live consultation groups to see equality and collaboration as the dominant story, with the implication that between experienced therapists, differences in the team—for example, with regards to race, culture, age, gender, or sexuality—can be negotiated and thought about without domination or oppression.

Halliwell (1996) interviewed team members about the meaning and experience of working in teams, drawing out themes related to attachment, use of differences and the importance of a shared belief system in the team about change and team practice. She suggests that where differences of professional hierarchy "have been eliminated" (p. 16) more personal differences around age, gender, and culture needed to be acknowledged in order to create a necessary level of difference to be creative. In her view, teams came together to manage the containment of anxiety, but—"as anxiety diminishes and containment increases, the ability to be aware of and use differences also diminishes" (p. 40). The dilemma for teams was therefore that difference was needed for creativity but the dynamics of the team pushed members towards conformity.

Experiences in peer consultation teams

I interviewed four systemic psychotherapists of different levels of professional position and experience (eight months to eight years) using a semi-structured interview format, and then analysed the interviews. The respondents in my interviews were mature individuals, three women and one man, all white British or European, and working in a multi-disciplinary child-focused setting, either in Social Services or CAMHS. I have named them Jo (49), Anna (47), John (58), and Cheryl (57). I saw these conversations as introducing the following themes: team structures; professional equalities and inequalities; the personal in the professional relationships; spaces for team reflection; and the impact on families in therapy.

Team structures and models

A number of the interviewees described what they do by virtue of the label given to their work within the agency, that is, "the family therapy clinic", which could involve live supervision, team and screen or dyadic in-room working, and often a reflecting team. It seemed an "internalized understanding" (Jo) of what family therapy involved, assumed rather than discussed. Where for Jo the phrase encompassed the use of a screen and team, and signified a greater intensity, depth, and complexity of therapeutic work, for John working in the room was preferred for its transparency and closer connection to the family.

Several of the interviewees used the words "formal" and "informal" in their descriptions of their work, referring to a perceived dominant discourse defining systemic therapy to which they more or less adhered depending on the context. The meaning of "formal" seemed to centre on a declared difference in role between therapist and co-worker, a commitment to pre- and post-session discussion and a break for reflection, either behind the screen or in front of the family, elements missing from the "informal" ways of working. However, beyond this, no-one named their practice as being a rigorous application of a particular model. Use of the reflecting team seemed the nearest, for example Anna felt a colleague saw it as "the most important distinguishing feature of family therapy".

What the interviewees reported was that in some teams there was very little reflection on the structures and models within which they were working. Jo therefore welcomed the differences in models between her and a co-worker as generative: "It means there is a rub, you know, and sometimes it's a very good rub, it's a very healthy rub about difference."

Overall it seems interviewees were positioning themselves as working systemically within the culture of their particular team, as well as drawing on an assumption of shared professional scripts coming from an accepted systemic paradigm, without much reflection or clarification of those assumptions.

Professional equalities and inequalities in peer relationships

At different times interviewees appeared to use the word "peer" in different ways—either meaning equality of experience or equality in professional status. There seemed to be a difference between those members where working as a peer was self-defined by the group despite external differences in status and hierarchy and where this was defined by the host agency. John explicitly contrasted his understanding of his peer working relationship with a colleague as separate from the formal hierarchies of the host agency: "it's a consultation rather than a hierarchical coming together".

Two participants in particular talked about the complications of working as peers in a family therapy team when one team member has seniority as a line manager in the host agency. Anna voiced her experience as a non-manager observing the positioning of two other team members, where she felt the inequality between them was not recognized or owned. She felt powerless to intervene and commented that she felt the senior person's attitude of certainty led to a closing down of the possibility of talking about the issue.

> "Sometimes I *had* experienced and felt very uncomfortable and not knowing how to kind of how to open my mouth about what I had seen, but sometimes [manager] could be very dismissive and derogatory to tiny statements that [another colleague] would make."

Cheryl was very aware of her power as a senior manager and her attempts to minimize the effects of this by taking what she felt was a one down position. Even with an experienced group of therapists, where there were complicated external lines of management inequalities, status was an issue.

> "I don't think it was a hierarchy top down sort of you know with the straightforward thing of 'Oh well that person's the boss so I've got to do what they say even if I don't, you know.' There weren't unsaid things like that ... There was very clearly 'you may be the boss but ... you may have more status, but actually this is a valid opinion.'"

All participants made a clear distinction between working with peers with a similar level of experience and situations where there was a large discrepancy. Where both or all team members were at a similar level of experience, two alternative repertories arose—of a competitive or collaborative interaction. Where this was collaborative, as John described it:

> "This is about peers explaining, able to be good in front of each other and able to be not so good in front of each other and able to *help* each other be the best they can on that day."

However, on the other hand, live supervision was also described in terms of "performance" by both Jo and Anna, and where this became competitive could become "who is the better therapist". As Jo explained:

> "If you have confidence and trust that the peer is working *with* you for the best for the families, it's a very different thing than if the peer is scoring points."

Jo also talked of one working relationship which felt unequal to her in terms of her greater experience and knowledge but was defined by her agency as a peer because of both being qualified family therapists. In this latter context, she emphasized that she struggled with what she could or could not say in her feedback about the therapy she was involved in. There seemed an issue about how inequality could be talked about. In another contrasting example Jo gave, involving another similarly less experienced worker, Jo's intervention was named as "helping" rather than teaching or supervising and so was able to be acknowledged and agreed between them.

This brings us to how people talked about the issues of responsibility and authority in these leaderless groups and dyads, with different teams negotiating the issue in different ways. One way was to bring in a repertoire about the "lead clinician". Both Jo and John commented on the idea that the therapist in practice becomes the leader of the group for that session. At the same time, teams seemed to show flexibility between sessions, and also a sharing of practical tasks for the smooth running of the therapy team.

It seemed that where inequality and difference were named and acknowledged they could then be explored, but where unacknowledged status differences existed—in relation to length of experience, or management responsibilities—people felt silenced. This seemed particularly so where a therapist felt him or herself to be relatively inexperienced or junior in some way—being able to name the differences depended on the position the more powerful team member(s) took and how self-aware they were.

The personal in the professional relationship

A number of successful peer relationships were identified by the interviewees, where respect, trust, and a depth of relationship built up over time had led to an ability to share personal and professional dilemmas in a process that benefited the therapeutic work. In talking about these relationships, they responded to potential criticisms of such relationships as "cosy" through a narrative that while emphasizing trust and respect between colleagues, put the family's needs first.

These successful relationships showed a working with difference in a way that looked for meaning beyond personal antagonism to allow the possibility of the relationship being sustained and growing in depth and understanding even at a time of potential conflict:

> "So you're very conscious all of the time that you know its not that I hate X today but that I'm somehow thinking of her within the framework of that family's problem and I've, you know, I've infused her with something that has no right to be there."
>
> (John)

For the three more experienced therapists, trust and respect together with an understanding of isomorphic processes between family and team were identified in a repertoire that described a linkage of personal and professional issues in the therapeutic work. Interestingly the most recently qualified interviewee spoke the least about personal professional development in this way. Through this identification, therapists felt themselves safer to work on therapeutic issues where the emotional intensity of the therapy or the closeness to the therapist's personal life issues made the work feel risky or particularly challenging in some way.

> "We knew each other very well. I would know what sort of case might raise issues for her and she would know what sort of case and we would be able to have a conversation about it."
>
> (Jo)

This process was named as "rescuing" in a couple of interviews; for example, John gives an evocative description of his peer colleague as a rescuer from "personal trapdoors", or from the emotional power of particular family dynamics.

In the dyadic peer relationships this linkage of personal and professional issues in the work seemed to happen informally. Cheryl spoke about times when peers could be "too close" to talk about certain issues. Even in a strong peer relationship there were limits with certain issues not being addressed. Her experience of a number of different therapy teams suggested a need with larger groups for a negotiated space where all group members agreed on the sharing of personal issues, for example through genogram work.

In a few examples, difficult peer relationships became hard to name. Jo talked about the difficulty of addressing a concern about the other person's practice in the context of being their peer. Because there was no explicit permission to critique the other's practice, any comments were in danger of becoming too "personal", in the sense of being seen as unwarranted criticism of their private self as opposed to a supportive critique of their professional self:

> "Because then it becomes more of a relational issue doesn't it? So for example if you went to supervise a student and you felt erm you had some issue with how the student was practising then there would be ways in which it doesn't become a personalized thing."
>
> (Jo)

Therefore in some peer working contexts, the interviewees saw a "personal" relationship with their co-worker as one in which to hold the possibility of conflict without threatening the relationship. However where the relationship was defined as purely professional this was not possible, and moving into the "personal" could even be threatening, if trust and respect were missing from the process.

Ability to talk about difference grew from respect between workers, as well as from the confidence of experience. Silence and not talking could therefore act as a sign that something was not working in the peer relationship. Worst scenarios for both Jo and Anna involved being silenced, with a feeling of no understanding, no connection, no respect, and even resentment at the person's presence, feeling that they were not being helped or supported, to a level where Jo commented, "Actually you think to yourself I'd rather see the family on my own because actually this is not teamworking." Thus in the examples of difficult working peer relationships a closing down of communication both personally and professionally led to the point where the therapeutic partnership could—or did—break down.

Spaces for team reflection

All four interviewees talked about a reflective space in which to consider their own functioning as a team as an important ideal, even if not always accomplished in reality. A frequent comment was that lack of time, and feeling overloaded, militated against sufficient reflection on the peer relationship. Informal "corridor" discussions and letting issues go unsorted were two ways of coping. Besides the possibility of using an external supervisor to open up conversations, Cheryl felt less public dyadic conversations outside of the group—"corridor conversations"—could be helpful in "speaking the unspeakable". On the other hand, John also put forward the position that not everything needed to be spoken about, provided that the therapists ensured that there was no lingering atmosphere from the issue arising between them.

It seemed that length of training and experience were also major factors in how much peer group reflection was possible, while interviewees varied in their stated need for a live supervisor. The consequence of the many opinions being expressed in Cheryl's experienced peer group was that it found itself in constant wrangles:

> "And we got to a point where we formally said, 'Julia's the person with the experience and the supervision experience, she should lead us.'"

However, particularly for teams bigger than dyads, the presence of an external supervisor/consultant to the team's process was seen as a positive step towards achieving a different level of reflection. Both Jo and Anna had this opportunity, with Anna feeling that this process flattened the hierarchy between her and her manager in the team in contrast to the perceived position of the consultant, although both described at times difficult intra-group relationships that still somehow had not been able to be addressed by this process.

The impact on therapy

All four interviewees spoke about the impact of team functioning on the effectiveness of the therapy undertaken. Jo contrasted her experiences as a therapist of positive and negative peer relationships, feeling very exposed in the latter and surmising that the experience was likely to have been a negative one for the family. She felt that the use of self involved in working with one's own vulnerabilities needs a strong positive team relationship in order to enhance therapeutic creativity:

> "It was a *positively* exposing experience … it's one which you learn from and you feel you get something offered to the family from it, but that that latter one for me is more erm one in which I felt I wanted to be less, I wanted to protect myself. So one encourages me to open up and take more risks and the other one just shuts me down in all levels really."

John also gave a long and powerful account of what he named as "bravery in therapy" that came from a strong peer relationship, leading to a confidence to work with risk and uncertainty, in his example in the area of sexual abuse.

Another way this creativity was described was in the "buzz" of a reflecting team, building new ideas in front of the family in a way which felt generative and affirming. Anna talked about "being in the moment", not knowing what would come but being able to trust in the others concerned and what would be produced. John however cautioned about the need to keep the family's response in mind:

> "I'm sure that at times you can get so enthusiastic about the line that's being followed and that you're both building on that actually you're waiting to be able to ask the next question before they've even had a chance of answering and … it becomes you know, one potato two potato with no filling, no family."

In contrast, all four spoke about the deadening effect of habitual patterns of interactions on the team's creativity, as Anna describes:

> "What, what *doesn't* work sometimes is the kind of shorthands that we can fall into. And forgetting to step back and step back and erm commit to fresh choices rather than kind of just go on where the track has been beaten."

Thus a team that was working well, with trust and respect between members, exhibited creativity and flexibility in response to the family's needs, whereas where habit or relationship difficulties were getting in the way there was a level of being stuck and simply closing down, with an inability to use the team to energize and invigorate the therapy with the family.

Discussion

Theoretically at least, peer family therapy teams are the "purest" form of providing "news of difference" through a binocular or polyocular vision without a hierarchical agency or professional context (see Selvini and Selvini-Palazzoli, 1991). In my experience and that of my interviewees this can be a powerful therapeutic tool, allowing families to be presented and challenged with news of difference in a supportive way. It is a process of bringing difference into the family, either through a reflecting team or via a team message, in a way that can be heard and thought about creatively by both therapists and family, so enabling family members to question their assumptions and patterns of interaction.

However, in practice, family therapy teams in the UK are largely working in public agency settings with very clear agency and professional hierarchies. They are expected to fulfil a number of other tasks in addition to providing therapy to families, most often by providing a family therapy clinic as a context for training junior professionals from a variety of disciplines. Even without the presence of trainees, a group of qualified family therapists bring with them relationships from the wider context of the host agency, as well as differences in race, gender, and so on which need to be addressed within the group (see Burnham, 1992; Divac and Heaphy, 2005). It seems to me that peer groups can have difficulty in negotiating ways to address these issues. This is especially so where the team context is one of assumed parity in terms of accountability and status within its members and of experienced inequality in ability or time since qualified. This can lead to a struggle to achieve relationships across these differences without domination. In addition, there is the bind that a worker may experience being defined as peer, for example by their employing authority, or other team members, but not actually experience the relationship themselves as peer. This of course may be particularly complicated for systemic therapists compared to other professionals because their dual qualification can mean that they have high status in one profession and lower status in the other.

The question of why people join live peer consultation teams is an important one. None of the interviewees in this research specifically talked about joining in order to be part of the "systemic club"; the interviewees were all clear that the purpose of the team was to enhance the therapy that they provided to families. At the same time, for membership to work and be successful in that aim, attention to group relationships and team functioning appears essential. Team members need to feel safe in order to take risks—to move to positions of "safe uncertainty" (Mason, 1993: 189)—and to avoid "stuckness". In this the interplay of the personal and professional in relations between team members appears, not surprisingly, as important as that between therapist and family. Strong personal relationships were seen as able to contain conflict in a way that allowed space for reflection and understanding rather than immediate, possibly hostile, reaction. However in general it did not appear that this was due to pre-existing "personal" relationships—rather they grew through a like-minded approach to therapy, similar values, or through the process of working together sometimes over several years.

I think that the meaning people give to the parity or disparity between them also depends on how they interpret the "personal" part of their relationship as they position themselves in conversation. In contrast to Halliwell's (1996) finding that "cosiness" in team relationships led to a lot being left unsaid, I found that the idea of the danger of cosiness could lead to an impetus to explore differences. In this I do agree with Halliwell that the ability to use conflict and difference to create new meanings depended on a shared belief that such issues could be safely explored within team relationships, encouraging creativity through multiple views of the issues that families bring to therapy. On the other hand, for some peer consultation teams, the danger was less from cosiness or uncontained conflict around difference and more from stultification through habit and unthinking patterns of behaviour. Reimers (2006) points out the process by which therapists can fall into narrowed styles of working through reliance on default positions based on habitual responses, responses to stress, and quests for novelty—and the same can be said of team functioning too.

As I look back over my career I can think of periods in my working life where this has happened, where relationships have become too cosy or unquestioning. A shift then occurred, often prompted by a change in the context—for example, a change of personnel, a challenge from a family to do it differently—that led to renewed self-reflection and subsequent regeneration. In my current working context in a live peer consultation team this research has given me the opportunity to review with my fellow therapists the history of the family therapy clinic team in which we work, our changing roles and expectations of each other, and to achieve a recognition that we had fallen into certain unreflective habits and ways of working.

There are additional complications in peer relationships where there is confusion or different assumptions about the basis on which a particular team is operating—do they see themselves as an interventive group sending messages to the therapist across the screen, or as conversational partners that communicate with therapist and family together through the reflecting team? How far have they talked through their expectations and aims of the therapy so that their approach, method, and techniques are coherent (Burnham, 1992)? From the interviewees' accounts, teams found a way of organizing themselves on a practical level so that the tasks of running a family therapy clinic were undertaken and families were actually invited and arrived. In terms of managing the therapeutic process teams seemed to be electing leaders either short-term for the duration of a session (often it seems the person in the therapist position) or more longer term by democratic vote or assumption of the "most experienced" or "most available" therapist.

I think that some of these issues are more difficult to manage informally for teams of more than two than for dyads, and it did seem that more structure appeared in the larger groups than in the dyadic relationships. For bigger groups there appeared a greater struggle around respect and trust with more ambiguity around distance and closeness between members. Halliwell felt that factors such as team size, too much diversity of experience and training, place a toll on "teamness" (1996: 54). In this research, it is interesting that both the closest and most acrimonious relationships were described by interviewees in dyads rather than larger teams. The crucial question in my view for live peer consultation teams is how far these differences are open to discussion: what are the team contexts where people feel able to speak and where they feel silenced? The participants' understanding of the meaning of these team contexts is central to how live peer consultation teams function. They are influenced by the meaning of interactions, power, and experience at professional and agency levels, by agency culture and beliefs about systemic therapy, as well as by the way people position themselves in relation to being part of the group.

Theoretically if one sees the team/observer as meta to the therapist–family dynamic, and a consultant/supervisor as meta to team–therapist dynamic, then live peer consultation teams can lose a level of observing difference. This absence can be brought back by use of sufficient reflective space either together as a peer group or with the help of an external consultant. In my own team context, we reviewed our working with the help of an external consultant (a colleague from another family therapy team in our organization)—which allowed us another level of self-reflexivity where different conversations about, for example, the way we use the reflecting team, and our differing positions on in-session interventions, were able to be voiced. The challenge for our team, in a context where there are differing and shifting hierarchies and seniorities, is, as I think it is for many others, to push ourselves to create this space so that the lure of cosy non-reflexivity is resisted and the "rub" of collaborative working maintained.

In a group as opposed to a dyad, there may be a greater need for this process of a consultant as facilitator, or it may be that more "informal" conversations about group process happen between individuals outside of the group. For peer group members to be reflexive in relation to self and team process, to use relational reflexivity (Burnham, 1993) in the absence of a live supervisor, requires, it seems to me, a certain level of training and experience in the group so that the importance of continuing personal and professional development and an understanding of isomorphic processes between team, therapy, and family is recognized.

In addition all the teams discussed in the research were CAMHS teams and it is interesting to consider, building on the ideas of isomorphism in therapy and supervision (Liddle and Saba, 1983), that the issues around authority and executive function which are often to be found in families with young children may also be a preoccupation of CAMHS teams in a way which is different from those working with adults only. This would be an interesting area to explore for adult teams in a future research project.

Implications for practice

I think the systemic field is ready for a new acronym which links PPD (personal and professional development), which has its more clearly defined role in the training context, and CPD (continuing professional development), which is part of the language of the helping organizations—that of team CPPD (continuing personal and professional development), a commitment to paying attention to the boundary between the personal and professional within the family therapy team. This is a position that acknowledges the bi-directional processes of isomorphism between team and family, and that models an openness to questioning team assumptions that is reflected in the therapeutic work with families who are being asked to question their own beliefs and assumptions.

Proctor (1997: 217) offers a format for a reflective space for peers, with a facilitator of the session (this could be an outside supervisor or a member of the group selected for the exercise), a presenter, a consultant (who helps the presenter explore and clarify issues), and observers who provide feedback, including comments on personal and professional "bells that ring". The exercise offers a way for workers to link the personal and professional in a non-confrontational and non-competitive context.

In order to help peer live consultation teams in this endeavour, I suggest the following guidelines can be useful:

- set up a working contract, giving permission as to what can be talked about—and review it!
- provide time and space to reflect on and review process

- recognize that to work creatively and to take risks involves an evolving process of trust and feeling of safety within the team
- aim for this atmosphere of trust and respect between team members through explicit ground rules of communication, time-keeping and so on
- aim for a collaborative rather than competitive ethos, for example, through the use of Proctor's (1997) model for reflection
- try to ensure sufficient knowledge and experience within the team to reflect on its own processes, particularly isomorphic processes between team and family
- provide periodic input from an external supervisor to review group process

In considering the above guidelines, teams may find the following questions useful. They can provide a starting point for self-reflection particularly for teams who have been working together for a long time in taken-for-granted ways.

What is the aim of working together like this?

Is "peer" defined externally by agency context or by the group? Do all members agree with the "peer" description?

How does the team pay attention to the similarities and differences between members?

How does the team talk about the inequalities that exist between members?

What model is the team following?

What orthodoxies have been established in the team culture?

What techniques/approaches (for example, reflecting team) is the team most wedded to? What do members fail to hear/pay attention to as a result?

If the team were to undertake something it does not usually do, what might that be?

And last but very much not least, what is the effect of the way the team is currently working on the families it is working with and vice versa?

In the CAMHS context at least, professionals are encouraged by government strategy and agency resource constraints to work more flexibly, outside of the clinic context, using "comprehensive" CAMHS, working in different settings such as schools, Behaviour Support Services, and Looked After Children teams. The orthodoxies of outpatient CAMHS teams and of family therapy clinic structures are being questioned. Family therapists need to be clear, both in their own thinking and in conversation/negotiation with their professional colleagues, as to the justification for using the "team and screen" (the current linguistic shorthand) to show the "added value" of the team setting in providing effective, evidence-based family therapy. If in our live peer consultation teams we prioritize family functioning to the neglect of team functioning we are ultimately doing families a disservice.

References

Andersen, T. (ed.) (1990). *The Reflecting Team: Dialogues and Dialogues About the Dialogues.* Broadstairs, Kent: Bergman Publishing.

Andersen, T. (1995). Reflecting Processes: Acts of Informing and Forming. In: Friedman S. (ed.) *The Reflecting Team in Action.* London: Guilford Press. Chapter 1.

Anderson, H. and Goolishian, H. (1988). Human Systems as Linguistic Systems: Preliminary and Evolving Ideas about the Implications for Clinical Theory. *Family Process.* 27(4): 371–395.

Biever, J.L. and Gardner, G.T. (1995). The Use of Reflecting Teams in Social Constructionist Training. *Journal of Systemic Family Therapies.* 14(3): 47–56.

Boscolo, L., Cecchin, G., Hoffman, L., and Penn, P. (1987). *Milan Systemic Family Therapy.* New York: Basic Books.

Burnham, J. (1992). Approach-Method-technique: Making Distinctions and Creating Connections. *Human Systems: The Journal of Systemic Consultation and Management.* 3: 3–26.

Burnham, J. (1993). Systemic Supervision: The Evolution of Reflexivity in the Context of the Supervisory Relationship. *Human Systems: The Journal of Systemic Consultation and Management.* 4: 349–381.

Clarke, G. and Rowan, A. (2009). Looking Again at the Team Dimension in Systemic Psychotherapy: Is Attending to Group Process a Critical Context for Practice? *Journal of Family Therapy.* 31(1): 85–107.

Divac, A. and Heaphy, G. (2005). Space for GRAACCES: Training for Cultural Competence in Supervision. *Journal of Family Therapy.* 27(3): 280–284.

Fine, M. (2003). Reflections on the Intersection of Power and Competition in Reflecting Teams as Applied to Academic Settings. *Journal of Marital and Family Therapy.* 29(3): 339–351.

Fine, M. and Turner, J. (1997). Collaborative Supervision: Minding the Power. In: Todd T.C. and Storm C.L. (eds) *The Complete Systemic Supervisor: Context, Philosophy and Pragmatics*. New York: Authors Choice Press. Chapter 16.

Friedman, S. (1995). *The Reflecting Team in Action*. London: Guilford Press.

Halliwell, C. (1996). *Towards an Epistemology of Teams: An Exploration of the Meaning and Experience of Working in Teams*. Unpublished thesis. London: Tavistock Centre.

Hawkins, P. and Shohet, R. (2000). *Supervision in the Helping Professions: An Individual, Group and Organizational Approach*. Milton Keynes: Open University Press.

Hoffman, L. (1993). *Exchanging Voices*. London: Karnac Books.

Hoffman, L. (2002). *Family Therapy: An Intimate History* London: Norton.

Kingston, P. and Smith, D. (1983). Preparation for Live Consultation and Live supervision When Working Without a One-way Screen. *Journal of Family Therapy*. 5: 219–233.

Liddle, H.A. and Saba, G.W. (1983). On Context Replication: The Isomorphic Relationship of Training and Therapy. *Journal of Strategic and Systemic Therapies*. 2(1): 3–11.

Mason, B. (1993). Towards Positions of Safe Uncertainty. *Human Systems: The Journal of Systemic Consultation and Management*. 4: 189–200.

Minuchin, S. and Fishman, H.C. (1981). *Family Therapy Techniques*. London: Harvard University Press.

Montalvo, B. (1973). Aspects of Live Supervision. *Family Process*. 12(4): 343–359.

Obholzer, A. and Roberts, V.Z. (eds) (1994). *The Unconscious at Work*. London: Routledge.

Proctor, B. and Inskipp, F. (2001). Group Supervision. In: Scaife, J. (ed.) *Supervision in the Mental Health Professions: A Practitioner's Guide*. Hove: Brunner-Routledge. Chapter 6.

Proctor, K. (1997). The Bells that Ring: A Process for Group Supervision. *Australia and New Zealand Journal of Family Therapy*. 18(4): 217–220.

Reimers, S. (2006). Family Therapy by Default: Developing Useful Fallback Positions for Therapists. *Journal of Family Therapy*. 28(3): 229–245.

Roberts V.Z. (1994). The Organization of Work: Contributions from Open Systems Theory. In: Obholzer, A. and Roberts, V.Z. (eds) *The Unconscious at Work*. London: Routledge. Chapter 3.

Selicoff, H. (2006). Looking for Good Supervision: A Fit between Collaborative and Hierarchical Methods *Journal of Systemic Therapies*. 25(1): 37–51.

Selvini, M. and Selvini-Palazzoli, M. (1991). Team Consultation: An Indispensable Tool for the Progress of Knowledge. Ways of Fostering and Promoting its Creative Potential. *Journal of Family Therapy*. 13(1): 31–52.

Shotter, J. and Katz, A. (2007). "Reflecting talk", "inner talk" and "outer talk": Tom Andersen's way of being. In: Anderson, H. and Jensen, P. (eds) *Innovations in the Reflecting Process*. London: Karnac Books. Chapter 2.

Smith, D. and Kingston, P. (1980). Live Supervision Without a One-way Screen. *Journal of Family Therapy*. 2: 379–387.

Vetere, A. and Cooper, J. (2003). Setting up a Domestic Violence Service. *Child and Adolescent Mental Health*. 8(2): 61–67.

White, M. (1995). *Re-Authoring Lives: Interviews and Essays*. Adelaide: Dulwich Centre Publications.

CHAPTER SEVENTEEN

Supervising across a theoretical divide: Systemic ideas in action

Gwyn Daniel, Maria Eyres, Sarah Majid and Andrew Williams

Introduction

In this chapter we explore some questions arising at the interface between systemic and psychoanalytic theories and practices in the context of a live-supervised systemic training group. This group, based at the Tavistock Clinic, ran for a year and consisted of weekly four-hour live supervision sessions for four specialist psychiatric registrars studying psychoanalytic psychotherapy. The Royal College of Psychiatrists' requirement, as part of this training, is for one hundred hours of practice in systemic psychotherapy. We chose to interpret the one hundred hours as the time that the trainee is actively engaged in clinical activity, either as therapist or as member of the observing or reflecting team. The remainder of the time is taken up with theoretical discussions, case reviews, clinical skills work, and personal development. The group consisted of two men and two women, whose cultural backgrounds were Indian, Polish, Welsh, and English, with a Welsh female supervisor. The supervisory contract was similar in some ways to that of a training one, with the exception that group members had not necessarily chosen to undertake this part of their training. They were also "accelerated" into a live supervisory context when most had very little experience of interviewing families and, with one exception, had not followed an introductory course in systemic theory. Added to this, the group was heavily committed in other areas; as well as their regular clinical practice, they were training in psychoanalysis, their preferred modality. From the perspectives of supervisor and three of the group members, we will discuss the opportunities within this context to make the year's experience valuable and durable, explore some tensions between systemic and psychoanalytic approaches in relation to therapy, supervision, and personal development; and describe aspects of the group's ethos and relationships that were helpful in sustaining a vibrant context for learning.

"Historically," writes Paolo Bertrando, "systemic therapy derives from psychoanalysis through differentiation but has maintained a relationship fraught with opposition throughout the years" (2002: 366). David Pocock (2006) argues that systemic therapy needed to maintain this opposition in its early years in order to develop its own identity but that it should now be mature and confident enough to engage in a richer and more positive relationship. However, what this "developmental" perspective omits is the extent to which psychoanalysis and systemic psychotherapy may indeed represent different paradigms in relation to modernism and to the political and ethical dimensions of therapy and therapeutic "expertise" in general. It is therefore important to acknowledge the ways that both history and on-going philosophical differences might exert an influence on our training relationship, especially within an institution dedicated to psychoanalysis. For a systemic supervisor, albeit with age, experience, and status within the systemic field, the group, albeit younger and inevitably less experienced as therapists, could nonetheless come to represent some of the oppositions in this historically and politically loaded paradigm.

Systemic and psychoanalytical theory

While systemic/family therapy emerged from the shadow of psychoanalysis and developed in opposition to many of its main premises, there has always been, within the field, a strand of psychodynamic family therapy (Box, 1979), and many prominent systemic therapists have discussed their continuing connection to and use of psychoanalytic ideas (Boscolo and Bertrando, 1996). In recent years, a number of theoretical contributions from the systemic field have sought to draw out connections between the two approaches (McFadyen, 1997; Pocock, 1997, 2006; Donovan, 2003). The increased emphasis on the self of the therapist (Flaskas, 1997) and the importance of the therapeutic relationship (Flaskas and Perlesz, 1996) have invited systemic practitioners to re-visit psychoanalytic ideas of transference and counter-transference (Bertrando, 2002) and to find new ways of conceptualizing emotional processes in therapy. Other points of connection have emerged in the form of attachment theory (Byng-Hall, 1995), feminism and intersubjectivity (Goldner et al. 1990; Benjamin, 1998), feminism and object relations (Leupnitz, 1997), and postmodernism (Larner, 2000). In the psychoanalytic literature, while approaches taking a relational perspective have emerged (Mitchell and Aron, 1999), they appear less likely to acknowledge the influence of systemic psychotherapy and its theoretical bases. In the pragmatic context of delivering therapeutic services within the public sector, the importance of engaging across disciplines and modalities is widely accepted (Speed, 2004).

Two papers, both written in 2002, illustrate different ways of engaging across this theoretical divide. In the first, a paper entitled "Minding the Gap, not bridging the Gap: family therapy from a psychoanalytic perspective", Brodie and Wright usefully summarize different models of thinking about family relationships as being inside out (states of mind projected outwards onto external relationships), or being outside in (the manner of relationships impinges on how individuals experience themselves and their thoughts and feelings). Exploring the links of systemic psychotherapy to psychoanalysis, they highlight Gianfranco Cecchin's concept of curiosity as being similar to Bion's (1970) notion of approaching the analytic encounter without memory or desire. They also connect the Milan team's ideas about neutrality to Freud's idea of evenly suspended attention. However, rather than engage with what contribution a systemic perspective can make, they describe families by using the same conceptual framework as for individuals, for example, family "characteristic methods of interaction", and families "projecting unwanted feelings onto the therapist", and are critical of a systemic therapist (Carmel Flaskas) in her use of psychoanalytic ideas. This illustrates how constructs of similarity and difference have loaded meanings depending on the standpoint of the discussant. For example, Brodie and Wright elide systemic ideas with pre-existing psychoanalytic ones (implying that there is nothing really new about systemic ideas) but emphasize difference when it comes to Flaskas moving onto psychoanalytic territory. For these reasons this paper seems to be a less helpful means of engagement.

In the second paper "The presence of the third party: systemic therapy and transference analysis", Paolo Bertrando takes the idea of transference and explores the different ways that systemic and psychoanalytic therapists might respond to times when clients/patients communicate about their relationship to the therapist. "Presentifying" the third party in individual systemic therapy is compared with the focus on the therapist/patient relationship in psychoanalysis. In psychoanalysis, external relationships end up being subsumed into the therapy room as the therapist/patient relationship is intensified, whereas in systemic therapy, invitations by the client to speak exclusively about the therapeutic relationship are expanded by the therapist into other relationships which are brought or "presentified" into the therapy room, thus de-centring the therapeutic relationship. While Bertrando makes clear his preference for the latter, he does not imply that one way of working is inherently superior to the other and thus difference can be engaged with more even-handedly.

Given the number of theoretical meeting places possible, one dilemma for a systemic supervisor training a group already immersed in the theory and practice of psychoanalysis is to what extent should she chose literature that introduces the systemic paradigm in all its newness and difference and to what extent should she go for "softening" the transition by selecting papers such as the above? Furthermore, given all the developments in systemic psychotherapy, what "face" of systemic psychotherapy (Boston, this volume) is most helpfully presented? What building blocks of our theory are useful? To what extent are "classic" papers essential? The supervisor was recently reminded of a cultural divide when she recommended a key paper and added, almost apologetically, that it was rather an old paper, being written in 1990. The group members laughed and said that they were more likely to be reading papers from the 1890s! This supervisor's choice was to opt mainly for key systemic papers rather than "bridging" papers for two reasons: first, it seemed important to emphasize difference rather than to too prematurely opt for similarity and, second, the earlier "systemic" papers are more likely to be helpful in learning to do therapy with families, whereas many later papers from narrative and social constructionist perspectives tend to privilege work with individuals (Minuchin et al. 1998). However, individual learning styles and preferences also come into play with some people feeling that they learn more easily by going for connections and others by engaging with difference. One member of the group commented that she thought it was better to choose papers which emphasize difference so that the group members themselves would have to make the connections.

Group processes

We will describe the processes of the group under the following headings, each authored by a different group member: Supervisory Dilemmas, The Demands of Changing Modality, Power and Authority in the Supervisory Process, and Personal/Professional Learning.

Supervisory dilemmas: Gwyn

For me, as supervisor, there were many contexts to address. It was important to think about the compulsory nature of the year's training, about what constraints and opportunities this created and to hold in mind, as described above, the tension between respect for existing theoretical frameworks and the wish to expose group members to the newness and difference of the systemic paradigm. Several factors combined to make this particular training context a useful challenge in terms of my own relationship to systemic ideas and to systemic processes in supervision. The obvious fact that, unlike most systemic supervision groups, I was in a clear minority regarding theoretical orientation had two consequences. First, as supervisor, I was challenged to reflect on my own "taken-for-granted" assumptions about the building blocks of systemic psychotherapy; ideas such as hypothesizing, positive reframing, the asking of questions, and the exploration of context, were vigorously contested and I had constantly to foreground my accountability for interventions and to hold my own ideas as contingent. On a more theoretically based introductory course, these ideas could be teased out and elaborated over time but in the arena of live supervised practice they had to be tested in action. Second, the supervisor's "minority status" had the important effect of mitigating a power imbalance where there can be a built-in tendency for systemic trainees to privilege the supervisor's ideas above their own or each other's. In this context, the dominant language of the group was that of psychoanalysis, a "natural" way of discussing certain emotional processes and a familiar one. In a culturally diverse group where all members were in any case at least bi-lingual, this metaphor had great potential and saliency. It opened up possibilities for reflecting on language as constitutive of realities, on the struggles involved in learning a "new language", and allowed for a more playful process where using only "systemic language" would be encouraged for certain team discussions and exercises and "psychoanalytic language" happily reverted to at every tea break!

While supervisory responsibility for the clinical work and for the functioning of the training group meant that I had to acknowledge my authority, the fact that the group had not chosen to do this training and that, other than completing the course, the Royal College of Psychiatrists had defined very few learning outcomes, created a paradoxical sense of freedom and mutuality. The question of what are realistic goals for training could be visited and revisited over the course of the year with the group's feedback about their expectations for themselves and my expectations of them contributing to the process in a way that, in the formally assessed qualifying level systemic training, can be more constrained. Whilst setting too rigid outcome criteria at the beginning of training might well have restricted the creativity of the group and the diversity of their personal learning goals, it is important to reflect on what realistic expectations a supervisor should have in this context. Such outcomes could range from a very modest one of knowing enough about systemic family therapy to be able to decide when to refer a family or couple for this treatment approach to a more ambitious one of understanding enough of the systemic paradigm to be able to integrate it into one's own therapeutic work. Other, more practical, outcomes could be the ability, to conduct a systemic interview, to understand the effects of the wider system and to take account of the observer/therapist's position and prejudices in the co-creation of meaning. Different group members had different connections to each of these possible outcomes.

However, what became increasingly evident to me was that the most effective way of engaging the group with systemic ideas was through giving them an experience of these ideas in action, not just in the clinical work, but in all aspects of the group's functioning. This included structuring discussion to bring forth ideas which developed and were enriched collectively, being open about my own premises, prejudices, and dilemmas, demonstrating the ability to reflect on or change a position in response to feedback, and addressing group process in ways that were direct and open without being blaming or pathologizing. Above all, an ethos of positive encouragement and optimism, while sometimes clashing with the culture of psychoanalytic training, enabled the group to experience personally the effects of positive connotation. While isomorphism between model of therapy and mode of supervision is generally taken to mean a (uni-directional) transfer of practices from therapy into the domain of supervision, in this context we could equally convincingly argue that learning about therapy is influenced by immersion in the processes of systemic supervision, so that isomorphism is properly experienced as bi-directional. Thus, for example, engaging with multi-realities, positive connotation, or playfulness, have more chance of purchase in therapy if they have first been experienced within the supervisory context.

Tensions inevitably arose between different therapeutic stances; such as taking family members' communication at "face value" versus looking beneath the surface at what might "really be going on"; between optimism and positive connotation and a more "tragic" view of human relationships; and between rigorous hypothesizing before a session and waiting to see what emerges. These tensions can be explored at different levels. One is that of the different theoretical perspectives, another is about the way the therapist's position itself brings forth certain processes which are then used as "evidence" and the third and perhaps most interesting is to explore the way that our own personal and cultural contexts dispose us towards certain theories and types of therapeutic activity. Theoretical frameworks are thus—rather than being challenged or refuted—explored from another standpoint, that of the way we all participate in the social construction of a favoured theory base. Perhaps the most realistic aim for the supervisor should therefore be, rather than trying to "sell" systemic ideas, to utilize them as a way of inviting group members to explore the contexts within which we all come to make choices about our therapeutic training and the ways we conduct therapy.

The demands of changing modality: Andrew

One of the major challenges expressed by the trainee group was that of switching from working from a psychoanalytic perspective to that of a systemic one. Whilst most of the group expressed feelings of being de-skilled upon entering the systemic domain, we did however reflect upon the familiarity of the experience, as doctors who had all negotiated the vicissitudes of medical training, of arriving at a new placement, and feeling oneself to be out of one's depth. I think that having survived the experience of engaging with a steep learning curve and "getting on with it", this was a helpful tool to bring to the systemic training. As the most recent member of the trainee group to join the psychotherapy training programme, I recall experiencing a tremendous sense of pressure in starting to work with a family, after coming straight from a psychoanalytically oriented team meeting to the systemic family therapy workshop. I initially felt disorientated and unsure of my skills, in feeling an expectation to be able to switch into thinking and acting in a very different way. Necessary adaptations which come to mind were of having to work harder during sessions to engage a family, and also being expected to prepare hypotheses about families in advance. A particular challenge that remains in my memory was that of moving swiftly from discussing the finer points of the death instinct in one psychoanalytic meeting to play-acting while wearing a hand-puppet snake in an attempt to engage a five-year-old girl and her mother only moments later!

One particular dilemma which emerged at the beginning of the systemic training was the discrepancy between our levels of confidence in working systemically compared to our more established confidence in working psychoanalytically. At this stage, different members of the group seemed to respond to this issue in very different ways. One of us expressed a wish to focus upon more theoretical reading and discussion, as she felt that this might give her a firmer theoretical basis upon which to start the work. Another expressed a wish to engage in role play in order to explore and practice some techniques that could be employed for working with the families.

A unanimous request was for a period of watching the supervisor work with a family, so that we could learn by observation. Some of these suggestions were taken up, but it was felt that overall there was no substitute for throwing oneself "in at the deep end" and working through doubts, uncertainties, and anxieties as they arose during the course of the clinical work. It was surprising how quickly our initial fears about working in a new modality dissipated, and it felt as if our initial shock at the idea that we would start seeing families ourselves within a few weeks of our initial meeting seemed to quickly turn into a cautious but enthusiastic spirit to learn.

Another struggle was that of negotiating the challenges of live supervision. Supervision as part of psychoanalytic training is carried out in the absence of patients and usually after the clinician has had time to write up and reflect upon the session; thus the experience of live supervision was in stark contrast to this usual experience. One trainee expressed her dislike for using the telephone whilst working with a family, finding it to be distracting and intrusive, and preferred a team member wishing to offer an intervention to knock on the door instead. I also found it very challenging to be interrupted by telephone during a session which required significant work to contain a distressed child. I remember feeling that the live supervision experience could leave one feeling criticized or self-conscious at times, compared to the more gentle experience of psychoanalytic supervision.

Different feelings were expressed within the group after a few months about our enthusiasm or reluctance to engage with the systemic approach. One member of the group expressed his irritation at being requested to prepare hypotheses about his family prior to starting the clinical session. Another stated that, although she had enjoyed some aspects of the experience, the training had reinforced her loyalty to psychoanalytic work. We all expressed our frustration at one time or another at having to leave our more familiar "psychoanalytic" formulations to one side in order to attempt to engage with a more systemic way of thinking about the families we saw. It was common to hear someone say, "I know that we're not supposed to think about counter-transference here, but ..." During a meeting held in order to review learning objectives and discuss our progress, it was generally agreed that these issues could be reframed and understood within a systemic model and that the two approaches need not be necessarily viewed as mutually exclusive. The experience of being asked to consider our own familial and cultural genograms proved to be one which we found initially to be daunting. We were unfamiliar as a group with disclosing much personal information to each other, and our initial attempts to do this task felt, at best, tentative. However, once we had relaxed into the idea of sharing as much as we felt comfortable with, the group expressed their sense of this as a stimulating and thought-provoking process.

During the final meeting to review our overall progress during the one-year training period, there were divided views amongst the group about whether we felt that we would want to develop our systemic skills further. I felt that I had developed many new skills in a relatively short period of time, such as those used in working with children, techniques to engage a whole family in discussion, and using a creative and collaborative approach to thinking about families. Towards the end of the training period, I felt that although I had learned a great amount, I was concerned about how to maintain the skills that I had acquired, particularly in the knowledge that I would be returning to working predominantly within a psychoanalytic framework for the foreseeable future. However, now that more than a year and a half has passed since the ending of the systemic training period, I have been surprised by the extent to which I have found myself continuing to use many of the insights and techniques that I learned from the systemic training. As a clinician working within a forensic mental health service, I have found that a systemic approach lends itself exceptionally well as a way of understanding violent patients within a family context, and my increased confidence in interviewing families has been invaluable in opening up new ways of engaging, understanding, and working with patients. The overall experience was a challenging but rewarding one, and something which will remain as a significant contribution to my overall training for years to come.

Power and authority in the supervisory process: Sarah

An inevitable challenge in shifting modality was to re-find a personal sense of authority as a clinician in the new context of systemic family therapy.

Coming from psychiatry, I had, in psychoanalytic psychotherapy training, to unlearn all kinds of "doctor" skills such as taking charge of meetings, investigating diagnoses, giving advice or feedback, making recommendations, offering hope, and enjoying the freedom to relate flexibly to the patient in a human and sometimes friendly way. Starting psychoanalytic work, I felt deskilled, trying to tolerate uncertainty and despair rather than come up with explanations or solutions, and struggling in sessions not to ask questions, give reassurance, or offer feedback – concretely known as keeping my mouth shut!

By contrast, in systemic work I was expected to be more active in the room—addressing a specific problem within a limited time frame. This involved taking responsibility for time management, ensuring the input of different family members, generating and testing hypotheses, making recommendations, and setting homework with feedback and follow-up. My struggle to assert a more active authority in the room was compounded by my unfamiliarity with systemic theory and practice and anxieties about my competence as a therapist in this new modality. The explicit context of live supervision and working as part of a reflecting team who would call in with suggestions, and whom I would consult during the meeting exposed me as very much a "trainee" in front of the family. And this, alongside "explaining my thinking", effectively deconstructed any transference or counter-transference as a therapist "who knows" which may have bolstered my confidence!

I felt this struggle for authority most strongly with my first family where the father was a tall, Caucasian, and successful consultant surgeon—stirring up all my inferiorities as small, female, ethnic trainee. He comfortably took charge of the interview, relating to me as a junior colleague discussing his emotionally vulnerable wife—undermining both her and my relationship with her before we had even begun. I thus felt even more undermined in role as family therapist. I was acutely aware how my personal struggle to assert authority resonated with the family's complaint about the father's controlling behaviour—particularly towards his wife who seemed to have lost all sense of personal worth and efficacy. I felt a pressure to demonstrate to the mother and children that I could myself stand up to this powerful figure in order to be able to help them move from a stuck bully-victim family dynamic. At the same time it seemed important not to take sides—to recognize the possibilities for agency in the mother and to be able to link empathically with the vulnerability of the father.

Between the authoritative voice of the father and the tearful complaints of the mother, I found myself struggling to assert clinical authority in the very concrete form of having to interrupt in order to speak. In a psychoanalytic setting I might have used my countertransference to make an interpretation about defence and projection of inadequacy, re-finding my voice and stance as therapist at the same time. In this new modality, I found it hard to conceptualize what I observed at the level of meaning within the family system. Not knowing what to say as an intervention compounded my difficulty in speaking at all. I tried to support the emergence of differing family narratives through encouraging the voices of individual members.

In working with this systemically, the live reflecting team supervision from behind the screen was crucial. First, I received concrete feedback; in the meeting I had experienced myself as fairly active—pushing myself to interrupt to a degree that felt unfamiliar and uncomfortable. But the impression from behind the screen was that I was quite dominated and hadn't taken sufficient control of the situation. Second, I received help reframing my experience systemically to comment on the family dynamics. Going back into the room I felt strengthened and supported by my colleagues behind the screen, giving me confidence to take more risks in challenging the family.

In the systemic training context I was encouraged to explore my struggle to speak and assert authority in the room in terms of my own family experience—I recognized a sense of helplessness and a tendency to retreat to silent observer in the face of a dominating voice. I was also reminded of childhood social situations where the dominant language might suddenly switch to a language or topics with which I was less familiar. I realized the sense of how having a different cultural family background also made me feel less entitled to comment on this upper-middle-class English family. However, in a systemic context, this acted as a prompt for active exploration—what is it actually like in this family? Within the supervision group our different personal family experiences could be explored as resources we brought to the work. Our team discussions also provided an opportunity to reflect on the dynamics of speaking within the "family" recreated in the reflecting team. We were encouraged to follow the discipline of reflecting conversation and circular questioning in all our discussions. In this warm and supportive atmosphere I became increasingly talkative and struggled not to interrupt!

From the other side of the one-way screen, I had the opportunity to watch a colleague grapple with his own "impossible-to-interrupt" family. This time a father and son constantly descended into rivalrous bickering while the mother looked on, rarely speaking unless invited by the therapist, and when doing so, being quickly shut down by the revived noisy arguing. Over the weeks I watched my colleague move from being repeatedly sidelined to actively taking charge of the situation, interrupting increasingly freely—and often raising his voice. The result was that it became possible for the family to stop talking and instead think and listen to each other—and new stories from their history had the opportunity to emerge, ones which shed light on the highly charged feelings in the room. It was inspiring to watch my colleague's transformation and I felt strengthened by his example.

I was inspired too by the modelling of our supervisor in her exercise of authority and her evident freedom to act—to pick up the phone, to test out a hypothesis, to decide on an intervention. She would come up with very creative suggestions, sometimes demonstrating a quite startling flexibility of frame—like the team all going in front of the screen, or dividing up, or sending in messages. This freedom and flexibility felt liberating and strikingly different to my experience of psychoanalytic work and supervision—where the free flow of impulse/thought to action is more subject to scrutiny, and the frame more rigidly defined.

Gwyn's assertion of authority as supervisor within the reflecting team inevitably met with our resistance—which mostly seemed to delight her! We varied over how far phone calls into the therapy room felt undermining or supportive of our authority as therapists. I was struck by how enthusiastically she engaged with the challenge of conflicting models, demonstrating her active valuing of the resources we brought as clinicians from another modality. Our lively discussions and disputes resulted in interventions that felt largely collaborative. This felt different to the tone of psychoanalytic supervision where the supervisor feels more "expert".

In this, Gwyn's approach seemed to demonstrate a systemic attitude in which the therapist's (or supervisor's) authority and activity is balanced by a genuine respect for the family's own resources and expertise. It took me awhile to really register the openness and curiosity within which a systemic hypothesis is only a hypothesis, that is, asserted as a question rather than as a solution. This seemed to be both more active but also less authoritative than a psychoanalytic situation—when you might only voice an interpretation when you believed it to be true (although it might take longer to arrive at). I could see how this could free up therapists and patients and make change feel more possible.

Over the months as I watched group members smiling, making jokes, forcefully interrupting, inventing homework, exchanging message cards with a little girl and developing skills in puppetry, I felt exhilarated and increasingly liberated as a clinician. I reconnected with a side of myself that I felt I had lost during psychoanalytic training—a capacity for spontaneity, creativity, and an ability to act. In the systemic work I enjoyed relating to patients more freely and pragmatically, and being allowed to hope and simply try to help things get better.

Psychoanalytic work does of course involve spontaneity, creativity, challenging interventions, flexibility, and a genuine wish to help. However, I was left wondering whether some combination of my personality and psychoanalytic training experience had restricted my sense of authority and freedom as a therapist. In the quiet thoughtfulness of analytic supervision I was attentive to how an expert thinks and works. By contrast, in the lively atmosphere of our systemic supervision I felt more able to be spontaneous, and was actively encouraged to challenge and take risks with patients. This freedom seemed importantly grounded by the presence of the reflecting team—with differing thoughts about the case and ready with honest feedback. This personal shift was a valuable aspect of the systemic training for me. Beyond "learning the model" I had a sense of myself as a clinician with the confidence to explore ideas in practice. Thinking about this experience psychoanalytically, raises further questions for me about the super-ego. Strachey (1933) emphasizes the therapeutic action of psychoanalysis through the analyst making mutative interpretations that modify the patient's superego by interrupting a harsh vicious circle. Functioning as an auxillary superego, the analyst's interpretations help the patient become aware of the distinction between a real benign object and an internal fantasy harsh object. This contributes to the lasting internalization of a more benign internal object through gradual and painstaking working-through over time. As a therapist in training, my superego was projected onto the supervisor and reflecting team (as it was also to the consultant father)—manifest in my initial anxieties about the one-way screen and anticipated criticism and inhibition .Fortunately, the supervisory projection was quickly ameliorated by the reality of active support, guidance, and positive feedback,. The transparency of the process helped me stay in touch with benign "reality" so that I could feel more freed up than in a more neutral analytic space where my projections remained more powerful and inhibiting. This could explain my sense of increased freedom and creativity as a clinician through the year of systemic training, but raised new questions about whether it could last. To what extent could a new "supervisory" object be genuinely internalized? Could there be any speeding up of the long struggle with my superego in personal analysis? The experience has certainly had an impact on my own practice in beginning to supervise junior therapists. And I think that, even if temporary, a lightening of superego restraints freed me up to experience real aspects of myself that I will remember and hope to consolidate in future work and training within any modality, including psychoanalytic work.

Personal/professional learning: Maria

Personal and professional developments are pivotal to any psychotherapy training and systemic training is no exception. The difference is that in this context they both take place in a very public arena and this is a challenging experience for someone coming from a psychoanalytic background.

Psychoanalytic psychotherapy trainees are used to a very rigorous supervision system; however, there is quite a distinction between what belongs to supervision and what belongs to the intimacy of the analytic setting. This means that every now and then we hear from our supervisors that we should take a certain issue to analysis rather then think about it in supervision. So, for example, if one mentions guilt in relation to the patient, one would be advised to take this issue to analysis in addition to thinking about it in the context of the therapy setting. This is not to say that what we bring into the therapy room is not a topic of supervision—one discusses the impact of one's nationality, gender, appearances, and so forth, on the patient—but this is done in relation to the material the patient brings in. We think about what it means for the patient in the context of their history and difficulties.

Yet, in systemic training, the ability to bring and openly discuss the personal is not only an option—it is a requirement. It includes self-reflection and openly thinking with the team about what we bring to the team and to the work.

The first head-on experience with this issue took place on the first day, when, after some preliminary discussion about organizational issues, our supervisor, in her signature optimistic and encouraging way, invited us to think what is it about our own families of origins that we will bring to our work. The initial silence is still ringing in my ears … This was a very complex issue to grapple with at the beginning; we didn't know each other that much and the supervisor was a complete stranger, contracted to run our group from outside of the department. There is a general belief that the majority, if not all of us, are working in mental health for our own, particular, and sometimes painful, reasons, often to do with our early experiences that touched us or those close to us. Some of those are difficult, personal issues, often taking us years to reveal fully in analysis. How are we to talk about them publicly and straight away in this newly formed forum? In analysis there is no pressure apart from one's internal one; things unfold in a gentle and un-rushed way. Here we were pushed beyond what felt comfortable. The dilemma we had was difficult; we wanted to be seen as keen and thoughtful, we wanted to learn, but clearly a balance needed to be struck.

While with time we got to know each other better and this task became easier, it still leaves me slightly uncomfortable. I can see how it can be helpful and can develop as the team gets to know and trust each other more; perhaps there was something about time limitations of our clinic and our background that made it less straightforward and more difficult.

This issue was further complicated by the diversity of our group; although we embarked on the systemic training together, we were at different stages of our core training, had different previous experiences of systemic practice, and one of us came from a somewhat different training. The only thing in common, apart from the fact that we all trained as medics (a very competitive and ambitious professional group to start with) and psychiatrists, was the fact that we all had siblings; no wonder that rivalry, competition, and envy were all at times present in our sessions. It would be an analytic view of naming those phenomena and I am sure that a systemic practitioner would describe them in a kinder, more positive way. This particular example perhaps also captures the differences we had to grapple with; it wasn't just the way that one works with the patients that was a challenge; we had to shift from one paradigm to another in every context; internal as well as external, personal as much as professional, individual as much as group.

Being thrown in at the deep end, starting to see the families almost straightaway, was an experience in itself. Having volunteered to do it first, as—at the time—the most experienced trainee, I spent a considerable amount of time trawling through my notes from the first year at the Institute of Family Therapy, trying to remember things. As it happened, I actually drew more on my own mothering experience, I think, than on any theoretical model and coupled it with a common-sense approach, which, together with my general therapeutic core, helped me survive the first session. But it was stressful ...

Writing our own appraisals was another challenge. In our core training it is mainly the supervisors' task; it is only occasionally that we are given an opportunity to discuss our appraisals before they are passed on to the panel which assesses our progress on a yearly basis. The conclusions of the panel discussion are then fed back to us by our tutors. This time we were confronted with our supervisor's request to write our own appraisals in addition to hers. The task was terrifying to start with; the job of balancing our harsh superegos with what at times felt like the omnipotence or manic defences of systemic practice was a high wire act. This is of course a caricature and an exaggeration intended to highlight the differences of approaches. Looking back, however, there was something very helpful about moving from being a rather passive object of appraisal in our core training to becoming a more active subject in the systemic training, particularly as one progressed through higher training and reached a consultant grade. The ability to look at oneself and to identify the area of strengths alongside the ones that need further development is vital when one becomes a more independent practitioner.

It was also at times hard to convince our supervisor that we really could not find enough enthusiasm or even conviction within ourselves to use the high art of positive reframing. However hard we have tried, there was one particular family which still looked stuck to us, and any attempts to present it differently had a whiff of emperor's new clothes. Our supervisor always put up a fight at times like those and we tried very hard to see things from her point of view, even though they were at odds with our more depressed, analytic, view of things. There were one or two "victories" when she admitted that we were probably more in touch with reality; "probably" was the word she would usually use in those circumstances!

Looking back, one thing that we have definitely learnt from those happy Tuesday afternoons was a confidence to try something new without the fear that we cannot manage but with the belief that we know enough as therapists, of whatever stable, to take a plunge and to try something new. This strengthened the belief in our own internal resources and the sense that we are capable of embracing totally new experiences. The enthusiasm for the new task was, in our particular group, influenced by our core training, which has a more cautious attitude to change and sees resistance to it as universal. The workshop also gave us the confidence to work alongside our systemically trained colleagues, support them as necessary, and to be able to apply some of the systemic principles to the wider context of working within organizations; something that is invaluable in the current climate. For example, keeping multiple perspectives in mind is particularly helpful while working within multi-disciplinary teams.

Reflections and recommendations

As well as systemic psychotherapy, group members' training requires the same number of hours of cognitive behavioural therapy, for which they also receive supervision. It would be possible simply to provide the practice required without considering a wider remit. However, it is hard for systemic supervisors, with their passion for context, not to invite reflexive awareness of the fit or lack of it between theories and personal philosophies and to be concerned with creating possibilities for an enduring effect in whatever way works best for the individual trainee. Therefore, as well as the clinical experience itself, it seemed important to pay attention to how well all the group processes reflected systemic practices and how they could evoke different meanings for each of the participants, as is reflected in these accounts.

Given that many systemic supervisors are engaged in this form of training, it is worth distilling some learning points from our experiences. First, there is the importance of paying attention to individual learning aims and to finding ways of monitoring how these evolve in the course of the year. Since many Specialist Psychiatric Registrars participating in this training have little background knowledge of family therapy or systemic theory, it can be more difficult to identify learning aims at the outset until they have an actual experience of the work. For a group actively committed to a different treatment modality, it was important to keep inviting reflections on how new systemic learning challenges or supports beliefs about psychoanalytically based therapy and to revisit and redefine learning aims and outcomes.

Secondly, the group's feedback that they would have liked more opportunity to watch experienced systemic therapists working led to a change this year when the supervisor and one of the trainees worked with the first family referred. This has the advantage of involving the group in the clinical work from the outset but from an observer perspective so that therapy and theory/practice links can be experienced in a less anxiety-driven context. It can also have the effect of reducing distance between supervisor and trainees as the supervisor's dilemmas, choices, and struggles around the work are made visible. However, the experiences reported in this chapter also suggest that being "thrown in at the deep end" had many advantages as trainees found creative ways to manage feelings of being deskilled, drawing upon competences such as being a parent or having been through medical training.

Thirdly, regarding personal development, it is worth remembering how very different the cultures are on psychoanalytic and systemic trainings. As systemic supervisors it is easy for us to take for granted our "benign" or normalizing intentions. The relationship between a positive resource-based approach to personal development and experiences of exposure when intimate questions are raised can however be another tension. The "slippage" between the supervisor's and Maria's memory of the question asked on that first meeting which the supervisor remembers as "What *resources* from your family do you think you will bring to family therapy?" is an interesting example of how our previous experiences, beliefs, and expectations create our realities, constituting language games in Wittgenstein's (1963) sense. This raises many theoretically based questions about what is a proper time frame and context for personal development, what are the boundaries between public and private domains, and how do these connect to assumptions about pathology, health, and resilience. Negotiating these processes and developing awareness of our own "systemic orthodoxies" and their effects is another rewarding "edge" when training in this context.

Conclusion

While in all training groups supervisors hope to enhance their own learning from the diverse skills and expertise of their trainees, this did represent a particularly rich learning experience for the supervisor. While all trainees make different gains according to their unique circumstances, in this context, with its particular combination of intensity and with its absence of fixed learning outcomes, the diversity of ways for members to attach themselves to varying aspects of systemic theory, practice, or group experience was starker and perhaps more exciting. The ethos of training across a theoretical divide created a great deal of scope for mutual enhancement and for questioning our own and each other's assumptions. The observational skills demonstrated by the group, especially in relation to discrepancies between verbal and non-verbal communication in families, were formidable and refreshing in our field, where verbal language is currently privileged and where making any kind of judgement is experienced as an unhelpful assumption of expertise. Reflecting back on her attempt to provide the group with an experience of systemic thinking-in-action and having read the contributions of the three group members has convinced the supervisor of the wisdom of assuming that the effects of any supervision, as of any therapy, are ultimately unpredictable and idiosyncratic whatever the prescribed learning outcomes and that, just as with therapy, the quality of the relationships, whatever model we use, is likely to be crucial and will evolve and acquire new meaning over time.

References

Benjamin, J. (1998). *Shadow of the Other: Intersubjectivity and Gender in Psychoanalysis.* New York: Routledge.

Bertrando, P. (2002). The Presence of the Third Party: Systemic Therapy and Transference Analysis. *Journal of Family Therapy.* 24(4): 351–369.

Bion, W. (1970). Opacity of Memory and Desire. In: Bion, W.R. (ed.) *Attention and Interpretation.* London: Tavistock. Chapter 4.

Boscolo, L. and Bertrando, G. (1996). *Systemic Therapy with Individuals.* London: Karnac Books.

Boston, P. (2009). The Three Faces of Supervision: Individual Learning, Group Learning and Positioning One's Own Accountability. In: Burck, C. and Daniel, G. (eds) *Processes in Systemic Supervision.* London: Karnac Books. Chapter 2.

Box, S. (1979). The Elucidation of a Family Myth. *Journal of Family Therapy.* 1(1): 75–86.

Brodie, F. and Wright, J. (2002). Minding the Gap Not Bridging the Gap: Family Therapy from a Psychoanalytic Perspective. *Journal of Family Therapy.* 24(2): 205–222.

Byng-Hall, J. (1995). *Rewriting Family Scripts: Improvisation and Systems Change.* New York: Guilford Press.

Cecchin, G. (1987). Hypothesising, Circularity, Neutrality Revisited: An Invitation to Curiosity. *Family Process.* 26(4): 405–413.

Donovan, M. (2003). Mind the Gap: The Need for a Generic Bridge between Psychoanalytic and Systemic Approaches. *Journal of Family Therapy.* 25(2): 115–136.

Flaskas, C. (1997). Engagement and the Therapeutic Relationship in Systemic Therapy. *Journal of Family Therapy.* 19(3): 263–283.

Flaskas, C. (2002). Comment on Brodie and Wright. *Journal of Family Therapy.* 24(2): 222–231.

Flaskas, C. and Perlesz, A. (eds) (1996). *The Therapeutic Relationship.* London: Karnac Books.

Goldner, V., Penn, P., Sheinberg, M., and Walker, G. (1990). Love and Violence: Gender Paradoxes in Volatile Attachments. *Family Process.* 29(4): 343–364.

Larner, G. (2000). Towards a Common Ground in Psychoanalysis and Family Therapy: On Knowing Not to Know. *Journal of Family Therapy.* 22(1): 61–82.

Leupnitz, D. (1997). Feminism, Psychoanalysis and Family Therapy: Reflections on Telos. *Journal of Family Therapy*. 19(3): 303–318.

McFadyen, A. (1997). *Rapprochement in sight?* Postmodern Family Therapy and Psychoanalysis. *Journal of Family Therapy*. 19(3): 241–262.

Minuchin, S. (1998). Where is the Family in Narrative Family Therapy? *Journal of Marital and Family Therapy*. 24(4): 397–403.

Mitchell, S. and Aron, L. (eds) (1999). *Relational Psychoanalysis: The Emergence of a Tradition*. London: The Analytic Press.

Pocock, D. (1997). Feeling Understood in Family Therapy. *Journal of Family Therapy*. 19(3): 283–302.

Pocock, D. (2006). Six Things Worth Understanding about Psychoanalytic Psychotherapy. *Journal of Family Therapy*. 28(4): 352–369.

Speed, B. (2004). All Aboard in the NHS: Collaborating with Colleagues who Use Different Approaches. *Journal of Family Therapy*. 26(3): 260–279.

Strachey, J. (1934). The Nature of the Therapeutic Action of Psychoanalysis. *International Journal of Psychoanalysis*. 15: 127–159.

Wittgenstein, L. (1963). *Philosophical Investigations*. Translated and edited by Anscombe, G.E.M. New York: Macmillan.

INDEX

Abela, Angela 289
Abstract conceptualization 55–56
Abusive situation 43
Acknowledging
  disappointment 177–178
Active experimentation 58
Adolescent disobedience 167
Adult Mental Health
  psychologists 327
Adult Mental Health Service 309, 316
Agency-based supervision 316
  position for 310
  ways forward 330–331
Agency-based supervisory
  practice 313
American Civil Rights
  Campaign 88
American Psychoanalytic
  Association 7
American Psychological
  Association 293

Andersen, Tom 15
Anderson, Christian, Little
  Mermaid 276
Approach, Method and Technique
  (AMT) 52
Asciak, Maestro Paul 304
Association for Family
  Therapy (AFT) 39
  and Systemic Practice code 293
  Blue Book 28, 196
  code of ethics and practice 115
  guidelines no. 14, 43
Authoritative doubt 14
Ayo, Yvonne 225

Bakhtin, Mikhail 20
Barratt, Sara 185
Basic Assumption (BA)
  fight/flight 132
Beckett, Samuel 219
Behaviour Support Services 355

Behind-screen dialogue
    and reflections 94–97
Bertrando, Paolo 3, 80
Bilingualism 219
Bionic theory 133
*Black Power: The Politics
    of Liberation in America* 250
Black social workers, development
    of programme 252
Blind spots 189
Blow off steam 112
Bion
    Basic Assumption (BA)
        dependency 130
    basic assumption
        fight/flight 132
    influences to individual
        and group process 124–134
    valency 131
Boston, Paula 27
Bowen theory 9
Bowenian supervision 9
Boyd, Elizabeth 203
Boyd-Franklin's (1989)
    idea 242
Brecelj-Kobe, Mojca 267
Bridges, Jeff 186
British Psychology
    Society (BPS) 293
Brown, Carla 110
Bruner, Jerome, metaphor
    of scaffolding 30
Burck, Charlotte 81, 141
Burnham, John 49
    relational reflexivity 142

Camhi, Claudia 185
Cecchin, Gianfranco,
    observation 176
Child and Adolescent Mental
    Health 188
Child and Adolescent Mental
    Health Service (CAMHS)
    337, 342, 355
    team 354, 356
Chilean story 191
Clarke, Grania 163
Client system to relationships 12
Client's therapy 7
Clinical practicum 252
Clinical psychologists 313–315, 331
    in mental health trust 309–331
    special needs 323–324
Coat hanger 72
Cognitive Behavioural Therapy
    (CBT) 52, 327–329
    therapist 328
Collaboration 337–356
Collective mind 340
Colonizing 89
Commission for Racial Equality
    (CRE) 251
Commissioning conversations
    316–317
Commissioning in agency
    settings 316
Committee of the International
    Psychoanalytic Association 7
Committee on Racial and Ethnic
    Diversity 305
Communication theory and
    research 311
Competition 337–356
Competitive dysfunction 340
Confidant trainee 34
Continued professional
    development (CPD) 141, 255,
    330, 354
Conversation stopper 249
Conversational process 312
Conversational tone
    and agenda 44

Coordinated Management
    of Meaning (CMM) theory 39,
    42, 113, 318
Corridor conversations 348
Cosiness 337–356
Cross-cultural
    working 109, 116
Cultural difference 226
Curiosity compass 61, 70

Dalal, Farhad
    influences to individual
        and group process 126–127
    "slippage in identity" 127
Daniel, Gwyn 163, 359
Decision-making
    responsibilities 259
Deconstructing Agnes 165
Delegated authority, power
    of 267–283
Demands of changing modality,
    Andrew 366–368
Deutsch, Helene 8
Diamond
    blunting 322
    defining relationships and
        positions using 321–322
    illustrate positions 320–321
Dilemmas and concerns, voiced
    by clinic team 254
Dilemmas re-storying 214
Diploma in Systemic Teaching,
    Training and Supervision
    (DSTTS) 50
    curriculum 51
Discordant discussions 43–44
Discourse theory 255–260
Discursive psychologists 257
Domains 40
Double voiced 208
Dutta, Sumita 103, 185

Egalitarian processes 179
Emotion
    as relational and contextual
        104–105
    Darwinian perspective 104
    defining 80–81
    discourses 79
    ending thoughts 115
    exploring in systemic
        supervision 104
    exploring 103–116
    limitations of language 105–106
    practice reflections 110–113
    prejudices exist 83–87
    questions from a supervisor's
        perspective 109
Emotional
    heat 112
    pre-supposing 89
    tone 82
Enthusiasm 88
Epistemological error 176
Ethical responsibility 241
Evaluation as enhancement 39–41
Eyres, Maria 359

Family stories 113
Family therapy 11, 45,
    90, 227–228, 314
    arena 29
    clinics 143
    contemporary 83
    diverse group of 203
    good 154
    party 199
    race and culture in 230
    service 291
    training supervisor 28, 38, 145
Family therapy teams, peer
    relationships in 337–356
    bravery in therapy 349

384   INDEX

development of peer
    consultation teams 339–342
impact on therapy 349–350
Milan team 340
on-going team relationships 338
personal in professional
    relationship 346
professional equalities
    and inequalities in 343–346
spaces for team reflection
    348–349
team peer consultation
    method 340
team structures and models 343
Feminism 269
Fernando, Suman 260
Fifth province Approach 317, 320
Foucault, influences to individual
    and group process 124–134
Foulkes, S.H., influences
    to individual and group
    process 124–126
Fox, Hugh 17–18
Fredman, Glenda 79
Functional Magnetic Resonance
    Imaging (FMRI) 207

Gasps behind the screen 90–98
Genograms 194
Genuine Occupational Qualification
    (GOQ) 260
Gilli, Gabriella 3
Gracious invitation 317
Grand narratives 317
Grasps experience 174
Gregory Bateson's (1972) emphasis
    on relationship 12
Gregory Bateson's terminology 5
Ground-breaking pioneer 88
Group analytic ideas 121–136
Group coherence 167
Group disruptiveness 167

Group narratives 151–153, 169
Group process 32–33, 34,
    121–137, 363–376
    demands of changing modality,
        Andrew 366–368
    evaluation 149
    methods to enrich 159
    personal resonances in 156–157
    personal/professional learning:
        Maria 373–376
    power and authority
        in the supervisory process,
        Sarah 368–373
    supervisory dilemmas,
        Gwyn 363–366
    theory 167
Group reflexivity 151–153
Group relational reflexivity 141, 148
Group supervision 14
    systemic 19
Group themes or preoccupations 28
Group's mistrust 172
Group–supervisee relationship 16
Guided dreaming 269

Harré, Rom, terminology 21
Hazardous to collaborative
    learning 141–159
Hecate, the Greek Goddess 27
    eye to responsibility,
        third face 38
Holloway 229

Imaginative isomorphism 53–54
Individual feedback
    conversations 44
Individual process
    influences from Foulkes, Dalal,
        Foucault, and Bion 124–134
In-front-of-screen dialogue 94–97
Ingrassia, Antonina 185
Inner conversations 107

Inner dialogue 116
Inner London Education
    Authority (ILEA) 260
Institute for Family
    Therapy 270
Institutionalized racism 250, 259
    British experience 251
    concept of 250–252
Instructional analysis 7
Intensive emotional reaction 43
Intergenerational
    supervision 9
    theory 9
Internalized other interviewing
    (IOI) 71
International Psychoanalytic
    Association 7
Interpersonal relationships 259
Interpretative Phenomenological
    Analysis (IPA) 209
Invisibility syndrome 239
Isomorphic transfer 72
Isomorphism 11, 13, 51, 250
    imaginative 53–54
    in therapy
        and supervision 354

Karamat Ali 226
Kelly, George 21
Kensington Consultation Centre's
    (KCC's) 49
    Foundation 51
Khan, Samra 71
Knowledge-in-action 50
Kolb and Schon, supervisory
    writing practices 68
Kolb and systemic/narrative
    practices, developing
    reciprocity 64–67
Kolb, David 50
    categories 71
    comfort zone 58
    concrete experience
        and abstract
        conceptualization 55–57
    contributions 54
    experience and transforming
        experience into learning 54
    experiential learning 54–55
    zone of proximal
        development 59
Kolb's model 55–56
    as a practical exercise 61–63
    as an abstract concept 60
    developing a relationship 60–61
    developing positional abilities,
        and abilities to position 61–63
    of learning 174

Larrington, Guy 185
Learning edges 179
Lewis, Penny 61
Linguagrams 317–318, 321
    exploring culture and moral
        orders using 318–319
    for supervision for senior
        psychologists 319
Live supervision 10, 338
    context of 275–276
Live supervision group processes,
    thinking
    systemically 141–159
Live supervision groups 142–144
    competition, conflict,
        and consensus 153–156
    connections within 149–151
    group narratives and group
        reflexivity 151–153
    in training 145–148
Live-supervision programme 249
Local emotional grammar 111
Looked After Children teams 355
Loss of identity 126
Love diagrams 61

386   INDEX

Majid, Sarah 359
Maltese Psychological
    Association 293
Maltese supervisor 294
Maturana's notion of domains 40
Mental Health Act Commission 260
Mental Health Foundation
    Trust 309
*Mental Health in a Multi-Ethnic
    Society* 232
Mental health service, child and
    adolescent 108
Mental health trust 309–331
Message-carrier, role of 10
Milan systemic group, original 12
Multicultural mental
    health team 237
Multicultural training,
    guidelines for 228
Multiculturalism 226
Multi-disciplinary assessment
    process 324
Multiple relationships 274–275,
    291–293
    dilemmas and challenges
        301–304
    disentangling the complexity
        of 293–295
    in supervision 289–305
    managing boundaries 295–299
    transformational possibilities
        304–305
Multiplexity 109, 115

Narrative therapy 33, 35
Nath, Reena 163
National Health Service (NHS)
    38, 199, 310, 313–314, 317, 319,
    330–331
Native informant 229
Neat conceptual system 56
Newnes, Kerri 70

Non-hierarchical supervisory
    relationship 13
Normalizing gaze 268
Numerous themes 35

Obsessive compulsive disorder
    (OCD) 327
One-way mirrors 10
Optimal supervisory practice 5
Othering 228–229
Outsider-witnessing practices 156

Panopticism 128
Paradoxes 14
Parks, Rosa 88
Partridge, Karen 309
Patron–client relationship 296
Peer consultation teams,
    experiences in 342
Personal and professional
    development (PPD)
    107, 112, 175, 354
Personal failing 149
Personal trapdoors 347
Personal/professional learning,
    Maria 373–376
Personally situated realities 229
Poor practice 39
Position taking talk 189
Positioning theory 255–260, 320
Post-Milan model 37, 45
Postmodernism 14, 172
    concepts in supervision 270–271
    inherent paradox of 268–270
Post-session
    discussion 36
    process 38
Post-structural critique
    of interiority 44
Power and authority
    in the supervisory process,
    Sarah 368–373

INDEX   387

Power and diversity 201
Practice development, ideas 87
Problem children 22
Problem-bearer 15
Problem-dissolving system 340
Problem-organising system 340
Procrustean bed of theory 19
Professional and organizational
   discourses 32
Professional artistry 50
Prominent therapy models 28
Protégé favouritism 297
Psychiatric social work
   service 260
Psychiatric social
   work team 252, 260
Psychic breathing 205
Psychoanalysis 11, 52, 268
Psychoanalytic
   method 8
   psychotherapy 56
   supervision 7, 9, 19
Psychoanalytical
   psychotherapist 4
Psychodynamic therapy 8, 275
   cornerstone of 267
Psychotherapists 3, 7
   self-awareness 11
   transparency 35

Racial awareness 228
Racial sensitivity 228
Racialization 227
Racializing process 255–260
Reciprocity 64–67
Recursive connections between
   families and groups 144–145
Reflection-in-action 50, 58
Reflection-on-action 50, 58, 68
Reflective
   conversations 316
   group 37–38

   observation and active
      experimentation 58
   relationships between
      practices 49
   space 134
Relational reflexivity 72
Relational responsibility 316
Researcher and participant
   relationships 241–242
Rich description 33
Rober, Peter 127

Safe enough conversation 35
Safe uncertainty 14, 134, 351
Scaffolding supervisor 30
Scale 1 Systemic Humility/
   Passionate Conviction 84
Scale 5 Emotional Closeness
   and Distance 84
Scerri, Clarissa Sammut 289
Second World War 219
Schön, Donald 19, 50
   concept of 'coaching' 70
   distinction "knowing- in-
      action" 56, 58
   professional artistry 72
   reflection 20
   reflection-on-action 58
Self-reflective
   processes 194
   space 151
Self-reflexivity 82, 158, 214, 219
   Sarah's 216
   supervisors' and therapists' 141
Self- silencing 111
Self-disclosure, experience 210
Self-supervision 107
Semantic polarities 84
Slovenian national identity 273
Slumdog Millionaire 225
Smith, Gerrilyn 79
Social constructionism 256

388 INDEX

Social GRRAAACCEEESS 53, 55, 228, 312
Special needs psychologists, diamond to illustrate positions for 325
Spellman, David 79
Streisand, Barbra 186
Strength-based conversation 13
Student responsibility, interview around the issue of 31–32
Subjugated discourses 326–327
Supervisee
　analytic relationship 269
　awareness 6
　blind spots 267
　collaborative relationship with 12
　discourses 236–240
　discussion on discourses 240–241
　non-hierarchical relationship with 13
　obligation to raise 243
　position 155
　voice entitlement narratives 216
Supervision 4
　across a theoretical divide 359–378
　as adult learning 312–313
　as learning to transgress 312
　as organizational development 310
　as primary participative research 311–312
　as primary participative research, for spiral process 314–316
　attention to the wider context 145
　collaborative model 231
　context of systemic training in Slovenia 270
　cross-cultural 85
　cultural and gendered influences on speaking and dilemmas in practice 203–220
　defining 81–83
　doing of 49
　ethical considerations 108–110
　examples in systemic practice 132
　focus of 7
　gender and multiple relations in 299
　giving directives 19
　goldfish bowl of live 127
　group discussions 127
　group learning 27
　group process 165
　group providing 143
　how works 19–22
　humour in 178
　ideas of 18, 114
　implications for practice 242–243
　increase of knowledge 18
　increase of points of view 19
　individual learning 27
　intergenerational 19
　intervention on the person of the therapist 19
　managing multiple relationships in 289–305
　modalities 14–18
　models 5
　of supervision 293
　one-to-one retrospective 88
　open dialogue 19
　postmodern systemic 19
　postmodern 12

prejudices exist 83–87
process in the context
  of multiple relationships
  274–275
process 32
race and culture in 225–243
race, culture and family therapy
  227–228
reflections and
  recommendations 376–378
reflective hand-over 278
responding to challenging
  feedback 276–277
retrospective 39
Shakespearian tradition 271
social constructionist 192
spiral process for 314–316
strategic and structural 19
strength-based models of 12
systemic group 19
systemic ideas in action 359–378
territory in 98
three faces of 27
training issues 228–230
vignette 1 277
vignette 2 279–280
vignette 3 280–283
voice entitlement narratives
  203–220
with the Brown family 108
Supervision and theoretical models,
  characteristics of 6
Supervision group
  double feedback 195–198
  getting on with it! 186–188
  reflecting 185–198
  Safria's experience 211–212
  the team 186
Supervision group experience
  acknowledging disappointment
    177–178

feedback and challenge (GD) 176
learning points 178–180
personal development 175–176
revisiting past, present, and
  future 163–182
theories, practices, and personal
  styles 172–175
Supervision-of-supervision (SOS)
  relationship, safe 301
Supervision, race and culture
  225–243
  terminology 226–227
Supervisor 166
  accountability 27
  African Caribbean 232
  authority of 12
  becoming 49
  clinical responsibility 41–42
  critical incident 103–116
  decentring 178–180
  dilemmas 157
  discourses 231, 235
  discussion on discourses
    235–236
  expectations 42–43
  ideas and knowledge 131
  influence positioning
    in groups 135–136
  interaction 53
  internal 164
  intervention 157
  learning 164
  obvious responsibility 234
  performing cooperation 147
  position of 134–135
  post-session discussion 42
  power 193, 242
  questions for 158–159, 216–218
  response and behaviour 29
  responsibility 144, 153, 231
  self-reflexivity maintaining 158

sought-after supervisors 303
South Asian woman 109
supervision group 276
supervisor-in-training 38, 142
thinking 44
trainee 147
Supervisor's narrative (GD) 170–171
Supervisor–supervisee
　dyad 167
　relationship 29, 249–250, 260, 274
Supervisory
　dilemmas, Gwyn 363–366
　locating practice in the Maltese cultural contex 290–291
　on-going practices 89
　practice through engaging with theories of education and learning 54
　practice 89
　process, Sarah 368–373
　questions 44
　relationship 107, 209, 235–236, 295–296
　response 36, 112
　therapeutic relationships 242
Systemic and narrative therapy 54
　practices 65–67
Systemic and psychoanalytical theory 360–363
Systemic club 351
Systemic conversations 314
Systemic psychotherapists 164, 309
　proper 192
Systemic psychotherapy 141, 163, 268, 290, 327
　clinical psychology 313
　qualifying-level 185
　supervisors' and therapists' self-reflexivity 141
　theory and practice of 4
　training 136

Systemic supervision 123–138, 165, 291, 312
　agency-based supervision, ways 330–331
　deconstructing "grand narratives" 317
　defining relationships and positions using diamonds 321–322
　exploring different positions in organization 320
　exploring discourses of emotion in 79–100
　exploring dominant and subjugated discourses 326–327
　exploring moral orders 318
　exploring teamwork and professional identities 322
　group 150
　in agency contexts 309–331
　joining the conversation as guest in culture 317
　theories of change and the practice of 3–22
　theories of learning and education 49–72
　using diamonds as way to illustrate positions 320–321
　using diamonds to become reflexive about positioning 324–326
Systemic supervisors 55, 290

Tavistock Clinic 291–292, 359
Team conversations 254
Team mind 172
Team peer consultation method 340
The Cybernetics of "Self" 176
The Dialectical Therapist 80
The Mirror Has Two Faces 186

Therapeutic system 12
Therapist to supervisor 51–52
Therapist–client(s) relationship 12, 16, 362
Therapist-in-training 11
Tokenism 238, 241
Trainee's/supervisee's emerging abilities 50
Training conversations 337
Trampuz, Dubravka 267
Transference and counter-transference 361
Transforming Emotion 79
Transitional understandings 341

Ventriloquation 208
Voice, development of 206
Video recordings 10–11
Voice entitlement concept
    emergence of 203–206
    examples of narratives 209–213
    last reflections 220
    Maria's story 209–210
    Safria's story 210–212
    Sarah's story 212–213
Vygotsky, Lev
    ideas 51
    thinking 30

Western society 257
White, Michael
    adaptation of Vygotsky's thinking 30
    ideas 17
Williams, Andrew 359
Wilson, Jim, *The Performance of Practice* 84

Ziminski, Jeanne 337
Zone of Proximal Development (ZPD) 50

For Product Safety Concerns and Information please contact our EU representative GPSR@taylorandfrancis.com Taylor & Francis Verlag GmbH, Kaufingerstraße 24, 80331 München, Germany

Printed and bound by CPI Group (UK) Ltd, Croydon, CR0 4YY
02/03/2026
02063581-0001